A Circus in the Paper

Stories of how a COLLEGE
ended up with a
CIRCUS

Russell Hany

ISBN: 9798622534201

This book is dedicated to my Parents.

Thanks to Illinois State University for allowing me to use massive amounts of media in this book.

Thanks to all of the *Vidette* reporters, editors, photographers, and those who assigned them to Gamma Phi stories.

Thanks to Jeff Gipe for his artful help with the cover.

Thanks to Bill Jaeger, the official Gamma Phi Historian, for all of his time and dedication through years of Gamma Phi historical research. Without his history lessons when I was a Pledge (and beyond), I wouldn't have ended up as interested as I am in this historical gold mine.

Thanks to "Coach" Jerry Polacek! Although his involvement is not documented in this book, he took over as Gamma Phi Director shortly after the point in which the book concludes. He provided selfless leadership to the organization through the good times and the bad. He also took the time to provide insight only he has in writing the Foreword for this book.

Also, a huge posthumous thanks to Clifford Horton, Arley Gillett, and all of the early Gamma Phi members who propelled the organization into the future so the rest of us could eventually share the experiences.

The many Gamma Phi members I have become friends with throughout the years fuel my fire to continue in the exploration of our shared history. I hope this book meets their approval.

About the Author

My parents met each other when they were in college and members of Gamma Phi. While raising us, they took my siblings and I to many annual Gamma Phi Circuses, as well as to the after show celebrations where I saw many of the people who are described in this book.

I wasn't really sure how my parents could have actually been in a circus. But then again, not many others understand how college students can actually be in a circus while in college—especially parents whose children have joined Gamma Phi.

Eventually, I joined that same organization, and ended up spending many years, and thousands of hours, as a performer, executive, coach, videographer, historian, and archiver. Most of my time, however, has been spent with the many friends I made during all of those year.

I started my Gamma Phi performing "career" as a Juggler and Unicyclist, and eventually learned many other circus skills including: Flying Trapeze, Fire Eating, Clowning, Skating, Gym Wheel, Acro Sport, Teeterboard, Rolling Globes, and Revolving Ladder.

My performances ranged from birthday parties up to large exhibitions and professional circus shows. I was in several competitions at The International Circus Festival in Sarasota, FL and have performed on national television many times.

Ever since joining Gamma Phi in 1984, I have been highly interested in its history. It's nice to actually be part of the history, but I've found it more interesting to uncover historical facts about the organization and to document them.

I hope others enjoy the stories in this book as much as I do.

About the Book

This book is the story of a collegiate circus, Gamma Phi, as told by a collegiate newspaper, the *Vidette*. The articles not only tell the story of the circus, but they also present the history through perspective on items of interest and language used in description.

Narration has been added to blend the newspaper articles into the complete Gamma Phi picture.

Author additions have a light grey background to help separate them from the newspaper articles.

Gamma Phi group pictures have been included from the Illinois State Normal University (ISNU) yearbook, the *Index*, and from formal Gamma Phi pictures in order to show the faces of the people chronicled in the Vidette articles.

About the Author -- vi
About the Book --- vii
Foreword --- xi
College Circuses -- 1
Gamma Phi at ISNU --- 6
The VIDETTE CIRCUS--- 8
COACH HORTON ARRIVES AT ISNU ---------- 12
GAMMA PHI BEGINNINGS ------------------------17
1929 – 30 School Year -- 23
1930 – 31 School Year -- 32
1931-32 School Year --- 37
1932 – 33 School Year -- 48
1933 – 34 School Year -- 62
1934 – 35 School Year -- 75
1935 – 36 School Year -- 85
1936 – 37 School Year -------------------------------------- 98
1937 – 38 School Year -- 111
1938 – 39 School Year -- 127
1939 – 40 School Year -- 152
1940 – 41 School Year -- 164
War Years --- 169
Gamma Phi Men Answer the Call to War --------- 174
1943 – 44 School Year -- 179
1944 – 45 School Year -- 184
1945 – 46 School Year -- 186
1946 – 47 School Year -- 191
1947 – 48 School Year -- 194
1948 – 49 School Year -- 197
1949 – 50 School Year -- 204
1950 – 51 School Year -- 213
1951 – 52 School Year -- 220

1952 – 53 School Year -------------------------------- 229
1953 – 54 School Year -------------------------------- 240
1954 – 55 School Year -------------------------------- 248
1955 – 56 School Year -------------------------------- 262
1956 – 57 School Year -------------------------------- 272
1957 – 58 School Year -------------------------------- 283
1958 – 59 School Year -------------------------------- 298
1959 – 60 School Year -------------------------------- 307
1960 – 61 School Year -------------------------------- 319
1961 – 62 School Year -------------------------------- 330
1962 – 63 School Year -------------------------------- 347
1963 – 64 School Year -------------------------------- 362
1964 – 65 School Year -------------------------------- 371
1965 – 66 School Year -------------------------------- 388
The Circus Continues -------------------------------- 399
Bibliography--401
Index--425

Foreword

Russ Hany could be a nearly normal person if it wasn't for his obsession and love for all things circus, especially Gamma Phi Circus. For decades, he has video-documented many Gamma Phi circuses, circus activities, and has spent literally thousands of hours editing those videos. Russ has also reviewed hundreds if not thousands of print articles in preparation for this publication. He is a past President of Gamma Phi, recipient of the Max Honn Service award which is the highest award that members of the organization can bestow on one of its own, and recipient of the Jerry Polacek Award in appreciation for his alumni contributions to Gamma Phi. His parents, Imogene and Darwin Hany, were also recipients of Gamma Phi Service awards. Russ's years of archiving all things Gamma Phi are very much appreciated.

The legacy that Gamma Phi Circus has left for Illinois State University (ISU) these 90 plus years is unmistakably positive. This publication will help to provide easy access to some of the history of Gamma Phi and the many contributions the organization has made to Illinois State University.

Through the years, those charged by the university with the responsibility of administering Gamma Phi have been referred to as sponsors, directors, coaches, etc. Here I will use the terms Directors and Assistant Directors. Point of clarification, Gamma Phi is the organization that Pop Horton brought to ISU. Gamma Phi Circus or "Circus" is the annual production presented to the public. Here the terms will be used interchangeably.

Russ has done a great job of documenting the arrival and history of Dr. Clifford "Pop" Horton at Illinois State University. Pop was a teacher, coach, administrator, and the originator of the ISU Chapter of Gamma Phi. Pop was not only a force at ISU, but he also was a founding father of the Illinois Association, for Health Physical Education, Recreation, and Dance (IAHPERD). He was president from 1950-51 and instrumental in writing the association's first constitution. In his honor, the IAHPERD created the Pop Horton Award for dedication, leadership, service and accomplishments.

In the late 1940's, Pop and faculty from the Special Education Department at ISU originated a camp at Lake Bloomington for children with physical disabilities. The children would attend the summer camp for two weeks. ISU students would receive course credit for being their counselors under the direction of ISU faculty and volunteers. Pop's vision of the camp was a place where children with disabilities could successfully participate in water & field activities, arts/crafts, nature walks, etc. without fear or anxiety. It facilitated rewarding experiences for hundreds of children. Easter Seals co-sponsored the camp with ISU.

Although he retired in 1961 before I arrived at ISU, I am grateful to have known Pop and his wife Garnetta. Pop was easy going. Even after his retirement he occasionally attended Gamma Phi Practices where he was always willing to provide coaching tips to circus members.

In Horton Fieldhouse, all male teachers and coaches used the same lockerroom. I had conversations with Pop as he prepared for his noontime swims. He was in his late 70's at the time. We agreed the benefits of being a member of Gamma Phi included importance of service, trust, perseverance, moral integrity, and hard work. When Pop passed away in 1981, members of Gamma Phi were among the pallbearers at his funeral.

As documented in this book, Dr. Arley Gillett was an early member of Gamma Phi and an outstanding wrestler. He was inducted into the ISU Athletic Hall of Fame in 1976 . Dr. Gillet was the Circus Director after Pop for 19 years. He was always a gentleman. In his role as an educator he was the consummate professional and commanded respect. By commanded I do not mean in a bombastic way, but rather from his demeanor. It was the way he treated people. An exceptionally kind and relatively soft-spoken man always treated people with respect. Held in high regard by his colleagues, Dr. Gillet was the Chairperson of the Men's Department of Health, Physical Education and Athletics from 1966-70 and Director of Athletics from 1968-70. He was promoted to Associate Dean of the College of Applied Science and Technology from 1970-72 and Associate Secretary of ISU from 1972-73. He and his wife Wynona always loved Gamma Phi. They attended most circuses. Later in their lives, Gamma Phi member Evan Brown helped Dr. & Mrs. Gillett by doing odd jobs around their home.

Dr. Gillett often spoke of the benefits of Gamma Phi as being a community with common goals; members helping each other to become better people/performers while providing service to others.

In 1967, I came to ISU as a graduate student pursuing a master's degree in Physical Education. Having been on the gymnastics team at Western Illinois University and competed against ISU's teams, I decided to become a member of Gamma Phi. I came in the Spring semester and according to the rules, I had to attain approval of the membership to be a part of the organization and perform in the circus. As it was for most of those before me, it was a great experience! I unofficially assisted with coaching the men's gymnastics team. Dr. Wayne Truex was the head gymnastics coach and Director of Gamma Phi and Alan Weith was his assistant in both organizations. The relationships we established helped shape the rest of my career.

Over the three years I was a student, I learned of the family ties between Dr. Truex and Dr. Gillet and his wife Wynona. Dr. Truex married Dr. Gillett's daughter Arlene. Arlene and her brother Jay were in Gamma Phi Circus shows as young children--interestingly enough, they were in the 1951-54 circuses with Russ's parents. Wayne & Arlene Truex had two children, Mike and Julie. Both were in circus shows as children as well. Julie became a member of Gamma Phi while she was a student at ISU. She was an accomplished gymnast and tumbler.

In 1970, I was hired by Dr. Gillett to become an Instructor of Physical Education, Assistant Director of Gamma Phi (under Dr. Truex) and Assistant Gymnastics Coach for Men (under Alan Weith). I am thankful for having been part of Gamma Phi for almost 50 years. I met my dear wife (51 yrs.) Marsha through Gamma Phi while preparing for a summer circus. We were adagio partners. We were married in 1968. There are many marriages resulting from Gamma Phi membership. Our daughter Lisa and son Adam are members of Gamma Phi. Adam was president and Max Honn Service Award recipient. They, of course, also performed in circus shows as children.

Both Pop and Dr. Gillet shared direct knowledge of the benefits of Gamma Phi membership. They independently expressed to me how grateful they were that ISU had continued to value Gamma Phi as a unique organization that projects a positive image of the University. They would be proud to see what the annual circus has become, and that the original values of the organization have remained intact. I am grateful that I have not only known Pop and Arley, but also all the Directors and Assistant Directors of Gamma Phi throughout its history.

Thank you again Russ for your love of Gamma Phi. I hope through your efforts, many more people will realize the contributions Gamma Phi has made to Illinois State University and to the lives of so many others. I hope readers will find the contained historical information as interesting as I did

Dr. Jerry Polacek
Illinois State University
Assistant Professor Emeritus
Gamma Phi Circus Director, retired

College Circuses

College circuses started over a century ago? Yes!

In 1899, Wellington Physical Training School, in New Zealand, had begun performing annual "Exhibitions of Gymnastics." The shows were similar to those of collegiate circuses to come.

Their shows consisted of performances by boys, men, girls, and ladies classes which were separated into different acts accompanied with music and stylish costumes. The female groups presented wand, dumbbell, and club exercises, as well as an Indian Club Duet. Both genders separately performed parallel bar, ladder, and vaulting horse exercises.

Back in the United States in 1899, Columbia University, in New York City, hosted the first "Intercollegiate Gymnastics Exhibition." Gymnastics teams from Yale, Princeton, and Columbia joined together to perform for thousands of cheering spectators. Traditional gymnastics events were performed including bars, rings, horse, as well as trapeze and swinging clubs.

At Ohio State University (OSU), they were also performing annual demonstrations of gym classes. At the turn-of-the century, they stepped it up from an exhibition to more of a show—even though they were still calling it a "Gymnastic Exhibition."

With the popularity of gymnastics and the sense of mental and physical discipline required to succeed in it, OSU founded a national athletic society designed for the advancement of physical culture and athletics. This organization officially began in 1901. It was called, Gamma Phi.[1]

The 1902 presentation included gymnastics, highlighted by tumbling, and also horizontal bar and incandescent Indian club swinging acts.

By 1903, the Universities of Wisconsin (UW) and Minnesota (UM) both had circuses. The Wisconsin show was created in 1901 to raise funds for their gymnastics team to travel. The "circuses" did feature gymnastics, but also relied on fraternities to compete in varieties of events which involved costumes, props, and sideshow acts.

The programs consisted of gymnastic events such as parallel bars, horse, and trapeze. Many clowns were present throughout the evenings. Upon conclusion, awards were given for best of the fraternity entries and best gymnasts. Their later circuses had additions of such things as boxing and wrestling matches.

Some praise came to the UW circus from Ringling Brothers' Circus members who were wintering in Baraboo in 1905. They attended the show and, "They were unanimous in declaring the performance the best amateur attempt they had ever seen." [2]

In 1906, Central Illinois became the home of a very large collegiate circus. The University of Illinois, in Champaign, had created an Interscholastic Circus, they called, "The World's Greatest Amateur Circus."

It began as a small fund-raising show presented to just a few hundred spectators, and grew to having nearly 1,000 student performers playing to regular annual crowds nearing 10,000 people.

They had two, three, four, and even five-ring outdoor shows with marching bands culminating with large fireworks displays. The acts in their repertoire compare to those of future Gamma Phi performances, ranging from traditional gymnastics acts through, tight and slack wire, trampoline, ladders, globes, unicycles, juggling, Rhon Rads (German wheel), perch pole, weightlifting, dancing, bullwhips, contortion, and aerial acts including flying trapeze.

On Apr 18, 1908, Ohio Wesleyan University (OWU) installed a new chapter of Gamma Phi in effort to further the interests of physical education. Ten members of the OSU Alpha Chapter completed the initiatory exercises for an OWU Gamma Phi chapter at the Sigma Chi fraternity house.

As a college Junior, future ISNU Gamma Phi founder, Clifford Horton transferred to OWU in 1917. He quickly joined the Gym Team and was involved in gymnastic exhibitions on campus, which were combinations of Gamma Phi and the Gym Team.

They performed High Bar, Parallel Bars, Horse, and Tumbling. Performances also involved Men's and Women's Gym classes, and basketball (which was still evolving) was included. The Gamma Phi Director, Prof. Dixon, commonly put on a well-received act of torch swinging.

Horton was officially initiated into Gamma Phi on Dec 4, 1917. He was hired as an instructor for the 1919-20 school year, and became a Co-Director of Gamma Phi. During the year, a decision was made to create a circus show.

On March 14, 1920 at 8:15 PM, the first Gamma Phi Circus was presented by Gamma Phi Members and the girls' gym classes, and was a great success. The student newspaper reported, "The circus was a revelation to many people who did not realize the excellence or work turned out by the Physical Education Department."[3]

For the next school year, Horton assumed complete control of the organization. Due to demands placed on the group, he put a three-fold constructive program in place.

The first phase was to make sure the Gamma Phi members were trained as athletic leaders and assist in athletic exercises.

The second phase was that Gamma Phi would absorb the old gymnasium team. Any man showing ability to make the gymnasium team was honored with a Gamma Phi membership. Under that phase of the work, members received advanced gymnasium training, conducted by Horton. They also worked on boxing, wrestling, and jiu-jitsu.

The third phase was something totally new. As requests were already being received, Gamma Phi would secure dates for presenting real athletic exhibitions in several cities. Horton noted, "That this organization can put on an interesting program of unusual stunts has been shown in the past years by its work at various school events." [4]

With the understanding that college circuses were fairly common in the early 1900's, let's delve into ISNU's Gamma Phi history.

Gamma Phi at ISNU

The Gamma Phi Circus is a collegiate organization. Most performers in the shows are college students with a few others being faculty and staff of the university.

In some instances, especially in the early days, people from outside the university performed in the circuses. Those people were in the shows, but were not members of Gamma Phi.

In the 19th Century, gymnastics was starting to become popular in the United States. Richard Edwards, President of ISNU, set a requirement in 1862 that all ISNU students must participate in "free gymnastics accompanied by music." That set into motion a gymnastics mindset in ISNU students. They became rooted in gymnastics skills, and those gymnastics skills evolved into circus skills.

Another circus component that spurred Gamma Phi's development evolved from the location of the university, Normal, IL, which has a twin city named, Bloomington. The Bloomington/Normal (B/N) community became the home of many professional circus troupes starting in 1875.

Circuses were a well-known form of entertainment through the country in the 18th century. Within the national circus performer community, B/N was an off-season mecca for circus performers. Many performers trained and lived there throughout the winter months.

"Flying Barns" were built by flying trapeze families in order to hone their skills and prepare acts for upcoming circus seasons. Several of these barns were built in the

Bloomington/Normal community.

In 1917, a Vidette reporter visited a popular Flying Barn in Bloomington.

March 21, 1917 (page 2)

G. D. C. on a Hike

The secret is out. Now we all know the surprise which the social committee had in store for us one Saturday afternoon recently.

Sixteen girls followed Miss Blake, our enthusiastic "hiker," down Broadway, and over to Emerson Street, where we soon came in sight of a most extraordinary looking barn. "The man is evidently boss here," remarked one girl, "and he thinks more of his stock than he does of his family." What was her surprise to find the guides leading the way to this very barn.

We entered the door, and then came a chorus of "Ohs" and "Ahs," for such another arrangement of trapezes, swings, rope ladders, and a strong rope net, we had never seen. Photographs of clowns, circus riders, and acrobats were noticed later and helped carry out the idea that we were on the "inside" of a circus. And so we discovered ourselves to be, for we were guests of the Flying Wards, who live in Bloomington during the winter and practice daily new stunts with which they startle "Young America," when it attends Hagenbeck's circus during the summer months.

But we feel we have an advantage over the small boys who will gather in the circus tents, for we have not only seen the hair-raising feats, but heard the good-natured joking of the actors, and found them to be quite human individuals.

After viewing the last triple somersault in mid air, we departed and tramped back to the home of our president, Miss Huxtable, where we enjoyed refreshments.

NOTE:

With so many circus performers located and training in one area, it's not hard to imagine that performances would occur. They did. Many of the flying trapeze groups practiced their acts at the Bloomington YMCA. To provide some payment for their many hours of practice, they put on circus shows for the community.

Performers in those shows consisted of the professional circus members as well as other performers from around Central Illinois, including some who would eventually be in Gamma Phi Circus including the founder of ISNU's Gamma Phi, Clifford Horton.

THE VIDETTE CIRCUS

While this book is compiled to chronicle the **Gamma Phi** Circus from the Vidette's perspective, the Circus we will start with is actually... The **Vidette** Circus! Seventeen years before the first Gamma Phi Circus, The Vidette had their own circus. It was created following The University of Illinois', "World's Greatest Amateur Circus."

March 3, 1915 (Front Page, 5, & 8)

VIDETTE CIRCUS BIG SUCCESS

A FEW PICTURES TAKEN FOR VIDETTE---SOME EXTRA GOOD ACTS GIVEN

THE DANCING GIRLS

From left to right the names are: Louise Place, Jo Hayes, Grace Moberly, Dorothy Burr, Nora Keogh, Beatrice Coolidge.

MISS LYDIA CLARK

DWIGHT M. RAMSAY

MR. HARRISON H. RUSSELL,
Director of Russell Troupe.

RUSSELL TROUPE—STATIONARY PYRAMID

RUSSELL TROUPE

A Circus in the Paper

March 3, 1915 (Front Page)
Should the Circus Become an Annual Affair?

The Vidette Circus of last Friday night, according to the consensus of opinion, was one of the best exhibitions of student talent ever displayed in Normal. So successful was the event from every standpoint that there is considerable talk of making it an annual affair. For a number of reasons let us hope that this will be carried out.

In the first place the circus was a success from a financial point of view. The auditorium was filled almost to its capacity. Although the expenses were fairly heavy, a large sum was realized. The money derived will go toward financing the Vidette; so the quarter the student spent for admission will come back to him in the form of a better paper.

The testimony is unanimous that the circus was worth seeing. Anything which thus affords an opportunity for recreation from the routine of student life is worthy of annual repetition. Humor, the oil of life, always makes the brain work easier.

Also, those who participated in the event were benefited. The physical exercise alone was worth the time spent in practicing. The values derived from all dramatic performances were realized. A certain mental stimulus—the joy of achievement—is felt by everyone who co-operates to make an enterprise of this kind a success.

Objection is made that with our basket ball and football games, and with our numerous plays, we already have too many student enterprises to attract the students' money. But with the new system going into effort this fall a great share of these enterprises will be paid for in the regular term fee. Furthermore, in the past all entertainments have been generously supported by the student body. This objection, then, is not serious.

While nothing so elaborate as the outdoor performance given at the University of Illinois could be given in Normal, the contest idea could be well carried out. Although we have no fraternities, the different clubs, the different departments or the different classes could give the stunts and the prizes be awarded as they are at Urbana. Let us hope that something of this sort will be given every year.

NOTE:
The Vidette Circus actually did become an annual event, but not as a circus. It was a big success on campus as the annual Stunt Show, which was much like a talent show. Many campus groups entered acts in the competition. The groups consisted of clubs, fraternities, dorm floors, and even Gamma Phi.

COACH HORTON ARRIVES AT ISNU

May 30, 1923 (Front Page)

Clifford E. Horton, Baseball Coach at Clark University, Named as Russell's Successor

Announcement was made late yesterday from the I. S. N. U. office that Mr. Clifford E. Horton, baseball coach at Clark University. Worcester, Mass., has been hired to coach athletics and direct physical education at the Normal University.

Although the Normal School Board met yesterday in Chicago to affirm the appointments recommended by President Felmley, the president had not returned to Normal at the Vidette's press time so the above announcement is not official. However it is understood that there is little doubt but what Mr. Horton was hired.

Mr. Horton comes to I. S. N. U. highly recommended. He has had four years of work at Ohio Wesleyan University, is a graduate of the Y. M. C. A. College of Physical Training at Springfield, Mass., and will receive his master's degree at Clark University this June.

Forty-seven different coaches throughout the east and middle west applied for the position here and Mr. Felmley feels assured that he selected a first class man, the best one available. Mr. Horton's coaching experience includes work in assisting with football and basketball at Ohio Wesleyan and at Clark, as well as having charge of baseball at the latter school while doing postgraduate work there. He is a young man, now 30 years of age.

June 18, 1923 (Front Page)

COACH HORTON TO STUDY UNDER DR. MEANWELL

Word has been received here from Clifford E. Horton, recently elected physical director and coach at I. S. N. U. to succeed Coach H. H. Russell, saying that he expects to spend the summer at the University of Wisconsin coaching school, studying the Wisconsin methods of conducting sports.

June 25, 1923 (page 3)

Dr. Meanwell, of the U. of W., is one of the veterans in the basketball game and has developed a very successful short passing game which has been used by Wisconsin teams extensively.

This type of playing has been used lately by Coach Russell and has proven very successful with Normal teams.

As a matter of duty every Normal ' student should help make Coach Horton's arrival the start of a new athletic period in I. S. N. U.—the most successful this school has ever enjoyed.

Coach Horton expects to pay Normal a visit before going to the Badger school. He is a successful coach, having been educated at Ohio Wesleyan, Springfield College of Physical Training and Clark University and having coached at Ohio Wesleyan and Clark. He comes here highly recommended and was President's Felmley's choice from among over forty candidates for the Normal coaching position.

June 25, 1923 (page 3)

COACH HORTON VISITS THE NORMAL, UNIVERSITY

Coach Clifford E. Horton, I. S. N. U.'s New athletic director, was a campus visitor last Thursday. He drove down from Madison, Wis., where he is attending the coaching school at the state university there.

Horton is not a large man, neither is a man of words, but he has had some excellent training in physical education work and was recommended to Dr. Felmley very highly by Prof. Douglas C. Ridgley, a former member of the faculty at Normal who is now at Clarke University, Worcester, Mass., where Mr. Horton coached the past year.

He is a graduate of Springfield Training school at Springfield, Mass, where he is rated one of the best gymnasts that institution has ever turned out. He played class football and soccer at Springfield, was captain of the senior class swimming team, and also played on the class hockey and baseball teams.

He has coached at Ohio Wesleyan University, handling freshman football and Varsity swimming and gymnastics teams.

At San Luis, Cal., he had full charge of all athletics in the public schools, coaching soccer, basketball, baseball and track. At Clarke he has coached soccer, gymnastics, and baseball, besides handling the gymnasium classes.

His high school career was spent at North Central High in Spokane, Wash., which is his hometown, where he captained the high school team in his senior year.

He has also done considerable officiating in the east in all branches of sport.

Sept 8, 1923 (page 3)
OUR NEW COACH
Old Normal welcomes you, Mr. Horton, and the old grads and the returning students are looking forward to a banner year in athletics. The School will stand back of the teams with more pep and enthusiasm than has been shown for some time.

Clifford E. Horton comes to us very well prepared for his duties as coach and instructor in Physical Education. He was recommended to Pres. Felmley very highly by Prof. D. C. Ridgley, a former member of the faculty at Normal who is now at Clarke University, Worcester, Massachusetts where Mr. Horton coached the past year.

He is a graduate of Springfield Training School at Springfield, Mass., where he is rated one of the best gymnasts that institution has ever turned out. He played class football and soccer at Springfield, was captain of the senior class swimming team, and also played on the class hockey and baseball teams.

He has coached at Ohio Wesleyan University, handling freshman football and Varsity swimming and gymnastics teams.

At San Luis, Cal., he had full charge of all athletics in the public schools, coaching soccer, basketball, baseball and track. At Clarke he has coached soccer, gymnastics, and baseball, besides handling the gymnasium classes.

His high school career was spent at North Central High in Spokane, Wash., which is his hometown, where he captained the high school team in his senior year.

He has also done considerable officiating in the east in all branches of sport.

During this summer he has been attending the coaching school at the University of Wisconsin under Dr. Meanwell, who is one of the veterans in the basketball game and has developed a very successful short passing game which has been used by Wisconsin teams extensively.

This system has been used very successfully lately by Coach Russell.

Let's all talk up football and help our new coach in every way possible.

Sept 16, 1927 (front page)
Introducing Coach Horton to New ISNU Men
To you older students this man needs no introduction. To you new ones we wish to present Mr. Clifford Horton, Director of Physical Education and head of the athletic department. But to both old and new, we wish to say that here is the man who is at the head of the department that is going to give I. S. N. U. the best athletic teams that she has had for many years.

Mr. Horton has had extended experience in his work and such that makes him a very fit man for the position. He has held positions at a great many places. He was physical Director at the Y. M. C. A. in Spokane, Washington; Michigan City, Indiana; Mittineague, Massachusetts, student instructor in Physical Education at Springfield College, Springfield, Mass.; Director of Playgrounds, Hamilton, Ontario.

Instructor in Physical Education, Ohio Wesleyan University, Delaware, Ohio; Director Physical Education, Public Schools, San Louis, California; Supervisor of Playgrounds, Gardener, Mass.; and Instructor in Physical Education and Coach of Baseball and Soccer, Clark University, Massachusetts.

Mr. Horton has been at I. S. N. U. for four years and those of us who are acquainted with him know that he is pleasant and willing to help at all times. We know from the past that Mr. Horton does his best at all times and if he could only do it all by himself, we would have teams that would whip any in the country but since he is powerless without our cooperation, it remains for us to supply the right kind of material for the team and then for us who do not make the teams to get behind our varsity and our coaches, Mr. Horton and Mr. Cogdal and push with all our might for the best teams that Old Normal ever put on the Athletic field.

MR. CLIFFORD E. HORTON.

Sept 16, 1927 (page 5)

GAMMA PHI BEGINNINGS

Coach Horton was heavily involved around the community with different physical education endeavors as well as being very busy with his job at ISNU. He was head coach of Football, Baseball, and Basketball, involved with intramurals, and also President of the ISNU Tennis Association.

Horton was, building relationships with people who would become involved in the organization and instilling his personality and ethics into the university. He received accolades for his work with the students, and was also well liked for his personality. He was kidded for being an "old man" and also for his Ohio roots.

During the 1927–28 school year, ISNU hired a new coach for football, basketball, and track. That provided Horton the opportunity to increase the scope of intramural athletics on campus (along with coaching the baseball team). He also began working with tumbling classes so they could provide entertainment during halves of football and basketball games. This was a big step towards forming a Gamma Phi organization to perform similarly.

The following Vidette article let's Coach Horton ("Pop"), himself, tell the story of the beginnings of Gamma Phi.

NOTE:
The article states Gamma Phi started at ISNU in 1926. The performances being described began in 1926, but Gamma Phi didn't start until 1929.

Clifford Horton: "Mr. Fieldhouse"
By Max Scherer
Sports Editor

It's no wonder after all these years that one of ISU's living athletic legends, Clifford E. "Pop" Horton is often called Mr. Fieldhouse.

After all, the former athletic coach and faculty member was university's first full-time athletic director, serving also as chairman of the men's health and physical department at the university for 38 years before retiring in 1961. That was the kind of service the was recognized in naming the new fieldhouse in his honor in 1963.

As the university's first full-time athletic director, Horton often had to contend with President David Felmley, an ISU president who prided himself on the academic achievement and the development of future schoolteachers.

Felmley, according to Horton, felt athletics were unimportant to a college's curriculum. As the athletic director, Horton couldn't schedule games on school days and once when Horton had scheduled 18 baseball games, Felmley wrote a letter Horton, wondering if 18 baseball games were a bit expensive.

Looking back on those days, Horton smiled about the former ISU president. "Dr. Felmley really didn't like athletics at all," he said. "When they named what is now McCormick Hall after him, he really was mad," Horton said. "They later named the science wing after him and renamed the athletic building after Henry McCormick."

Another memory Horton has about the former ISU president was when Felmley got upset about $105 electric bill for the gymnasium, which was then housed in Cook Hall. "I wrote back to Dr. Felmley and told him that besides the gym, the auditorium and the physics lab were on the same line as we were and that I tried to conserve as much energy as possibly Horton said.

Despite all of the run-ins that Horton and Felmley had, the former ISU athletic director thought highly of him. "Dr. Felmley's main

Former ISU athletic director Clifford Horton is often called Mr. Fieldhouse by many ISU fans just as much as he is affectionately called "Pop" by others at the university.

Photo by Steve Cardot

July 23, 1976 (page 8)

concern was one of academic concern," Horton said. "He was concerned that the students got the best education possible and that nothing should interfere.

"Dr. Felmley was a very charming and interesting man," Horton added, "and after he retired, I often went to see him."

Besides being athletic director, Horton was responsible for development of the Gamma Phi Circus which today is recognized around the country as one of the best college circuses in the nation. According to the former Redbird director, he had circus blood in him.

"I fell in love with the circus in 1908 when I entered high school," Horton said. "There at the YMCA, I introduced to tumbling and work with the apparatus."

His love for gymnastics and circus continued through his education particularly at Springfield College in Massachusetts where he was a member of the gymnastics exhibition team. There, he and other gymnasts went around the Eastern part of the country, giving exhibitions to large crowds.

Horton has two pictures of those days in two old yearbooks that he keeps in his ISU office in his basement. In the first one in 1917, he is on the top of a pyramid but the next year he was on the bottom. Horton explains the change rather humorously. "It had to do with the captain in 1918," he said with a smile. "He felt he deserved to be on top."

After college, Horton's love for the circus continued when he taught at Ohio Wesleyan. Nearby Ohio State had an organization also known as Gamma Phi. Wesleyan students were interested and started their own group with the encouragement of Horton.

Encouraged by the success at Wesleyan, Horton organized another Gamma Phi here at this university in 1926 with the first performance at Cook Hall as well as during the halftime of basketball games. Cook often was cramped when Horton used the hanging apparatus for some events. "We couldn't use that during basketball games *because it would interfere with the crowd," Horton said about the crowd which sat over the gym on a track on top.*

Through the years, the circus continued at ISU with growing success. Helping the program at first was the ability of ISU students to work out with professional aerial stuntmen at the local YMCA.

Horton said that it was the interest of the students that made the circus, successful. "You could be interested in this personally," he said, "but the circus won't be a success unless the students are interested in it."

Today, Horton enjoys going to the circus, which is now over 40 years old. "The show is a lot more fantastic these days," he said. "When I show some of the kids pictures from the old days of the circus, they laugh."

But the laughter stops when people think of the things Horton has done for the university. The distinction of being called Mr. Fieldhouse demonstrates the respect he has just as much as the nickname "Pop" demonstrates the affection people have for him.

Jan 31, 1928 (page 3)
Horton's Tumblers Please Crowd at DeKalb Game
There is never a dull moment during a basketball game held in the Felmley Gymnasium. Even between halves there have been attractions. Among the greatest of these attractions has been the performance of Coach Horton's tumbling class. This class is composed of young men who have as their pet avocation tumbling, and who under the direction of Coach Clifford E. Horton, have made this hobby of theirs something more than just a mere hobby. They have become quite adept at the art of "flip-flopping."

This class is usually aided and abetted by the august personages of "Tiny" and his brother Roy. Roy and Tiny come to supper when called Moore. At a recent game Tiny was evidently having a little trouble with his vertebrae, hence the visit to "Dr." Roy Benjamin Moore, "D. C." a recently expelled student of the Bone Crusher

Academy of Chiropractors. From the method of exit which the patient and "Doctor" made it was left entirely up to the audience as to whether or not the pennies which were thrown at "Tiny", presumably to pay his doctor bill, were spent for a worthy cause. "Tiny" seems to be O. K. today.

The rest of the program was given over to barrel rolls, half "Immelmans," nose dives and short zooms on the part of the Tumbling class. The members of the class are—Arthur Glasgow, Maurice McEhliney, Roy Moore, Glenn Moore, and others from the Physical Education department.

Mar 7, 1929 (page 2)
Tumbling, Boxing, and Wrestling to be Featured.

The men's advanced classes in Physical Education are presenting a program of boxing, wrestling, and tumbling next Wednesday evening at 7:00 o'clock at the Felmley gym. (Note: Felmley Gym would later be re-named McCormick Gym.) This program is the result of a term's work in the respective classes.

The Tumbling class coached by Mr. Horton has given exhibitions between halves at the games, but Wednesday night they will have a new exhibition which will not be limited to the customary ten minutes. Most of the class of twenty-five will take part in this program.
...

GAMMA PHI IS APPROVED AS A FRATERNITY AT ISNU!

Pop's interest in getting men interested in doing something for themselves not confined to competitive athletics; his participation in Bloomington YMCA circuses; and the focused desire of a couple ISNU students to form a new chapter of Gamma Phi, culminated in the official approval for the Alpha Chapter of Gamma Phi on Nov 5, 1929.

Gamma Phi practices, and future circuses, take place in McCormick Gymnasium until 1964.

Nov 11, 1929 (page 3)
GAMMA PHI, NEW FRATERNITY MEETS
The Gamma Phi, a new honorary gymnastic fraternity, was approved at the last faculty meeting. This fraternity was instigated and will be sponsored by Mr. C. E. Horton, head of the Department of Physical Education, for men, and its objective is to stimulate interest in a better all-round development of the body. It does not propose to promote teams or social activities.

Any man who has three Physical Education credits is eligible, provided he meets all the requirements to become a member.

Requirements Stated
According to the constitution, he must: have leadership ability, be able to teach gymnastics, strive at all times to have good posture, know sportsmanship code and practice it religiously, do a number of stunts on parallels and horse, have Physical Education grades averaging 80, know the Normal nine, be able to teach ten of the unit pyramids shown in the physical education syllabus for the winter

term, have voice 80 percent proficient on volume, clarity, and ability
to command, pass a physical efficiency test in the following events:
first, 100 yd-dash, 12 seconds
second, running high jump, 4 feet, 4 inches
third, throw baseball 217 feet
fourth, throw a baseball accurately, four strikes out of five
fifth, running broad jump, 14 feet
sixth, punt a football, 35 yards
seventh, forward pass accurately to man running in lateral
    zone
eighth, make 7 out of ten free throws
ninth, rope climb, 18 feet in 8 seconds
tenth, hand spring successfully

NOTE:
In a 1975 interview, Pop confessed; "At the time it
seemed necessary to indicate the qualifications for
membership. The list was more or less idealistic on my
part." [5] If pledges came close they could still join. Later,
the test was modified to be more gymnastic and circus
oriented.

Nov 18,1929 (page 3)
GAMMA PHI PLEDGES HOLD FIRST MEETING
Aims And Ideals Of New Organization Discussed By Mr. Horton
*Gamma Phi pledges together with Mr. C. E. Horton, sponsor, met
last Monday evening to talk over and formulate plans for the new
fraternity.*

*Melvin Story was selected to serve as temporary chairman owing to
the fact that there are no members, just pledges, consequently
officers can not be elected.*

*Mr. Horton explained the aims and ideals of the fraternity and also
stated briefly the requirements that must be met on the horse, on
parallels, and in tumbling, all indoor tests.*

Several of the men faculty members have indicated a desire to join the fraternity and all are eligible to honorary membership.

The pledges are to be initiated on December 5 and 6, with a banquet on the night of December 6, when they will be formally initiated into Gamma Phi.

This new fraternity, planned and made possible through the efforts of Mr. Horton, has created a furor of interest on the campus because of its high ideals and standards of ability that one must have in order to become a member.

Men pledged the past week are G. Moore , Drum, LaMance, Shiner, Covey, Graack, Arnold, Aeillo, and Professors Holmes and Hudelson, and Coach Douglas.

Dec 9, 1929 (page 3)
GAMMA PHI TUMBLERS SHOW THEIR CLASS IN EXHIBITION THURSDAY

Three Gamma Phi pledges together with their instructor, Mr. C. E. Horton, gave a finished exhibition in tumbling during General Exercises at the auditorium Thursday morning. All the men showed excellent coaching and performed the many difficult feats with ease.

The program was given under the auspices of the Student Council with "Peg" Reynolds in charge. Roy Moore explained the ideals of the new fraternity, Gamma Phi. Mr. C. E. Horton, of the department of education, sponsor, was a member of this society at Ohio Wesleyan University, and will initiate the pledges, said Mr. Moore. "The boys will now word the song, 'Sweetheart of Gamma Phi'."

Tiny Moore, who as a comedian is in a class by himself, kept the crowd in an uproar with his impersonations of a golfer.

The tumbling team consisting of "Bill" Muhl, "Rus" Carter, Carl Unsicker, and Mr. Horton, will also entertain between halves of the home basketball games.

Dec 16, 1929 (page 6)
GAMMA PHI, P. E. FRAT, HOLDS INITIATION BANQUET
The new fraternity Gamma Phi in the Physical Education curriculum held an invitation banquet at the Rogers Hotel Thursday night at 7:30. This banquet was given in honor of the new pledges following an initiatory service held at the gym before going to the hotel.

A dinner was served and the young men and faculty pledges were entertained with music and speeches.

About eighteen pledges were given their frat pins at this banquet. The group included Roy Moore, Louis Striegal, Edward Covey, Gene Hill, Melvin Story, William Muhl, Gerald Drum, John Shiner, Forrest Steelsmith, Carl Unsicker, Jack Mooney, Ray Copeland, Bill Bryan, James Stables, George Graack, Bob Rowe, and Scott, also the faculty men, Tommy Douglass, Jr., M. J. Holmes, and C. W. Hudelson.

Jan 13,1930 (page 3)
P E. MEN ARE BEING TAUGHT TAP DANCING
Fifteen students who are enrolled in the Physical Practice class under Mr. C. E. Horton are being taught tap dancing two hours a week by Miss Margaret Barto, head of the Physical Education department for women.

Mr. Horton says that "the entire class is evidently preparing for the stage". From the actions of "Tiny" Moore at time little doubt of this assertion can be entertained.

Jan 13, 1930 (page 3)
GAMMA PHI PREPARES FOR DEMONSTRATION AT COOKSVILLE
Members of Gamma Phi, newly formed fraternity in Physical Education, are preparing for a demonstration to be given at Cooksville sometime next month. The demonstration according to Director C. E. Horton will be one in methods of conducting various classes in tumbling, marching, and different games.

Jan 30, 1930 Edition 02 (page 3)

When the Gamma Phi boys marched out between halves in immaculate white outfits some rowdies in the crowd shouted remarks about the boys being "Whitewings" and asked where were their street cleaning- brushes. This hoodlum element at games is thoroughly shocking and should be discouraged. Write your Senator about it immediately.

The wand drill presented by these same Gamma Phi lads was decidedly interesting. The closeness of the contest kept the crowd on edge throughout but finally Story managed to gain a comfortable lead and finished well ahead of the other entrants. Shiner also ran.

Feb 10, 1930 (page 4)
Editorial - Deems Conduct Unsportsmanlike
Last week the column conducted by "Stretch" and "Bill" whoever they may be, carried a number of wisecracks about the wand-drills given by Gamma Phi at the Dekalb game. It may have lacked coordination, but it was given in the right spirit by men who had backbone enough to get out and do their best and it seemed to me that the sallies were wholly out of place.

Feb 10, 1930 (page 6)
GAMMA PHI TO GIVE ATHLETIC DEMONSTRATION
Members of Gamma Phi, honorary physical education fraternity for men, will go to Cooksville on February 12 and to Saybrook on February 21 to give exhibitions in tumbling, wand drills and stunts on parallel bars. The organization is also sponsoring a boxing and wrestling tournament to be held the second week in March, details to be published later.

The Gamma Phi fraternity has received all concessions for the district tournament for high schools which is to be held at Normal the latter part of March. Members of the fraternity will operate a check room and the sale of candy and will furnish ushers for the games.

During the business session at the last weekly meeting it was decided to hold monthly instead of weekly meetings on the first Wednesday night of the school month at 7:30.

Mar 3, 1930 (page 6)
GAMMA PHI TO HOLD PLEDGE MEETING

On last Wednesday evening at 7:30 p. m. Gamma Phi held a special meeting to consider new pledges. Four pledges and two honorary pledges were nominated for membership. Upon the initiation of the new men Gamma Phi will contain eighteen active members and five honorary members.

The four new men nominated for pledges are: Burton Carlock, of Carlock, Carrol Cade of Normal, Clark Starr of Downs, and Arthur Hill of Decatur. The two faculty men nominated are Professors Richard Browne and Russell Packard.

A pledge meeting will be held next Wednesday afternoon at 4:30 p. m. in room 126 in the Felmley gymnasium. At this time the new pledges will be formally pledged to Gamma Phi.

At this time plans will be completed for caring for all concessions at the High School District Tournament to be held at the Felmley Gym on March 6, 7, and 8.

Gamma Phi will have a check room and all candy concessions. During the more important sessions of the tournament the members will also have charge of the ushering.

Plans have almost been completed for the boxing and wrestling tournament to be sponsored by the Greek letter fraternity. The date for the event has not yet been decided upon. Watch in the next issue of the Vidette for the time of this event.

1930 Index (page 149)

Apr 7, 1930 (page 3)

Gamma Phi Athletic Show Draws Large Number of Sporting Fans Despite Inclemency of Weather

Judges from Y. W. Have Had Experience in Boxing The unexpected return of Old Man Winter failed to dampen the ardor of the goodly crowd that attended the Athletic Show, sponsored by the Gamma Phis; Physical Education fraternity of I. S. N. U. The show was held in the Felmley gymnasium, Tuesday night, March 25.

Judges of the meet were Lou Houser and Art Shelton of the Y. M. C. A. Both men are well versed in the art of boxing and wrestling, and are well known by Normal and Bloomington sport fans. Harry Carter of I. S. N. U. officiated as referee and Carl Leonard as timekeeper.

The first event was a middleweight wrestling match of a six minute time advantage between "Louie" Striegal and "Jimmie" Orr, Louie winning in one fall after five minutes and forty-five seconds of wrestling.

Winebrenner Wins Lightweight In the lightweight division, Winebrenner threw Griffin in one minute and thirty seconds, in an easy match.

Roy East tossed Arthur Armbruster after four and one half minutes, to take the title in the heavyweight division. The struggle was very close and aroused much interest among the spectators.

The fourth event was a heavyweight bout between Roy Moore and Irwin Perrill. Moore weighed in at 164 pounds while Parrill was checked at 160. The match was scheduled for three rounds to a decision. According to the attentiveness of the crowd, the boys put up a good scrap. First blood was drawn by Perrill in the initial round by a left hook to Moore's face. Perrill seemed to have the advantage in the first and third rounds, while Moore looked best in the second. At the end of the thrilling bout the judges awarded Perrill the decision.

Smith Outclassed by Pitts
Tommy Smith met Hank Pitts in the middleweight division and was outclassed in a fast bit of boxing. Pitts weighed 158 pounds while Smith registered at 150. According to the judges, "Tommy" took the opening round, but "Hank" staged a comeback in the last two to win the decision.

An exhibition match of clever boxing featured the sixth event of the meet. Two Y. M. C. A. boys, Clarence Croutcher and Bud Wheat, weighing 131 and 134 pounds respectively, put on a fine demonstration, which clearly showed the wonderful training which they had received under the guidance of Lou Houser and Art Shelton, coaches of the Y. M. C. A. boxing and wrestling teams. No decision was offered.

Webb vs. Van Schoick in Finals In the final event, "Charlie" Webb met "Bob" Van Schoick in a clever exhibition of wrestling. Although no decision was made the match was very close and was a fine conclusion for the meet.

Regardless of the fact that this is the first year boxing and wrestling have been taught extensively at I. S. N. U., the plan for their continuance has met with great approval.

June 23, 1930 (page 3)

Eugene Hill, Track Star, Appointed to Normal Coaching Staff Ex-Captain Eugene Hill of Illinois State Normal University's 1930 track edition has been appointed by C. E. Horton, director of physical education and all athletics, as a member of his alma mater's coaching staff, and will assume his duties on September 1. Mr. Hill has just graduated from Old Normal with an enviable athletic record.

He captained this season's track team, which finished fourth in the Little 19 conference meet, climaxing his fourth year of running with a place himself. In addition to his track ability he competed on the Varsity football team and was a member of the Varsity basketball team throughout his entire four year curriculum. He has been awarded the "N" blanket, for four years of athletic work on one Varsity squad and for having received the resultant four letters. He holds the all-time records in the half and mile runs at Normal.

"Gene" is a member of the Gamma Phi fraternity, an athletic group, and of the Jesters, a dramatic organization. In addition he is a member of the Illinois State Normal athletic board and belongs to the "N" club, a group of letter men.

His scholastic work has found him completing all of the courses in education, particularly in physical education and coaching, with high marks. He prepared for matriculation at I. S. N. U. at Leroy high school, where he was a star in track, football, and basketball.

The exact duties for Mr. Hill have not been announced yet, but it is expected that he will assist in football and track besides handling some education classes. Mr. Horton and Mr. Cogdal have been overburdened with work the past year and so Coach Hill's appointment will relieve some of the burden from their shoulders.

1930 – 31 School Year

Gamma Phi members are very active and successful in intramural sports. They perform in many exhibitions and in the annual Bloomington and Peoria YMCA Circuses.

Several Gamma Phi members also represent the YMCA in a large Bloomington parade by performing on parallel bars on top of a float.

1931 Index (page 150)

Oct 10, 1930 (page 3)
Bill Muhl and Shorty Unsicker would like the attention of every man who is interested in tumbling to be called to the class in tumbling which meets the sixth and sevenths hours on Thursdays. These two boys have done much toward the growing interest in this sport at Normal and it is probable that members of this class will perform between halves of the home basketball games this winter.

Oct 27, 1930 (page 3)

GAMMA PHI GROUP IS TO STUNT AT NEXT GAME

A group of 32 men are being trained by Melvin Story and William Muhl to participate in a drill feature during the half at the football game between I. S. N. U. and Macomb here November 1. The feature will be in the form of a zuave drill, at double pace time with the accompaniment of the drums.

This drill is one of the efforts of the Gamma Phi, physical education fraternity, to encourage the men students in gymnastics. It will also give the participants an idea of drilling and of how to obtain exactness and unity in mass action.

Nov 3, 1930 (page 3)

Gamma Phi is Host to Physical Education Men

Gamma Phi, the men's physical education fraternity on the campus was the host to the members of the physical education curriculum at a party held last Monday evening in McCormick gym.

Forrest Steelsmith, president of the organization gave a speech of welcome in which he presented a short history of Gamma Phi and its purposes, the speech appears at the last of this article. William Muhl and Melvin Story entertained the audience with a demonstration of a zuava dance with members of the freshman gym classes aiding in the work. The dance is done to the beating of a tom tom, Mr. Muhl and Mr. Story being responsible for the training of the dancers.

"Shorty" Unsicker, William Muhl, and Director C. E. Horton then gave an exhibition of tumbling and parallel and high bar work. Refreshments in the form of ice cream and cake were served after which the boys played games. Following are excerpts from a talk given by Mr. Steelsmith.

History of Gamma Phi
"Our object in bringing this fraternity to life was to promote the interest, of Physical Education among the students and to honor the gymnastic excellence of the individual members of the student body and faculty.

"While we have not been in existence long and our history is short, we have made what I believe is a good beginning. The men in this chapter have been and are those who have with work accomplished a high degree of proficiency. Last year we took a worthy place in the Y. M. C. A. circus in Bloomington. In addition we gave several programs at High Schools near by. We believe that not only did the men giving these programs receive something worthwhile, but that we had an excellent part in advertising our school. Though we are still too young to point to any of our members, who have graduated and say they have accomplished much, we are confident that in the future our members will greatly aid in dissemination of physical education throughout the schools of the state.

"For the current school year we are planning to receive into our midst those men who have developed themselves to meet our rather rigid requirements. Further we are going to repeat at some of the schools our presentations of last year and also perform before a number of other student bodies. There are three purposes we have in mind in so doing.

A degree of knowledge will be acquired by those performing which could not be obtained elsewhere. We expect to interest the schools in better physical education, thus opening a wider field for future graduates, and we believe the University and teaching profession will profit by our performances. In that more men will be interested in entering schools and graduating into the teaching profession."

Dec 8, 1930 (page 3)
GAMMA PHI TO ENTERTAIN WOMEN'S P. E. CLUB TONITE
Gamma Phi, gymnastic fraternity, will hold a joint meeting with the women of the Physical Education department. Monday night at seven o'clock in Henry McCormick Gymnasium. All of the women of the physical education department are cordially invited.

There will be various demonstrations and talks by the members of Gamma Phi. There will also be a social period with games, dancing and refreshments.

Jan 19, 1931 (page3)
The basketball squads from Forrest Township and Bloomington High Schools were guests of the I. S. N. U. Athletic Association at the Charleston game. As an added feature Gamma Phi, the men's gymnastic fraternity, put on some splendid tumbling acts between halves of the contest.

Mar 16, 1931 (page 4)
Intramural Finals: Gamma Phi wins Handball, Bowling, Twenty-one, and team point total - came in second in Volleyball and Free Throwing.

Mar 23, 1931 (page 4)
Intramural Track: Gamma Phi "Thinlies" win track meet. Wardell 2nd in 220 dash; Raymond 1st in shot put; Muhl 1st in 880 run; Unsicker and Sweet 2nd in Pole Vault; Raymond 2nd in Javelin; Raymond 3rd in Discus; Moore, Starr, Sweet 1st, 2nd, 3rd in 120 high hurdles; Moore 1st in 220 low hurdles.

Mar 23, 1931 (page 4)
TWENTY-FOUR TO BE INITIATED INTO GAMMA PHI
Twenty-four candidates will be initiated into the Gamma Phi at their formal and informal initiation ceremonies to be held at McCormick gym in the evening of March 26.

The candidates have qualified for entrance by passing a number of tests prescribed by the organization. The members to be initiated are:
> *James Tatman, June Van Gundy, Philip Bavo, Hugh Pinkstaff, Donald Wardell, Arthur Sitwiller, Lloyd Fricke, Glen Raymond, Cecil Fosdick, Dorrence Darling, Wayne Scott, Ray Copeland*

In addition to these regular candidates three honorary candidates will also be initiated. They are President H. A. Brown, Prof. John F. Fraley, and Prof. C. A. Harper of the faculty.

Coach Horton is sponsor of the club, Forrest Steelsmith is president and will preside over the ceremonies.

June 8, 1931 (front page)
Awards Presented to Students In General Exercises Tuesday
...
Prof. W A. L. Beyer awarded to John E. Shiner, William Muhl and Carl Unsicker special awards in recognition of their work in the Gamma Phi during the past year. The pins are slightly different from the regular pins of the society and are the first of their kind to be awarded.

1931-32 School Year

As the school year starts, no circus is in the works. The first Gamma Phi Circus comes together late in the school year. The members continue with heavy intramural involvement and many gymnastic exhibitions.

1932 Index (page 64)

THE
GAMMA PHI
TUMBLERS

For the third year this group appeared at the Peoria Y.M.C.A. Annual Circus Thursday, March Thirty-first.

1932 Index (page 233)

GAMMA PHI,
INTRAMURAL
WINNERS

Gamma Phi, intramural champions in Bowling, Volleyball, and Twenty One.

This group defeated the "N" club for the Volleyball and Bowling championships, and the Holly Hawks for the Twenty One title. From left to right: Raymond, Starr, Muhl, Mooney, Copeland, Shiner, Van Gundy.

1932 Index (page 233)

Oct 5, 1931 (page 5)

C. E. Horton Speaks at Stag Party Held by Varsity Club
Pres. Brown, Hancock, Cogdal, and Harpster also Talk to Men

A stag party for the men of the school was held in McCormick gym Wednesday evening, Sept. 30. The party was sponsored by the Men's Varsity Club. About 150 men were in attendance.

Rudolph Leasman, president of the organization, presided at the meeting of which the members of the faculty connected with athletics gave short talks C. E. Horton stressed the importance of each student getting into some form of physical activity as a means of getting "athletic minded" and to link the student participating with the institution. C. E Harpster told of the importance of friendship among students in the building of a school. Other speakers were Pres. H. A. Brown who stressed the importance of clean athletics, Coach H. J. Hancock, and Coach J. T. Cogdal.

The Gamma Phi represented by Philip Bova, John Shiner, "Shorty" Unsicker, and Joe Mooney, entertained on the mat and bars. Philip Bova then led the group in a few Normal cheers.

Refreshments of doughnuts and cider were served by a committee of the club.

Oct 12, 1931 (page 3)

GAMMA PHI SPONSOR GET ACQUAINTED PARTY

A get-acquainted party for all GM majors was held in the McCormick gymnasium Tuesday evening from 7:30 until 9:00 and was sponsored by Gamma Phi, honorary athletic fraternity.

About 30 men of the school attended and an effort to have everyone become acquainted was made after which various games were indulged in. Badminton, volley ball, handball and gymnastics were the main attractions of the evening.

Carl Unsicker, chairman of the program, called the men together and introduced Mr. C. E; Horton, head of the department, who outlined the aims and plans of the organization, with the proposal winter program.

Mr. Horton, in covering his outline, Stated that Gamma Phi would meet each Tuesday night from seven until eight-thirty and that all physical education majors and their friends interested in the participating and learning of games that are not so widely known or performed, or in gymnastic stunts are cordially invited to attend these meetings.

Continuing Mr. Horton explained the purpose and aim of the organization in promoting good sportsmanship and honesty." Not because it's wrong," he said, "but because we believe it's the right thing to do," was his statement concerning both honesty and sportsmanship.

He also stated how Gamma Phi gymnastic teams had at various times given performances and exhibitions before Business club and high school audiences, and annually participated in the Bloomington "Y" circus and in functions about the university, mainly the annual stunt show held each spring. It was also mentioned that this would be a good opportunity for all those men who have had special yearnings to learn and master some trick on the bars and ropes, or be able to play some game which heretofore they have not been able to play.

After the fun and introductory talk refreshments of ice cream and doughnuts were served to all those who attended. It is being planned to have refreshments each meeting night and this will be brought about by the cooperation of all those interested.

Feb 29, 1932 (page 3)
The Gamma Phi, athletic fraternity, at Normal university, are at present completing plans for a circus to be staged at McCormick gym on March 11. This is the first event of its kind ever sponsored on the campus and it is expected to bring out a large crowd. The price will be reasonable and the Gamma Phi hope that everyone will cooperate to make it a success.

THE McCORMICK GYMNASIUM IN NOVEMBER

On misty autumn days, when the pattern of light and shade, which every architect expects to set off his building to best advantage, is weakest, the new gymnasium still presents a strong, but somewhat ambiguous style of architecture.

1932 Index (page 176)

Celebrate Winter Term Ending

SELL YOUR BOOKS AND PUT SOME MONEY BACK INTO CIRLATION FRIDAY NIGHT—

Gamma Phi

Mammoth Gym Circus

10 BIG ACTS

STARTING 7:30

VARSITY CLUB

School Party and Dance

—INTRODUCING—

BILL McQUEEN and HIS SERENADERS

STARTING 9:15

SINGLE ADMISSION—CIRCUS 25c— DANCE 25c
COUPLE ADMISSION TO BOTH — 75c

Mar 7, 1932 (page 5)

1932 Index (page 231)

Mar 7, 1932 (front page)
First Annual Circus to be Given by Gamma Phi Friday
One of the Most Outstanding Events on Any Campus Held in Gym
PROGRAM IS GIVEN

"Lay-deeze and Gentilmun, you are going to witness one of the most outstanding spectacles ever witnessed on any college campus in the United dates." It won't be long until "barkers" will be screaming and shouting for the first annual Gamma Phi circus to be held in McCormick gymnasium next Friday, March 11.

During the last four or five years, men representing Gamma Phi, a gymnastic fraternity, have exhibited tumbling acts, pyramid building, and various gymnastic maneuvers until they developed a reputation among students of the school. Because it was felt that basketball was enough attraction for one evening exhibitions have stopped. However, the fellows have practiced hard and are going to make a concentrated effort to put on a program never witnessed before. Mr. Horton expects it to be exceptionally good.

The evening will resemble a characteristic circus and Mr. Fletcher and his band will furnish music.

Following is the complete program:
1. *Tap Review—by Women's Physical Education Department.*
2. *Mel Story's World Review Zoave.*
3. *Egyptian Troup—Pyramid building.*
4. *Russ Carter and his Famous Flying Rings.*
5. *Barr Brothers on the double horizontal bar.*
6. *Razewell Troup—will do tumbling.*
7. *Gamma Phi Unparalled Bar Pyramids.*
8. *Russ and Carl—Revolving Ladder—death-defying feat in mid-air.*
9. *The finale will be a typical— Grand leap for life over the elephant.*

Innumerable clown acts will be led by June Van Gundy. A giant strong man promises to exhibit monger muscles.

Jake Ward, a veteran ring master or many of the leading circuses in the U.S., will handle the same duties for this circus. Don Warded is in charge of advertising, while Frank Muhl has been delegated to manage properties. Pop corn, peanuts and candy will be sold.

Immediately following the circus, the Varsity Club is cooperating with Gamma Phi in staging a dance. The admission for a couple to both the circus and the dance will be seventy-five cents. Single admission is twenty-five cents for each event. Bill McQueen's greater Band will play.

1932 Index (page 231)

1932 Index (page 231)

1932 Index (page 231)

Apr 4, 1932 (page 3)
GAMMA PHI TO PEORIA
*Gamma Phi, national gymnastic fraternity and two girls from the
women's physical education department took part in the Peoria Y. M
C. A. Annual Circus Thursday night March 31. This is the third time
that Gamma Phi has' appeared at that circus.*

*Mr. Forest Cockerill '28 and member of Gamma Phi is an instructor
in the Peoria Y. M. C. A.*

*Those making the trip were Shiner Van Gundy, Muhl, Unsicker,
Carter Anderson, Warded, Mooney, Martin Lauderback, Sweet,
Starr, and Muleloon.*

Apr 4, 1932 (page 3)
INTRAMURAL TROPHIES AWARDED BY MANAGER
*Immediately preceding the final match of the boxing and wrestling
carnival, the intramural trophies were awarded by senior manager
Melvin Story.*

*Owen Barclay, Charles Sweet, Louis Smolak, and Paul Hutmacher
received sweaters with their class numerals, as a reward for their
services as sophomore intramural managers. Donald Wardell and
June Van Gundy were presented with sweaters having the intramural
monogram attached for acting as junior intramural managers. Mr.
Hill awarded Melvin Story a handsome pin as his senior manager
reward.*

*Following these presentations, the various sport trophies were
presented. The Gamma Phi scored the highest total of points for the
winter term, entitling them to have their name engraved on the
permanent trophy. The fraternity boys won the championships in
team volleyball, team free throwing, and team bowling.*

*The Hollyhawks, an independent organization, received handsome
trophies for winning the basketball and twenty-one titles.*

*Clark Starr of Gamma Phi received a cup as a reward for securing
the individual bowling championship. Clark also maintained his lead*

*in the race for the individual point trophy, which is to be awarded at
the end of the spring term.*

Apr 11, 1932 (page 6)
Gamma Phi Will Meet To Select Pledges In Its Spring Initiation
*Illinois Alpha chapter of Gamma Phi, which was installed at Illinois
State Normal university in 1930 and whose Objectives are to
promote the interest of physical education among the students of the
school and to honor gymnastic excellence in the individual members
of the student body and faculty of the school by election to
membership, has named their pledges for this year following the
results of a meeting held Tuesday night, April 5.*

*Plans for the passing of certain tests which are required of all
pledges have been started. At some near future date pledges will be
given these tests and if successful will be taken into the organization
by both informal and formal initiation ceremonies.*

*As has been the custom in the past, the names of student and faculty
pledges are not announced publicity until after both initiations.*

*This organization of men has taken part in many all-school activities
in the past and are planning an even more extensive program for the
future.*

May 2,1932 (page 6)
GAMMA PHI TO HAVE CLUBROOM IN GYM
*Gamma Phi has been given the space in the northwest corner of the
men's locker room in McCormick Gymnasium for a club room. The
north tier of lockers has been moved south a few feet, thus leaving a
small room enclosed on the west and north sides by the brick wall of
the locker room, on the east by the wire enclosure of the supply
room, and on the south by the north tier of lockers. These lockers are
being rapidly vacated and rented by Gamma Phi members.*

*To make the enclosure complete wall board has been used in the
partition above the lockers and around the door which is located
between the locker tier and the west side of the supply room. Keys*

for this door are being made and will be issued to each member soon.

Although nothing in the way of furnishings has been procured, plans are underway to obtain some furniture as soon as possible.

Until the room is completed, the Tuesday night business meetings will continue to be held in room 126.

May 9, 1932 (page 3)
GAMMA PHI HOLDS SMOKER
Gamma Phi, physical education fraternity, is holding its monthly "dinner and smoker tonight at 6:15 in the newly decorated party room of the Alamo building. Mr. John A. Kinneman will speak on a topic concerning recreation, following the dinner. Pledges to the organization have been rapidly completing their tests and will be present at the smoker.

May 16, 1932 (page 5)
John Ad Kinneman Reads Paper Before Gamma Phi Members Brings Out How Schools May Effect Use of Leisure Time
Mr. John A. Kinneman read a paper on leisure time to Gamma Phi members and pledges last Monday night at a smoker held in the newly decorated party room of the Alamo building, The paper created quite an interest among those present and much discussion followed the many questions that were asked Mr. Kinneman at the conclusion of the paper.

Many men, according to the paper, have a tendency to "play" in some manner or other when time permits. One tinkers with his automobile, another raises fancy poultry, one reads, arid still another gathers antiques. There are also many, however, who do riot know what to do with their leisure time. They do not know how or what to play. The result is that probably they patronize commercial recreation or simply waste their time doing nothing but loaf.

...

After the reading of the paper, a discussion followed. Among the points discussed was the "carry over" value of school sports. The final feeling was that the average or below average coordinated person needs participation in the activities of the playground and intramural type, while the athlete, even though in most instances a star in one or two sports, develops the interest necessary at the time he needs it, if his particular game or games cannot be continued throughout life. An example of this is the football star who loves competition and has the spirit of play well-developed. Activity is life for him, and being unable to continue football, takes up tennis, golf, or any of the other numerous activities which one can continue throughout life.

Faculty members and pledges present included Mr. Tom Douglass, Mr. Richard Browne. Mr. Howard Hancock, and Mr. C. E. Horton, sponsor.

May 31, 1932 (page 5)
GAMMA PHI TO INITIATE AND HOLD BARBEQUE
Gamma Phi pledges are gradually completing their test and initiation, and those qualifying will be given their formal initiation tonight after school. Immediately after the initiation, which makes them members of this organization, the fraternity and guests will leave for a cabin at Lake Bloomington where a barbeque will be held. This outing is an annual affair and many of the men who are not in school now, return for it. Pledges who have completed the initiation so far are:

M. Hanson, Elliot
E. White, Bloomington
S. Anderson, Bloomington
Paul Madigan, Longview
W. Kenneth Martin, Taylorville
John Lafferty, Taylorville

Carl Unsicker, Deer Creek, is president and Mr. Clifford E. Horton is sponsor. This is the fourth year in which this organization has been in existence on the Normal university campus.

June 6, 1932 (front page)
P. E. SENIORS ENTERTAINED

With the graduation of Melvin Story, Bloomington; Walton Ruebush, Bloomington; Clark Starr, Downs; Louis Striegal, St. Anne; John Shiner, Hudson; and Carl Unsicker, Deer Creek, Gamma Phi will be left with no charter members. Following the banquet an election was held and Junior Van Gundy, Normal, was elected president, Frank Muhl, Bloomington, vice-president, and Donald Wardell, Normal, Secretary.

June 6, 1932 (page 2)
HONOR GRADUATES

Gamma Phi members who will be in school next year honored their graduating brothers" with a banquet at the Alamo Wednesday night of last week. Donald Wardell, Normal, was toastmaster for the evening. Those members who are leaving were asked to give suggestions as to activities planned for next year, as were the new members who have just been initiated.

1932 – 33 School Year

Building on the success of the first Circus, Gamma Phi moves forward with the second annual circus. This year, however, they introduce a new feature—The Queen. Over the next few decades, the Gamma Phi Queen attracted much of the attention and publicity of the Gamma Phi Circuses.

The traditions of the organization/fraternity begin to take shape. Practices, meetings, and pledging all start following patterns. In addition, a Service Award is introduced to honor individuals who contribute outstanding service and leadership within the organization.

1933 Index (page 141)

48

Sept 19, 1932 (page 3)

Brown to Speak to Men at Stag Party for All Men Tonight

A Stag Party for all the men of the university will be sponsored by the Varsity club at McCormick gymnasium Monday evening, September 19, at 6:45. The party will give the men on the campus, and especially the Freshmen, in opportunity to become acquainted with other men and to learn to know more of the various faculty men and campus leaders that are concerned with the activities of the men of the college. During the course of the evening many of the campus leaders among the men will be introduced, several faculty men will speak, and an excellent program will be presented.

President Brown will be present to welcome all the men and speak to them. The president has been very much interested in the activities of the university and most of all those concerning the men. He is an enthusiastic sports follower and he Is doing all within his power to forward the interests of not only sports but also all of the other activities that will further the interests of the school.

In addition to President Brown, the men will hear Professor Horton, Director of the Division of Health and Sports; Coach J. T. Cogdal, cross country and basketball coach; and Howard J. Hancock, director of Intercollegiate athletics. Each of these men will talk of the field in which he works and the athletic outlook for the coming year. The captains of the athletic teams of the fall term will be introduced.

Program is Planned
A program is being arranged that promises to be very entertaining. Theodore Colteaux, a magician, who recently received a high award from the association of amateur magicians of the United States for the excellence of his work, will be present to mystify the men with his conjurer's tricks. Fred Fissell, a local man who has received wide acclaim as a master of the piano accordion, will play a group of selections. Gamma Phi will present a gymnastic act. Professor Admire will use his skill in aiding the men in group singing. Food is to be served by the Four Chefs in an unusual and interesting as well as appetizing manner.

Oct 17, 1932 (page 2)

GAMMA PHI TO HAVE CHANGE OF NORMAL CHEERLEADER

In an effort to stimulate the cheering it the football games and to bring about cooperation through the medium of tumbling in cheerleading, Gamma Phi, the men's honorary gymnastic Fraternity has taken over the business of training the cheerleaders.

At a meeting held recently, Kenneth Martin of Evanston was appointed by the club to take charge and since that time as evidenced by the splendid showing at the football games, the yell-leaders have been working together.

Five men, in addition to Martin will comprise the cheerleading team. They are, Arthur Litwiller of Hopedale, John Guthrie of Lexington, Charles Jordon of Clifton, Clifford Scott of Normal and Clifford Tanglois of Manteno.

In the future this group hopes to introduce new cheers to entertain and pep-up the crowd and with the cooperation of the student body they will be able to make the cheering of Normal crowds noted.

Nov 4, 1932 (front page)

Homecoming Festivities are to Open This Evening at 8:15

...

After the Homecoming play at 8:15 and dance at 8:30. Jester-Theta Alpha Phi's reception for cast of the Homecoming play will be held, with the Gamma Phi Midnight Luncheon following at 12:00.

...

Nov 14, 1932 (front page)

TUMBLING TIME HAD AT CONVOCATION

Twas short and snappy! Everyone seemed to be having a tumbling good time at the convocation Wednesday morning, November 9. At 9:50 o'clock when the doors were closed, the auditorium was filled nearly to capacity.

"Just a Bunch of Bums Returning from Homecoming," starring Carl Unsicker, Bill Muhl, Richard Nelle, Frank Muhl, Cecil Fosdick, Kenneth Marlin, Joe Mooney, Edson White, Junior Van Gundy, Russell Anderson, Arthur Litwiller, and Donald Warded, brought a storm of applause, to say nothing of those tumbling, tapping lasses—Jessie Marie Lucas, Caroline Wolf, Charlotte Jackson, Jean Wilder, Helen Royce, Marjorie Cook, Rachel Noe, Betty Baird, Thurley Voelkel, and Dorothy Harmon.

And can that Muhl boy swing a wicked Indian club? Um-um.

Pep, originality, with a dash of the Four Marx brothers for seasoning, were the ingredients that went into the making of that joint performance presented by. members of Gamma Phi and the Women's Athletic Association last Wednesday.
...

GAMMA PHI IS ON THE RISE
The Gamma Phi presence on campus is growing larger than just the Intramural teams and small shows they've been doing, to include the annual Circus.

ALONG WITH THE START OF THE CIRCUS, THE GAMMA PHI QUEEN IS STARTING
The Gamma Phi Circus is a big thing on the ISNU campus. This year, the Gamma Phi Queen is just starting. The Queen integration with Gamma Phi begins to grow much larger for a long time.
...

Jan 9, 1933 (front page)
Second Annual Gym Circus To Be Presented Feb. 16-17
Circus Queen to be elected by Student Body to Preside
"Step right up close, Ladies and Gentlemen, you are about to witness the greatest show on earth", or words to that effect. While the barker's language may be a bit strong, he is merely informing the public that on Thursday and Friday, February 16 and 17, the second annual Gym Circus will be held at McCormick gymnasium.

*Last year Gamma Phi, the gymnastic fraternity on the campus,
staged the first circus and it proved such a success that another is to
be given this year. However, Gamma Phi, having been the guiding
force in instigating the circus movement is incorporating with the
other departments in school in staging this year's performance.*

Greatest of its Kind
*This year's presentation promises to be the greatest of its kind.
Drills, tumbling, gymnastic exhibitions, tap dancing, pyramid
formations and a dozen other types of entertainment will be offered.
All the departments at the gymnasium are assisting and both the men
and women physical education majors will play leading roles.*

*In addition to these headliners a professional act is being brought to
the campus which promises to be a great treat.*

*Clowns galore, peanuts and pink lemonade, a stentorian-mouthed
ring master (in the person of Jake Ward) and numerous other
features that are typical of a real circus will be included.*

To Pick Circus Queen
*A special feature of this year's circus will be the election of a Circus
Queen by the student body. A young lady, a member of I. S. N. U.
undergraduate body, will be chosen by popular vote to preside over
the proceedings.*

*Nominations for the Queen must contain twenty-five signatures and
the first twelve names received will be on the ballot for the final
voting.*

*Begin circulating your petition now for the Queen of the Circus.
Turn the petitions into either Donald Warded, June Van Gundy, or
Campbell Miller.*

More details will be given later

Jan 16, 1933 (page 6)

CIRCUS PLANS ARE GETTING UNDERWAY

*Plans for The Second Annual Gym Circus Are Taking Form
Nominating Petitions for Queen are Due by Noon, Jan. 20 With all
the committees hard at work on their particular line of duty the plans
for the Second Annual Gym Circus to be presented at McCormick
gymnasium, Thursday and Friday, Feb. 16 and 17, are rapidly
nearing their final form.*

*The student body is fortunate in having on the campus Mr. Charles
Holloway, assistant boy's secretary at the Bloomington Y. M. C. A.,
who is doing graduate work at Normal this year. Mr. Holloway has
charge of this year's program and is ideally fitted for the position.
He received his bachelor's degree in Physical Education at Y. M. C.
A. college in Chicago where he made a special study of gym
circuses. Under Mr. Holloway's guidance the program for this
year's circus promises to be even greater than the splendid one
presented last year.*

Seventeen Numbers on Program
*Indications are at present that the program will contain seventeen
numbers, each one chock full of thrills, laughs, and entertainment.
The Grand March, a colorful parade of all the participants, will
open the proceedings and accompanied by Mr. Kenyon S. Fletcher's
State Normal band, the program will spring into life with a rapid-fire
appearance of class drills in pyramids and other intricate
formations, sport demonstrations, tumbling, parallel bar
performances, feats on the flying rings, smooth and machine like
Indian club exhibitions, gymnastic dancing, ladder pyramids, and
numerous other special treats that should hold the audience
entranced until the grand finale, the Sports Tableau to climax the
evening.*

*Close to seventy-five individuals will take part in the circus. Mr.
Harold Frye is in charge of the men's classes who will present the
class projects, Dr. Joseph Cogdal will handle the ports
demonstrations, and Mr. C. E. Horton's Gamma Phi gymnasts will
present the bulk of the tumbling, Indian club drills and the like.*

Joe Mooney is in charge of the tumbling, Russell Carter, Charles Sweet and Joe Mooney will conduct the parallel bar and ring exhibitions, while Bill Muhl, who many remember or his prize winning performance in the stunt show, will direct the Indian Club spectacle.

Miss Barto has charge of the women's program which promises to be novel and entertaining. While Bob Brumett will be the head clown without which no circus would be complete.

Committees in Charge
"Stretch" Miller is in charge of the publicity for the affair, with Frank Muhl handling the tickets and programs and Donald Warded in charge of decorations, properties, and arrangements.

With a number of nominations already in the hands of the committee in charge, the deadline for the nomination of Queen of the Circus is drawing closer. On next Friday, Jan. 20, It noon, all names, in order to be considered, must be with Donald Warded, June Van Gundy, or Campbell Miller. In order to nominate a girl for this honor her name must be accompanied by twenty-five signatures. The first twelve named on petitions received will be considered in the final all-school balloting.

Feb 27, 1933 (page 5)
ILL. NORMAL BAND AND CIRCUS TO JOURNEY TO MACOMB THIS WEEK
The "Red Birds", with a host of followers, including the school band and possibly a troupe of the Gamma Phi tumblers and parallel bar men will entrain Thursday evening for points west, with Macomb as the stopping place, where this year's hardwood battle between the Teachers' colleges is to be fought.
...

"Pop" Horton has been communicating with the officials at Western, and it is very probable that he will take a group of the actors from the recent circus out west with him, where they will give the people who are not fortunate enough to see a circus very often, a treat in the *way of stellar acrobatic performances on the mats and on the parallel bars.*

NOTE:
Throughout the years, the process of joining Gamma Phi has varied.

In 1929, all of the men except Pop were considered to be Pledges. Not being Members of Gamma Phi, those men were required to pass the requirements to the extent Pop felt they were qualified to become official Members.

Once formally initiated, those new Members were in control, along with Pop, of how future prospects could themselves become Members.

Members and Directors through the years have altered the qualifications, pledging requirements, and rituals.

At this point, and for the next several years, prospective members committed to pledge the organization. If they completed the requirements of an Informal Initiation, they were formally initiated a couple weeks later. Once initiated, Members (new, current, and past) joined in celebrating.

Mar 21, 1933 (front page)
GAMMA PHI, HONORARY GYM FRATERNITY, PLEDGES 22

Twenty-two men have been pledged to Gamma Phi, national honorary gymnastic fraternity, according to an announcement made Friday by the organization's secretary. The men pledged are:

Clifford Cozart, Normal
Barney Lewis, Carrollton
Gerald Slusser, Villa Grove
Ralph Seitz, Sullivan
H. Clifford Scott, Normal
John Guthrie, Lexington
Herbert Litwiller, Normal
Tom Kerrick, Bloomington
Homer Rice, Cerro Gordo
Campbell Miller, Chicago
Glenn Roberts, Rankin
John D. Murdock, Normal
Edward Fitzgerald, Springfield
Charles Marsh, Normal
Carl Marquardt, Bloomington
Robert Reynolds, Paw Paw
Leroy Van Brannan, Bloomington
Robert Brumett, Saunemin
Harold Swartzbaugh, Canton
Richard Bennett, Decatur

Mar 27, 1933 (page 7)
GAMMA PHI MEETING

Gamma Phi, local gymnastic fraternity, held a short meeting Monday, March 20, for its pledges. Talks were made by President Harry Van Gundy. C. E. Horton, sponsor and director of the Health and Sports Education for Men, and by Donald Wardell. Each member was assigned to a pledge, entrance requirements were read, and the members withdrew after a short business meeting.

Apr 3, 1933 (page 2)

Gamma Phi Gym Fraternity Stages Initiation Services

Gamma Phi, physical education fraternity, held an informal initiation Monday, March 27, for its pledges.

New members taken into the organization include:
Harold Swartzbaugh, Robert Brummitt, Charles Marsh, Van Brannan, Richard Bennett, Tom Kerrick, Howard Litwiller, Kenneth Sykes, Kenneth Rice, John Murdock, Dick Reynolds, Glen Roberts, Barney Lewis, Sam Slusser, Ed Fitzgerald, John Guthrie

A group of actives kidnapped four of the pledges and drove them out in the country, whereupon the car ran out of gas and the pledges caught a ride home and the actives pushed their automobile home.

Formal initiation will be held Monday April 13, in the new Gamma Phi clubroom in McCormick gymnasium. C. E. Horton, director of Health and Sports Education for men, is sponsor.

Apr 10, 1933 (page 6)

Gamma Phi Stages Formal Initiation for Seventeen Men

Gamma Phi, the national honorary gymnastic fraternity on the campus, initiated seventeen new members at formal services held at McCormick gymnasium last Monday evening.

New members are:
Howard Litwiller, J. Van Brannan, John Guthrie, Russell Anderson, Glenn Roberts, John Murdock, Kenneth Seitz, Robert Brumett, Richard Bennett, Edward Fitzgerald, Tom Kerrick, Jerry Slusser, Charles Marsh, Robert Reynolds, Charles Sweet, Clifford Cozart, Kenneth Rice

A dinner was served at the Alamo following the initiation services at which faculty members and students spoke briefly. Henry Van Gundy, the president, was toastmaster.

Prof. C. E. Horton, director of the department of health and sports education, and sponsor of Gamma Phi awarded service pins to four members who have been outstanding in activity in the organization. Those who received pins were Henry Van Gundy, Milford Hanson, Donald Warded and Melvin Storey.

Apr 17, 1933 (page 6)
GAMMA PHI PUTS ON EXHIBITION AT PEKIN
The members of Gamma Phi, local physical education fraternity, under the supervision of C. E. Horton, director of Health and Sports Recreation for men at Normal, journeyed to Pekin Wednesday, April 12, to put on an exhibition. The work was a part of the physical education demonstration sponsored by the Douglas School of Pekin.

The Gamma Phi exhibition consisted of tumbling acts, floor pyramids, Indian club swinging and several wand drills. The Indian club drill was especially well received by the audience. "It is part of our work to promote and help special physical education activities in surrounding communities," said Mr. Horton.

Monday evening, April 17, the organization will do a similar demonstration at Waynesville High school, Waynesville, Illinois.

The following members made the trip to Pekin and will go to Waynesville tonight: Russell Anderson, Richard Bennett, Van Brannan, Clifford Cozart, Glen Higginbothan, Tom Kerrick, Arthur Litwiller, Joe Mooney, Frank Muhl, Bill Muhl, Dick Nelle, Sam Slusser, Carl Unsicker, and Edson White.

May 1, 1933 (front page)
Announcement Made of Groups Chosen for V. C. Stunt Show
The announcement of the selection of the groups to participate in the annual Varsity Club Stunt Show in the Capen Auditorium May 13 was made Monday by Glenn Roberts, chairman of the Varsity Club Committee.

Synopses were submitted by a number of organizations and competition was keen for places on the program. The Women's Athletic Association, The Art Club, Gamma Phi, Blackfriars, and Jesters submitted the synopsis that were selected by the committee.

The Women's Athletic Association will present "Moon Interpretations"; the entry of the Art Club is "Marionettes"; "Marble Statuary" will be staged by Gamma Phi. A stunt called "Rhythmic Variations" will be the Blackfriars stunt and the Jesters will give "Paul's Reverse Ride or The Red Menace."

These organizations are now busy preparing their skits. Many new features in lighting are to be included in the stunts as well as novel presentations of the stunts themselves. The Poster contest that is also sponsored by the Varsity Club has provided an incentive for creative effort. The contest closes May 3.

May 8, 1933 (front page)
On Friday night the annual Stunt Show will hold the spotlight in Capen Auditorium. The Art Club, the Women's Athletic Association, the Jesters, the Blackfriars, and Gamma Phi will vie for honors in presenting the most original, the best executed, and characterized stunt. Judges will rack their brains to decide which one of the presentations will be awarded the cup for this year, while the faculty will present their annual attraction.

May 8, 1933 (page 8)
GAMMA PHI AWARDS CIRCUS QUEEN SISTER PIN
Gamma Phi, local physical education fraternity, held its monthly meeting Monday evening May 1 at the Alamo. Dinner was served at 6:30 o'clock. Guests included Miss Doris La Master, senior in the Women's Physical Education curriculum, and Miss Margaret Barto, head of the Women's Physical Education department, and Mr. Eldred Sleeter, Illinois Wesleyan swimming instructor, and a former aerialist with Ringling Brothers-Barnum and Bailey Circus.

Miss La Master, who was queen in the Second Annual Gamma Phi Gym Circus held last winter was awarded a "sister" pin for her service in the circus.

Mr. Sleeter, principal speaker of the evening j discussed "Circus Performers I Have Known." Mr. Sleeter told of the routine life of the circus and his own work in connection with the circus.

Plans were discussed for the spring party which will be at Lake Bloomington in the near future.

W.A.A. AND ART CLUB WIN TOP HONORS IN ANNUAL STUNT SHOW
...
Gamma Phis Present Statuary
"Marble Statuary" presented by the Gamma Phi was an effectively lighted display of the possible developments of the human body given by groups of the men students. In the last of the statuary groups of four members displayed red letters of I. S. N. U. on their chests. A new type of lighting was used in the Indian Club demonstration which typified the accompanying musical selection. "The Glow Worm.."

May 15, 1933 (front page)
W.A.A. AND ART CLUB WIN TOP HONORS IN ANNUAL STUNT SHOW
...
Gamma Phis Present Statuary "Marble Statuary" presented by the Gamma Phi was an effectively lighted display of the possible developments of the human body given by groups of the men students. In the last of the statuary groups of four members displayed red letters of I. S. N. U. on their chests. A new type of lighting was used in the Indian Club demonstration which typified the accompanying musical selection. "The Glow Worm."
...

June 5, 1933 (front page)

GAMMA PHI HOLDS PICNIC AT LAKE BLOOMINGTON

The members of Gamma Phi, local physical education fraternity, held their annual picnic, Monday, May 29, at the Scout camp at Lake Bloomington. Twenty couples were present, along with James Carnahan, instructor at Normal Central Grade School, and Prof, and Mrs. C. E. Horton and family.

After the picnic lunch, Mr. Carnahan guided the group over the scout trail, which is two feet wide and extends over a distance of two miles. According to various members of the party making the trip, they were forced to keep to the "straight and narrow".

A short business meeting was held after the hike, and - officers were elected for the ensuing year. Frank Muhl was elected president, Gerald Slusser vice-president, and Kendrick Martin, secretary-treasurer.

1933 – 34 School Year

Intramural involvement has faded away and more time is spent performing in exhibition shows.

1934 Index (page 65)

Sept 29, 1933 (front page)
GAMMA PHI IN PARADE

Gamma Phi, physical education fraternity', was represented in the NRA parade by a group of supple stunters who thrilled the crowds with their daring maneuvers. Standing on their heads and making every kind of artistic figure, they added greatly to the part that Illinois State Normal University played in the parade.

Participants were Clifford Cozart, Kendrick Martin, William Muhl, Melvin Story, Richard Bennett, Frank Muhl and Robert Brummitt, chauffeur.

Oct 27, 1933 (front page)
GAMMA PHI BANQUET

The second annual banquet of Gamma Phi, physical education fraternity, will be held at Lutie's party house across from McCormick gymnasium on University avenue, at 12:15 Saturday night after the dance. Plates should be reserved with Frank Muhl or Kendrick Martin. The plates are 50 cents per couple.

Oct 27, 1933 (front page)

GAMMA PHI TAKES PART IN LEGION SHOW

*Gamma Phi, physical education fraternity, gave the opening
performance at the American Legion show Friday evening, October
20, at Normal Community High School, The performance was a
parallel bar number and was participated in by William Muhl, Tom
Kerrick, Frank Muhl, Kendrick Martin, Richard Bennett, Carl
Unsicker, Carl Marquardt, Vincennes Bowers, and Howard
Litwiller.*

Nov 10, 1933 (page 3)

GAMMA PHI OFFERS RECREATIONAL PROGRAM

*Coaches of the high schools of Normal and Bloomington and towns
nearby are invited to bring four or five boys to McCormick
gymnasium on Monday nights to participate in recreational program
offered by Gamma Phi.*

*The program, says Prof. C. E. Horton, head of the physical
education department, is designed to provide an opportunity for hoys
who are not on interscholastic teams to engage in sports activities.
The program will also aid the man in the teaching field to build up a
program of sports and games. Coaches, as well as students, may
enter the games. Boys are not entered as teams but are mixed for the
indoor activities.*

Dec 8, 1933 (page 3)

GAMMA PHI TO HOLD REGULAR MEETING NEXT MONDAY AT GYMNASIUM

*Gamma Phi, physical education fraternity under the direction of C.
E. Horton, director of Health and Sports Education, will hold its
regular meeting next Monday evening at 7:30 in Room 126 at
McCormick gymnasium.*

*The meeting is to be a real attraction with Dr. Markowitz,
Bloomington city health officer and also a noted pathologist,
delivering a talk on venereal diseases.*

Dr. Markowitz is very well known throughout Illinois and the gymnastic fraternity Was fortunate in securing him to speak.

The members of Gamma Phi have decided to make the meeting open to everyone in school and cordially invite anyone interested.

Dec 15, 1933 (page 3)
GAMMA PHI ENTERTAINS AG. SMALL GRAIN SHOW

Gamma Phi, physical education fraternity at Normal, entertained the delegates to the Small Grains Show which was held in the Old Castle Thursday, December 14. The delegates, which numbered Ag. students from Central Illinois high schools, showed their appreciation of the tumbling acts and pyramids put on by the Gamma Phi members, by applauding the members heartily. Frank Muhl, Bill Muhl, Cozart, Murray, Elinger, Sweet, Martin, Bennett, Litwiller, Collins, Slusser, and Cooper were the men who put in the exhibition of tumbling routines and pyramid building.

Dec 19, 1933 (page 3)

Gamma Phi, physical educational fraternity at Normal, made such a hit last year at the Normal School Basketball Tournament, at Macomb that they have received an invitation to give an exhibition of tumbling and pyramid building, between halves of the James Millikan-Macomb basketball game, January 31.

Jan 16, 1933 (page 2)
NOTICE!

The members of Gamma Phi, gymnastic fraternity, have been working hard in preparation for the 3rd Annual Gamma Phi Circus to be held February 23, 24 at McCormick gymnasium. Anyone interested in participating should get in on the workouts, which are held from 4:30 to 5:00 p. m. every afternoon.

Jan 16, 1933 (page 3)

A group of Gamma Phi boys have been asked to perform for the Chow Club show Thursday, January 18, at Bloomington. Indian club swinging will be a feature of the Gamma Phi act.

Jan 19, 1934 (page 3)

Gamma Phi Group to Be Busy During the Remainder of Month

Gamma Phi, local physical education fraternity, faces a very busy schedule during the remainder of the month of January.

Last night the Gamma Phi fraternity put on an Indian club drill before members of the Chow club at McBarnes Building. The clubs were lighted by neon and the drill was well received by an enthusiastic audience.

Next Monday, January 22, the Gamma Phi troupe will put on a tumbling and pyramid-building act at the First Methodist church in Bloomington.

As an added feature of the Annual Circus this year the Men's Glee club and the Normal University Band will be on hand to deliver several programs. The dates of the circus this year are January 23 and 24. The circus will be held in McCormick gymnasium.

Jan 19, 1934 (page 3)

Gamma Phi Troupe to Show Before Macomb Students January 31

Gamma Phi, local physical education fraternity has accepted an invitation to appear at Macomb to give an exhibition of tumbling and pyramid building before the students of Western State Teachers College. The Gamma Phi troupe will appear at Macomb on January 31

A short business meeting will be held at the home of Mr. C. E. Horton, Wednesday night, January 24 for the purpose of discussing the annual circus which will be held February 23 and 24.

Jan 30, 1934 (front page)

DIGEST HAS NORMAL PICTURE

This week's issue of The Collegiate Digest contains a photograph of the Gamma Phi tumbling team from I. S. N. U. It is to be found on page three. More pictures of Normal activities will appear in the near future.

12 Picas

"They tumbled into their jobs." They also tumbled into the rotogravure section of "The Collegiate Digest." Yes sir, tumbling must be the rage right now.

In keeping with the fashion the thermometer took a tumble, and it is a well-known "can't get around it" fact that grades, values, and even humor took their tumbles all about the same time.

The Gamma Phi boys confine their tumbling to acrobatic performances, but most of the tumbling done by the rest of us could he defined equally well by the little word, "falls"!

Feb 2, 1934 (page 3)

Gamma Phi, local physical education fraternity, put on an exhibition between halves of the Western-Millikin game at Macomb last Wednesday and members of the troupe reported that the ball game was a great battle. Western won by a score of 42-40 and the Leathernecks firmly perched themselves in second place with a mark of six victories against one defeat.

Feb 9, 1934 (front page)

PLANS MADE FOR ELECTING GAMMA PHI CIRCUS QUEEN

Petitions, bearing nominations for circus queen, should be circulated right away, according to Gerald Slusser, head of publicity for the Gamma Phi Annual Circus. The Gamma Phi circus, which is an annual affair, promises to be better than ever this year.

According to Mr. Slusser, a paper bearing the name of a student's choice should be circulated among the students, and as soon as twenty-five names have been signed to the petition, the girl of the choice is eligible for the position of queen. All petitions must be in at the telephone desk in the Mail office by noon on Tuesday, February 13.

An all-school election will be held ii the Main office on Thursday, February 15.

Miss Doris La Master, of Mendota who received her degree last June, was the Queen of the Gamma Phi circus last year.

The circus will be held on February 23 and 24, this year.

Feb 2, 1934 (page 3)
Gamma Phi, local physical education fraternity, put on an exhibition between halves of the Western-Millikin game at Macomb last Wednesday and members of the troupe reported that the ball game was a great battle. Western won by a score of 42-40 and the Leathernecks firmly perched themselves in second place with a mark of six victories against one defeat.

Feb 9, 1934 (front page)
PLANS MADE FOR ELECTING GAMMA PHI CIRCUS QUEEN
Petitions, bearing nominations for circus queen, should be circulated right away, according to Gerald Slusser, head of publicity for the Gamma Phi Annual Circus. The Gamma Phi circus, which is an annual affair, promises to be better than ever this year.

According to Mr. Slusser, a paper bearing the name of a student's choice should be circulated among the students, and as soon as twenty-five names have been signed to the petition, the girl of the choice is eligible for the position of queen. All petitions must be in at the telephone desk in the Mail office by noon of Tuesday, February 13.

An all-school election will be held in the Main office on Thursday, February 15.

Miss Doris La Master, of Mendona who received her degree last June, was the Queen of the Gamma Phi circus last year.

The circus will he held on February 23 and 24, this year.

Feb 9, 1934 (page 3)
Edson White, physical education director at the Soldier's and Sailor's Childrens' school, will have a group of tumblers in the Gamma Phi annual circus. White has a bunch of fine performers and has entertained at the Western Avenue Community Center and various other places in Bloomington and Normal. Scotty was a leading member of the physical education fraternity during his sojourn at Normal.

Feb 9, 1934 (page 3)
Gamma Phi Circus Scheduled To Appear Feb. 23-24 At Gym
To be Third Annual Presentation of "Big Top" Performance
Strike up the Band! The circus is coming to town. The list of events has been completed for the annual Gamma Phi Circus which will be held February 23 and 24 at McCormick gym.

The State Normal Band will open the circus and the Men's Glee club has also been secured to furnish music for the occasion.

In variety and novel features this year's circus promises to surpass all of the other performances given in past years.

The selection of the queen will he held Thursday, February 15, in the Main office and the choice will be crowned and rule over the circus both nights.

Two clowns will be on hand to furnish plenty of laughs throughout the performances.

A host of entertainers including the Gamma Phi performers, the Metcalf girls' tumbling team and members of the Women' Physical Education department have been working for several weeks on their various acts and will have them in tip-top shape for the circus performances.

Order of Events
1—Overture—I. S. N. U. Band
2— Selection—Men's Glee club
3— Coronation of Queen.
4— Selection—Men's Glee club.
5— High Bar—(Horizontal) Murray, Sweet and Cozart.
  Clown - Cats
6— Tumbling— I. S. and S. C. S.
7— Class Procedure—Metcalf 5th and 6th grades.
  Clown - Lion Act
8—Flying Rings—Cozart, Murray. W. Muhl
9—-Limber Back—-Grade school girls, tumbling and back bends.
10— Military Tap Dance—Miss Barto's Class (Carolyn Wolff, Jessie M. Lucas, Jean Wilder, Marjorie Cook, Marie Donovan, Charlotte Jackson)
11— Novelty Juggling—Bennett and Martin.
  Clown - Cat Pic
12—Parallel Bars—Sweet, Cozart. Murray.
13—Arkadsky—W. Muhl, Cozart, Murray—Russian Dance (from Program).
14—Ladder Pyramids—I. S N U. gym class.
  Clowns - William Tell
15—Novelty Tap (Miss Barto's Class (Carolyn Wolff, Jessie M. Lucas, Marjorie Cook, Marie Donovan, Charlotte Jackson))
16—Tumbling—Gamma Phi.
  Clowns - Osteopath
17—Lighted Indian Clubs—W. Muhl, Cozart.
18—Mickey and Minnie Mouse—Bennet. Martin—Comedy skit.
19—Comedy Tumbling—Neil Marquardt.
  Clown - Balloon Bounce
20—Parallel Bar Pyramid—-Gamma Phi.
21—Leap for Life—White Elephant— Gamma Phi and I.S & S. C. S.
Closing Spec

Feb 13, 1934 (front page)

TO CHOOSE QUEEN BY ALL - SCHOOL VOTE THURSDAY

The deadline for petitions for Circus Queen was at noon today and an all-school election will be held Thursday, February 15 in the Main Office to determine the choice of the student body for the exalted position of Queen of the Annual Gamma Phi Circus.

The Circus this year has drawn a wide variety of talent. There will be performers from the Physical Education fraternity, the Women's Physical Education department, Thomas Metcalf grade school and the Soldier's and Sailor's Children's School.

Edson White is in charge of physical education at the children's school and has a group of tumblers that are "par excellence". The Children's School tumblers have been on exhibition throughout Bloomington and Normal, These little fellows will furnish one of the acts for the circus.

Music will be furnished by the State Normal band and by the Men's Glee club.

The coronation of the Queen is always a beautiful spectacle. The identity of the queen-elect is kept secret until the opening night of the circus when she is crowned as the ruler of the circus.

According to the chairman of the committee in charge of arrangements, the polls will be open all day Thursday and every one in school has the privilege of casting a vote for his choice for Queen of the circus. The election will be held in the Main Office and the pictures of the candidates will be posted on the Bulletin Board by Wednesday.

Feb 16, 1934 (front page)

Queen Chosen by Vote for Gamma Phi Gym Circus

The Queen of the Annual Gamma Phi circus was elected yesterday in the Main office by popular vote of the student body. The identity of the Queen will remain secret until the opening night of the circus which is next Friday, February 23.

Five nominations were petitioned by students and the Queen was elected from these nominations. The Misses Verna Satterfield, Margaret Watson, Rosamond Tierney, Dorothy Mindrup, and Ruth Pritchett were the nominees.

Mr. Clifford E. Horton is sponsor of the Gamma Phi fraternity and is a nationally known authority in Physical Education. He has been instrumental in staging the circus for several years.

The Gamma Phi group has given many exhibitions of tumbling and pyramid building throughout Central Illinois and the tumblers have proven extremely popular in all of their exhibitions.

"The Leap for Life" is an amazing spectacle which concludes the evening's entertainment.

The Circus is to be held at McCormick gym on the nights of February 23 and 24.

Mar 9, 1934 (front page)
GAMMA PHI MAKES TEN DOLLAR GIFT TO STUDENT LOUNGE
The executive committee of Gamma Phi, men's gymnastic fraternity, agreed to donate ten dollars to the student lounge at a meeting and banquet held a Lutie's party house, Wednesday, February 28 at 6:00 p.m.

It was also decided at the meeting to advance money for the intramural awards this year, if money for this purpose can not be secured from other sources, and to give twenty-five dollars to the band. Each year the proceeds of the Annual Gamma Phi circus have been distributed to various deserving organizations of the school. Last year the sum of forty dollars was given to the student loan fund and fifty dollars was given to the band to finance the trip to Macomb where it played at the Teachers College basketball tournament.

Members of the executive committee of the Gamma Phi circus were, Prof. C. E. Horton, sponsor; Robert Brummett, Kendrick Martin, Frank Muhl, William Muhl, and Gerald Slusser.

Mar 9, 1934 (page 3)

Edson White, physical education director at the Soldier's and Sailor's Childrens' school, will have a group of tumblers in the Gamma Phi annual circus. White has a bunch of fine performer's and has entertained at the Western Avenue Community Center and various other places in Bloomington and Normal. Scotty was a leading member of the physical education fraternity during his sojourn at Normal.

Mar 30, 1934 (page 3)
GAMMA PHI PLANS TUMBLING EXHIBIT FOR THIS MONTH

Now that the Gym Circus is over, husky bunch of tumblers and pyramid builders, known as the Gamma Phi" will take to the road once more according to their sponsor, Prof. C. E. Horton. Two exhibitions and probably three will be given next month.

On April 6, they will journey to Peoria where they have been invited by Mr. Arthur Ridenour, physical director of the Peoria Y. M. C. A., to appear in the annual gymnastic circus of that organization.

Rutland, Illinois will be the scene of their next appearance which will take place April 16. Another invitation has been received for a performance at Lexington, Illinois on April 20; the last invitation has not yet been definitely accepted but this will probably be done at the next meeting.

Apr 20, 1934 (page 3)
TO ATTEND BANQUET

Gamma Phi will put on their tumbling and pyramid building exhibition at a banquet at Lexington on Friday night, April 20th. They have been requested to appear by Harris Dean, Normal

*graduate, who will be remembered by many as basketball captain
and all-round athlete during his years in school here.*

May 1, 1934 (front page)
VAUDEVILLE ACTS, MUSICAL COMEDY TO BE PART OF MAY FETE

...

*The first vaudeville act, at 9 o'clock, will feature a group of physical
education women of the university in folk and tap dancing selections,
directed by Miss Margaret Barto, head of the department of physical
education for women. A tumbling and pyramid building act by
members of Gamma Phi, men's gymnastics fraternity, will follow.*

May 18, 1934 (front page)
GAMMA PHI TO DEMONSTRATE

*Gamma Phi, men's physical education fraternity, under the direction
of C. E. Horton, head of the Health and Sports Education
department will give a series of demonstrations at 8:00 o'clock
Monday in front of the gym, including tumbling, advanced acrobatics
and pyramid building.*

*The Normal University Band under the direction of Kenyon S.
Fletcher will present a program at 8:00 o'clock in the evening.*

May 23, 1934 (page 3)
GAMMA PHI IS TO ADD ANOTHER CHAPTER

*Another chapter will be added to Gamma Phi, honorary gymnastic
fraternity, soon it is believed, as Mr. C. E. Horton, sponsor has just
received a letter from a student at Cortland Normal, Cortland, New
York, inquiring of the manner in which they might institute a chapter.*

*The student, a transfer from the University of Illinois read an article
concerning Gamma Phi in the May issue of the "Journal of Health
and Physical Education" and immediately wrote to Mr. Horton
requesting such information that they might be able to organize in
the New York institution.*

May 29, 1934 (page 2)
CONFINED IN HOSPITAL
Jerry Slusser, junior at I. S. N. U., is quite ill at Brokaw hospital following an appendicitis operation. Jerry is a member of The Vidette staff and is active in athletics and Gamma Phi.

NOTE:
He got better.

1934 – 35 School Year

The annual rhythm of Gamma Phi activities continues in the year of the fourth circus.

The eventual second Gamma Phi Director, Arley Gillett, pledges this year.

Mr. Horton, Murray (Pres.)
Litwiller, McDaniels, Hall, Sweet, Ayres, Ellinger, Christensen, Stoneker
Deetz, Armitage, Gillet, Cozart, Brannon

1935 Index ([page 128)

Oct 25, 1934 (page 3)
Gymnastics, another hobby hour feature is meeting with a great deal of approval. Every Monday afternoon from four to six o'clock and Friday evening from three to five, the men take the gym floor. In addition to enjoying themselves, they are preparing for the Gamma Phi circus to be held later in the year.

Nov 6, 1934 (page 3)
Gamma Phi Members Prepare for Circus

Gamma Phi members are working out regularly in the gym in preparation for the circus. Fifteen new members have been installed and the committee in charge is looking for more material. The Gamma Phi organization is now equipped with natty new uniforms. The first performance will be staged Thursday evening, November 15, in the Old Castle for the Hopkins Agriculture club.

USES TIGHT ROPE
Kendrick Martin, '35, has become interested in tight-wire walking. He now has a complete outfit, but the apparatus has not yet been installed. Anyone interested in taking up tightwire walking should see Mr. Martin or C. E. Horton, director of the physical education department for men.

Nov 23, 1934 (page 3)
Intramural Party Gives Fellows Chance to Show How Unskilled They Are

All of the boys in school had an opportunity to show how unskilled they were Wednesday evening, when the First Annual Intramural party was held in McCormick gymnasium, Most of the contestants showed their weak points.

Each of the men present had his chance at twenty different games and there was not a contestant that scored in every event.

"Deacon" Gorens hosed out Les Murray for individual honors, while one Mr. Goodsen nosed the raspberries out of the pie in the best time to win the pie-eating laurels—a string of berries from ear to ear.

A group of Gamma Phi boys put on a tumbling act and Sweet, Murray, and Cozart did some work on the bars. Harold Fry, instructor in physical education, paced the faculty members to the apple stand, where everyone eventually wound up.

Dec 14, 1934 (page 3)
LOOKING FOR MATERIAL
C. E. Horton of the Physical Education department announces that he is still looking for new material to join the Gamma Phi, physical education fraternity.

The members have been putting on a number of exhibitions and have received several calls to entertain in Bloomington and neighboring towns.

They entertained a large crowd at the Association of Commerce building in Bloomington on December 10, and appeared at the Christian church in Normal for a program last Wednesday evening.

Feb 8, 1935 (front page)
Ten Men Initiated into Gamma Phi at Meeting This Week
The initiation of pledges for Gamma Phi, honorary gymnastic fraternity, was held Monday evening at 6:30 p. m. in the men's gymnasium.

Ten men, John Armitage, John Ayres, Otis Barclay, Myers Christenson, Ralph Deetz, Arley Gillet, Harold Hall, Harland King, Clement McDaniels, and D. Snow passed all tests requested of them by the twenty-one members present and are now full-fledged members of the organization.

The next meeting will be held Monday evening, February 11 at 7 :30 p.m. in the Gamma Phi room.

Feb 12, 1935 (page 3)
HAVE BUSY WEEK
Members and pledges of Gamma Phi, honorary gymnastic fraternity, enjoyed a busy week from February 4 to February 8.

Monday evening pledges were initiated in to the organization; Wednesday evening between halves of the' St. Viator basketball game the organization was represented by a clown act and a parallel bars act by Leslie Murray, Clifford Cozart, and Clement McDaniels. Thursday evening the group gave an exhibition at the parent teachers meeting held in Raymond school in Bloomington; and Friday evening they gave an exhibition on the "Family Night" program at the Bloomington consistory.

The members of this group are working diligently in preparation for the annual Gamma Phi circus to be held March 21 and 22 in the men's gymnasium.

Feb 15, 1935 (page 2)
WANTED — A QUEEN
The Gamma Phi Circus, which is to be presented at McCormick gymnasium March 21 and 22, is looking for a Queen to rule over it. All petitions for nominations must be filed by Friday, February 22.

Petitions should have at least fifty signers and should be accompanied by pictures if possible. Turn these in to Ralph Deetz on or before the deadline is Friday, February 22.

Feb 15, 1935 (front page)
Gamma Phi Fraternity Presents Acts; Prepares for Annual Gym Show
Gamma Phi, in an effort to arouse an interest in gymnastics, continues to travel and give exhibitions. Tomorrow evening the honorary gymnastic organization will present an exhibition of tumbling and pyramid building at the El Paso high school between halves of a basketball game.

This work by the group, from all appearances, is beginning to bring about the desired result. Activities of a similar nature are now in progress in Maroa, Pontiac, and Rutland and it is hoped that this work will develop into something of importance in other communities visited by the organization.

The annual Gamma Phi circus will be presented two nights, March 21 and 22, by all-school talent. One of the outstanding numbers of the circus has already been announced, "The Leap for Life."

Mar 5, 1935 (front page)

SIX ARE NOMINATED TO RUN FOR GAMMA PHI CIRCUS HONORS

Clowns, Tumblers Prepare for Annual "Big Top" Event

Time is approaching for the Annual Gamma Phi circus. Members of the fraternity are spending most of their time preparing for this event, which will be presented two night, March 21 and 22, by all school talent.

Six candidates for the circus queen have been petitioned. One of these six fair ones must be selected to reign over the circus. This decision will be made during registration for the Spring term, March 11, in the McCormick gym by popular vote of the student body.

The following girls have been nominated: Margaret Naffziger, Lois Elliot, Mary Pluxtable, Eva Van Winkle, Alice Crush, and Aline Burgess. It has been the custom "since the first circus to have the Queen reign. Doris La Masters was elected in 1933 as the first. Last year Ruth Pritchett was Queen.

Clowns begin practice this week in preparation for the event. Clifford Cozart and Leslie Murray are at work on a new "thriller" to take some of the spotlight away from the famous "Leap for Life" and the "Wampus."

As a warm-up, the Gamma Phi boys are to perform at the finals of the District Tourney Saturday night at Memorial gym.

March 19, 1935 (page 2)

Music, always a part of us will be heard as the I. S. N. U. band furnishes the background for the "muscle-men" of Gamma Phi. The weight-lifters are in great shape and Thursday and Friday evenings will be filled with the "body beautiful" . . . Ah! what could be more divine . . . military music accompanying the rhythmic ripplings of a symmetrical physique . . .

Mar 22, 1935 (front page)

MARGARET NAFFZIGER CROWNED QUEEN OF GAMMA PHI CIRCUS

Will Also Preside over Tonight's Big-Top Event

Miss Margaret Ann Naffziger, crowned queen of the Gamma Phi circus last night, will preside again at tonight's performance beginning at 7:30 p. m. in McCormick gymnasium. Miss Naffziger was chosen by student vote on registration days as 1430 students took part in the election. She is a junior in I. S. N. U. and has been prominent in campus activities.

The colorful coronation ceremonies of last night will be reenacted tonight. The queen's attendants are: Eloise Bordner, Virginia Deetz, Helen Alarie Bowers, and Gladys Wiseman. The entire program, as given in the opening performance, will be repeated tonight.

The highlights of the program were the clowning by King and Barclay of Gamma Phi; the "Leap for Life", and the tap-dancing by the Duncan-Citron team, and by the W. A. A. women; and the perilous tumbling acts of the Gamma Phi boys. The troupe from the Illinois Soldiers' and Sailors' Orphans Home were very well received.

Miss Naffziger is the third queen of the annual Gamma Phi circus to be chosen from the Women's Physical Education department. Her two predecessors, Doris La Masters, queen in '33, and Ruth Pritchett, queen in '34, both majored in that department.

Tickets for tonight's show will be available at the door. The admission price is twenty-five cents.

Mar 2, 1935 (front page)

APPRECIATIVE AUDIENCE GREETS FINAL GAMMA PHI BIG TOP EVENT

Cozart, Murray Furnish Crowd Some Real Thrills

A crowded house greeted the final performance of the Gamma Phi circus last Friday evening at the gymnasium.

All available seats were filled as the show opened with the overture by the Illinois State Normal University band. The crowd was not in the least hesitant about expressing its approval of the various stunts and acts.

Duncan and Citron in their dance number, and Bill Muhl with the electric light Indian clubs proved to be very popular. Duncan and Citron responded to the applause with a novelty dance in which they were chained together. The Children's School tumbling and pyramid building troupe surprised many by their exhibition in which they compared favorably with the Gamma Phi boys.

Cozart and Murray produced the real thrills of the evening with their daredevil antics on the revolving ladder. The tensest moment came as Murray stood on his hands on the rungs of the ladder which was extended in mid-air and balanced there by Cozart, who was nonchalantly perched on the opposite end. It was a very clever exhibition of balance.

The boys gave very creditable performances on the flying rings and on the high bar. Martin stole the show from the clowns, who were all just silly enough to be good.

Mar 29, 1935 (page 3)
Professor C. E. Horton Principal Speaker at Anchor High Banquet
C. E. Horton, head of the Health and Sports division of education at Normal and director of Gamma Phi, men's physical education fraternity, was the principal speaker at an athletic banquet at Anchor High School last Thursday, March 28.

Mr. Horton delivered a talk on "The Value of Athletics in a School Program." Four of the members of Gamma Phi accompanied Mr. Horton and entertained the hosts with a series of tumbling exhibitions. Les Murray, Clifford Cozart, Otis Barclay, and Harland King were the participants.

The banquet was given in honor of the Anchor basketball team which has had a successful season under the direction of Coach Abell.

April 5, 1935 (page 2)
Gamma Phi Tumblers Schedule Three Shows
The Gamma Phi tumblers and acrobats, who are still very much in demand for exhibitions, are scheduled for three local appearances this week.

They gave a demonstration last night at the local Methodist church and are booked to repeat the performance tonight. For their third appearance they will be cavorting about at the University High school circus Saturday night.

May 21, 1935 (page 2)
GAMMA PHI BANQUET
Thursday of this week will be the last day to make reservations for the banquet at the Y. W. C. A. given after the Gamma Phi formal initiation, Monday, May 27. All members should be present to vote on the service award to be given the most valuable senior.
C. E. Horton

May 24, 1935 (front page)
Elephants, Gamma Phi Don't Forget; Walking Back Part of Ritual
"Let Me Call You Sweetheart" was the theme song of the pledges for Gamma Phi as they were conducted about the campus and to various other parts of town during the informal initiation held Monday evening.

Tradition demands that an initiation should be impressive and something that the candidate will never forget. According to one of the candidates, the pledges who were impressed at this august event will have no trouble remembering the emphasis placed on the ritual and stressed by a barrel stave, board off a barn, or a table leaf.

To guarantee that the lucky neophytes would have an appetite and be able to indulge, in a heaped up fresh strawberry sundae, they were taken out in the country and ordered to be back at the Alamo within a given short time. The horrible penalty for being late was not inflicted because no one was late.

*The final installment of the spring initiation will be held in the form
of a formal banquet at the Y. W. C. A. Monday night.*

May 31, 1935 (front page)
EARLY HABIT FORMATION ASSET FOR ATHLETES BIG LEAGUER BELIEVES

*Burleigh Grimes Speaker at Gamma Phi Banquet Monday Burleigh
Grimes, manager of the Bloomington Cardinals, was the principal
speaker at the Gamma Phi annual banquet held at the Y. W. C. A.
Monday, May 27.*

*Mr. Grimes stated that habits are the most important things that a
person has to deal with, He emphasized the fact that these habits
should be formed young and illustrated his point by comparing the
habits of various ball players with whom he had come in contact
during his twenty-five years of big league baseball.*

*The period in an individual's life between the ages of eighteen and
twenty-four were referred to as the "moon stage"—a stage when a
person may go to bed at night building air castles and being puffed
up like an over-inflated balloon, but when the alarm goes off in the
morning he may feel like a flat tire.*

Must Learn to Take "Raps"
*"The ability to take it," said Burleigh, "is one of the greatest assets
to a ball player or any one else. When I worked in logging camps at
the age of seventeen and lived with several hundred men of all types,
including Polocks and Bohunks, I learned the value of being able to
take a rap and get up for more."*

*Being a baseball player, Burleigh stated that he could see a great
resemblance between that game and the game of life. That both must
be played with the best of one's ability, in order to get all that either
has to offer.*

*Mr. Grimes closed his discussion with a bit of advice to the members
of Gamma Phi: "Never give a person a kick in the pants when it is
just as easy to give him a pat on the back."*

Coach "Pop" Horton gave introductory and explanatory talks for the members that were short of words.

Martin Given Senior Award
Following the lecture by Mr. Grimes, Les Murray, the retiring president, presented Miss Tish Nafsiger with the queen award which consisted of a pin and membership to the fraternity. Kenneth Martin was given the honor and award for four years of active service in the organization. This is an honor that is given to a senior member each year, the individual being chosen by ballot.

Mr. Grimes was puzzled by one thing, because of the number of girls present, and said he wasn't sure whether the organization was a fraternity or a sorority.

June 7, 1935 (page 4)
GAMMA PHI ELECTS OFFICERS
Gamma Phi announces its selection of officers for the coming year. Clifford Cozart will serve as president of the organization, Ralph Deetz as secretary and treasurer, La Verne Christianson, vice president and Fred Kearney as publicity manager.

Mr. Clifford Horton was chosen as advisor and sponsor.

1935 – 36 School Year

The regular schedule of Gamma Phi activities continues. The group has, however, secured a club room in McCormick Gymnasium. It has a lounge with a radio.

R. Deetz, C. Horton, J. Ayres, J. Ellinger, H. Hall, F. Kearney, W. Lewis, L. Murray, M. Naffziger, D. Reid, W. Sloneker, H. Snow, D. Wene, J. Fraley, C. Hammerlund, E. Hill, C. Hudelson (1936 Index - page 202)

September 20, 1935 (page 2)
Gamma Phi, honorary gymnastic fraternity, will hold its first night meeting Tuesday, September 24, at the Campus Inn, beginning at 7:30 p. m. Present plans call for a dinner, after which there will be an important business meeting.

Sept 27, 1935 (page 3)
Coach Harold E. Frye "Pop" Horton Plans Big Year at First Gamma Phi Meeting
Arrangements Underway for All-School Dance
"Pop" Clifford Horton and his tribe of Gamma Phi tumblers held their second meeting of the year Tuesday evening at the Campus Inn. The meeting was in the form of a banquet, followed by a business meeting.

Members of the group were appointed by president Clifford Cozart to make arrangements for an all-school dance to be sponsored by the organization. Plans were also discussed for a high school competitive gymnastic contest to be held prior to the Gamma Phi Circus. The group made plans for the refurnishing of the old Gamma Phi room at the gym. "Pop" and the boys say that they are going to make 1935-36 one of the biggest and most interesting years in the Gamma Phi history.

The boys work out almost every afternoon at four o'clock and according to a statement made by "Pop" there is room in the organization for a few more members and all men interested are urged to come down and get acquainted.

An historian has been appointed and a scrap book is being purchased to keep an up-to-date record of the activities of Gamma Phi.

Oct 8, 1935 (front page)

Gamma Phi to Present All-School Dance in Women's Gym Saturday
Gamma Phi, honorary physical education fraternity, is sponsoring an all-school dance Saturday night, October 12, at. 8:30 p. m , in the women's gym.

Rose Marie Orr, popular dance orchestra leader, and her orchestra from Dwight, will be the main feature of the evening. Mr. Ralph Deetz, president of Gamma Phi, states that this orchestra is highly recommended in the northern part of the state.

Those serving on the decorating committee are Harold Hall, Dempsey Reid, Donald Wene, Fred Kearley, and Lavern Christensen.

Chaperones for the evening are Mr. and Mrs. Harold Frye, Mr. and Mrs. Howard Hancock, Mr. and Mrs. C. E. Horton. Mr. Horton is sponsor of Gamma Phi. Admission will be twenty-five cents per person.

Oct 25, 1935 (page 6)

Hobby Hour Drawing More Recruits, Director Says

Gamma Phi hobby hour is being conducted every Monday and Wednesday afternoon o at 4 o'clock. There has been an average attendance of fifteen men, and Mr. C. E. Horton invites any man interested in tumbling to join the group.

Oct 25, 1935 (page 8)

NOTICE

Gamma Phi, honorary physical education fraternity, will hold the annual midnight Homecoming banquet at the Campus Inn, on Sunday morning, October 27, at 1 a. m. immediately after the dance. All active and alumni members and guests are invited to attend the Gamma Phi reunion.
Pres. Clifford Cozart.

Nov 12, 1935 (front page)

Snake Dance Friday

Gamma Phi will sponsor a bonfire and snake, dance on Friday, November 15, at 7:30 p. m., just east of the football field. According to Mr. Ralph Deetz, arrangements for the events were placed in the hands of Clifford Cozart and Gamma Phi and the Student Council are in full charge.

Nov 15, 1935 (front page)

Gamma Phi Sponsors Snake Dance, Cheers BonFire, Tonight

Gamma Phi is sponsoring the annual Snake Dance and Bonfire to be held Friday night, 7:30, on the campus just east of McCormick Gymnasium.

Wood and other material which will make a big blaze are being gathered for the event and all contributions will be accepted provided they are not valuable property.

Clifford Cozart and Ralph Dietz are the leaders in this movement and they urge that the entire student body turn out for this annual affair.

Nov 26, 1935 Edition 02 (page 3)
Gamma Phi Tumblers to Make Third Bow
According to Ralph Deetz secretary-treasurer of Gamma Phi, honorary physical education fraternity, this organization will make its third appearance of the current year al Chenoa high school on December 6th.

Jan 10, 1936 (page 5)
Ring Queen to be Chosen Soon by Popular Vote; Clowns to be Super
Gamma Phi, gymnastic fraternity, has been working overtime to get ready for the fifth annual circus. The plans have been altered so the circus will not be a repetition of those of previous yrs. Preparations have been made for the biggest circus ever staged at Old Normal.

This year, the Circus Queen will be selected by popular vote of the student body, just as was done last year. The petitions for queen nominees must have 25 signatures, and a picture accompanying the petition. These pictures must be in by January 20, 1936, and should be turned in at the telephone desk in the main office or to Ralph Deetz, secretary and treasurer of Gamma Phi.

Jan 24, 1936 (front page)
Circus Queen Poll on Registration Day
Voting for the Queen of the Gamma Phi's annual circus will take place on registration day. The results of the election will not be made public until the opening night of the circus when the Queen, surrounded by her attendants, is coronated in McCormick gymnasium.

At the present time, five girls have been nominated for the honor. They are: Miss Vangine Sicks of Peoria who will represent the

*western section of Illinois; Miss Geneva Mien of Staunton,
representing the southern section of the state; Miss Grace Mikel of
Bloomington, central Illinois; Miss Betty Hart, of Decatur, also
representing central Illinois, and Miss Virginia Jacquath of Chicago,
representative of northern Illinois.*

*The circus is annually presented by the members of Gamma Phi,
men's gymnastic fraternity and includes acrobatics, tumbling,
trapeze stunts and group drill work besides other acts.*

*The circus will be held on the evenings of February 27 and 28, at 8
p. m. Admission will be 25 cents.*

Feb 14, 1936 (front page)
Normal Tumblers Show at Lincoln
By Staff Reporter
*Coach "Pop" Horton and a band of his "tumblers put on an
exhibition of tumbling, pyramids, hand to hand, and clowning for the
spectators of the Clinton vs. Lincoln high school basketball game at
Lincoln, Friday, Feb. 7.*

*"Pop" and his gang were slated to give an exhibition at Coal City on
Saturday night, but because of stormy weather and slick roads the
date was changed to Feb. 17.*

*The boys, under Coach Horton's critical eye. are practicing every
available night, to work up a varied routine for the annual Gamma
Phi circus that is to be held in the gym, Thursday and Friday nights,
Feb. 27 and 28.*

*Cozart and Murray and their revolving ladder will be featured again
this year. The boys have been working hard and risking their necks
every time they practice in order to put in the-thrills that make this
act bigger and better.*

*If you are not suffering from a weak heart, or are not confined in the
hospital, you will miss one of the biggest opportunities in your life if
you fail to see this year's circus.*

Feb 14, 1936 (page 4)

Not Sailors, But Acrobats Prove to Be Best Dates for Fell Hallers

Getting in After Hours Simple—Just Know Right People

By Staff Reporter

An upperclass co-ed has just revealed an escapade of her freshman year which she feels might interest the present residents of Fell Hall.

According to the story, this "freshie" went to a Gamma Phi party which lasted longer than she had expected. When the men and their guests clambered out of the truck which brought them to the gymnasium after the party, the clock of Old Main testified to a rather late hour.

To ring the doorbell of Fell Hall would have necessitated a lengthy explanation and might have caused some embarrassing moments, so the entire party gathered back of Fell Hall to consider the situation.

The men soon solved the problem. They made a pyramid under the late-comer's window, while an anxious roommate opened the window and pushed two beds in front of it.

The culprit then climbed to the top of the pyramid and was pitched through the window onto the beds.

The co-ed dedicates the story to the women of Fell Hall who cannot reach the door before closing time.

Feb 18, 1936 (page 2)

Cliff Cozart

Rates High Among Tumblers, Writes Who's Who Reporter in Review of His Activities

By Maurine Blum

The man who carefully slid down the table leg in assembly some few weeks ago is in the spotlight this week. President of Gamma Phi and tumbler supreme. You may see Cliff Cozart in a circus some day.

"Ever since I was a little shaver I've been turning somersaults on piles of leaves 'n around," Cliff laughed. "I didn't really learn any

correct tumbling until I came to I. S. N. U., though. 'Pop' Horton has taught us Gamma Phi boys a good many tricks of the trade. "

Cliff is a Normal boy, a senior majoring in physical education and industrial arts. His ambition is to coach in a high school in the winter and tumble in vaudeville or circuses during the summer.

Drawn by Gamma Phi
When he was attending Normal Community High School, Cliff saw the Gamma Phi boys perform, and decided right then to come to I. S. N. U. Now Cliff, Les Murray, Arley Gillett, Harland King, and Owen Barclay (the last two are members of the class of '35) have formed a tumbling troupe whose schedule during the month of August will be arranged oy a Minnesota booking agency.

"Sure. I eats me spinach," Cliff admitted. "I eat Wheaties for breakfast, too," he grinned. In spite of this Cliff maintains that brawn isn't the chief ingredient of a good tumbler. Timing and balance are more important, he claims, and constant practice, too.

Courage Necessary
To the average spectator, tumbling looks a bit difficult, but Cliff says anyone with good coordination, persistence, and a genuine enthusiasm for the sport can master it. When Cliff admitted that he knocked himself out every week or so, practicing, we added courage to the list of prerequisites.

Ping pong, swimming, and diving share honors with tumbling in Cliff's preferences. Electrical construction is the most interesting course he ever took, and, as you may have guessed by now, "Pop" Horton is his faculty hero.

Difficult Back Flip
The most difficult number in Cliff's repertoire is a back flip from the spring hoard which lands him standing on a table. The trick is landing on the table, Cliff explained, and had any number of "skun" elbows to prove his point.

The big event in Cliff's immediate future is the Gamma Phi circus which comes off in a few weeks. He says it's bigger, better, and funnier than ever before; magnificent, gigantic, colossal, stupendous, titanic, tremendous . . . you know. (But he doesn't know who the queen is).

Gathering Gags
The funny business in the Gamma Phi acts is thought up by different members of the troupe. If some one thinks of a gag during the routine, he pulls it. If the rest laugh, it's put into the routine.

Cliff is full of hair-raising anecdotes about stunts on the revolving ladder, the parallel bars, and the spring board, but you'll have to wait for his auto-biography. This is only a column.

Cliff likes the good fellowship he has found on the campus, but when asked if he'd be glad to graduate, he sighed, "Oh, yeah," with some conviction.

Feb 21, 1936 (front page & page 5)
Gamma Phi Circus Lists Elaine Good
By Staff Reporter
One of the highlights of the forthcoming Gamma Phi Circus will be the performance of Miss Elaine Good, twelve year old Thomas Metcalf eighth grader, who will indulge in some aerial antics aboard a suspended ladder.

Two of the mid-air maneuvers which Elaine will include in her routine are the Arm Balance and the Leg Balance. Both stunts fall into the category of those attempted only by polished performers. The Arm Balance consists of having both feet stretched in midair, perpendicular to the hanging ladder, and parallel to the ground.

While the Leg Balance, which is sort of a running mate to the Arm Balance, is a feat whereby both feet together with the legs, are all that keep the young Miss from gravitating downward. In this act, her arms and body are outstretched away from the ladder.

Elaine is by no means an amateur at this stunt stuff. She has performed in three YMCA circus offerings in Bloomington, and had

*also contributed an acrobatic dance to the Gamma Phi Circus of
1934.*

Stars in Circus

Elaine Good, eighth grade pupil, contributes ladder act to Gamma Phi Circus.

Vidette Feb 25, 1936 (front page)

Feb 25, 1936 (front page & page 4)
Gamma Phi to Reveal Ring Queen as Prelude to Aerial Features
By Lee Poklaske

Coronation of the Gamma Phi Queen will be the entree of the melange of entertainment to be offered by the Circus of 1936. Which young lady has been elected to the throne is a carefully, guarded secret, and will remain a secret until this next Thursday evening.

But in addition to viewing the Queen the audience will have the pleasure of viewing some very fancy aerial and earthly gymnastics by a cast including local and imported talent. In addition, the Normal Community High School Band will blow on their horns and furnish tunes for the two evenings.

Immediately after the Queen takes her place on deck, a horde of Gamma Phi-ers will come out and do a tumbling act. Following this will be offered a parallel bar act. Arlie Gillett, Glenn Kidder, and George Burnett are scheduled to pick on the parallel bars.

An imported act will next be on tap. Harold Gardner, Mason City, will show-off a unicycle act on the floor of McCormick gym.

A wand-drill executed by the tumblers of the I. S. S. C. school is to follow Gardner and his cycling.

Murray, Cozart, and Gillette will next hold hands or something and go through a stunt known as the "Hand to Hand."

The Imperial Act, composed of an imported troupe from Pontiac High, will, perform an Adagio dance.

Solo efforts are to be donated by the following: Anna Frances; Duncan, sometimes known as Anna Frances Duncan, is booked for an exhibition with her highly talented and trained feet. A xylophone will be subjected to some delicate tapping at the hands of Doris Kunkel. William Muhl is to go through some queer antics with Indian Clubs. And young Elaine Good's suspended ladder act is to be the last of the individual efforts.

Once again this year, Murray and Cozart team up to present their revolving ladder act. A tableau by Gamma Phi is to be the finale of the performances on both Thursday and Friday night.

Gamma Phi Goes Through Paces

No, these boys are not painting the roof of McCormick gymnasium but are getting in their licks for the third annual Gamma Phi circus to be held in the gym Thursday and Friday evenings. Working on the difficult ladder tricks are Les Murray (left) and Cliff Cozart, aces of the tumbling and acrobatic squad.

Vidette Feb 25, 1936 (page 3)

Apr 24, 1936 (page 6)
John Finds That Gym Is No Place for Killing Time
By John Dohm
Those persons who think that the men's gymnasium is nothing but a good place for holding the Homecoming dance, should have been around the muscle factory last Tuesday afternoon about five o'clock.

I, harmlessly enough, went down there for purely observatory purposes, and emerged about thirty minutes later feeling somewhat like the rum-pot who was run over by a steam roller and when his pals brought him home to his wife, they shoved him under the door-sill.

To say that the gymnasium was crowded would be cheating the issue. It was jammed, filled, packed, gorged, glutted, stuffed, and occupied. In fact, there were quite a number of persons there. And what is more important, those who were there were all wrapped up in some game or sort of practice.

Gets Free Shave
I walked up the backstairs to the gym and as I reached the top step, a baseball whizzed by my head so close that I could read the guarantee on the cover. (The first one: Baseball).

On one side of the floor a game of paddle tennis was in progress and about the time that I was crossing this area, one of the tumblers from the Gamma Phi squad who were practicing, jumped on my back— mistaking me, no doubt, for one of those wooden horse affairs—and I went to the mat. (The next two: Paddle Tennis and Tumbling).

More Athletes!
In the center of the gym, about forty ruffians were playing what looked similar to basketball, but when a loose ball rolled over to where I was standing and they had finished getting off the pile-up of which I formed the base, I decided that it was a mock war. (Fourth game: Basketball).

Gene Hill picked the pieces of me up and stood me against a wall. But it was altogether the wrong wall. Two lunatics were playing handball directly in front of me and all I could see was a little black ball coming towards my chest and leaving the same with much backspin. (Fifth: Handball).
...

May 5, 1936 (page 4)

Gamma Phi Banquet at Maplewood Today

Gamma Phi men's physical education fraternity, will hold its annual Spring banquet at Maplewood Country club Tuesday, May 5. At this time the plebes will be formally initiated. Miss Grace Mikel, queen of the annual Gamma Phi circus, will be initiated also.

Dr. F. W. Hibler will be the speaker, and Leslie Murray will be toastmaster.

At the last regular meeting of the year, Laverne Christensen was elected president for the year 1936-37. Other officers are Wendel Lewis, vice-president, and Arley Gillett, secretary-treasurer.

1936 – 37 School Year

Gamma Phi is still not large enough to put on an entire show using only Gamma Phi members. This year, four Pontiac High School acts are included in the Circus. Their coach is Jack Haskins, who will eventually start the Flying High Circus at Florida State University.

A big campus controversy erupts involving the Gamma Phi Queen. It isn't totally clear what the controversy was though. It has something to do with how the voting is done and seems to also involve who was elected.

The Queen admitted she was so nervous that she couldn't speak. Some evidence supports it evolved into a larger conversation about hair color and intelligence. (That is speculation from 80 years later though.)

1937 Index (page 160)

Oct 30, 1936 (page 12)

Only a short program will accompany the annual Homecoming dinner of Gamma Phi, men's gymnastic fraternity. Because of the football players who are members of the fraternity only two short speeches and a few toasts will be heard.

Arley Gillette, secretary, announced that the dinner will be held Saturday at 12:00 o'clock noon. This is a change from the usual time, which has been in other years at 12:00 o'clock midnight.

Jan 15, 1936 (page 6)
Gamma Phis Have Dinner-Then Hear Fingerprint Talk
With James Christensen as guest speaker, the Gamma Phi fraternity held a dinner meeting Monday night, Jan. 11. The speaker, a member of the Bloomington Fingerprint Bureau, gave a talk on the needs and uses of fingerprinting. He placed special emphasis on the necessity of obtaining records of the prints of everyone so that police work may become more efficient.

After the dinner the members of Gamma Phi put on a tumbling exhibition for the Legionnaires at the Masonic Temple in Normal.

Jan 19, 1937 (front page)
Gamma Phi Circus To Be March 10, 11
Candidate for Queen Must Be University Senior
Gamma Phi, the gymnastic fraternity, following the precedent of other years will present its annual gym circus on March 10 and 11. This will be the sixth year that Gamma Phi has held its circus and will be the fifth year that a queen has been chosen, announced Ralph Deetz.

Regulations for the nomination of the queen have been changed this year by the managing committee, Mr. Deetz reports. This year all candidates must be seniors at Normal. Application blanks are to be turned in to the telephone desk not later than 4 p. m. Friday, January 22. Misses Doris La Masters, Ruth Pritchett, Margaret Nafsiger, and Grace Mikel have previously been chosen.

Jan 22, 1937 (front page)

On March 10, Fell Hall will sponsor "The Man on the Street".
Tumbling in true Gamma Phi style will be the program

Jan 22, 1937 (front page)

To Elect Gamma Phi Circus Queen
Ask Organizations to Put Candidate in Contest

With plans for the biggest circus ever staged the Gamma Phi
fraternity is anxious to have anyone interested in being in the circus
to meet in men's gym at 7:30 Monday night, January 25.

With the election of the circus Queen on registration day, Feb. 1, the
club is hoping that the organizations will each sponsor a girl for
Queen in order that the race and interest will be keener.

The petition must be accompanied by 25 signatures and a picture.
These will be placed at the four corners, so every one may see who
has been nominated. The girl selected as queen will become a
member of the Gamma Phi organization.

Jan 26, 1937 (front page)

Gamma Phi Circus Queen To Reign For Two Nights
A circus queen is to be elected!

Mary Huxtable, Doris Angleton, Gladys Wiseman, Lois Elliot, and
Starkey Hunt are the candidates. All of the girls are seniors and the
one elected will reign for two nights as Queen of the Gamma Phi
circus.

On registration day, the ballot box will be open for the votes for the
queen, states Ralph Deetz.

Feb 12, 1937 (page 4)

Annual Circus To Be Planned
Gamma Phi Holds Session At Campus Inn

Gamma Phi's and senior physical education majors will meet in a
joint committee on Monday evening, February 15, at the Campus

Inn. They will make definite plans for the Gamma Phi Circus which will be held on April 2 and 3.

The Gamma Phi's will pick the queen of the circus who will in turn choose four maids of honor.

Don Adams, '37, is head of the committee. Ralph Dietz, program chairman, says that some of the most popular acts' in the past will be produced again. The adagio dancers from Pontiac, the hand-to-hand act, and the unicycle act are to be a part of the program. Sailors and Soldiers Children School, Women's Physical Education, and Men's Physical Education will participate.

"We plan to use more school talent than we have in the past," states Mr. Dietz, and he promises more clowns than ever before.

Mar 5, 1937 (page 7)
Men Discuss P. E. Change
Gamma Phi to Increase Membership Roles
A committee composed of C. E. Horton, director of the division of Health and Sports for men, William Moore, Don Adams, Ralph Deetz, Wendell Lewis, Laverne Christensen, Arley Gillett, and Curtis Smith has been discussing the proposed enlargement of Gamma Phi, honorary Physical Education fraternity. This would be accomplished by opening membership to all majors and minors in physical education and any others who wish to promote professional interests in physical education.

The committee hopes by this action to bring more closely together those men interested in athletics and to furnish another connecting link between alumni of that department and the present active students.

A constitution and by-laws have been drawn up and await the approval of President R. W. Fairchild. Upon receiving his approval plans will be made to take effect at once so as to have a larger group from which to draw the performers of the Gamma Phi circus.

Mar 19, 1937 (page 8)

*There will be a meeting of all Men who have a field in Physical
Education and any others who are interested in joining Gamma Phi
Monday, March 22, in the gymnasium of Old Castle. A program will
be given and refreshments will be served.*

Lavern Christensen, Pres.

Apr 2, 1937 (front page)

*GAMMA PHI, the new P. E. fraternity, seem to have something up
their sleeves for this year's circus. Just what it is, no one seems to
know, but it will be new, anyway. There is one fellow who knows, but
he has been known to change his mind, so it may be some time before
the veil is lifted.*

*THE GAMMA PHIS are going to try their old trick of entering all
intramural activities. I see they have a team or individual entered in
most every intramural sport event. More power to them.*

Apr 6, 1937 (page 3)

Gamma Phi Circus | Promises Thrills; Queen Kept Secret

BY JOHN ROSS

*The "greatest edition of the annual Gamma Phi circus ever
produced" will be presented to the public on Friday and Saturday,
March 16 and 17.*

*In presenting this entertainment Gamma Phi, honorary physical
education fraternity, has imported the best talent appearing in
current circuses in all parts of the state. According to Ralph Deetz,
who is in charge of the program, several spectacular acts of Jack
Haskin's Pontiac circus are to be shown. These will include an
adagio trio and whirlwind aerial acts.*

*Gamma Phi, in presenting this circus, is trying to bring to the
campus the better entertainers in school within the state coupled
with such local performers as Christenson and Gillett who are
making their third appearance this attraction.*

Also appearing under the local colors will be "Sandpaper" Lewis who is one of the better springboard artists in the collegiate world.

To Select Queen
As has been the custom in the past the members of Gamma Phi will vote and select the most popular woman in I. S. N. U. and present her as queen of the circus, along with her maids of honor. The selection is to be withheld from publication until the first performance of the current circus.

The ticket sale will be handled through the members who will accost everyone they meet, so that all may have an opportunity to see this attraction. The price of tickets is twenty-five cents and there will be no reserved seats.

Apr 9, 1937 (page 7)
Circus Plans Now Complete
Gamma Phi Annual Show Includes Outside Acts
Final arrangements for the annual Gamma Phi circus have been made, according to program chairman Ralph Deetz. The programs as it will be presented will include four acts from Pontiac, one from the Illinois Soldiers and Sailors Children's school, two by the Women's Athletic association, one from Decatur, and two from Normal.

Schools to be represented in the program by groups are: Eugene Fields School of Normal, Bloomington High School, Adeline Bach School, and I. S. N. U. Appearing as an outside act, Bennett of Decatur, a juggler of some fame in the midwest, will present his stock of tricks.

Pontiac brings to us two spectacular aerial acts done upon high trapezes. These acts were the most popular to be found in the Pontiac circus.

There will be two performances. The first will be Friday, April 16, and will be repeated Saturday, April 17. Tickets will go on sale Monday, April 12, both at I. S. N. U., and at W. B. Read's in Bloomington.

Apr 13, 1937 (page 3)
Gamma Phi Circus
BY JOHN ROSS

"Who's the queen?" seems to be the prevalent question this week and of course students are referring to the queen of the annual Gamma Phi Circus to be held next Friday and Saturday. The answer to this query will be released only during the performance of the attraction.

The coronation will be the highlight of the evening's entertainment which includes nineteen stellar acts, including the four hit acts of the recent Pontiac circus.

The acts to be presented by the northern prep school students are the Ballerinas of the clouds, the Imperial Pour, an adagio act, the Five Queens of the Air, and the Perch pole. These attractions were chosen by program chairman, Ralph Deetz, because of their grace and daring of action and their difficulty in performance and should give those in attendance an unforgettable thrill.

Tickets for the Gamma Phi Circus are on sale now and can be obtained from any member. The admission is twenty-five cents.

Apr 16, 1937 Vidette (page 7)
Ace Stambach To Introduce Circus Acts
Dons Garb of Civilization For Leading Part In Show
BY JOHN ROSS

"And in this corner, ladies and gentlemen, we have the Illinois state amateur grappling champion, Ace Stambach, taking on another of his many roles, that of ringmaster."

P. T. Barnum relied upon Bailey. In presenting their annual circus Friday and Saturday evenings, Gamma Phi puts its trust in the Ace as ringmaster of this colorful production. Stambach, trading his wrestling togs for those of a civilized human being, will present the acts to the public.

It is not possible for all of us to see the coronation of the queen of England, but we can be in step with the cream of society by attending a crowning this year, that of the ruler of the Gamma Phi circus.

The varied program, to be presented will include music by the band, the coronation of the queen, tumbling, tap dancing, the Six Queens of the Air, Bennett, juggler supreme, a double parallel bar act, the Adelaide Bach school, Fell Hall act, pyramid building, the Ballerinas of the Clouds, and roller skating, springboard and bronze figure acts.

GAMMA PHI, in presenting their annual circus, bring a great deal of unusual talent to the campus. Among these acts the Six Queens of the Air is a feature attraction. These artists are members of the Jack Haskin troop of Pontiac, which have been billed all over the state, including an engagement in Chicago.

The men's physical education class is to present the bronze figure study which promises to equal the work of Ted Shawn and his famous troop. These men, chosen for their muscular development, are under Miss Theilen of the women's physical education department, leader of the Orchesis group.

The community of Normal will send a well-trained colored dance and comedy troupe which has been popular in several shows given recently.

Tickets for this all-star production may be purchased from any member of Gamma Phi, or in the main office, and at W. B. Read's Sporting Goods Co., in Bloomington. The admission is twenty-five cents. There will be no reserved seats.

Apr 16, 1937 (page 8)
Women's I-M Department Aids Gamma Phi
The women's intramural program is cooperating with the Gamma Phi circus and is presenting two dance numbers. Nine women will participate in a tap dance and a comedy dance.

Miss Barto is the faculty member in charge, and Helen Belknap is the student head.

Apr 23, 1937 (page 3)
Gamma Phi Queen Thrills to Annual Fraternity Circus
N. U. Physical Education Group Honors Queen, Her Attendants
"My greatest thrill was walking across the floor of McCormick Gymnasium to the platform," exclaimed Miss Clar Myers, circus queen. "I got the biggest buzz' while walking from he door to the chair." Miss Myers added: "I had a hard time keeping it to myself, since I knew it for two weeks. I was so tickled, because I had never made a public appearance at Illinois State Normal university before."

"I wasn't so nervous until they handed me the flowers and then lost absolute control of my speech."

Clara Myers

Miss Myers, a senior from Armington, is in the music curriculum. She plays both the piano and the violin and is a member of the Lowell Mason club. LaVern Christensen crowned Miss Myers and presented a bouquet of flowers to her.

Her attendants were Lois Davis, Marion Holt, Bernadine Benson, Don Imhoff, Dorothea Radmacher, John Ross, Kathryn Porter, and Vayne Fasse.

Each woman was presented with a corsage, from Gamma Phi.

Paul Ives was the escort of Miss Myers. Gamma Phi selected the girls and they chose their escorts.

Apr 23, 1937 (page 7)
Gamma Phis Give Chase
I wondered why the Gamma Phi clowns chased the cat so diligently last Friday night when it escaped from their exaggerated hypodermic needle. Recently, I discovered that these four circus entertainers, Orville Evans, Allen Alldridge, Robert Clendenin, and Louis Zelip, had paid twenty-five cents for the creature. However, the feline was later found.

Incidentally, the Gamma Phi boys are in great demand at the present time. Last week they went to Camp Point, where Les Murray, one of their members, is now acting in the capacity of athletic director; this week they journeyed to Colfax; and they are scheduled to appear in Fairbury on Friday, April 30.

May 7, 1937 (page 7)
CHAIR BALANCERS
Since the recent 'Gamma Phi Circus, Walt Switzer, Glenn Kidder, and Jimmy Thorson have worked up a chair-balancing act which without doubt eclipses any of the stunts which they performed during their annual affair.

When they did their bit at Fairbury last Friday, April 30, they attempted a pyramid atop two tables and a stack of chairs. When Mr. Thorson finally clambered to the top of the heap he couldn't raise his hand very far above his head to acknowledge the acclaim of the crowd—the ceiling interfered.

Jangled and "coffeefied" nerves have no place in the lives of these boys. Their act is tops.

May 11, 1937 (front page)
Elect Gamma Phi Frat Head
Vote W. Lewis to Head Club; Gilford Parsons Vice-President
Wendell Lewis Junior in the department of physical education, was elected to the presidency of Gamma Phi, honorary physical education fraternity, at the regular meeting of the club Thursday,

May 6. Lewis has been active in the annual circus since coming to I. S. N. U., specializing in the springboard gymnastics. He is from Marseilles.

On the same ballot, Gilford Parsons, Monticello. a junior was chosen for the vice-presidency. Parsons was a letterman in football in '35 but injuries forced him from this year's squad.

James Thorson, freshman, of Gardner, was elected secretary/ treasurer of the organization. Jim, also a springboard' artist had a leading part in this year's circus.

The officers will take office at the first regular meeting in the fall in place of president Lavernne Christiensen, vice-president Wendel Lewis, and secretary Arley Gillett.

Plans for the coming banquet and initiation were also discussed at this meeting.

May 14, 1937 (page 7)
Banquet Planned By Gamma Phi's
The annual Gamma Phi Banquet will be held Wednesday evening, May 19 at 6:30. The place has not been determined as yet but will probably be Maplewood Country Club in Normal.

The organization under the sponsorship of C. E. Horton announces this is the biggest event of the year for those persons interested in physical education. A program of interest is being arranged by Fred Guttstein.

Houston to Speak
The principal speaker of the evening will be Dr. Victor Houston of the Education department. Dr. Houston will choose a topic from his many fields of interest to present. Other speakers will be C. E. Horton, head of the department of physical education and sponsor of Gamma Phi, and Lavern Christensen president of the organization. A musical organization under the direction of Fred Stephenson has been acquired to furnish the music for the occasion. They will endeavor to give their version of swing music at I. S. N. U.

Those Eligible
All persons signifying an intention to join Gamma Phi are eligible to attend this banquet. The price is fifty cents a plate and the affair is to be "stag" or "drag" as one prefers. At five o'clock on the same afternoon Gamma Phi will hold the formal initiation. All men interested should get in touch with Lavern Christensen.

May 18, 1937 (front page)
Clara Myers To Be Guest Of P. E. Frat
Gamma Phi to Honor Circus Queen, Initiate New Members
Clara Myers, senior from Assumption, will be the guest of honor of Gamma Phi, honorary physical education fraternity at the annual banquet to be held Wednesday, May 19, at 7 o'clock at Maplewood Country club.

Miss Myers was recently chosen as queen of the Gamma Phi Circus. At the banquet she will be presented with the queen's pin given each year by the organization to the circus queen.

Later in the program the award of the Gamma Phi service badge to the senior member doing the greatest service for the fraternity during his membership will be made.

Tickets to the banquet which is to be held in conjunction with the formal initiation of new members are on sale in the main office. The initiation will be held in McCormick gym at five o'clock.

June 12, 1937 (page 3)
Horton, Hancock to Study At University of Indiana
C. E. Horton, director of health and physical education for men, and Howard J. Hancock, director of athletics and head football and baseball coach, are spending their summer in Bloomington, Indiana, where they will attend Indiana university to work upon their doctor's degrees.

Mr. Horton at the end of this term will have finished his work with the exception of his thesis.

1937 – 38 School Year

This year, the Gamma Phi Queen participation is cancelled due to the controversy from 1937.

Several Gamma Phi members join professional circuses for the summer.

They're All Alive and All Inside

. . . Jimmy Thorson, a Jack-of-all-trades in any circus, who is shown at the left just "cutting up" on the rings. He hails from Gardner, Ill. and we all know him from his work in the Gamma Phi the last two years.

. . . Our big hero, "Samson" "Sandy" Lewis, president of the Gamma Phi, depicted as clinging on the "crows nest" of the tent while um-m-pphing a heavy dumb-bell.

. . . Robert "Tony" Clendenin, who, besides pulling many clowning antics such as the one pictured here (He has just swung through the top of the tent), will become the envied "Man on the Flying Trapeze."

. . . Jess Parsons and Glenn Kidder, who will innovate the giant swing on the eight-foot bar.

. . . Jack LaBounty, the other half of the "wit" role.

. . . Poble and Eastbrook, newcomers who will shine Friday and Saturday nights of this week.

. . . Herbert "Red" Smith and Ruth Parkinson who will present an intricate acrobatic tap routine to the music of Once in a While."

. . . A host of other stars of the first magnitude, far too numerous to be included in the above picture, along with a galaxy of the weaker sex.

The queens elected for the last three years were respectively Miss Margaret Nafzigger of Peoria, Miss Grace Mikel of Bloomington, and Miss Clara Myers of Assumption. Queens automatically became members of the Gamma Phi. This year, however, the electing and crowning ceremony has been ruled out.

The hands you see pictured are of the photographer, to whom applause was so urgent that he dropped his camera as a result.

Mar 4, 1938 p6

Oct 1, 1937 (page 7)
Gamma Phi Holds Meeting Thursday
*Gamma Phi, honorary physical education fraternity at I. S. N. U ,
will hold their first meeting of the year on Thursday, October 7, at
7:30 p.m.*

*Wendel Lewis, president of the organization, states that it is of the
utmost importance that all members be present as plans for the
pledging of new members will be discussed. It is also desired to get
an early start on the plans for the annual circus to be held during the
second semester.*

*President Lewis also expressed a desire, to see the heads of the
various committees before Monday noon.*

Oct 12, 1937 (page 3)
Gamma Phi Holds Meeting For All University Men
*Gamma Phi. honorary physical education fraternity, is to hold a
meeting open to all men in the university interested in physical
education. The get-together will he held tonight, Tuesday, October
12.*

*After a short program and pledging activities, refreshments will be
served. It is the desire of the organization to entertain as large a
number of new men as possible. The time of the meeting is 7:30 and
the place McCormick gym.*

Oct 15, 1937 (page 6)
Fred Young Speaks To Men's Group
*Gamma Phi honorary physical education fraternity held their annual
pledge meeting Tuesday evening October 12 in McCormick
gymnasium.*

*Wendel Lewis president of the organization opened the meeting by
welcoming the new men and explaining to them the purposes of
Gamma Phi.*

The feature of the evening was an informal discussion of the football rules by Fred Young, sports editor of the Bloomington Pantagraph. Mr. Young illustrated his talk with several experiences during big games he has officiated. Gamma Phi pledged twenty new men. A record class for that organization. The rest of the evening was spent playing games. Refreshments of cider and doughnuts were served.

Oct 29, 1937 Edition 02 (page 11)
NOTICE
Gamma Phi, honorary physical education fraternity will hold a smoker for alumni and members at Ralph Deetz's residence at 301 South Fell avenue after the game Saturday. Refreshments served. Tickets 25 cents.

Wins Second Place

—Courtesy of Pantagraph

ARLEY GILLETTE, Red Bird wrestling captain poses as Lord Normal in the annual Homecoming Hobo Parade. A big game hunting scene depicting the Red Birds bagging a victory over Carbondale was presented by Gamma Phi and won second prize. Other members of the organization served as chair bearers.

Nov 4, 1937 (page 3)

Nov 19, 1937 (page 3)

Judging Contest Draws Candidates From 25 Schools

Spectators to See Movie, Gamma Phi

Representatives of more than twenty-five schools doing Smith-Hughes work will be on our campus today in cooperation with the annual sectional agriculture judging contest to be held in Cook Hall. The judging will start at 9:00 a. m. and there will be contests in the judging of poultry, corn, small grains and in weed identification.

The Gamma Phi tumbling team under the direction of Clifford E. Horton, head of the physical education department, will entertain with several acts during the morning.

The contest is open to the public and, during the noon hour the spectators will be entertained by a motion picture show, "A Midsummer Night's Dream." Members of the Alpha Tau Alpha, national honorary agricultural fraternity, will have charge of a refreshment stand.

The schools represented in competition are Chenoa, Colfax, Cornell, El Paso, Eureka, Fairburv, Heyworth, Hopedale, LeRoy, Metamora, Mackinaw, Minier, Minonk, Normal, Pekin, Pontiac, Stanford, Washburn, Green Valley, Lexington, and Gridley.

Dec 1, 1937 (page 7)

Gamma Phi, honorary physical education fraternity will hold a regular meeting Thursday, December 3 at 7:30 in room 103 of McCormick gymnasium. It is important that all members be present in as much as a definite date for the formal initiation of new members will be set. Other business must also be transacted at this meeting, according to President Wendel Lewis.

Dec 10, 1937 (page 6)

President Wendel Lewis has his 1937 crop of Gamma Phi boys working out regularly now. Ten fellows constitute the main section of the corps. Among these are Wendel himself, Jimmy Thorsen, an able little hand-walker, Laverne Christensen, of football fame and last year's Gamma Phi president, and Jesse Parsons, a freshman from Bloomington who shows real promise on the parallel bars. This group of rollers and tumblers is planning a series of exhibitions to be given in conjunction with several of the basketball "games during the course of the winter. An exhibition has already been scheduled for some time before Christmas, to be given at the Normal Community High school.

Jan 14, 1938 (page 6)
Physical Education Group to Present Tumbling Show Gamma Phi, honorary physical education fraternity, will make their first appearance of the season when they give a tumbling exhibition Saturday night at McCormick gymnasium. The troop will entertain between the halves of the Normal-Charleston basketball game.

Professor C. Horton, head of the physical education department and sponsor of the fraternity, has been engaged for several weeks in working out a suitable routine, entertain between the halves of the basketball squad, the members of Gamma Phi have worked out every night and are now able to put on a different and entertaining act.

Following the example of other members of his department, Horton has dressed up the members of his troop in new suits which will get their first showing Saturday.

Men who will participate in the exhibition are Wendel Lewis, James Thorson, Porter Powell, Merle Rivord, Herb Smith, and Roger Easterbrook.

Lewis, who is president of Gamma Phi, says that this year's tumbling squad is the best since he has. been affiliated with the organization. In the light of this statement the exhibition will undoubtedly furnish some activity during the usually dull half period of the basketball game.

Jan 18, 1938 (page 3)
Gamma Phi Entertains
The half-time entertainment furnished last Saturday by Gamma Phi,

physical education fraternity, was of the highest quality. Doing a variety of stunts in their routine, the boys gave the spectators something to enjoy during the intermission.

Jan 21, 1938 (pages 6 & 7)
Gamma Phi to Entertain At Intermission of Game
Due to the way in which the Normal basketball fans acclaimed the gymnastic exhibition during the intermission of the Charleston game, Gamma Phi is practicing a new routine which will be tried during the DeKalb game.

It is not known yet just what the nature of this exhibition will be. C. O. Horton, sponsor of the organization, stated that it may take the form of a parallel bar act featuring Jesse Parsons and Ernest Pohle. Parsons is noted in this part of the country for the ease with which he performs such difficult feats as a one-arm lever and a one-arm hand stand.

Another possibility is a hand-to-hand routine featuring the entire troop of Gamma Phi gymnasts. The complete repertoire of the organization has been made up by the performers, under the direction of Mr. Horton.

Jan 25, 1938 (page 3)
The half exhibition put on by Gamma Phi, men's physical education group was a parallel bar routine featuring Jesse Parsons and Wendel Lewis. The act culminated with a one arm lever by Parsons that was acclaimed by the fans.

Feb 4, 1938 (pages 6 & 8)
Gamma Phi to Present Annual Circus in March
Gamma Phi, honorary physical education fraternity for men, will present the annual gym circus this year on Friday and Saturday March 4 and 5.

The troupe has begun working out in McCormick gymnasium under the direction of Professor C. E. Horton, sponsor of the organization.

They are working out several routines including hand to hand and parallel bar stunts.

The addition of Jesse Parsons to the Gamma Phi roster makes prospects look good as he is considered as is in the middle-west. He appeared in the circus last year while attending Bloomington high school

It is the plan of the organization to have only university students in the show and so they are inviting anyone in school who has talent in any line to get in touch with either Mr. Horton or Wendel Lewis, president of the organization.

As usual the election of a queen will precede the circus performance and the show will be built around the crowning of her Highness. Last year's queen was Clara Meyer who graduated and is now teaching. The four girls ranking next to the queen in the voting will again be maids of honor.

Feb 18, 1938 (page 7)
Gamma Phi Busy Preparing Circus
Gamma Phi, honorary men's physical education fraternity, is busily engaged in preparing a routine for the annual gym circus to be held Friday and Saturday, March 4 and 5. After Friday when the troop will cooperate with the fee party committee in helping to put on the program they will get down to the serious business of arranging their stunts in circus ardor.

The organization, under the direction of Prof. C. E. Horton, head of the department of Physical Education, has traveled to various cities throughout the state putting on exhibitions in tumbling and apparatus work. It is the present plan of the group to combine these routines and add acts by other campus organizations and the affiliated schools.

For the first time in the history of the circus the plan is to be built around a regular circus parade instead of the entrance of the queen. This year the members have decided against electing a queen in as much as serious comment arose last year over the affair.

A Circus in the Paper

Definite plans for the circus will be announced in a later issue of The Vidette as will the method of ticket sales.

Feb 22, 1938 (front page)
Gamma Phi Acts Rehearse in Gym
Springboards are creaking, parallel bars are groaning under straining bodies, flying, rings whistle across the McCormick stratosphere and contortions of face and body distort athletes as Gamma Phi, invitational fraternity for gymnasts, prepares for the annual Gamma Phi Circus, listed for March 4 and 5 in McCormick gymnasium.

One-hand stands, difficult pyramids, unusual hand-to-hands, brilliant buffoonery have come to be accepted standards of Gamma Phi exhibitions. This year's show will be benefited by ability of several talented newcomers to the fraternity, states Wendell Lewis, president. Jess Parsons, parallel bar artist, Porter Powell and Wayne Van Huss are among the better performers.

Arley Gillett and Jimmy Thorson have a unique revolving ladder routine, which is expected to draw a large quota of "oos" and "ahs" from the crowd.

Feb 25, 1938 Vidette (front page)
Gamma Phi to Present 20 All- Student Acts in Annual Gymnastic Circus March 4-5
Feature Clowns
Tumbling, Trapeze Work, Ladder Act, Dances On Bill of Fare
Training is in full Swing for the annual Gamma Phi Circus to be held March 4 and 5 in McCormick gymnasium. Both performances start at 8:15 p. m. Gamma Phi is the invitational fraternity for men talented in gymnastics.

Many veterans of former shows are included in the cast of gymnasts who will present this year's entertainment. In the list are: Glenn Kidder, Wendel Lewis, Jimmy Thorson, Bob Switzer, Tony Clendenin, Jack La Bounty, Porter Powell, Lavern Christensen and others. Jess Parsons and Wayne , Van Huss are outstanding newcomers.

Plenty of Clowns
Clowning for the show will be interspersed with the twenty acts. Jack La Bounty and Tony Clendenin who spent a summer with Cole Brothers circus, will lead the large band of funsters. La Bounty and Clendenin promise several new gags for the entertainment of the anticipated crowd.

Departing from precedent of former years, no outside talent will lie used. All acts will be drawn from the university and affiliated schools. Gymnasts from Illinois Soldiers and Sailors Childrens' school, Eugene Field School, Victory Hall and Norma! Central will present acts, from tumbling to pyramids, says Wendel Lewis, president of Gamma Phi.

Twenty Acts Listed
The complete program is as follows :
Parallels (Parsons, Poble, Kidder, Thorson); Rings (Eastbrook, Thorson); Trapeze; Swinging ladder; I. S. S. C. S., Pyramids, Tumbling; Bronze act, hand to hand act; Spring-board act; Rope spinning, whip cracking; Cloud Swing.

Tight wire, clown; High bar; Chair and table act; Wampus; Tumbling, Gamma Phi; Eugene Field School; Tap Dance; Revolving ladder; Victory Hall; Folk Dance; Parallel bar pyramids.

Seats are being sold by all members of the fraternity and will be offered in the Main office starting Monday, February 28. Admission will he 25 cents a person for each performance.

Circus Man

CLIFFORD E. HORTON, head of the Physical Education department, is faculty sponsor and coach of Gamma Phi, men's gymnastic fraternity, which will present its annual circus in McCormick gymnasium March 4-5. Mr. Horton has directed this organization for several years, offering the circus as its annual feature.

Feb 25, 1938 (page 8)

Gamma Phi tumblers at State Normal are working at fever heat for the annual Circus, which will be held March 4 and 5 in McCormick gym. Among the 20 acts will be some difficult stunts never attempted before by Normal tumblers.

Mar 1, 1938 (front page)
Giant Swing, Dance Team, Flying Trapeze to Hold Circus Spotlight

Swinging around the horizontal bar with utter disregard for the law of centrifugal force, or their necks, Jess Parsons and Glenn Kidder will present for the first time in Gamma Phi Circus history, Friday and Saturday nights, the giant swing on the eight-foot bar. The giant swing starts with a handstand on the high bar. The gymnast holds the handstand for a short time, then leans forward, to rotate around the bar, bunching the muscles on the down swing to give enough momentum to carry over the bar. The momentum increases with each turn and soon the gymnast is twirling around, like a giant pinwheel, at a dizzy pace.

The giant swing is brought to a halt by gradually tightening the hands, only means of support in the 'round and 'round episode. Some performers end the swing with a graceful flip in the air, landing on the mat below.

Deserting his usual clowning for a brief time, Robert "Tony" Clendenin, will become the "Man on the Flying Trapeze." According to Wendel Lewis, president of Gamma Phi, Clendenin's role will be enacted gymnastically rather than romantically.

Following the acrobatic motif, but in a varied style, Herbert "Red" Smith and Ruth Parkinson will present an intricate acrobatic tap routine to the music of "Once, in a While." Miss Parkins is a freshman prodigy of terpischore, while "Red" needs no introduction to Normal students, having performed in several Blackfriar productions and at other occasions.

Studded with stars of the first magnitude, acrobatically speaking, the Gamma Phi Circus cast this year will present a varied and fast moving show, says Lewis. Tickets are on sale by all members, in the main office and, will be available at the doors at 25 cents a person.

Wendel Lewis

May 10, 1938 (front page)
Gamma Phi Plans Dinner Dance for May 20
William Anderson, a junior in the Health and Physical Education curriculum, was elected to the presidency of Gamma Phi honorary physical education fraternity, last Thursday evening in a meeting held at the gymnasium. Robert Shields was chosen for the vice-presidency and Lowell Johnson is secretary and treasurer.

During the course of the meeting, plans were formulated for the annual spring dinner. It was decided to have a dinner dance this year and the Hotel Rogers in Bloomington was named as the site for the festivities.

The party is to be held May 20, and all members of Gamma Phi are urged to attend. On Sunday, May 15, the organization will hold a

*stag picnic at Lake Bloomington. President Wendel Lewis is in
charge of the arrangements and states that reservations for both the
picnic and dinner dance may be placed with Gilford Parsons at the
post office window in the Main office.*

*It is the practice of the fraternity to select the member doing the
greatest service to the organization during the year and to present
him with the Gamma Phi service pin at the spring dinner. Ralph
Deetz was the winner of the 1937 award. His successor will be
chosen and announced on May 20.*

*Tickets for the dinner dance may be had for one dollar and forty
cents per couple.*

May 20, 1938 (page 6)
P. E. Group Holds Dinner
Gamma Phi to Convene For Annual Social Function
*Gamma Phi, physical education fraternity, will have its annual
banquet tonight beginning at 7:00 o'clock at the Hotel Rogers in
Bloomington. The doors are open to all present members, to the new
pledges, to alumni who once belonged to the organization and to
their guests.*

*The program which has been arranged by Harry Barclay and Lewis
Kerwood begins with a three course dinner at 7:00 p. m. Afterwards
recognition will be given to Wendel Lewis, president; Gilford
Parsons, vice-president: and James Thornson, secretary-treasurer;
all officers of the organization during the year of 1937-1938. A place
on the program will also be given to Prof. Clifford E. Horton,
sponsor of Gamma Phi and head of the department of health and
physical education.*

*Walter E. Switzer will give a review of the years' activities: and then
the officers for 1938-1939 will be introduced. The president for next
year is William Anderson, the vice-president is Robert Shields, and
the secretary-treasurer is Lowell Johnson. After this introduction of
the new officers for the coming year there will be a presentation of
the annual service award.*

When the clock strikes nine everyone is invited to sway to the rhythm of Chuck Tursan and his orchestra from Peoria.

The guests of the evening are Mr. and Mrs. Charles E. Decker, Mr. and Mrs. Ralph W. Fogler, and Mr. and Mrs. Eugene L. Hill.

June 23, 1938 (page 6)
Make Plans For Circus
Affair Attempts to Show One Type of Free Entertainment

Plans are being made for the first summer school gym circus to be held on Thursday night, July 14, according to a recent announcement by Wendel Lewis, president of Gamma Phi.

Because many students on the campus this summer have never seen the circus that is presented during the regular term each year, this experiment should prove especially interesting, Mr. Lewis said. It will be an attempt to show the type of work carried on by the men's physical education department in the form of a free show for everyone.

Although only a few of the men who appeared in the regular circus are enrolled this summer, enough new men will be added to the group to make most of the larger acts possible. The list of participants is not completed, but Porter Powell, Herbert Smith, Harold Stambach, Gilford Parsons, Floyd Schwenn, and Wendel Lewis comprise an early nucleus of the group.

"This is an excellent opportunity for those people already in the field," according to Professor C. E. Horton, inasmuch as the gym circus is the coming thing in small schools. This activity, Prof. Horton says, will give the persons interested some insight into how a circus is conducted.

July 7, 1938 (page 3)
McCormick Gymnasium Is Scene of School Circus
Show to Include Balance Acts on Tight Wire, Flying Rings
Summer time is circus time.

The carnival spirit will prevail here Wednesday night, July 13, when McCormick gymnasium will take on all the color of the genuine "big top" for the showing of the first summer school gym circus. All acts are entering the final week of rehearsal, and according to Prof. C. E. Horton, director of the gymnasts, and Wendel Lewis, president of Gamma Phi, the principals in the big one-ring affair will be in top form to entertain all who come out for the free show. Few Regulars

Although only a few of the circus men are enrolled this summer, an attempt will be made to feature practically every major act of the regular term circus, with a smaller number of participants in each act.

The trio of Thorson, Kidder, and Lewis will demonstrate some feats of balance in their chair and table number and their triple hand balancing stunt. Lewis will team with Powell and Easterbrook for the special tumbling performance. These same men have also been practicing for some time on the springboard and are all set to perform in a few fancy dives.

Easterbrook and Kidder are paired as the "daring young men" in the flying rings performance, and Powell and Lewis are planning to soar to dizzy heights on the revolving ladder.

Tight Wire Act
The tight wire walker will be Red Smith, who will also be featured in a tap dancing exhibition. William Muhl is scheduled to demonstrate his prowess as a tosser of the Indian clubs.

The Gamma Phi circus has always featured several displays of pyramid building. This phase of the program will be handled by a group of boys from the Illinois Soldiers and Sailors Children's school.

Big Top

The girl on the flying ladder gives some insight into the nature of the acts to be presented by Prof. C. E. Horton and his troupe when they entertain the student body with the first annual summer gym circus on Wednesday, July 13, at McCormick gymnasium.

July 7, 1938 (page 3)

Note:

Yes, this is the same picture from 1936 with a different caption.

1938 – 39 School Year

The Gamma Phi Queen participation is brought back with stringent voting rules.

1939 ISU Special Collections

Aug 4,1938 (page 5)
Normal Gymnasts Present Exhibition at CCC Camp
A quartet of Gamma Phi gymnasts entertained the men on duty at the LeRoy CCC camp, Wednesday night, July 27. The four men, Lewis, Powell. Murray, and Cozart. performed several acts in tumbling, fancy diving from the springboard, and demonstrations on the parallel bars. Prof. C. E. Horton, who accompanied the men to LeRoy, presented a motion picture which featured the sensational chair and table act presented by the men in the recent gym circus.

Oct 4, 1938 Vidette (page 4)
Gamma Phi Week to End With Stag Party
Gamma Phi, men's honorary physical education fraternity, is holding the annual Gamma Phi week beginning October 3 and ending with a stag party at Lake Bloomington on October 9, according to Mr. William Anderson, president of the organization.

Anyone interested in physical education is eligible for pledgeship to the organization.

During the week, the active members will wear official Gamma Phi shirts, will have pledge slips, and will answer questions of pledge applicants.

This organization is for the purpose of furthering the interest of men in physical education on the campus and sponsors, each year, the Gamma Phi circus.

Nov 8, 1938 Vidette (page 3)

Physical Education Seniors Meet, Outline Year's Schedule of Events

With the aim of providing periodic entertainment for physical education majors, the seniors in this field of study met last Tuesday evening at the home of Dr. C. E. Horton, head of the physical education department.

Thirteen seniors (not superstitious) attended the meeting, including William Anderson, president of Gamma Phi, men's honorary physical , education fraternity; Howard Lester, Marvin Hamilton, George Matthews, Lindsey Morris, Clair Stine, Francis Griffith, Sheldon Robinson, "Rocky" Shields, Gene Lientz, James Shearer, Forrest Reid, and Lowell Johnson. Besides Dr. Horton, the faculty was represented by coaches Eugene Hill and Harold Frye.

An informal discussion was held, during which plans were made to throw open the Gamma Phi meetings to all physical education majors, in the hope of fostering a spirit of comradeship and sociability.

The meetings will be sponsored by the four classes, beginning with seniors. Dr. Horton will act as advisor for the senior group, Mr. Frye for the juniors, Mr. Hill for the sophomores, and Mr. Struck for the freshmen.

After Dr. Horton had started the ball rolling, a spirited discussion

*took place, led by the loquacious "Rocky." The group finally decided
to hold a basketball clinic as the feature of the first meeting, with
prominent members of the local sporting world as head-line
attractions.*

*President Anderson appointed two committees, one to arrange the
program and the other to take charge of distributing tags to all
physical education majors. Howard Lester will serve as chairman of
the program committee, with George Matthews, Claire Stine, and
Lindsey Morris as his aides. The tag committee consists of Lowell
Johnson, chairman, Francis Griffith and George Matthews.*

*Mr. Horton provided a pleasant surprise at the conclusion of the
meeting, furnishing everyone with a generous helping of pumpkin pie
with whipped cream and coffee.*

*The definite plans and date for the clinic will be announced in the
next issue of The Vidette. This meeting will be closed to everyone
except male physical education majors and Gamma Phi members:
President Anderson and the rest of the seniors are planning to make
the clinic one of the year's most interesting events. In addition (if the
treasury holds out) refreshments will be served.*

Dec 2, 1938 (front page)
Gamma PM Holds Formal Initiation in Gym Monday
*Gamma Phi, men's honorary physical education fraternity, will hold
its formal initiation at 8 p. m Monday in the W. A. A. room of
McCormick gymnasium.*

*All those who have turned in their pledge slips and all physical
education majors are eligible for membership. The dues of 50 cents
must be paid before the initiation ceremonies.*

*As this will be the last initiation of the first semester, President
Anderson urges that all those eligible attend. The initiation will he
absolutely formal in nature, with no paddling or mental tortures.*

Horton Elaborates on Background Of Coming Gamma Phi Production

BY BOB SMITH

Hearing a rumor that the Gamma Phi circus is coming to town, our city editor called me in and said, "Smith, here's your big chance. Go down and see Dr. Horton and get a little inside stuff on this business."

Armed with a notebook and pencil, I trekked to McCormick gymnasium and was fortunate enough to find the object of my search.

It seems some eleven years ago physical education students here at I. S. N. U. under the careful guidance of Dr "Pop" Horton wanted to organize a physical education club. After much deliberation a chapter of the Gamma Phi was proposed.

With the Gamma Phi chapter organized, the members began to practice faithfully and soon exhibitions were given between halves of basketball games. This went over so well that the members of the organization decided to expand. With the experience gained by the exhibitions behind them, the Gamma Phi organized the first "Gamma Phi circus."

It was just eight years ago that the first circus was held, and it was, quoting Dr. Horton, "A big success from start to finish." Since then it has been an annual affair and it has played to large and attentive audiences. Each year the student representation in the different acts has improved so much that the circus rivals any of its kind in the state.

Helps Teachers
Much has been gained by the circus, in that it prepares students for teaching. Several physical education graduates and ex-Gamma Phi's have inaugurated similar circus in the high schools in which they teach. This is a good example of the fine work the physical education department is doing at Normal.

Every year some outside talent has been brought in to help make the " circus a success. This year, however, an effort is being made to make the circus as thorough an all Normal event as possible. Many new acts are being worked on and this year's circus looks to be the best yet.

Elect Queen
The revival of the election of the Queen of the circus will be one of the added features of the circus this year. Although the method of election has not been decided upon as yet, I am informed that everyone will have equal rights in the voting and that age and mental ability will not stand in the way of one's casting the fatal ballot. Further particulars concerning the election of the Queen will appear in the near future, in the Normal "scandal sheet."

Wiping the sweat from my brow, I bade Dr. Horton adieu and strolled leisurely back to, my abode where, after seeing those pink elephants on the wall the other night, I vowed to go to the Gamma Phi circus after this to see the animals.

Feb 17, 1939 (front page)
Selection of Gamma Phi Circus Queen Set for Party on March 3
Through the collaboration of the Cooperative council, the election of the Gamma Phi circus queen will take on an air of pageantry.

At the Cooperative party on March 3, the dance programs will be furnished with an attached ballot. All the candidates for queen will be introduced to the crowd of dancers, and the ballots will then be cast and placed in the various ballet boxes scattered throughout the gymnasium. The identity of the winner will be kept secret until the opening of the circus, when the queen will be crowned.

Nominate by Petition
In order to nominate a candidate for the honor, a petition with twenty-five signatures must he turned in to John Scott, chairman of the election committee, has the printed petitions. 'These must be obtained and filled out by the deadline Tuesday noon, February 21.

The queen, besides presiding in state over the circus, becomes an honorary member of Gamma Phi.

While preparations for selecting the queen are in full sway, students concerned directly with the circus are laboring day and night. Thorsen, Parsons and Morrisey made a preliminary appearance at the U High-Bloomington game the other night, and were well-received by the crowd.

Murray Brings Performers
Former and present Gamma Phi members in the surrounding high schools are planning to bring their prize gymnasts to lend color to the show. Les Murray, who will be remembered as one of Normal's immortals, will have a group of performers.

Other campus organizations have also signified their desire to participate in the festivities, and Director Stine, is confident that this year's circus will eclipse all those of the past.

Feb 21, 1939 (front page)
Gamma Phi Issues Plea for Redhead
Although the influenza epidemic has seriously crippled their fighting forces, members of Gamma Phi still putting forth every effort toward the perfection of plans for this year's circus.

The illness of John Scott, who was in charge of the much-heralded election of the circus queen, slowed down the machinery, but his duties have been assumed by William Anderson, Gamma Phi prexy, and Lindsey Morris, publicity director for the circus, and the nominations were closed today at noon as previously announced.

Several of Normal's fairest flowers have been nominated for the honor of presiding over the circus, and the list will be announced in Friday's Vidette.

Some of the petition-passers have put forth an indication that they wish to be recognized as gentlemen, by the act of nominating blondes, while others have distrusted the peroxide and genuine types, pinning their hopes on some dark-eyed brunette.

The selections made guarantee that the queen will be worthy of her honor, hut those in charge had hoped fervently that the Lord would send them at least one red-head.

Charter Member

EUGENE HILL, physical education instructor and intramural director, sits in a thoughtful mood. Perhaps he is concentrating on the Gamma Phi circus to be held in McCormick gym, March 10 and 11. Hill is a charter member of the organization, and along with Prof. C. E. Horton, helps direct its activities.

Vidette Feb 24, 1939 (page 4)

Hill Gives Views On Gamma Phi
BY BOB SMITH

"Peanuts," "Popcorn," "Crackerjack," will soon be heard resounding through the rafters of McCormick gymnasium, because the Gamma Phi circus is coming to town. Your editor, needing something to fill up today's paper, called upon your truly to get another story about the spectacle, which is to be presented on March 10 and 11.

Retracing my footsteps to McCormick gymnasium, I was able to corral Mr. Eugene Hill, physical educator instructor. With my pencil thoroughly sharpened and my notebook squarely planted in front of me, I was able to jot down the following details concerning the past activities under the "big top" of the Gamma Phi circus.

Mr. Hill, although he informed me that the circuses were not inaugurated until after he graduated, was a charter member of Gamma Phi. Most of us know that "Gene," as he is called by those near to him, became a member of the I. S. N. U. faculty upon his graduation from the Normal institution, and has helped with all the circuses.

First Circus
In commenting on the first circus, he said, "It wasn't very good. The acts were short, and of very little variety and no outside talent was brought in to lengthen the program." He also stated, "Due to the fact that the circus was new to the people in this vicinity, the attendance was very poor."

However, since the first circus the crowds have increased so much that this year's attraction is expected to fill the "big top" to overflowing.

It was made plain to your reporter that the circus is strictly on a non-professional basis and most of the acts are practiced and performed by members of the different physical education classes. The different exhibitions lack the finesse and dress of similar acts of the professional type, but show the ability of the performers as well as the training that the physical education students are receiving through the efforts of Mr. Horton, Mr. Hill and the other gym instructors.

Each year the different acts which will be part of the circus are generally exhibited in neighboring towns, mainly for practice as well as advertisement for the circus.

Ex-Grads Perform
In commenting on the achievements of students who have graduated and who have taken part in past Gamma Phi circuses, Mr. Hill stated that "several boys have joined show troupes and circuses, and have exhibited their ability in this way."

Some of the ex-grads who have had this experience are Arlie Gillette, LaVern Christensen, and Les Murray. King and Barclay also joined a show troupe and performed a revolving ladder act similar to the one they did in the past circuses. These men, most of whom are teaching in different high schools throughout the state, are now putting on circuses of their own in their respective schools.

Another young man bearing the name of Tony Clendenin, quoting the words of Mr. Hill, "was offered a job as a clown in the great Ringling Brothers circus." Tony, as you know, accounted for the laughs of last year's circus, with his clowning antics.

Revival of Queen
In stating his opinion about the revival of the election of the queen of the circus this year, Mr. Hill informed me that he thought "the presentation of the queen was one of the highlights of the circus and added a great deal of color to the event." The queen is made an honorary member of the Gamma Phi fraternity and will receive a pin symbolic of the fraternity.

In closing a very interesting interview "Genial Gene" told your reporter that "through the efforts of Mr. Horton the Gamma Phi circus was organized, and if it hadn't been for his great interest in the circuses, they would have died out."

Feb 24, 1939 (page 6)

The Gamma Phi has been hesitant about supplying half-time entertainment, but the faculty is not backward. A charming half-time exhibition of basket shooting was given during the Chicago Teachers game with such notables as Messrs. Linkins, Marzolf, Ivens, Holmes, Johnson, Browne, Fogler, Struck, and Gooding performing. Mr. Marzolf won the lead-plated tin cup for the most wicked shots. If he were only eligible, but, at that, Hibler is the toughest of them all. Stretch Miller of the radio and Fred Young of the press also took a crack.

Feb 24, 1939 (front page)

Gamma Phi Selects Five Nominees For Annual Circus Queen Contest

After lengthy hours of deliberation and argument, the election committee for the Gamma Phi circus queen has finally managed to arrive at a decision.

In order to guarantee that the queen will be truly representative of the coed ranks, and to forestall most of the chances for disappointments, five candidates were selected.

The girls who received the contested posts are Clarabelle Huggins, Lois Davis, Helen Shippy, Ruth Parkinson, and Mary Brumbach.

Miss Huggins is a sophomore from LeRoy in the French curriculum. She is serving as associate editor of the 1938-39 Index.

Miss Davis is a junior from Auburn in the commerce curriculum, and was a candidate for Homecoming queen in 1937.

Miss Shippey is a sophomore from Decatur, also in the commerce curriculum.

Miss Parkinson is from Ipana and is a sophomore in the health and sports for women curriculum.

Miss Brumbach, secretary-treasurer of the sophomore class, is from

Dwight and enrolled in the four year elementary curriculum. She was a candidate for Homecoming queen in 1938.

Following the announcement of the committee, none of the nominees could be reached for a statement.

The five candidates will be introduced at the Co-operative Party on March 3, at which time the voting will be done, through the courtesy of the Co-operative Council.

The winner of the election will be crowned queen of the Gamma Phi circus on Friday night, March 10, and will preside over both the Friday and Saturday night festivities.

In addition, she becomes an honorary member of Gamma Phi, quite an achievement for a member of the weaker sex, and receives a pin.

The remaining four girls are given the distinction of serving as maids-of-honor to the queen at both performances of the circus.

Voting for the queen will be carried on only at the party on March 3. Ballots will be. attached to each program, and after the nominees have been introduced, it will lie a simple matter to mark the ballot and drop it in one of the numerous boxes provided for the occasion.

The committee fervently hopes that the selections meet with the approval of the student body. Every effort was made to make the best choices possible.

Feb 24, 1939 (page 8)

Tumblers Go To Towanda For Program
Gamma Phi to Present Preview of 1939 Circus

Clair Stine, director of the Gamma Phi circus, announces that the plans for completion of the circus program are moving definitely toward a climax.

Members of the various committees have been giving freely of their time and energy to assure the fact that this year's affair will eclipse any of the past performances.

Troupe Travels

In order to "warm up" for the show, individual performers of the Gamma Phi troupe have been busily engaged in offering performances at various towns in the vicinity.

For those who desire to get a preview of some of the circus acts, a trip to Towanda on Wednesday night would prove beneficial.

Thorsen, Parsons, Morrisey and the other members of the cast will give a special performance at Towanda high school on that date.

The occasion will be a benefit basketball game, in which the Gamma Phi cagers, including Dave Rydeen, Barney Leigh, Art Cox, and other stellar hoop artists will meet an opponent whose identity is yet to be disclosed.

Thrilling Events

The Tumblers will not offer the entire repertoire which has been planned for the nights of March 10 and 11, but will endeavor to thrill the audience with a few technical tricks.

Performers in the circus are exerting themselves to the utmost to attain perfection in order to make sure that their deeds will not be eclipsed by the beauty of the circus queen.

Mar 3, 1939 (front page)

Bevy of Beauteous Brunettes Appear at Party, Aspire to Honor of Selection as Circus Queen

"La-deez and gentlemen! In this corner we have"—In a modified form, this cry will resound through McCormick gymnasium tonight, as the candidates for queen of the Gamma Phi circus are introduced to the public.

Five representatives of the female population of Old Normal have been selected to vie for the honor of presiding over the annual March festivities. They will be presented to the crowd tonight, with an appropriate background furnished by Bill Bardo. Curiously enough, the tradition that gentlemen prefer blondes received a jolt when it was revealed that none of the quintet. of aspirants can escape being classed in the brunette ranks.

Proceeding alphabetically, we discover Mary Elizabeth (Diddy) Brumbach, sophomore from Dwight. Miss Brumbach is the possessor of brown eyes, decidedly dark brown hair, and claims the distinctive height of five feet two. Lois Davis, the lone junior on the list, has unusual hazel eyes, a. lighter shade of brown hair, and fs in the immediate vicinity of five feet four. Miss Davis is a native of Auburn. Clarabelle Huggins, sophomore, from the nearby town of LeRoy, owns very large brown eyes, very dark brown hair, and is an inch taller than Miss Davis.

Ruth Parkinson, sophomore from Ipava, is the nearest approach to a blonde that we can offer. In addition to her light brown tresses, Miss Parkinson is "five feet two, eyes of blue."
Finally, we have Helen Shippey, sophomore from Decatur. Miss Shippy adds to the majority of brown-eyed lasses, has dark brown hair, and is five feet seven.

These five young ladies, attired as befits the occasion, will appear before the Co-operative party audience tonight. Members of Gamma Phi have been using every vestige of effort and inventive genius to make the presentation striking and unusual, and it is fairly certain that a deep impression will be made on those present.

Ballots attached to every program will make it a simple matter for dancers and non-dancers to cast their votes for 'the girl they believe to be most truly deserving of the honor of presiding over the circus. Ballot boxes will be placed at convenient spots about the dance floor.

The utmost effort will be exerted to keep the results of the election a secret until the night of the coronation. Members of the committee on election are bracing themselves for the expected flood of curious questioners.

Mar 3, 1939 (page 6)

Veterans Perform in Gamma Phi Circus

Thorsen, Parsons Return To Action on Bars, Balancing
BY BOB SMITH

Three boys will be featured during the Gamma Phi circus on the night of March 10 and 11. These boys have made quite a reputation for themselves in this locality due to their gymnastic ability.

Jimmy Thorsen, a junior from Braceville, Jesse Parsons, a sophomore from Bloomington, and Bill Morrissey, a sophomore from Pontiac are the three boys referred to.

Thorsen Veteran

Thorsen has appeared in every Gamma Phi circus since his arrival on the Normal campus. Having no high school experience in gymnastics Jimmy gives all the credit for., his ability to perform on the parallel bars, the flying rings, etc.to Dr. Horton. Other specialties in which Mr. Thorsen contributes his ability to are the three man balancing act, and a new specialty, the perch pole. Jimmy, a commerce major, calls gymnastics his hobby and hopes upon his graduation to have a circus of his own.

Outside Performances

Jesse Parsons, a Bloomington boy started his gym work about four years ago while in high school. He has participated in the last two Gamma Phi circuses here at Normal, Y. M. C. A. circuses have taken much of his time as he participated in two such affairs while in high school. Lewis Probasco, a former gym captain at the University of Wisconsin, taught Jesse nearly everything he knows concerning gymnastics. He will thrill this year's circus crowd with his feats on the parallel bars, high bar, three man balancing act, table and chair act and the new perch pole act. Jesse is considered a veteran when it comes to

Jack La Bounty

performing his outstanding specialties and was offered a job with a circus "troop but preferred an education to circus life.

Star at Pontiac
Bill Morrissey, the last of the boys mentioned has a great reputation in circus work.

He has performed two years in the Pontiac circus, which is a very outstanding circus, his specialty being on the parallel bars. Adagio dancing has also taken up two years of "Bill's" time, and he has had the honor to show his talent twice at the Blackhawks restaurant in Chicago. He has also participated at the State Fair in Springfield. Bill started his gym career when a junior in high school. Mr. Haskins, gym instructor at Pontiac, helped Bill and taught him to perform on the parallel bars. Bill participated in the Normal circus, while a member of the Pontiac circus, a year or so ago. Morrissey has been specializing in circus work for five years.

Mar 3, 1939 (page 7)
Clowns Galore Display Talent To Circus Goers
Laugh, clown, laugh. This procedure will be somewhat reversed next week when, at the Gamma Phi circus March 10-11, it will be the spectator's opportunity to laugh and the clown's duty to supply the necessary mirth-provoking stimulus.

The merry makers participating in this year's epic of under the big top are headed by that diminutive bundle of vivacity, Jack La Bounty, possessor of six years' clowning experience. Mr. La Bounty will be ably assisted by a competent crew of fellow funnymen, including Walter "King Kong" Selberg, Boots Herrick, and Don Fitzsimmons. Mr. Selberg is the lone member of this group who is a newcomer to the art of rib-tickling.

For several years the trio of La Bounty, Herrick, and Fitzsimmons have done semi-professional clowning in central Illinois, banded under the name of The Stooges. They have "worked" carnivals, fairs, shows, and assemblies, being great crowd pleasers at each performance.

As in any other line of work, many amusing instances also arise in the art of making people laugh. Slap-stick comedy involves a great deal of rough treatment when, for example, one clown is kicked in the face, stomach, or some other part of his anatomy by another, it is no joke to the recipient who must act as though he enjoys it. At one performance a lusty whack on the seat of Mr. La Bounty's britches caused that worthy gentleman to eat his meals from the mantlepiece for two days.

After adding many acts to their already overflowing repertoire, this year's users of grease paint and slap-stick assure us of at least a laugh a minute from the start to the finish of the "Show of the Century, the Gamma Phi Circus of 1939."

Mar 15, 1939 (front page)
Large Crowd Sees Gamma Phi Circus
Thorsen Draws Applause With Perch Pole Act; Brumbaugh Queen
After two nights filled with much "hub-bub" and excitement activities around and about McCormick gymnasium have settled down to their natural trend. All gymnastic equipment may be seen resting in its proper storage space and some of it will not be used until next year when another Gamma Phi spectacle will be staged.

This year's circus was a big success. Rainy weather kept attendance down to a certain extent but a goodly crowd witnessed both shows.

Variety of Acts
A great variety of acts thrilled an attentive audience, and each performance, from the minuet dancers of Thomas Metcalf, to the climax of the evening, the perch pole act, kept everyone in suspense from start to finish.

The perch pole act was undoubtedly the outstanding act of the circus with little Jimmy Thorsen going through his daring feats high in the air amidst the well-deserved applause of the audience. Jesse Parsons had the important job of holding up the heavy iron pole on top of which Thorsen performed.

The tumblers from Towanda, Lexington, Victory Hall, and the Soldiers and Sailors home showed considerable ability in their tumbling and pyramid building.

Every act should be complimented and the way they were enacted Friday and Saturday nights shows that many hours of diligent practice were needed to perfect them. Several acts, namely, the parallel bars, the high bar, the swinging ladder, the tight wire, the bronze act, and the importation from the Pontiac circus were very good.

Horton Receives Clock
Jack LaBounty, Don Fitzsimmons, "Boots" Herrick, and Walt Selberg kept the crowd laughing with their clowning antics and would without doubt prove an asset to any big time circus.

During the festivities Saturday night, "Bill" Anderson, president of the Gamma Phi, introduced Dr. "Pop" Horton, head of the physical education department and overseer of the circus, to whom he presented an electric clock, a well-deserved token of appreciation for the undaunted work which he so cheerfully donated toward making the Gamma Phi circus the success that it was.

"Diddy" Brumbach, queen of the circus, and her attendants presided over the activities both nights. Clair Stine, director of the circus, Ray Heckel, ringmaster, Mr. Eyre of Bloomington, boss of the properties committee and those boys who donated their services by taking care of the equipment and seeing that each act was run off smoothly, carried out their work in fine style and are to be complimented on their endeavors.

March 31, 1939 (page 3)
Parsons Member Of Gymnast Team
Represents Bloomington In National YMCA Meet Jesse Parsons, ace sophomore, gymnast who is noted for his stellar performances on the horizontal and parallel bars, is a member of the team that will represent Bloomington in the National Y. AI. C. A. meet tomorrow at Fort Wayne, Indiana.

Jesse received the bulk of his training from Clifford 'Pop' Horton, director of the physical education department. He excels in any type; of bar work and is exceptionally good in balance acts. He was one of the big 'guns' in the Gamma Phi circus and was on the ground-end of the newly famous pole-balancing act. Jesse has been appearing nightly in the great Gym Circus of the. Bloomington Y. M. C. A.

Jesse is the second I. S. N. U. athlete that has carried his banner in a national meet; Warren Sperry being the other.

April 14, 1939 (page 8)
Gamma Phi, men's physical education fraternity, will hold an important meeting Tuesday, April 18, at 7:30 p. m. in G-103. All members are urged to attend.
Wm. Anderson, President.

May 5, 1939 (page 7)
Trio of Acrobats Appear in Circus
The Gamma Phi is scoring again. Again its members are participating before strange audiences.

In the near future Jimmy Thorsen, Jesse Parsons, and Bill Morrissey, present Gamma Phi stalwarts, will perform at LaSalle-Peru in a circus given and directed by Arley Gillett, a former Redbird and Gamma Phi expert.

This is the first circus ever attempted by Mr. Gillett. Arley as you may remember was former wrestling captain, and star performer of past Gamma Phi circuses. He has used the experience gained through participation in these circuses to bring to the people of La Salle-Peru a glimpse of the fine things that can be done by his students.

May 23, 1939 (page 3)
Gamma Phi Dance Routine Is Popular

Dr. C. E. Horton has announced that a request has been made by the Mendon, Illinois grade school, asking for a return engagement of the Gamma Phi's three high and acrobatic dance routines. The occasion is the Mendon grade school revue which is part of a school reunion sponsored by the community of Mendon.

A request has also been made by the fall festival committee of Berry, Illinois, wanting members of the Gamma Phi to participate in a festival to be held in September.

Both invitations will he accepted if possible and the following performers have been asked to take part in both affairs; Ruth Parkinson, June Kosnick, Jimmy Thorsen, Jesse Parsons, and Bill Morrissey.

June 22, 1939 (page 6)
Gamma Phi to Present Gymnastic Carnival

For the purpose of promoting the interests of gymnastics and physical education, the Gamma Phi, honorary gymnastic fraternity, is presenting a summer circus on Friday evening, July 14. The circus will consist mainly of skillfully performed acts which have been given in prior circuses.

Several alumni members of Gamma Phi, all past circus performers, have returned to summer school and will aid in the presentation. Wendel Lewis, former Gamma Phi president and performer, is among this group; also William Muhl, who is directing waterfront activities at East Bay Camp, will be with the performers.

There will be no admission charge.

June 29, 1939 (page 7)

Metropolitan Tenor Carter Appears on Artist Series
Brass Symphony Date Changed

The fourth lecture board number, Herbert Petrie's Symphony in Brass, scheduled for tomorrow evening has been postponed until July 14. The changing of this number necessitated the postponement of the Gamma Phi circus until July 28.

July 20, 1939 Vidette (front page)

Gamma Phi Holds Circus
Thorson, Parsons, Parkinson Perform

Circus day is just around the corner!

July 28 will be an unlucky Friday for the fellow who fails to see and hear the seasoned troupers in Gamma Phi imposing outdoor summer circus. Gamma Phi and the Physical Education department have spared neither effort nor expense in bringing before the student body, free of charge, a performance that will compare favorably with professional shows under the big tops.

Breath-Taking Act
Jimmy Thorson, Gamma Phi president, and Jesse Parsons will risk bones and necks in their gravity defying perch pole balancing stunt. Doing a headstand on bicycle handlebars atop a 25-foot pole, balanced by Parsons, is an everyday occurrence in Jimmy's life. Full of indoor perils as this feat is, these men will be making their first attempt under the stars. It requires the perfect timing and coordination of both performers, and adjustments will have to be made for even the slightest puff of wind.

And all for the same price, Charles Hall will team with Parsons, Thorson, Switzer, and Lewis in the unparalleled table and chair balancing act. Hall will convince his audience that the seemingly impossible can be done, and—climaxing this act—Thorson and Switzer will do handstands on top of four and six chairs stacked above a wobbly table. "We have reason to believe," said a high ranking circus official, "that this act has never been performed in any other amateur show."

Lewis in Fire Dive
Wendell Lewis, former Gamma president, will terminate a unique and dangerous springboard performance with a dive through a flaming kerosene soaked hoop. Lewis has his life insurance up to date, but so far he hasn't done more than singe a few hairs.

According to manager Jimmy Thorson, Jack LaBounty is secretive about just what he will do until the day arrives, because he doesn't know. And that is one of the secrets of LaBounty and his crew of half a dozen wise-cracking clowns. LaBounty has never failed to get a big hand, and he and his gang are reported better than ever this summer.

The popular Ruth Parkinson needs no introduction to students on the campus during the regular year. Her natural grace as a dancer, and her artistic balance and daring on the tight wire rated her as a star even after the first of her many performances. Her tight wire partner, Herbert Smith, also ranks among the top performers in the amateur ranks.

Twenty scintillating performers, in 13 or more acts, will treat the spectators with an hour and a half show.

"Don't forget it is all under the sky's big top, and our elephants don't eat peanuts," was a clown's final reminder.

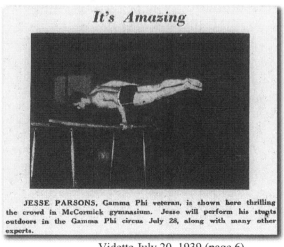

It's Amazing

JESSE PARSONS, Gamma Phi veteran, is shown here thrilling the crowd in McCormick gymnasium. Jesse will perform his stunts outdoors in the Gamma Phi circus July 28, along with many other experts.

Vidette July 20, 1939 (page 6)

Hope No One Sneezes

JIMMY THORSON, shown here as the apex of the human sky-scraper, is responsible for the operation of the Gamma Phi circus, which will be aired on July 28. Jim is next year's president of the men's physical education fraternity.

Vidette July 20, 1939 (page 8)

July 27, 1939 (page 14)

Gamma Phi Holds Outdoor Gym Circus Friday Night

Summer Festival Is Free Affair Circus going folks will view a high class performance when they attend the Gamma Phi summer circus at 8:15 tomorrow evening. The site is the athletic field just south of McCormick gymnasium. Aerial and tight-wire acts, four-man balancing feats, clown capers, and--well, just about everything the big circuses can offer will he yours without charge. All the fan needs to do is walk in, sit down, open the peanut bag and be prepared for a full evening of pleasing surprises.

Parkinson-Smith Team Up
According to witnesses of previous performances, the team of Ruth Parkinson and Herb Smith have always received ovations in their several appearances on the I. S. N. U. campus. In their last appearance here, which was in February, they danced with Joe Sanders and his distinguished band. Tomorrow night they will do an adagio which promises to be both artistic and amusing.

Besides their dance numbers, this pair will demonstrate various difficult steps and stunts on the tightwire, taught to them, it is said, by the famous Balletti of the circus world. Red Smith, the male member of the team, also works a clown routine on the unicycle.

Horton-Muhl-Parsons
Clifford Horton, popular director of physical education and Bill Muhl, director of East Bay waterfront activities will swing electrically lighted Indian clubs in their matchless interpretation of how these clubs should be swung.

Also, Jesse Parsons, parallel and horizontal bar expert, will execute some maneuvers that won places for him in the national Y. M. C. A. meet held at Ft. Wayne in May of this year. Daggett and Kidder, co-performers with Parsons, are also experts on the bars.

Many Other Features
The famous perch pole and balancing acts of Thorson, Parsons, and Morrissey, which have been mentioned in previous issues of the Vidette will be among the many features. Also Rinkenburger,

*Easterbrook, and Thorson on the flying rings, and Parkinson on the
flying ladder have never failed to please in former shows. Wendel
Lewis, ex-president of Gamma Phi, Miller, and Switzer, all Gamma
circus veterans, will team with Parsons and Thorson in the much
publicized chair and table balancing act and in the performance of
difficult stunts on the high bar.*

*The thrills will not be over until Lewis and Powell, the bouncing
boys of the springboard, do their daily dozen over dizzy distances,
and "don't forget us," was the final reminder of the funny LaBounty
and his daffy company of clowns in the persons of Fitzsimmons,
Hoyl, Selberg, and Herrick.*

Aug 3, 1939 (page 13)
Gamma Phi Circus Held; Audience Numbers 1500
Performers Show Varied Skills
*About fifteen hundred spectators viewed the 13 feature acts and half
dozen clown skits of the Gamma Phi amateur circus, which was held
on the university athletic field Friday night.*

*Bleachers placed on both sides of the small arena were packed
before the opening number, and late comers stood three deep around
the ends, while others watched through the iron bars of the fences.
The field was lighted by floodlights which played upon gay
decorations.*

*The audience was brought to attention when, with "oh's" and
"ahs," they watched the Smith-Parkinson team open the show with a
colorful performance on the light-wire. Although their tightwire act
brought much favorable comment, it was their adagio dance, later in
the evening that brought the most applause.*

Thorson-Parsons Favorites
*Jimmy Thorson's daring headstand on top of an 18-foot pole, held in
the air and balanced by Jesse Parsons, climaxed an act that brought
forth more applause than any single exhibition of the evening.
Performed for the first time outdoors, their stunt was made more
difficult by a stiff breeze.*

The chair and table balancing act, in which the venturesome Lewis - Thorson - Switzer - Parsons quartet performed hand-stands on chairs placed five high above a table, also brought the unanimous approval of the house.

Running closely parallel to this in popularity was the performance of Powell and Lewis on the springboard, climaxed by Lewis' dive through a flaming, kerosene-soaked hoop. The three-man balancing act of Morrissey, Parsons, and Thorson, and the Indian club swinging of Muhl, although lacking the reception of some of the more dangerous feats, were no less dexterously done.

The Parsons-Dagget-Kidder parallel bar team, and the Parsons-Thorson-Miller horizontal bar trio turned in almost professional performances, hut it took the giant swings to capture the spectators.

Clown Acts
Get Hand LaBounty with his clown company of Fitzsimmons, Selberg, and Herrick, kept the fans in good humor with their imitations of most of the serious stunts. Their mimicry of the Park-Smith team on the wire and the little medicine show skit, with Chief Horseshoe (the full-blooded half-breed) as the center of attraction, were the most vociferously received.

Red Smith, clowning on the unicycle, captivated the assemblage from his first appearance. His antics on the unicycle and the combined buffoonery of himself and Miss Parkinson in the clowned dance received some of the biggest ovations of the evening.

The Rinkenburger - Easterbrook: combination on the flying rings and Miss Parkinson on the swinging ladder added much of the color to an all-around good amateur circus production.

1939 – 40 School Year

Membership into Gamma Phi is opened to women. Previously, Gamma Phi Queens were given honorary membership, but now the regular membership is open to all.

Not only is this a good thing for the organization as a whole, but the timing also turned out to be critical. In 1942, most of the men left ISNU to fight in the war...

Oct 13,1939 (page 3)
Notice
Gamma Phi formal initiation will be held Monday, October 16, at 7:30, in the W. A. A. room of the gym. All old members are urged to attend.

Oct 13, 1939 (page 5)
Gamma Phi has taken a progressive step in setting a new precedent by admitting the feminine gender to its fold. Never before in the history of the organization has a woman been even considered for membership. But now, by invitation, the once-called "weaker sex" will be pledged to the only athletic fraternity on the campus. Someone is making use of talent that would have otherwise gone for naught—hats off to him.

Oct 20, 1939 (page 6)
Nine Pledges Get Gamma Phi Honors From Initiation
Gamma Phi, physical education fraternity, held its formal initiation Monday, Oct. 16, in the W. A. A. room at the gym.

The initiates were Stanley Breen, Don Fitzsimmons, Jack LaBounty, Max Haughey, June Kosnick, Ruth Parkinson, William Morrissey, Lyle Rinkenburger, and Charles Thomas.

For the first time in the history of the organization, women have been invited to become members. This step is expected to bring a variety of new talent to the annual circus.

Ruth Parkinson and June Kosnick, who were members of the traveling troupe last year, are the first women to be honored in this capacity it was announced by James Thorsen, president of the organization. Membership in Gamma Phi is limited and by invitation only.

Nov 10, 1939 (page 6)
Gamma Phi Invites Women to Become Acrobats, Tumblers

"The men's gymnasium will be buzzing with activity if all women in school interested in tumbling and acrobatics will come down next Monday night at 7 p. m. to start practice for Gamma Phi," announced Jesse Parsons, circus director of Gamma Phi.

"No previous experience in acrobatics is needed," Mr. Parsons continued, "only the determination not to mind being a bit stiff and sore at times."

Meetings will be held every Monday between 7 and 9 p. m., and there is opportunity to learn tight wire walking, swinging ladder acts, as well as the more down-to-earth gymnastic feats.

"There may be a chance to make the traveling squad later on," Mr. Parsons said, "And these trips we take are really worth the time spent in practice."

Last year there were only two co-eds, Ruth Parkinson and June Kosnich, who traveled with Mr. Horton and his boys, but the Gamma Phi's want to improve their acts this year by having more women in them.

Nov 17, 1939 (page 6)
Gamma Phi Men's Invite Accepted
Gamma Phis initial practice Monday night "uncovered" a wealth of strength and beauty among the so called weaker sex, as well as exposing some male ability.

The youthful and eager lady acrobats outnumbered more bashful male advocates of the aesthetic but interesting circus activities by quite a margin.

Phases of the graceful arts of tight wire walking, ground tumbling, of working the swinging ladder, the flying rings, and even the spectacular perch pole were introduced to the new candidates.

Succeeding Monday nites from 7 to 9 will again offer the above activities in the men's gym. Expert instruction is to be given, and no previous experience is necessary— interest and enthusiasm being the prime prerequisites.

Dec 1, 1939 (front page)
Second Co-op Party Features Ted Fio Rito
WJBC Broadcasts Normal Hit Parade
A very excellent floor show, promised by the orchestra, consists of 15 members, each a talented musician in his own right. A short Gamma Phi act will also be presented

Dec 12, 1939 (page 3)
Gamma Phi Works
Gamma Phi enthusiasts under the capable direction of C. E. Horton have been practicing regularly every Monday evening in order to be ready for the numerous engagements which they are asked to fill.

Membership in Gamma Phi is not a complicated thing, anyone interested in gymnastics and wishing to perform the many acts in its repertoire may join. Meetings are held each Monday night for the purpose of perfecting individual feats.

The tight wire, the parallel bars, the balancing ladder, the perch pole, juggling, and many other interesting acts are just a few of the many fine events at the gymnasts' disposal. Last Friday evening a group entertained at the Sheridan school in Bloomington. Ruth Parkinson and June Kosnick were featured in their sparkling acrobatic dance.

'He Floats Through the Air'

JESSE PARSONS, one of the most active of the Gamma Phi satellites, gives out with a bit of ring work. Jesse is tops at this part of the game and is also the foundation of the famous perch-pole act of the athletic fraternity. The above act is only one of his large repertoire which he will show at the big Gamma Phi circus to be held in March.

Vidette Dec 20, 1939 (page 5)

Feb 2, 1940 (page 6)

Intramural Cagers Prepare For Boom on Hardwood
Donated three Nights in February For Tournament

Again we are confronted with the question, "Why doesn't this university have a separate intramural building, or better still, why doesn't it have a student union building which would house the intramural department.

There is so much happening these days in McCormick gymnasium that the entire intramural program, probably the largest on the campus, is being thrown around haphazardly.

It looks like an organization of this type, which occupies the time of nearly every man on the campus, should be shown more consideration. The second basketball tourney is a fine example of this undue treatment. Only three nights are available during the month of February for play in this tournament.

Special clubs, varsity and "B" team basketball practice, High school games, and Gamma Phi practice are just a few of the examples why the gym is always crowded.

It is however, necessary to have the above groups carrying out their various duties. The Gamma Phi gymnasts, hard at work preparing for its annual circus are also being slighted, having only one evening a week for their preparation.

Passing judgement against these groups is entirely out of the question for they are undoubtedly as much of 4 part of the school activities as an intramural sports program and for I this reason one can see the serious need for a structure that will take care of all intramurals and extra-curricular activities that look, to McCormick gymnasium for housing.

As has been mentioned before, only three nights in February are available for basketball games. The month of March presents a similar problem with Gamma Phi circus taking two weeks for practice and presentation. After the activities in the big tent are over, we are faced with spring vacation which will put the hardwood game on the spring calendar instead of its customary spot on the winter chart.

A union building would be just the thing to remedy this, as well as many other situations which confront the students during the year. Why can't something be done?

Feb 9, 1940 (pages 6 & 7)
Gamma Phi Prexy Receives Call to Arms; Accepts Professorship
Latest addition to the professional teaching field is Jimmy Thorsen, Gamma Phi prexy, widely known for his perch-pole, chair-balancing, and other coordination achievements.

Thorsen graduated in mid-year and was planning to attend the U. of I. to work on his degree, when he was notified of his appointment to teach commerce at Valier.

Besides teaching commercial subjects, he is sponsoring the school newspaper. Old friends are predicting that before long Jim will also be inaugurating and sponsoring a school circus.

Walt Switzer, former Vice-president, automatically becomes the new Gamma Phi president.

Feb 20, 1940 (front page)
Circus Queen Petitions Are Due Friday
Election Precedes Annual Gamma Phi Spectacle
Who will reign as queen of the Gamma Phi circus for 1940?
Gamma Phi, men's physical education fraternity, sponsors annually a local-talent circus featuring near-professional acts that fairly smack of the odor of sawdust and the atmosphere of the big-top. Highlight of the circus each year is the queen who is' elected from the student body.

Candidates for queen are selected by petition, and the queen is elected from these by the students at large. The circus is to be held this year on Friday and Saturday, March 15 and 16. Petitions for queen candidates are due in the main office no later than 4 p.m. on Friday of this week, February 24. Blank petitions are now available in the main office.

Queen Made Honorary Member
The girl receiving the most votes is declared queen and those next four in order of votes garnered are appointed maids of honor to serve as her majesty's court. The queen is made an honorary member of Gamma Phi and is presented with a Gamma Phi pin.

The queen and her court will be introduced to the public at both showings of the circus and will reign over all the festivities of the carnival era while sitting in especially-constructed thrones which overlook the arena.

Brumbach Queen Last Year
Miss Diddy Brumbach served as first lady of Gamma Phi for 1939, and her court consisted of Helen Shippey, Clarabelle Huggins, and Lois Davis.

Co-chairmen in charge of publicity, Kenneth Haughey and Don Fitzsimmons, urge all interested men to get their girls' petitions in immediately, since the deadline is only three days away.

Feb 27, 1940 (front page)
Gamma Phi Queen Will Be Chosen At Friday Dance
Six girls have been selected by petition as candidates for the Gamma Phi queen who will reign over the Gamma Phi circus which is to be held this year on March 15 and 16.

Candidates are the Misses Betty Lou Cox, Eleanor Dalton, Kay Hinman, Betty Ann Smith, Jean Strange, and Mary Turnbull.

Voting for the queen (to be chosen from the above candidates) will take place at the Co-op party this Friday. At that time the candidates will be introduced from the stage.

The girl receiving the most votes is declared queen, and the remaining five will serve as her attendants. The queen is automatically made an honorary member of Gamma Phi and is presented with a Gamma Phi pin.

The queen and her court will view all circus festivities from a royal throne situated at the north end of the gym.

Mar 13, 1940 (page 45)
Cox to Occupy Throne Of Honor at Circus
Betty Lou Cox, freshman from Edelstein, has been elected to reign as queen! of the Gamma Phi Circus which is to be held this Friday and Saturday, March 15 and 16.

Eleanor Dalton, Kathryn Hinman, Betty Ann Smith, Jean Strange, and Mary Turnbull were chosen by popular vote to serve as attendants to Queen Betty Lou, and the whole group will observe both nights of the circus from the royal throne situated at the north end of McCormick gym.

With the above girls furnishing the glamour, the circus, further delves into the depths of big-top lore, and the outcome promises to present every possible version of spine-chilling feats usually - viewed only in regular saw-dust shows.

La Bounty Is M. C.
Jesse Parsons is director-in-chief of this year's production, and Jack LaBounty has been appointed master of ceremonies. Mr. LaBounty will introduce the varied acts in a manner entirely his own.

This year's show includes a multitude of new acts in addition to several favorites of long standing. Most of the performers come directly from within the university, although many are graduates, and a few are courtesy acts.

One highlight of the circus is the perch-pole exhibition—an old setting with new faces. Parsons is the bottom man, and Marilyn Bauman, University High School sophomore,' performs at the top. Precarious balancing 'positions by Miss Bauman atop a slender 18-

foot pole held in a belt socket by Mr. Parsons, feature this act.

Switzer Slides
Climax of this; show, is the "Slide for Life" with Gamma Phi president, Walter Switzer, whizzing down a 50-foot wire slide, suspended only by his teeth. Another wire act features Ernest Jarke and June Kosnick performing on the tight wire.

A new feature this year is the "Cloud Swing." Ruth Parkinson stars in the swing which consists of a single rope suspended from the rafters, and climaxes it with a spectacular dive ending only a scant distance from the floor.

Dancers who performed at the homecoming football game last fall, Patti Lovelock and Jean Bliss, will present their "Symposium of Dance" which, reputedly, surpasses their former exhibition. Girls from the Whitmer School of the Dance will present two of their numbers, and Marilyn Bauman will give a tap routine.

Ladders Revolve
Men physical education majors will present a "leap over the elephants," always a favorite with circus-goers, while a revolving ladder act featuring Adrian Sieh and Charles Thomas will further thrill the crowd. Lucille Heaton and Beverly Sellers, newcomers to Gamma Phi, will tumble through a difficult routing.

Don Smith, former. State Normal football player, will bring five Piper City girls who will put on a limber back tumbling routine. Three university women will perform on the swinging ladders, namely, Betty Von Allman, Lois Eyer, and Eleanor Young, while Betty Lou Cox Warren Frink, rated by C. E. Horton, Gamma Phi sponsor, "as much at home on a single wheel as two," will give an exhibition on the unicycle.

The Allison brothers, University High School students, billed as performing cowboys, will spin ropes and put on other: tricks usually seen only at home on the range. An acrobatic number featuring children from the I. S. & S. C. school, will be given. This act is under the direction of John Foy.

Some Funny Clowns
*Parsons, Switzer, and Sieh will give a horizontal bar exhibition,
while Parkinson and Kosnick will dance through a new acrobatic
routing. Charles Thomas and Betty Von Allman will thrill the
audience with a professional-appearing knife throwing exhibition,
and general humor will be furnished by the clowns. This year's
group of funny men includes Don Fitzsimmons, Max Haughey, Buell
Herrick, Tony Clendenin, and Virgil Hargis.*

*Roger Easterbrook, Warren Frink, and Jesse Parsons feature in a
flying rings act, while a parallel bar exhibition presents Waters,
Greenwood, and Parsons as its headliners.*

*Tickets are now on sale in the main office and the price is set at 25
cents advance sale. All seats are reserved, and admission at the door
will be 40 cents.*

Mar 15, 1940 (front page)
Curtain Goes Up on 1940 Gamma Phi Circus Tonite
**Parsons Is Director-in-Chief — LaBounty Is Master of
Ceremonies —- Cox Is Queen of AH**
*The first showing of the 1940 Gamma Phi circus will be held in
McCormick gym tonight starting it 8 o'clock. Another performance
will be given tomorrow night.*

*Many new - acts are featured this year, along with famous old
standby thrillers such as the perch pole, pyramids, revolving ladder,
tight wire, tumbling, and various clowning acts. New performances
include the "slide for life," "cloud swing," knife throwing, and rope
spinning in addition to many others.*

Parsons Is Director
*Emcee of this present production is Jack LaBounty, a circus
performer of long tradition, who will better utilize his abilities this
year as ringmaster. Jesse Parsons is the circus director who does
many-fold duty by enacting difficult ring feats in addition to seeing
that everything functions smoothly.*

Beauty is not forgotten, and Queen Betty Lou Cox along with her court attendants, Eleanor Dalton, Kathryn Hinman, Betty Ann Smith, Jean Strange, and Mary Turnbull, will reign over the entire festivities from the royal throne.

The university band will provide perfect circus toe-tapping music which all aids in carrying out a big-top atmosphere. Popcorn and peanuts will be available for the voracious, while reserved seats assure all attending ample parking space.

Mar 15, 1940 (page 3)
Want to Join Gamma Phi? Horton Gives Low-Down
Several misconceptions concerning membership in Gamma Phi are entertained by the student body at large, and, accordingly, C. E. Horton, advisor to this physical education fraternity, desires to clarify these erroneous ideas.

In the first place, membership is open to anyone — that is, anyone interested in physical education and possessing enough initiative to demonstrate this interest in some form of a stunt. The stunts may be of varied type — tumbling, bar work, acrobatics, juggling, clowning, rope spinning — anything remotely connected with physical education or circus lore.

Persons interested need only approach the gym on any Monday night and express their desire of joining Gamma Phi to Mr. Horton (he's the little guy without much hair) and tell him wherein their interest lies. Gamma Phi members will help everyone with their stunts whether they intend joining the organization or not.

Membership is open to both men and women. The addition of the weaker sex is an innovation added only this year, the fraternity formally consisting soley of men. There are no dues or initiation fees, the only requisite for initiation being the aforementioned interest and an honorable standing in the university (passing grades).

Gamma Phi is entirely self-supporting. It is not affiliated with the activity fund, and its only source of income is from the annual circus, which is being staged this year on the present week-end, Friday and Saturday, March 15 and 16.

The organization will put on acts for any school in the state, having at present covered schools within the limits of Chicago Heights and Camp Point. In this way Gamma Phi has proven an excellent advertisement for the university and, at the same time, has provided he participants with a great deal of enjoyment.

May 21, 1940 (front page)
Gamma Phi Elects

Officers for the ensuing year were elected at the regular meeting of Gamma Phi Monday evening. Retiring prexy, Walter Switzer, presided over the gathering and announces that Jesse Parsons was unanimously named as the new president. Ruth Parkinson and Warren Frink were selected to fill the vice-president and secretary/ treasurer seats for next year.

1940 – 41 School Year

Gamma Phi is finally large enough to perform the entire Circus with no outside acts. Everything is looking good… until December 7, 1941.

Feb 21, 1941 (front page)
Gamma Phi Opens Contest For 1941 Circus Queen
Petitions May Be Obtained at Office
Petitions are now available at the main office for Gamma Phi circus queen aspirants.

The Gamma Phi circus, an annual affair, will be held this year on Friday and Saturday nights, March 14 and 15, in McCormick gymnasium. Sponsored by Gamma Phi, men's physical education fraternity, the circus consists of near-professional big-top acts, including tightwire walking, parallel bar work, strong-man acts, clowns, and various feats of skill and strength.

Anyone Eligible
The circus queen is elected by the students and is chosen from the group of girls whose petitions have been entered in the contest. Any girl in school is eligible to enter the queen contest except previous Gamma Phi circus queens.

Jesse Parsons, president of Gamma Phi, outlines the procedure to follow:
1. Get a petition from the post office window in the main office.
2. Have the petition signed by 25 students.
3. Turn the petition back in to the main office by 4 p. m. next Friday, February 28.

Picked in Election
At an all-school election, the following Friday, students may vote for their choice for queen. The girl receiving the most votes will be named queen, and the next four girls, in order of votes garnered, will serve as the queen's court and sit with her on the royal throne during performances of the circus.

Circus queens are made honorary members of Gamma Phi, regally presented to the public on both nights of the show, and given corsages of honor as symbolic of their rating. Betty Lou Cox was queen of the circus in 1940 and her court consisted of Eleanor Dalton, Betty Ann Smith, Kay Hinman and Jeanne Strange.

Feb 28, 1941 (page 4)
Notice
The closing date for entries for the Gamma Phi Queen contest has been extended until Tuesday, March 4, at 4 p.m. Petitions may be obtained at the post office window.

Mar 7, 1941 (front page)
Nine Petitions in For Circus Queen As Deadline Nears
Nine girls have already announced their intentions of running for 1941 Gamma Phi circus queen, but the date on which petitions will be due has been extended to Tuesday, March 11, at 4 p.m.

Genevieve Gantz, Patricia Gould, Jane-Graves, Joyce Jacobs, Hope Jones, Gerry McCain, Norma Morris, Betty Tobias, and Lorraine Welch are the contestants to date, from whom will be elected the lady who will reign over both nights of circus festivities, Friday and Saturday, March 14 and 15.

To Vote at Assembly
The queen candidates will be presented at next Wednesday's assemblies, and the voting will take place at this time. The girl receiving the most votes will be declared queen, and the next four contestants in order of votes garnered will serve as maids of honor.

The candidate who is chosen queen will be made an honorary members of Gamma Phi and will view the circus both nights on a specially-constructed throne while surrounded by the bevy of beauties that comprise her court. The queen and all attendants will be presented with corsages, while her majesty, alone, will wear a golden crown.

'Pop' a Barnum?
The Gamma Phi circus is an animal event on the State Normal
campus that has been one of the variety highlights for the past
decade. C. E. "Pop" Horton serves as the sponsor for Gamma Phi,
and the circus is more or less his brainchild.

This year's show includes all the old standard sawdust acts plus a
number of new specialties that will please both young and old, so
promises Jess Parsons, Gamma Phi president. Glib-tongued Kenneth
Haughey will present the queen candidates at the assemblies.

Girls desirous of competing for this year's queen must turn in to the
telephone desk, before the deadline, a paper signed by 25 students
nominating her for 1941 Gamma Phi queen.

Mar 14, 1941 (page 6)
Meet the Misses
Ruth Parkinson — Gamma Phi Favorite; Commends Punctuality;
Prefers 'Tall, Dark, Handsome'
By Elizabeth Halane
As "a tall, dark, and handsome man" is usually the ideal Prince
Charming of every young woman, Ruth Parkinson, to be in vogue,
prefers men of that type. Although Ruth, has gone to ISNU for four
years, she still wouldn't change her mind on that point.

Is Dancer
Ruth's interests are varied but the rhythmic patterns and grace of
good dancing appeal to her more than anything else. Be it social
dancing, tap dancing, acrobatic dancing, Orchesis, or just dancing,
Ruth is sure to be enthusiastic about it. Among the various sports
Ruth would choose swimming as her favorite. Much of her time
during the summer is devoted to swimming in outdoor pools.

Active in Circus
People who can't keep appointments "gripe" Ruth. If persons say
they are going to be at a certain place at a certain time, Ruth would
like for them to be there.

Ruth is probably known best on the campus for her work in Gamma Phi. Her skill in acrobatic dancing is the envy of many. She is also very active in the women's physical education department.

Likes Traveling
Ruth likes going places and seeing things. "She has been in California, Mexico, and through the West, but she would like to travel more extensively. She has a great desire to go to the Hawaiian islands— on her honeymoon (this came as an afterthought).

A teaching position in an elementary school would be Ruth's choice. She prefers working with younger children better than with those of high school age. As to a geographical location, she would like teaching in the West.

Jesse Parsons, president, muscle man, property man and general manager of the Gamma Phi circus, does find time to give out with a few skyward endeavors himself, as well as direct proceedings of to-night's activities under the big top.

Vidette Mar 14, 1941 (page 5)
Same picture from1939 -- different caption)

Andy Kamp Deserts Texts for Tents
Soph Comedian Active In Plays, Gamma Phi

Pink lemonade! Fluff candy! Elephants and pink tights ! For more information concerning these things, contact Andrew' Kamp, a sophomore in speech from Watseka; Illinois. Andy goes with a circus this summer.

The first appearance before Normal students of this long, tall comedian was in the freshman assembly a year ago when he regaled us with a tuba solo. His next show of versatility was in playing the part of the "chicken clucker" in the all-school play, "Our Town." And who will forget the gyrating discus thrower in the hilarious farce. "You Can't Take It With You."

Andy also crowded into his two years here at Normal a part in "Family Portrait," a part in the Blackfriar "Propaganda Piece," extensive radio work over station WJBC, backstage work, and he prophesied the professional status he shall attain this summer by his clown work in the Gamma Phi circus.

The Monday that the lordly seniors are receiving their sheep-skins, Andy Kamp opens in Pittsburg as a professional clown with a two-ring circus (rumored to have the best cook-house of any circus . in the United States!)

Anyone who is interested in following in such illustrious footsteps need only answer sundry acids in Billboard or Variety, listing certain requisite characteristics—a naturally humorous face, a bull-frog voice, an elongated torso, a twinkle, a "grin, and a twenty-four hour sense of humor. Andy has them all!

War Years

Gamma Phi started the 1941 - 42 school year as any other even though everyone knew a war was going on overseas.

Sept 30, 1941 (page 3)
Gamma PM Meets

The first meeting of Gamma Phi, honorary physical education society for men and women, was held Thursday, September 25. President Tony Fedanzo called the meeting to order and plans for the preparation of the annual circus were discussed. Lois Eyer is vice-president this year, and Warren Frink is secretary.

The only entrance requirement for membership in this organization is the desire to learn how to tumble and do apparatus stunts. All freshmen and others who are interested in anything of this kind are urged to attend the meetings.

Meetings are held twice weekly; on Monday and Thursday evenings in McCormick gymnasium.

Sept 30, 1941 (page 3)
Gamma Phi had a "Bronze Men" float in the Homecoming parade. Vice President Lois Eyer was, to a large measure, responsible for it. It received so many favorable comments that it was thought that it could revolutionize the classification of parade entries.

Oct 17, 1941 (page 7)
Fedanzo Is Gamma Phi Star, Former Marine
Varied and interesting has been the career of Tony Fedanzo, the little dynamo from Chicago's west side.

Tony is a senior in P.E. and works as a recreation director of the NYA camp. This is the same post that he held this summer at the

Social Studies laboratory at East Bay. The outdoors holds great allure for Tony and for the last two summers he has been a lifeguard at the Bay. For the three previous summers he counselled at the Chicago Commons' Michigan camp.

Those who saw the Gamma Phi Circus will remember Tony's daring on the whirling ladder. This feat won for him the presidentship of Gamma Phi this year. Besides the hours for studies, work and the circus, he squeezed out time to get his pilot's license last fall. Other campus activities include U club, Social Science club, and B team football in '37 and '38.

In addition to all this, Tony spent four years in the Marine reserves, took one semester off to travel through the eastern states and has been a factory worker, truck driver, night watchman, salesman, and many other occupations.

This tells a lot about Tony Fedanzo hut in answer to the question what his hobbies are he said laconically, "O, travel, fishing, hunting, and dancing, I guess" and he added with a chuckle "And I'm another person who likes poetry and isn't afraid to admit it."

Nov 18, 1941 (page 3)
New equipment is installed for use in the 1942 circus.
The plans for ceiling rigging which would support apparatus as far as 10 feet on either side of the center beam were written up by Jesse Parsons. National Defense Training (NDT) classes under the supervision of A. C. Baulck, NDF Instructor, installed the new system of welded pipes.

Dec 2, 1941 (pages 3 & 4)
Know the Students
Lois Eyer Is Top Gamma Phi Star
"I'm not a very interesting person," is the assurance of Lois Eyer, the golden-haired queen of the Gamma Phi circus performers.

Lois was graduated from Bloomington high school and started at

ISNU as a "special." She is now a junior, in the commerce department, minoring in English, and is an active member of both the Commerce club and junior advisory board.

Being vice-president, Lois takes much interest in Gamma Phi, the physical education fraternity. Although she is not connected with the PE department in her regular school work, she has become proficient in the tight wire and revolving ladder act's, highlights of the annual circus.

She was, to a large measure, responsible for the beautiful "Bronze Men" float in the Homecoming parade this year. It received so much favorable comment from the students, faculty and alumni that it may revolutionize the classification of the parade entries.

As for hobbies, Lois is quite original. She has a collection of miniature horses, originating with her fondness for horseback riding.

To add to the variety of her interests, almost every list of play committees contains the name of Lois Eyer, a typical busy campus co-ed

The War has Begun

Dec 12, 1941 (page 3)
Horton's quote about the war: *"I think that this surprise attack has not caught us unprepared. Our production and preparation for it is not generally known. We are better prepared than we think. Things will settle down, and we'll see an adjustment made."*

Feb 20, 1942 (page 8)
Now's the Time to Reorganize ISNU's Extracurricular Life

The meeting of organization sponsors and presidents Tuesday evening brought the extracurricular problem into sharp focus for the first time.

The crowded, disordered activity life at Normal university has long been the school's weakest part. But only recently has it become the center of legislative attention. It consists, and has consisted of two painful extremes — the large percentage of students who join so many organizations they get activity indigestion, and the still more alarming percentage of students who belong to no organization.

Expansion and Conflict
From the meager social life inaugurated at the school's founding, the extracurricular program at ISNU increased to a point at which regulation and proportion were lost sight of. One club after another joined the roster and sought a place on the calendar. This group, and that one, found nice-sounding "purposes" to justify their functioning. The calendar board accepted them hopefully but dubiously, finally found themselves, frantic trying to schedule all the requested meetings in four week-nights. It hasn't worked, and it won't. Fifty organizations on a campus like Normal's are too many. And the problem isn't one only of people belonging to too many clubs.

Problem of the 700
It is of vital concern that the seven hundred students on campus who avoid extracurricular activities develop socially and spiritually as well as scholastically. But the student who doesn't join a club is not the only person to whom the university has an obligation. What about the girl or fellow, who joins one organization after another, spreading loyalties thinly but over a wide surface — just to get an extra picture or two in the yearbook or a few advantageous items for graduate credentials? It is obvious that action must follow in order to restore the extracurricular program to standard quality — but it must follow now, while attention is keen.

Then came Prof. Harper's no sponsor project. Admitting that his idea might be absurd, Harper suggested that a removal of faculty domination would prove a good test for the ability of a club to survive. In support of his contention, partially or wholly, were Miss Isaacson, Geneva Meers, Louise Sternberg — but Tony Fedanzo (Gamma Phi) believed sponsors were indispensable, at least for teaching a parallel-bar flip, and Wade Hannah declared that "we would have a mess if organizations were turned loose without sponsors."

Mar 18, 1942 (page 7)
Gamma Phi Takes Over Sponsorship Of Physical Fitness Program
Prof. Horton Directs Class Twice Weekly

A program of General Physical Fitness, instigated by the War Activities program, is being sponsored by Gamma Phi, Physical Education fraternity. All men in school are invited to come to the meetings which will be held Monday and Thursday evenings at 7:15 p.m. in McCormick gymnasium.

Participation in various sports, under the direction of Prof. Clifford E. Horton, head of Men's Physical education department, will be featured to help develop physical fitness in connection with military service. If enough interest is shown, a class in the fundamentals of marching will be given.

At the present time the Principles of Physical Education classes are learning fundamental marching procedures. This class has been carried for several years. Members of the class in the past, who are now in military service, found this knowledge of marching tactics a great help to them in the present war situation.

Gamma Phi Men Answer the Call to War

While these individuals are not specifically called out in the Vidette, it is still important to commemorate them in a Gamma Phi historical document. Please excuse this break in Vidette documentation.

The men put their lives on line to defend our country, and were forced to leave the university. Gamma Phi was put on hold, as were so many things.

Warren Frink
Bomber Pilot. Died in the line of duty in a training accident in 1944.
(Gamma Phi 1940 & 41: Secretary/Treasurer, Flying Rings, & Decorations Committee)

John Lafferty
Warrant Officer. Assistant to the Captain. Entered the Navy after leaving ISNU in 1932. Died on the Cruiser Houston when it was sunk on March 1, 1942 in the Battle of Sundrea Straight.
(Gamma Phi: 1931 & 32: Zouaves & Floor Pyramids)

Robert Parsons
LT. USN. Pilot. Killed in Action - in European area October, 1943.
(Gamma Phi: 1941: High Bar, Flying Rings, Chair Balancing, Parallel Bars, Hand Balancing.)

Vic Aldridge
Ensign in Naval Aviation.
(Gamma Phi: 1938: Clowns)

George Brauer
B-24 Pilot. Completed 29 missions over France and Germany, then returned stateside to train other B-24 and B-29 pilots. Received the Distinguished Flying Cross Medal and many others.
(Gamma Phi: 1941 Parallel Bars)

Ed Covey
US Navy.
(Gamma Phi: 1929 – 31)

Tony Fedanzo
Navy Pilot.
(Gamma Phi:1941 Revolving Ladder)

Don Fitzsimons
Ensign US Navy. Attached to the Communication staff of the Commander of the Pacific Naval Air Force.
(Gamma Phi 1940: Clowns, Advertising Committee, & Queen Candidate Committee)

Chuck Foster
Aviation Machinist's Mate 3rd Class at Navy Pier, Chicago, IL.
(Gamma Phi: 1940 Juggling and Rope Spinning Deluxe)

Arley Gillett
PFC US Army.
(Gamma Phi: 1935 – 38, 1947 - 66: Director, Assistant Director and practically everything else)

Chuck Greenwood
PFC US Army. Infantry in Europe for 6 months and was injured. Received Purple Heart, Good Conduct ribbon, European Theater of Operations ribbon, and Pre-Pearl Harbor ribbon.
(Gamma Phi: 1940, 41, 46: President, Parallel Bars and High Bar)

Kenneth Haughey
US Navy
(Gamma Phi: 1940: Clowns & Queen Candidate Committee)

Ernest Jarke
Aviation Machinist's Mate 3rd Class. Critically injured in a crash of a Navy blimp on Catalina Island, CA in Oct 1944.
(Gamma Phi: 1940 & 41 Tightwire)

Gene Keltner
US Navy for 3 years.
(Gamma Phi: 1941 Vaulting)

Lyle King
Army Corporal. Went overseas in Nov 1943.
(Gamma Phi: 1938 – 41)

Ike LaBounty
US Army Paratrooper in the weather corps in Brazil.
(Gamma Phi: 1941 & 46 President, Parallel Bars)

Arthur O'Byrne
U.S. Marines.
(Gamma Phi: 1939 – 41)

Jesse Parsons
US Navy.
(Gamma Phi: 1938 - 41: Director, President, VP, Clowns, Perch Pole, Chair Balancing, and Parallel Bars)

John Perring
Martin Aircraft.
(Gamma Phi: 1941 Tightwire)

Edward Schram
Pullman Aircraft.
(Gamma Phi: 1941 Parallel Bars)

Adrian Sieh
Army Air Corps.
(Gamma Phi: 1941 High Bar & Revolving Ladder)

Walter Switzer, M.D.
Lt Col, U.S. Army. WWII, KO, VN.
Received five battle stars of WWII, the Army Commendation Medal, and Legion of Merit Award. Served in three Wars. Started as a Bomb Group Armaments Officer in 1941 and eventually ended his military service in 1966 as Chief of Surgery in Zama, Japan.
(Gamma Phi: 1937 - 40 President, Hand Balancing, Vaulting, Table and Chair Balancing, High Bar, Iron Jaw of Death)

James Thorson
Lt Col, U.S. Army Air Force
Received two Distinguished Flying Crosses, Silver Star, Purple Heart, and many other medals. Started as a B-17 pilot in WWII and eventually ended up retiring in 1970 after serving with the Strategic Air Command.
(Gamma Phi: 1937 - 40: President, Sec/Treas, Hand Balancing, Springboard, Flying Rings, Chair and Table Balancing, Perch Pole, High Bar.)

Howard Waters
Private Airborne artillery.
(Gamma Phi: 1940 & 41 Parallel Bars & Hand Balancing.) He joined The Flying Lamars after the war.

Eugene Hill
American Red Cross. Went to Washington DC where he received two week's training prior to getting sent to an overseas appointment as a physical education director in the American Red Cross.
(Charter Gamma Phi member. Gamma Phi Director and ISNU varsity wrestling and tennis coach.)

Clifford Horton
American Red Cross. Taught courses for American Red Cross swimming and first aid to V-12 Unit at ISNU. Pop also served in WWI.
(Gamma Phi Founder)

1943 – 44 School Year

A free summer show is organized by the university. As the war is still on, the number of performers on campus is low. Pop and two Gamma Phi members (Esther Hileman and Irene Bookwalter) perform in the show. Wayne Sherrard, band director for Gamma Phi Circuses, is the director of the band for the summer show.

While the 1944 & 45 summer shows were not actual Gamma Phi Circuses, they were significant in that they kept some Gamma Phi continuity intact with continuing and new students from the beginning of the war through re-starting Gamma Phi afterwards.

Oct 13, 1943 (page 4)
Gamma Phi will hold its first meeting Wednesday evening, October 13, at 7:15 in the men's gym. Gamma Phi is an athletic organization, which learns and practices circus type activities. No spectacular abilities necessary. Anyone interested is invited to come to the gym on Wednesday evening ... a special invitation is extended to the navy men.

Dec 8, 1943 (page 2)
Verse Vogues
Conducted by Mona Eisenhower
...

The Gamma Phi circus was a special event
Which no longer is seen by our residents;
Their costumes so bright, and their acts of daring
Put your heart in your stomach and your head to swimming.
There was popcorn and candy and clowns oddly dressed,
Who walked through the bleachers and begged to be kissed.
From ladders way high in the top of the gym
Swung ladies so lovely and men so trim.
...

July 19, 1944 (page 4)
Notice
Girls! Civilian men! Sailors! All those wishing to try out for the forthcoming Gamma Phi circus in summer school show should see Prof. C. E. Horton at the gym.

Aug 2, 1944 (page 2)
Summer Session Show Coming; Circus, Music, Magic, Other Acts
Finale Features Entire Cast in Patriotic Number
Fun? You bet!

Money? You don't need any.

A big smile is the price of admission to the big summer session show which is slated to be packed from beginning to end with fun and entertainment.

It's not a circus to compete with Barnum and Bailey, nor a carnival to show up the Royal American company—there's not even a tent. It's just an evening chock full of thrills, laughter, and amazement. That's what the big show has in store for students and faculty Wednesday, August 9 — Thursday evening in case of rain.

Typical Circus Music
Typical circus music will follow the specially featured Navy V-12 Review and will announce the beginning of the big event. Under the direction of Prof. Wayne F. Sherrard, the band will be featured.

The baton twirling sisters, Esther and Jane Hileman, are scheduled to demonstrate their skills at the performance. Both girls have won state and national honors in baton twirling and have participated with American Legion groups.

Drake Contributes Cake
A cake is the contribution of Edgar A. Drake, magician by hobby, and everyone in attendance will be given a chance to help name the delicacy.

Contemporary with Mr. Drake in the field of magic is Prof. O. L. Young, whose slate will perform miracles. There will be no trickery, he promises; all will be done slowly before your very eyes.

Cooperation is the theme of Metcalf Training school's number, as pupils, teachers, and band work together to show the spirit permeating our school system today.

Bleyl Milks Snakes
Among other features Dr. Karl Bleyl will defy the laws of nature as he "milks the rattlesnakes." An exhibition in mid-air will be given by Irene Bookwalter, student at ISNU, as she performs on the swinging ladder.

Additional acts include the full skirts and the bobbing straw hats of "Ye Olde Countree Dance,"' the Indian club demonstration by Dr. C. E. Horton, an animal act arranged by the agricultural department, and a fireworks display under the direction of Dr. R U. Gooding.

The finale will be of a patriotic nature, everyone participating.

The Hileman Sisters

Jane and Esther Hileman, acrobatic baton twirlers, familiar figures who lead the ISNU marching band, will be on hand for the summer show August 3. They will demonstrate the skills that have won them state and national honors.

Aug 2, 1944 (page 4)

Band, Navy Drill Are Featured In Summer Show This Evening

Finale Displays Flags Of 38 Allied Nations

The flags of the 38 Allied nations will be on display tonight as act number 12 of the big summer show to be held on McCormick athletic field at 7:30.

Thirty-seven girls from ISNU and six girls from University high will take part in this patriotic finale which is under the direction of Women's league.

Another attraction different from the original plan discloses that the Flying Rene's" has become two aerial performers as Lucile Fechter joins with Irene Bookwalter, both ISNU summer students, to appear on the swinging ladders in a midair exhibition.

Miss Allen Writes Script
The script for the show has been written by Miss Mabel Clare Allen, assistant professor of speech, and members of her speech class.

Beginning at 7:30 sharp, there will be an appearance of the Navy men from the V-12 unit. This feature includes the V-12 review and a V-12 signaling demonstration.

Admire, Master of Ceremonies
Following the Navy appearance, the ISNU concert band under the direction of Wayne F. Sherrard will open the show proper with the "Iron Count Overture"' by K. L. King. Barney M. Thompson will sing "Somewhere a Voice Is Calling" by Tate.

Master of Ceremonies Harry F Admire will present the following acts: "Young America on the March," which will be given by 150 children from Thomas Metcalf training school; "The Magic Slate,' a miracle directed by Prof. O. L Young; and a "Parade of the Bluebloods," by pedigreed specimens from University Demonstration farm.

Agile coeds and their escorts will 'swing their partners" in "Ye Olde Countree Dance." The Hileman sisters, winners in national competition, will do "Baton Twirling." A magic novelty, "The Victory Cake of 1945," will be conducted by E. L Drake, district supervisor for Division of Juvenile Delinquency.

Bleyl Milks Snakes
Next in line, Dr. Karl Bleyl from the science department will present his "death-defying act," "Milking the Rattlesnakes." Irene Bookwalter and Lucile Fechter, ISNU students, become "Flying Renees" or the swinging ladders. Prof. Horton of the physical education department will demonstrate "Spiral Electrics" with his glowing Indian clubs.

The "Flaming Niagara Falls," a fireworks display, will precede the grand finale in which Women's league will present "Flags of the Nations."

If the weather should prove unsuited for the show tonight, it will be given at the same time tomorrow evening at McCormick field.

1944 – 45 School Year

A second war-time summer show is held. Not much other Gamma Phi activity is taking place, but having a summer show does keep the Gamma Phi flame burning.

July 25, 1945 (front page)
Prize Stunt Will Be Given
Summer Show Slated;
Public Invited
...

Typical Circus Stunts
Returning to the show for the second season are those well-known baton twirling experts, the Hileman sisters Circus acts featuring a revolving ladder, tumbling, and clown acts, plus an Indian club exhibition, "Balls of Fire," will lend zest and variety to the program.

The ISNU band under the direction of Prof. Wayne F. Sherrard will furnish music throughout the program which will be climaxed by a fireworks display under the direction of Dr. Ralph U. Gooding.

Aug 15, 1945 (page 4)
Crowds of 3,500 Applauded Talent Acts Of Last Week's Summer Show at Field
Clowns Thrill Juvenile Audience
By Vidette Reporter
An airplane winked by overhead as the barren bleachers slowly came to life. Gay streamers fluttered lazily in the evening breeze. Unexpected backstage glimpses gave promise of treats to come. With the arrival of the master of ceremonies the show was "on."

A bursting torpedo introduced the clowns and the university band. All the acts were made more circus-like by the toe tapping rhythm of the band under the direction of Prof. Wayne F. Sherrard.

"Mommie, where are the clowns?" queried members of the small pigtailed, be-ribboned group, when those laugh provoking pranksters stayed behind the curtain too long.

Visions of steaks, chops, ham, and bacon passed before the eyes and drooling mouths of the audience during the "Red Points on Parade."

A record audience of 3,500 applauded the antics of the Victory hall boys in their tumbling act, as well as their ability on the horizontal bars.

The Fumbling Faculty Four lived up to their reputation with appropriate singing, swallow tail coats, and silk hats. They were accompanied by a long blast from a railroad train in answer to their vocal plea, "Blow your horn!"

The "Balls of Fire" were a colorful sight, as Dr. C. E. Horton performed on the darkened stage before a bushed audience. The red and green lights made strange designs in the black background.

Small hands clapped (also size seven and up) at the "Revolving Ladder," "Metcalf Trampoline," and the "Baton Twirlers." Among the numbers sung by the "Summer Session Songsters." was "Cindy," a favorite with everyone.

The skit, "Dear Mom," prize winner of the ISNU stunt show, was the highlight of the evening.

An applause meter would have checked 1000 for the "Patriotic Salute" and "The World United."

A dazzling array of fireworks, reminding the spectators of pre-war Fourth of July days, ended the show.

The decided opinion of the diminutive spectators was "Gee, it was just as good as a real circus."

1945 – 46 School Year

The war is over and it is hoped that everything can now go back to normal. A homecoming is held in McCormick Gym. Almost nobody attends. Not much activity happens throughout the year.

At the point of the year when Gamma Phi used to put on the Circus, it was decided that a show should go on! With two prominent Gamma Phi members (Ike LaBounty and Chuck Greenwood) back from the war, a successful show is imminent.

With the baton passed from the summer shows and support from Pop Horton and Gene Hill (Gamma Phi Charter Member who is now on the ISNU), Gamma Phi does put on a successful show with the assistance of other community groups.

Gamma Phi is back!

Oct 17, 1945 (front page)
Gymnastic Organization Begins Year's Activities
It was recently announced that the Gamma Phi gymnastic organization would commence activities for the coming year. The group has usually had an annual circus, but as they have been almost inactive the past two years because of the shortage of men on the campus, this event has been cancelled for the present.

The Gamma Phi originated the queen idea, here at Normal, by having a queen for their second circus in 1933. The Gamma Phi, itself, has been operating since before 1930.

Some of the gymnastics accomplished by the group are working on the flying swings, the tight wire, the cloud swings, tumbling, juggling and acrobatic dancing. Anyone interested in activities of this type is invited to join. Meetings are held every Monday night from 7 :30 p.m. to 8:30 p.m. in the gym.

Mar 13, 1946 (page 7)
The Gamma Phi circus is scheduled for April 6th. Plan now to see "Pop" Horton and the men in intramurals in this big show. Orchesis is practicing a sword dance for the circus.

Mar 20, 1946 (page 3)
Gamma Phi To Plan A Circus
Plans to hold their eleventh annual circus April 6 are being made by Gamma Phi, ISNU chapter of the national physical education fraternity. This organization, inactive since 1941, elected Charles Greenwood freshman art major, and C. E. Horton, professor of health and physical education, its president and sponsor, respectively, at the first reorganization meeting last week.

Before the war the Gamma Phi circus was an annual affair. This year, however, it will be sponsored jointly with the Intramural class, according to Mr. Horton.

Participants in the circus will be selected from the student body. Previous experience is not necessary. In fact, anyone with a desire to walk a tight-wire, swing from a trapeze, or throw knives is welcome, invites Mr. Horton.

General practice for the acts will be held at 7:30 on Wednesday nights in McCormick gymnasium.

The customary practice of electing a Gamma Phi queen from the student body to reign over the circus will be discussed at the next meeting of the fraternity.

Apr 3, 1946 (front page)
Gamma Phi Plans Circus Saturday
The intramural circus, featuring Ike LaBounty and Chuck Greenwood on the parallel bars, Virgil Gaffney on the trampoline and numerous other students as clowns and performers, along with several non-school athletes, will be held Saturday April 6. at 8 p.m. in McCormick gymnasium. It is under the direction of Mr. C. E, Horton and Mr. Eugene Hill of the physical education department. This year the circus is sponsored by the intramural classes and Gamma Phi jointly and students will be admitted on activity tickets.

The men in the physical education department, under the direction of Mr. Harold E. Frey will present an act, "White Elephant," and Orchesis, under the direction of Miss Catherine Patterson will present a sword dance.. These and many other acts are on the program, promising an evening, of thrills and entertainment Music will be furnished by the University band under the leadership of Mr. Wayne F. Sherrard.

Apr 10, 1946 (page 2)
Gamma Phi Circus Returns
Last Saturday night the Gamma Phi circus made its first return appearance on the campus since the war. The circus had been discontinued in 1941. Congratulations and praise are in order to the men and women's physical education department for reviving and producing the circus.

To many of us it was our first Gamma Phi circus and we at least got a taste of what they have been in the past. The return of the circus mark another way in which ISNU is returning to normal. This should serve as an incentive to other organizations to revive some of their activities that were abandoned during the war. We are looking forward to a bigger and better gym circus next year.

Apr 10, 1946 (page 3)

Gamma Phi Circus Smashing Success
Orchesis Performed Colorful Sword Dance

McCormick gymnasium was the scene of clowns and gymnastics Saturday night at the first Gamma Phi circus since 1941. The chief clown, Virgil Gaffney, provided humorous interludes between acts.

Illinois State Normal university band played throughout the program. The first act was by the Anderson Tots from the Second Presbyterian church of Bloomington. Four girls did tumbling. The program turned to the comical side with the clowns from ISNU playing Let-her-Fly.

Coach Harold Frye's class of PE majors staged the White Elephant. This was followed by two girls on the swing ladders from Normal Central Grade School. The girls swung on the ladders and did stunts while they were in the air.

Boys from Normal Central performed on the high bar. The boys were assisted by Charles Greenwood.

The clowns were back again. This time they were going to do a very difficult act, according to Virgil Gaffney. He asked the audience to be still so they wouldn't make the performer nervous. One of the clowns was going to jump from a board to a chair on another clown's head but when the clowns stepped on the board it broke in two.

The Orchesis, under the direction of Miss Catherine Patterson presented a sword act which consisted of marching and forming a square with the swords.

Trampoline act was the next feature of the evening. This was done by students from Normal Central and Virgil Gaffney.

PE majors built pyramids. They were under the direction of "Ike" LaBounty.

This was followed by May Martin from Danvers and a boy from Metcalf grade school. They did tumbling acts.

Shooting a hen was the next thing the clowns thought of doing. Last on the entertainment was "Ike" La Bounty and Greenwood doing gymnastics on the parallel bars.

Ike LaBounty and Chuck Greenwood are shown performing on the parallel bars as they did in the Gym Circus Saturday night.

Vidette Apr 10, 1946 (page 3)

Note:
In 1947, this 1946 show was not counted as an official Gamma Phi Circus show. No indication is given as to why. So, the milestone show years celebrated years later could all be off by one.

1946 – 47 School Year

Arley Gillett becomes the Assistant Director. He will eventually become the second Gamma Phi Director. With Pop and Arley still in charge, Gamma Phi returns to a similar routine as in pre-war times.

At this point, Gamma Phi has completely made it to the next level. Almost every other collegiate circus vanished. They didn't make it through the WWII years.

Only Pop's old Springfield College and ISU's Gamma Phi Circus survived the war! Springfield College has a "Home Show" for homecoming. They are older than ISU's Gamma Phi Circus. However, they aren't a "circus." They still resemble the early Gamma Phi days of gymnastics exhibitions.

Jan 29, 1947 (page 4)
WRA Playnight Features Games, Gymnastic Skit
The first play night of this, semester will be sponsored by the WRA on Friday, January 31, from 8 to 11 p.m., in McCormick gym.

Gamma Phi, honorary gymnastic fraternity, will present a short skit as prelude to their annual circus. In addition to the usual games and entertainment, bingo will also be played.

Feb 5, 1947 (front page)
NOTICE
The 12th annual Gamma Phi circus will be held March 21 in McCormick gymnasium. All men and women students wishing to participate should report to a tryout session to be held Monday, February 10, in the men's gym.

Gamma Phi Circus Marks Highpoint on Fun Calendar

*Step right up folk and see the greatest show this side of the big time!!
So cries the barker, announcing the campus circus to be presented
March 21, at 8 p.m.*

*This time the "big top" will be McCormick gymnasium, and instead
of Barnum & Bailey or Ringling Brothers as sponsors will be
Gamma Phi, honorary gymnastic fraternity. All the thrills of a
professional circus, from popcorn and clowns to thriller diller
trapeze acts and tumbling stunts are to be featured. Special event of
the evening will be the coronation of the circus queen, to be chosen
in an all school election, Tuesday, March 18.*

Petitions Available
*In charge of the queen's election is Henry Wendell. Nominating
petitions will be available at the main office desk, Thursday, March
13. Those submitted must contain twenty-five signatures. Faculty
sponsors of the circus are C. E. Horton, head of the physical
education department, and Arley Gillette. Master of ceremonies will
be G. B. Barber of the speech department.*

*Handling publicity for the affair is Ken Buss, and in charge of tickets
is Lyle Ball. Rosemary Ortman heads the committee for decorations,
and Louella Johnson is chairman of costumes. In charge of
properties is Bob Dickey.*

First Circus in 1932
*Participants to date include members of Gamma Phi, physical
education majors, junior high boys from Soldiers and Sailors
Children's school, and girls from Normal Central school.*

*The idea of the circus at ISNU was inaugurated in 1932, and the
initial circus was presented through the work of "Pop" Horton, with
cooperation of Gamma Phi. The following year the scope was
widened to include the entire physical education department. This
year's presentation will be the first real post-war revival of the
popular program, although a gym circus was sponsored last year by
the intramural department. This year's presentation will be the first*

real post-war revival of the popular program, although a gym circus was sponsored last year by the intramural department. This year's presentation will be the first real post-war revival of the popular program, although a gym circus was sponsored last year by the intramural department.

1947 – 48 School Year

Pop Horton steps down from directing Gamma Phi and Arley Gillett takes over. However, Pop stays involved as an advisor. For the most part, he still coaches the girls while Arley works with the boys.

Seated: Hrehovcsik; Witherspoon; Hartshorn; R. Meyer; L. Johnson; E. Hileman; L. Ball. Standing: Mr. Gillett; Daley; De Groff; Madrey; French; Buss; Yorr; Weber; Thomas; Abbott; Mr. Horton.

1948 Index (page 106)

Oct 31, 1947 (page 8)
to direct Gamma Phi publicity . . .

Gamma Phi On Way Back After Wartime Shortages
Gamma Phi, first organization on the ISNU campus to have a queen, is working to become the foremost club on campus.

"More people are out than ever before," stated Arley F. Gillett, sponsor and former member of Gamma Phi. "Some of the people coming out are looking very good," he added. Total membership is 18 active members and 25 pledges.

Gamma Phi was organized in 1927 by Clifford E. Horton and patterned after similar organizations at Ohio Wesleyan. These are the only two organizations of this kind in the country. Eugene L. Hill,

194

*present assistant professor of health and physical education, was a
charter member.*

*At first, the organization was for men only and primarily for physical
education majors. Now membership is open to men, women and
faculty members. Requirements for membership are being reworked
at the present time. Previous experience is not necessary, for
instruction is given in all types of entertainment of a gymnastic
nature every Monday night. This includes instruction in dancing,
clowning, and aerial work.*

*Exhibitions have been scheduled throughout the entire state to fulfill
the purpose of Gamma Phi, that of fostering an interest in
gymnastics. Last year, members performed before the Illinois
Physical Education Conference, before a benefit basketball game, at
Play Nights, and at Chanute Field.*

*Former members have been active in circus work, some having
become professionals and others sponsored circuses while teaching.*

*The big event toward which each member of Gamma Phi works is
the circus. Eleven such circuses have been held. They were
discontinued during the war because of lack of personnel. Only one
old member was back last year when the circus was resumed. The
circus will be presented on two nights this year, March 19 and 20. A
queen will reign in Gamma Phi tradition. Gamma Phi had a queen of
the circus before Homecoming had a queen.*

Mar 3, 1948 (front page)
Gamma Phi Holds Circus March 12-13
*Gamma Phi, ISNU's gymnastic organization, will give two
performances of their annual gym circus this year on Friday, March
12, and Saturday, March 13, at eight' o'clock in McCormick
gymnasium. Admission for the circus will he 60 cents for adults and
40 cents for children.*

*A circus queen with her court will reign during the show which
promises to be an even greater performance than that given last
year. Any girl on campus wishing to become a candidate for the*

*position of queen may do so by simply leaving her name at the
telephone desk in Old Main before March 4. Each candidate is urged
to put up at least one or two posters publicizing the fact that she is
running for Gamma Phi queen.*

*The voting will take place all day Tuesday, March 9. On the
following day the five leading candidates will be introduced in
assembly. However, the one from this group who, has been elected
queen will not be announced until the night of the circus.*

*Gamma Phi, an organization for students interested in gymnastics, is
sponsored by Mr. Arley Gillett, supervisor of boys' physical
education at the Thomas Metcalf school.*

Mar 10, 1948 (front page)
Hi Ho Come To The Fair; Circus Friday
*All roads lead to McCormick gym Friday and Saturday evenings,
when the annual Gamma Phi circus will hold forth. The big event
promises to rival Ringling Bros., et al, for masterly showmanship
and daring performances.*

*Mr. Sherrard's circus band, trapeeze performers, Hindu rope fakirs
and many diverse campus tricksters and oddities will catch the eye.*

*Seven pretty candidates vied yesterday for a chance to share the
circus spotlight as reigning queen of the proceedings. Her highness
will be one of the five lucky choices presented in this morning's
assemblies. The runners-up will be attendants.*

*The queen will be crowned Friday night after Mr. Sherrard's band
provides the opening hot licks. Each performer will receive special
acknowledgement from the royal personage, herself, and the queen's
recessional will end each program.*

*The candidates were Ruth Anne Nolan, East Alton; Norma Reeser,
Mendota; Phyllis Young, Shelbyville; Mary Louise Strejcek,
Edwardsville; Marilyn McCarthy, Sterling; Delores Maile, Chicago
and Pauline Bury, Milford.*

1948 – 49 School Year

Things are back on a regular schedule again. This year's show is the first one to be filmed.

Lucy Lanham, treasurer; Robert Thomas, president; Joan Sterling, secretary; Kenneth Buss, vice-president.

1949 Index (page 89)

Mar 5, 1949 (page 5)

Competition for Gamma Phi queen seems to be exceptionally strong. Didn't know that there were so many "potent" gals here at ISNU. Campaigns for many different club officers are also being set into motion.

Mar 15, 1949 (front page)

Gamma Phi Opens Big Top For Annual Circus Frolics
Gym Midway Scene For Acrobatic Antics
BY BETTE SOLDEWEDEL

"Ya, and it's going to be a bigger and better show this year," was the early prediction sent out by Gamma Phi concerning its annual circus to be presented March 18-19 in McCormick gym. To illustrate

ground for this statement, it has been revealed that Gen Witherspoon who stole last year's show with her daring air acrobatics, has a new "perch pole" and will be able to stand on her head 25 feet up. Wheee . . .

Another startling act will feature Jack Daley and is called "Iron, Jaw." Jack will be hoisted to the ceiling, hold on to a support with his teeth, and spin to the floor.

Pro Clown Gets in Act
In exchange for the exhibition Gamma Phi put on in Minonk, a 70-year-old former professional clown will take part in the circus. He will give the boys new angles on clowning and is to assist with make-up.

Lyle Ball, last year's Gamma Phi prexy, and now a graduate student in education at the University of Illinois, will serve as MC for the show. Ken Buss is general manager and his committee includes Lou Johnson, publicity and program; Phil Weber and Lucy Lanham, queen and court; Gen Witherspoon, decorations; George Youngren, and Ken Darr, custodian of costumes.

Jesters in Gay Attire
Jack Daley and Phil McBain will don the gay suits as jesters.

Arley Gillett, instructor at Thomas Metcalf and ISNU, is a sponsor of the organization.

Circus tickets will go on sale Wednesday noon in Old Main.
The tentative program released is as follows:
1. Opening concert, circus band
2. Coronation of queen
3. High bar
4. Pyramids, ISSCS, Friday
   Tumbling, TMA, Saturday
5. Trampoline
6. Rings
7. Tumbling, Gamma Phi men
8. Pyramids, Gamma Phi girls

9. The ball, Phil Weber
10. The Web
11. Perch Pole
12. Ladder Pyramids
13. Parallel Bars
14. Acrobatic Dance, Val Hunter
15. Tumbling, Pat and Rose Meyer
16. Iron Jaw, Jack Daley
17. Chair and table, Arley Gillett, Jo Sterling, Mel DeGraff, Ken Buss, Lucy Lanham, Lou Johnson
18. Cloud Swing, Gen Witherspoon
19. Queen's recessional

Mar 15, 1949 (page 2)
ON THE AIR WJBC Tower Studios Cook Hall
Friday, March 18 — 4:30 p.m. CAMPUS NEWS. News of campus activities. Don Ferguson and William Tipler. "What to Expect of the Circus." Interview with Ken Buss of the Gamma Phi.

Mar 15, 1949 (page 4)
Lowell Kuntz Heads Gamma Phi Band
BY BARBARA FINDLEY
What is a circus without a circus band? When you go to the Gamma Phi circus this Friday or Saturday, try to imagine what it would be like without the stirring processional march for the queen, the Tiger Rag for the clowns, and the swinging lilt of the Blue Danube accompanying the aerial acts.

Under the direction of Lowell Kuntz of the music department,. the circus band has been rehearsing strenuously for the past two weeks. The 50 hornblowers who make up the band are the 30 long-suffering, unsung heroes of the Pep band plus 20 recruits from the ISNU concert band.

At the Charleston game a couple of weeks ago the Pep band had a good preview of what circus life will be like this weekend; for they never got a chance to finish any number they started.

Two of the band members have been in close contact with the team during basketball season this year; Gordon L'Hiereux and Roy Salzman served as shock absorbers for the same forward, three times each! Last semester Wayne Sherrard, who was then sponsoring the pep band, spent a lot of time worrying about the bass drum. But nothing ever happened to it. He should have worried about the bass clarinet—during the DeKalb game it speared a basketball and got temporarily disabled.

It may not happen in the circus, but last semester when Mr. Sherrard's wielding arm got tired, he used to turn the baton over to a band member and carry on with his cornet. The pinch-directors were the following: Arthur Ewing, Michael Kmetz, Robert Allan, Richard Veselack, Don Sherrard, and Raymond Montross. Watching these fellows conduct was a favorite diversion during the half for many of the basketball fans.

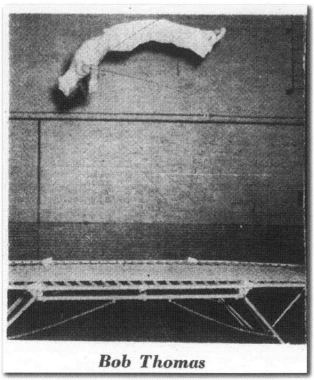

Bob Thomas

Vidette Mar 15, 1949 (page 7)

Gen Witherspoon

Vidette Mar 15, 1949 (page

Mar 22, 1949 (page 3)
Gamma Phi Performers Thrill Capacity Crowd

Gamma Phi, honorary gymnastics fraternity, threw open the big top last weekend in McCormick gym and presented its thirteenth annual circus before a standing-room-only crowd.

Preceded by a circus band concert under the able baton of Lowell Kuntz, the circus was officially underway with the coronation of Beverly Olson, this year's Gamma Phi queen, per majesty's court consisted of Mary Nicewander, Rosalyne Tweet, Betty Casner, and Phyllis Bjorkman.

Rosemary Ortman and Gen Witherspoon provided audience thrills with their flying ring act, which was preceded by a quartet of excellent acrobats on the trampoline.

Phil Weber as the "Globe Trotter" completely mystified the capacity crowd by walking up inclines, jumping the rope and trotting around, all of which was done on a big plastic ball.

Jack Daley's iron jaw act and the Gen Witherspoon - George Maddrey perch pole stunt proved a highlight of the circus

201   A Circus in the Paper

performance. Both feats were accompanied by audience gasps, and the stirring applause seemed little compensation for the daring performers.

The tumbling trio, composed of the Meyer sisters and little Arlene Gillett, daughter of Gamma Phi sponsor Arley Gillett, astounded the crowd with their agility. The Meyer sisters furthered the enthusiasm as they did wheel-like double forward rolls around the circus arena.

Exhibiting remarkable acrobatic talent, Gamma Phi members performed with professional skill in the "Flip Flop Boys," the "Ladder Pyramids," and on the parallel bars.

Ken Buss, Jack Daley, Phil McBain and John Shryock furnished plenty of laughs as circus clowns.

Lyle Ball, last year's Gamma Phi president, acted as master of ceremonies for the evening's entertainment.

BOB THOMAS, president of Gamma Phi, is pictured above as he crowns **Beverly Olson** queen of the thirteenth annual Gamma Phi Circus. The royal court include from left to right **Phyllis Bjorkman, Rosalyn Tweet, Mary Nicewander** and **Betty Casner.**

Vidette Mar 22, 1949 (page 3)

Mar 22, 1949 (page 5)

We liked that Gamma Phi circus. The boys and gals looked mighty good—as usual. Hear that Big George had a little trouble getting the perch pole to balance. Also had some good looking queens reigning over the affair.

Mar 22, 1949 (page 6)
Circus Sidelights

. . . . Mrs. Thomas had her young 'un to see Gamma Phi Prexy Bob perform.
. . . Andy Perhach was sporting a new topper for the affair. It was strictly the "College Look."
. . . Arley Gillett's little boy is learning to be an acrobat also, and he and his sister should be putting on the circus in ten or so years.
. . .Congrats to the fellows who set up and took down the apparatus. Without them the show would last all night.

Mar 22, 1949 (page 5)

We liked that Gamma Phi circus. The boys and gals looked mighty good—as usual. Hear that Big George had a little trouble getting the perch pole to balance. Also had some good looking queens reigning over the affair.

Mar 22, 1949 (page 6)
Circus Sidelights

. . . . Mrs. Thomas had her young 'un to see Gamma Phi Prexy Bob perform.
. . . Andy Perhach was sporting a new topper for the affair. It was strictly the "College Look."
. . . Arley Gillett's little boy is learning to be an acrobat also, and he and his sister should be putting on the circus in ten or so years.
. . .Congrats to the fellows who set up and took down the apparatus. Without them the show would last all night.

1949 – 50 School Year

Arley Gillett takes a year of leave to do graduate study at Indiana University, so Pop Horton takes over again.

Bottom row: R. Meyer, A. Holzman, M. Fager, P. Meyer, B. Putnam, L. Lanham, J. Sterling, L. Buss, S. Spellerberg, G. Hale.
Second row: J. Reynolds, C. Churchill, J. Baldwin, J. Archibald, E. Chapman, M. Lighthall, L. Hartshorn, E. Shumaker, M. Whitlock, M. Reed.
Third row: B. Wolf, E. Bunte, F. Weituschat, L. Logan, L. Brandstetter, G. Cunningham, E. Irving, F. Brooks, V. Hunter, C. Frederick.
Fourth row: T. Douglass, R. Swayze, K. Buss, W. Taylor, M. DeGraff, P. Weber, J. Wilson, K. Crotchett, J. Shryock, G. Youngren, D. Hany.

1950 Group Picture Gamma Phi Circus

Oct 11, 1949 (page 6)
Gamma Phi Initiates Three
Gamma Phi, gymnastic fraternity, initiated three new persons at its meeting last Monday night. They are Janice Fager, Al Buckowich, and John Shryock. The ceremony was conducted by president Phil Weber, who was assisted by Ken Buss and Melvin DeGraff.

The troupe is busy taking the polish off new equipment, including a swinging perch pole, a tight wire, and heel swing. Other club members are busy working up new acts and ideas for the annual circus held each spring.

Any persons on campus who are interested in or skillful at tumbling antics are invited to attend the weekly meetings and participate in the activities of the organization, Mr. Weber declared.

Oct 11, 1949 (page 10)

Gamma Phi Movies Shown At Reception

Movies of last year's Gamma Phi circus will be shown at the homecoming reception of Gamma Phi. The reception will be in Federal building 6, immediately after the parade.

Pat Meyer and Wally Zimmerman, co-chairmen of the reception, announced that refreshments will be served to all present members, alums, and their families and friends.

Lou Johnson, Ken Buss, Sue Spellerbreg, Phil Weber, and Herb Voights have been appointed to the homecoming float committee.

Nov 1, 1949 (page 15)

P. E. POINTERS

By Margaret Eggenberger

Physical Education club and Gamma Phi members are planning on attending a performance of the Danish Gym team, November 15 at Huff gymnasium in Urbana. This troupe has 32 members, and has performed in Madison Square garden during its tour. They excel in all gymnastics, balancing acts, and folk dances of many lands.

NOTE:
Due to a coal miners' strike, ISNU was closed for 2 weeks, as the buildings were heated by coal.

Mar 8, 1950 (page 3)

Gamma Phi Circus Dates Postponed; Practice Held

It's even too cold for a circus! Because of the two week vacation. Phil Weber, president of Gamma Phi, announced that the circus has been postponed. The circus will be held on ISNU campus March 31 and April 1.

The circus will appear in Mendota on March 17 and in Serena March 18 as was planned. Weber also stated that the members of Gamma Phi would be notified later as to rehearsal time.

TEETH ARE vitally important, as shown above, when the Gamma Phi Circus comes to town. This act, with many others to draw the oohs and ahs of the crowd, are a part of the circus. ·

Vidette Mar 21, 1950 (page 3)

Mar 21, 1950 (page 3)
Gamma Phi Sets Up The Big Top
Change Dates to March 31-April 1

Phil Weber, president of the Gamma Phi gymnastic fraternity, announces that the Gamma Phi circus will be held March 31 and April 1. With McCormick gym serving as the "big top," an array of 22 acts will be performed for her majesty, the queen of Gamma Phi.

George Youngren offers valuable information for queen aspirants: petitions may be secured from the switchboard in Old Main and must be returned by Friday, March 24, by 4 p.m. Any girl on campus is eligible to be a candidate for queen.

New features in this year's program will include a roller skating act, triple trapeze act, a "foot loop the loop" act by Rosemary Ortman, the gal who performed in "flying rings" last year, and bronze posing act by boys of ISSCS.

Tickets, at 60 cents per person, will be sold March 29, 30, and 31, in the main office. They may also be purchased from any member of Gamma Phi.

Officers of the organization are Phil Weber, president; Melvin De Graff, vice-president; Jean Putnam, secretary; and Herbert Voigts, treasurer. Dr. Clifford E. Horton, head of the division of physical education, is the sponsor of the club.

Committee members appointed by the officers include the following; publicity, Lucy Lanham, Sue Spellerbreg, and Jean Putnam; queen, Geroge Youngren and Jan Fager; decoration, Jean Putnam and all circus members; tickets, Jack Daley and Russ Taylor; program, Ken Buss and Melvin De Graff.

GAMMA PHI ACROBATS and tumblers, pictured above, are practicing for the annual performance which will be given at McCormick gym this Friday and Saturday.

Vidette Mar 28, 1950 (front page)

March 28, 1950 (front page)
Gamma Phi Queen Heads Weekend Panorama
Adds Voice to Circus Nerve Shattering Fun Professional Barker

With the blasting of trumpets and the rolling of drums, the ISNU circus band, under the direction of Lowell Kuntz, will strike the opening notes of the Gamma Phi Circus. Performances will be given March 31 and April 1 at 8 p.m. in McCormick gymnasium.

An added attraction to the 14th annual circus will be Gene Enos, professional circus barker, who will serve as master of ceremonies. It will be his first appearance on the ISNU campus.

Adding hilarity to the circus crowd will be a group of clowns whose job it will be to spread the "giggling germ." Those chosen to act as fun-makers are John Shryock, Phil McBain, Ken Buss, and Jack Daley.

Competing for the honor of reigning over the two-day circus are Jeanne Wilson, Lois England, Jan Turley, Margaret Batman, Joan Hodel, Pat Killian, Dorothy Coatney, Joyce Archibald, and Christine Jablonski.

After the queen has commanded the performance to begin, Gamma Phi members will scatter and the tangled ropes at the top of the gym will take form in an array of trapezes, rings, and other circus equipment.

PROGRAM
> *1. Hi Bar: Phil Weber, Les Park, Tom Douglass, Russ Taylor.*
> *2. Miniature Tumbling: ISSCS boys, Thomas Metcalf boys.*
> *3. Swinging Ladders: Barbara Wolf, Irene Hartshorn, Marilyn Reed, Edna Mae Chapman, Jan Pager.*
> *4. Balancing Sextette: Ken Buss, Lou Johnson, Lucile Lanham, "Muff" DeGraff, Sue Spellerbreg, Tom Douglass.*
> *5. Perch Pole: Tom Douglass (Russ Taylor).*
> *6. Trampoline: Phil Weber, Russ Taylor (Rose and Pat Meyer).*
> *7. Madam Oats and her Co-ed Colts: Lucy Lanham, Pat Meyer, Jean Putnam, Jan Fager, Barbara Wolf.*
> *8. High Bar: Les Park, Tom Douglass, Phil Weber, Russ Taylor.*

9. *Parallel Bars: Jack Daley, Tom Douglass, Les Park, Russ Taylor.*
10. *Triple Trap: Carol Frederick, Eileen Shumaker, Marzetta Whittlock.*
11. *Table Balancing: Valerie Hunter.*
12. *Swing Perch: Ken Crotchett, Sue Spellerbreg, George Youngren, Lucy Lanham.*
13. *Rings: Rosemary Ortman, Sue Sue Spellerbreg, Les Park, Chuck Harraden.*
14. *Iron Jaw: Jack Daley.*
15. *Living Statuary: ISSCS.*
16. *Globe Trotter: Phil Weber.*
17. *Foot Loop the Loop: Rosemary Ortman.*
18. *The Web: Adrienne Halzmen.*
19. *Advanced Tumbling (twists and turns): George Youngren, Ruse Taylor.*
20. *Cloud Swing: Rosemary Ortman.*
21. *Evolutions on the Mat: Gamma Phi Men.*
22. *Co-Ed Acrobatics: Gamma Ph: Women.*
23. *Rolling Spins: Dave Wilson, Ireen Hartshorn.*
24. *Simple Balancing: Connie Churchill, Bill Hrebik.*
25. *Clowns: Phil McBain, John Shryock, Ken Buss, Jack Daley.*
Master of Ceremonies: Gene Enos (ex-professional circus ringmaster).

Joan Hodel, Queen of Circus, Reigns With Court of Four

Joan Hodel, a freshman elementary major from Metamora, reigned over the annual Gamma Phi circus, held in McCormick gym last Friday and Saturday nights. The queen's court included Jeanne Wilson, Pat Killian, Dorothy Courtney, and Jan Turley, as attendants.

The show, with all of the "bigtop" gaiety, was the usual top calibre performance of Gamma Phi members. Spectacular performances were turned in by the Meyer sisters, Pat and Rose, who were last on the program, but who "stole the show" with their rapid and breathtaking tumbling stunts.

Rosemary Ortman provided "ohs" and 'ahs" by her daring aerial acrobatics, and Tom Douglass, by his perch pole act and chair balancing, was outstanding.

"Madam Oats and Her Coed Colts" gave the circus a real horse act, while "The Three Bobs" performed an authentic 'slapstick" number, between regular acts.

Of course, the clowns were present, adding circus flavor with their slightly off-color remarks and painted faces.

Gene Enos, professional circus man, who had a bit of trouble reading dialogue for the vivid ISSCS "Living Statuary" number, otherwise gave a professional air to the entire production.

JOAN HODEL, FRESHMAN, was crowned queen of the Gamma Phi circus Friday night by Phil Weber, president of the organization. Her attendants, left to right, include Jan Turley, Jeanne Wilson, Bev Olson, last year's queen, Pat Killian, and Dorothy Coatney.

Vidette Apr 4, 1950 (front page)

Apr 11, 1950 (page 2)
Heard tell of war weary veterans who fought for months and came out without a scratch. Then they came home and met with some domestic accident. A Gamma Phi circus performer, Jack Daley, is the ISNU version of the above. He came out of his "ironjaw" circus act with flying colors only to injure his leg in another less dangerous act. Result—no more gym work for the rest of the semester.

Apr 18, 1950 (front page)
Gamma Phi Circus to Give Weekend Benefits; Serena, Mendota to Play Hosts
All major acts of the Gamma Phi Circus will be presented in benefit shows out of town this weekend.

For the third consecutive year the performers will give the circus in Mendota to aid the hospital there. This trip is scheduled for Friday evening.

Serena is the destination of the troupe Saturday. Proceeds from the show there will go to the Parent Teacher association. Last Friday evening the circus was presented at Canton in a benefit production for the newly organized Chamber of Commerce.

May 9, 1950 (front page)
P.E. Club Wins Stunt Show
By Joan Bonney
The women's Physical Education club "slid into home" with the first place trophy for their performance in last Friday's Stunt show, sponsored annually by the University club.
...
Here's to Normal
The PE club depicted the life of a college girl at Normal in a five-act "Here's to Normal" theme, using as their topics registration day, a camping trip, a class in recreational activities, the Gamma Phi circus, and homecoming.

211 A Circus in the Paper

The last scene was the most effective as cheerleader Mary Mulkern led the audience in two choruses of the Normal loyalty song, and a group of girls on the stage representing football fans spelled out I-S-N-U using large red and white square cards. The Meyer sisters in the Gamma Phi circus scene were their usual entertaining selves as they tumbled in baggy overalls.

May 23, 1950 (page 8)
Russell Taylor Head Gamma Phi Executive
Members of Gamma Phi, honorary gymnastic society at ISNU, met Monday evening to elect officers for the 1950-'51 school year. Russell Taylor, Streator, was named as president of the group. Others selected were Jack Daley, vice-president; Mary Janice Fager, secretary; and Edna Mae Chapman, treasurer.

1950 – 51 School Year

Arley Gillett comes back as Director.

Mar 7, 1951 (front page)
*MEMBERS OF THE GAMMA PHI CIRCUS TROUPE take time out
from practice to gather for this group shot. The troupe will present
its annual frolic in McCormick gym Friday and Saturday nights.
Arley Gillett, extreme right, back row, is the sponsor.*

1951 Group Picture Gamma Phi Circus

Sept 28, 1950 (page 2)
Gamma Phi President Taylor Sends Out Call for Gymnasts

*President Russ Taylor has announced that Gamma Phi, the
gymnastic fraternity here on campus, will hold its first meeting of the
year next Monday evening at 7:30 in McCormick gymnasium. All
you guys and gals interested in joining Gamma Phi should attend
this meeting, as well as those who are already members. Movies will
be shown of past performances and refreshments will be served.
Arley Gillett is the faculty sponsor of the group.*

Oct 3, 1950 (page 7)

Gamma Phi to Meet Tonight Can you stand on your head or balance a ball on your nose? Are you interested in tumbling, special apparatus work, or specialty circus acts? If so, Gamma Phi, a gymnastic fraternity, is looking for you.

Russ Taylor, president of Gamma Phi, announces that an open house will be held October 2 at 7:30 p.m. at the McCormick gym. Movies of last year's circus an annual event, will be shown and refreshments will be served.

Officers for this semester include, besides Taylor, Janice Fager, secretary, senior from Easton; and treasurer Edna Mae Chapman, sophomore from Clinton. Taylor is a junior from Streator.

Arley Gillett is the sponsor of this year's group.

Nov 8, 1950 (page 5)
Homecoming
Gamma Phi mobile float comes in 9th place and is awarded $7.00.

Feb 14, 1951 (page 8)
Gamma Phi Circus Set for March 9,10; Arley Gillett Heads Gymnastic Troupe
Eight Committees, Chairmen Begin Work On 15th Annual Production of 'Big Show'

March 9 and 10 have been announced as the dates for the 15th annual Gamma Phi circus.

Committees are now working on plans for the "big show" to be staged in McCormick gymnasium under the direction of Arley Gillett, Gamma Phi sponsor. Mr. Gillett returns as sponsor of the organization after a year's leave of absence.

Committeemen and chairmen appointed at the February 5 meeting include publicity, Nancy Quimby, chairman, Doug Smith and Gene

Phillips; queen, Charlene Patterson, chairman, Jan Fager and Ginger Fager; and decorations, Barbara Wolf, chairman, George Youngren and Jack Daley.

Other committees and chairmen are tickets, Jack Daley; program, Charles Harradan; and costumes, Eileen Shumaker, chairman, Romaine Zehr, Lois Kafer, Ann Kennedy, Valerie Hunter, Jan Hoffman, and Louisem Hrebik.

Concluding the committeemen list are animals, Jean Putnam, chairman, Jack Daley, Rose Meyer, and Jan Fager; and clowns, Jack Daley, chairman, and John Shyrock.

JACK DALEY, left, and Russ Taylor work out on the parallel bars in preparation for next week's Gamma Phi circus performances. The election of the queen to reign over the affair will be held next Monday in the West Bridge.

Vidette Feb 28, 1952 (page 6)

A Circus in the Paper

Queen, Court of Four Will Reign Over Circus; Gamma Phi Members Prepare for March Shows

The circus is coming! Petitions for the Gamma Phi queen arc still available at Francis Wade's office in M206, but they should be turned in by 4 p.m. today.

Only ten candidates are eligible to run for the queenship and any woman on campus may enter the contest.

Elections will be held all day Monday, March 5, in the West bridge of Old Main.

As in previous years, the court will be composed of five girls having the largest number of votes. The candidates will be notified of the results Monday evening, but who is queen will remain a mystery until the Friday night of the circus.

The coronation ceremony will take place on both nights of the performances. Tickets for the event will go on sale soon. Dates of the circus are March 9 and 10.

Committee chairmen working on the arrangements include Nancy Quimby, publicity; Charlene Patterson, queen; and Barbara Wolfe, decorations.

Others are Jack Daley, tickets; Charles Harradan, program; and Eileen Shumaker, costumes.

Additional committee heads are Jean Putnam, animals; and Jack Daley, clowns.

Committeemen and other committee workers were named at the February 5 meeting of the gymnastic fraternity. Arley Gillett is sponsor of the group. He returns to the organization after a year's leave of absence for further study.

GAMMA PHI CIRCUS OPENS FRIDAY NIGHT

*Queen, Court of Four Will Reign Over Annual Frolic in McCormick
Queen of the annual Gamma Phi circus will be coronated at the
opening performance Friday night in McCormick gymnasium. The
co-ed who will reign will be from among the five selected at
Monday's all-school election.*

*Top vote getters were Mary Alderson, senior from Chicago; Mary
Margaret Cabalek, senior from Villa Grove; Barbara Handy,
sophomore from Riverside; lane Hinshaw, senior from Hudson; and
Sylvia Lemanski, freshman from LaSalle.*

*Opening of the big circus will be the ISNU band under the direction
of Wayne F. Sherrard. Gene Wendland, senior from Wauwatosa,
Wis., will be ringmaster.*

*Twenty-three different numbers are included in the circus
performances to be given both Friday and Saturday evenings at 8
p.m. in McCormick gym.*
1. *Open Concert — Circus Band, Wayne F. Sherrard, Director*
2. *Parade and Coronation of Queen— Circus Troupe*
3. *High Bar — Milan Jablonovich, Les Park, Russ Taylor*
4. *Tumbling Small Fry — Thomas Metcalf boys, ISSCS boys*
5. *Swinging Perch Poles — Eileen Shumaker, George Youngren,
    Barbara Wolf, Ken Crotchett*
6. *Clowns — Jack Daley, John Shryock, John Macek, Phil
    Martin*
7. *"Just Horsin' Around" — Rose Meyer, Pat Meyer, Jan Fager,
    Ginger Fager, Ann Kennedy, Charlaine Patterson, Jean
    Putnam, Romaine Zehr, Valerie Hunter, Esther Day,
    Imogene Lindberg, Barbara Wolf, Phyllis Turner*
8. *Hand Balancing and Low Parallels — Les Park, Dick Carr,
    Arley Gillett*
9. *Tumbling Tumbleweeds — Darwin Hany, George Youngren,
    Ken Crotchett*
10. *The Web — Nancy Quimby*
11. *The Gilletts — Arley, Arlene, Jay Gillett*
12. *Parallel Bars — Russ Taylor, Jack Daley, Les Park, Ken
    Crotchett*

217   A Circus in the Paper

13. *On the Ball* — *Doug Smith*
14. *Clowns*
15. *Swinging Ladders* — *Jan Fager, Romaine Zehr, Valerie Hunter, Charlaine Patterson*
16. *Foot Revolve—Nancy Quimby*
17. *A Balancing Duet—Louise Hrebik, Bill Hrebik*
18. *Trampoline* — *Russ Taylor, AI Buckowich, Darwin Hany*
19. *Clowns*
20. *The Flying Four* — *Eileen Shumaker, Nancy Quimby, George Youngren, Gene Phillips*
21. *Wild Animal Act*
22. *Bronze Motion on the Rings* — *Les Park, Charles Harraden*
23. *Clowns*
24. *The Meyer Sisters* — *Rose and Pat Meyer*
25. *Recessional* — *Circus Troupe Master of Ceremonies: Gene Wendland*

June 6, 1951 (front page)

Honorary Gymnastics Initiate 17 Pledges Into Gamma Phi Fold

Gamma Phi, honorary gymnastic fraternity, initiated 17 pledges recently. At the candlelight ceremony the initiates took the Gamma Phi pledge and received their emblems.

The pledges include:
> *Dick Carr and Esther Day, Clinton*
> *Phil Martin, Springfield*
> *Imogene Lindberg, Rockford*
> *Janette Hoffman, Forest Park*
> *Charles Headley, Alton*
> *Herb Snook, Bloomington*
> *Ginger Fager, Easton*
> *Charlaine Patterson, Fithian*
> *Milan Jablonovich, Chicago*
> *Yvonne Garry and Phyllis Turner, Momence*
> *Ann Kennedy, Peoria*
> *Gene Phillips, Pontiac*
> *Louise Hrebik, LeRoy*
> *Doug Smith, Joliet*
> *Mary Ann Gallagher, Chicago*

Willis Frink of Normal, who is now in the U. S. Navy, was also initiated in the organization a week earlier.

1951 – 52 School Year

Back Row: Warren Stephey, Robert Merdian, Doug Smith, Dick Carr, Milan Joblonovich, Al Szczepaniak, Konstantin Morhun, Roger Kirkton, George Chaudoin, Dick Gifford, Ralph Windle, George Youngren, Jim Winans, Darwin Hany, Bob Hoff, Arley Gillett
Row 3: Al Larson, Celio Bongiani, Dick Wuthrich, Dave Kirkpatrick, Merrill Kallenbach, Ray Catenacci, Bob McKinley, Evan Borchers, Wayne Arnold, Conrad Aschenbrennen, Phil Somers, Tom Kerrihard, Dick Stephey
Row 2: Gloria Hickman, Francis Curtis, Lydia Almquist, Edie Ice, Darlene Nemitz, Nancy Quimby, Eileen Shumaker, Romaine Zehr, Esther Day, Jun Ann Husir, Imogene Lindberg, Pat Meyer
Front Row: Arlene Gillett, Jay Gillett

(Not Pictured: Phil Martin, Rose Meyer, Leslie Murray, Les Park

1952 Group Picture Gamma Phi Circus

Sept 26, 1951 (page 8)
Gamma Phi Schedules Workout, Open House
Members of Gamma Phi, honorary gymnastic fraternity, will welcome all newcomers interested in the organization at an open house and general workout scheduled for Monday, October 1 at 7 p.m. in McCormick gymnasium.

The organization is open to both men and women and participants do not need to be physical education majors or minors. Officers of the organization are Darwin Hany, president; Ken Crotchett, vice-president; Eileen Shumaker, secretary; Pat Meyer, treasurer; and Mr. Arley Gillett, sponsor.

Oct 3, 1951 (page 4)
Gamma Phi Opens Doors To Aspiring Gymnasts
Gamma Phi, honorary gymnastic fraternity, extends an open invitation to students interested in gymnastics to attend practice sessions each Monday evening at 7 p.m. in McCormick gym. No previous experience in gymnastics is required. This invitation is open to men and women in the university.

Each year Gamma Phi presents a circus in the spring on campus and takes the circus on the road to several towns in central Illinois. They are often called upon to present programs for small organizations and school groups. Mr. Arley Gillette is director of Gamma Phi and Darwin Hany, a junior, is president.

Regular practice meetings begin Monday.

Oct 31, 1951 (front page)
Homecoming
Gamma Phi mobile float comes in 5th place and is awarded $10.00.

Feb 13, 1952 (front page)
Gamma Phi Sets Dales For Annual Circus
Tentative dates for the annual Circus Carnival were set and publicity pictures were taken at the last meeting of Gamma Phi, Monday evening, Feb. 4.

The Carnival will perform, at McCormick gymnasium on March 14 and 15. It will travel to Clinton on March 22 and to DeKalb on March 28.

New pledges have brought new ideas into the club to make the festival a bigger attraction this year. A total of 20 acts have been formulated thus far.

Feb 20, 1952 (page 4)

Candidates for Queen May Pick Up Petitions

Petition blanks for candidates for the 1952 Gamma Phi Circus queen are now available and may be obtained at Arley Gillett's office in the gym.

According to Dick Carr, publicity chairman, the petitions must be signed by at least 25 people and must be turned in to Mr. Gillett's office by 4 p.m., Monday, in order to be valid.

The queen candidates will be presented in the March 5 assembly.

Feb 27, 1952 (page 8)

Gamma Phi to Preview Circus in Assembly

The presentation of candidates for queen and a preview of some of the acts of the Gamma Phi circus will comprise the March 5 assembly program.

The names of the candidates have not yet been released, but 25 acts have been billed, all of which should prove interesting. Outstanding among these listings, for example, is to be an "Old Timers" hand-balancing act, featuring Leslie Murray, now principal of Gridley high school; Arley Gillett, coach and sponsor of the Gamma Phi circus; and Clifford E. Horton, head of the physical education department, who will perform an Indian dance.

Rose Meyer, teacher at Elgin, will return to complete the tumbling act with her sister, Pat Meyer. The loss of two graduates, Russ Taylor, last year's president and trampoline artist; and Jack Daley, winner of last years' Service Pin award, will leave these two attractions somewhat weak. Some students who might contribute are now teaching off campus or have entered the armed forces.

Despite the vacancies, there are seven veteran performers and three outstanding beginners with the troupe this season. These include the Meyer sisters; Darwin Hany, trampoline, balancing and tumbling artist; Eileen Shumaker, daredevil, trapeze, and perch poles artist; Milan Joblonovich, high bar artist; Dick Carr, high bar, parallel bar, and balancing artist; and beginners Ralph Windle and James Winans, parallel bars; Celio Bongiani, heavyweight tumbler; and Konstantin Morhun, German-born gymnast.

Mar 5, 1952 (front page)
Students to Elect Gamma Phi Queen Today, Tomorrow

Voting on the candidates for 1952 Gamma Phi circus queen presented this morning in assembly, will take place this afternoon and tomorrow morning. Students must present their activity tickets in order to vote.

The chosen queen and her court will reign over the circus at the March 14-15 performances.

Those competing for the honor are Cecilia (Cel) Cardosi, a Kankakee senior in physical education; Joan Allen, an elementary sophomore from Chicago; Carol Hunsinger, an elementary sophomore from Staunton; Lois Kafer, a Fairbury elementary sophomore; Lawanda Dillon, an Alton elementary freshman; and Beulah Smith, a Taylorville home economics freshman.

DARWIN HANEY AND PAT MEYER are pictured above practicing for one of the acts making up the Gamma Phi Circus which is to be presented in McCormick gym this Friday and Saturday nights. The program will offer 25 acts with the act by the Gilletts one of the outstanding features.

Vidette Mar 12, 1952 (front page)

A Circus in the Paper

Gymnasts Present Annual Circus This Week
Meyer Sister Act To Highlight Gamma Phi Program

Members of Gamma Phi will present their interpretation of the Big Top show to members of the ISNU student body, faculty, and members of the community this weekend.

Offering competition to any well-known circus, the Gamma Phi artists will present a program of 25 separate numbers.

The program for the evening's entertainment is as follows:
1. Opening concert
2. Coronation of the Queen
3. Circus Troupe
4. Animal Act
5. Swinging Ladders
6. Tumbling and Pyramids
7. The Old Timers
8. Rolling Along
9. Clowns
10. Tumbling
11. The Web
12. Swinging Perch Poles
13. Horizontal Barr
14. Clowns
15. Trampoline
16. The Plying Four
17. Clowns
18. Parallel Bars
19. The Gilletts
20. Triple Trapeze
21. Rings
22. Clowns
23. Tumbling and Balancing
24. Cloud Swing
25. Meyer Sisters

Horton Founder Of Honorary Group On ISNU Campus
By Don Patterson

The 16th annual gymnastic circus will be presented by members of Gamma Phi at 8 p.m. this Friday and Saturday in McCormick gym.

Gamma Phi is a national honorary gymnastic organization. It was founded at ISNU in 1928 by Dr. C. E. Horton, present head of the physical education department. Only men were allowed to become members until 1941, at which time the fraternity became coeducational.

The purpose of the club is to promote the interest of physical education among the students, and to honor gymnastic excellence in the individual members of the student body and faculty by election to membership. Arley Gillett, assistant professor of health and physical education, is the present sponsor and coach. He has held this position since 1947.

The present membership totals 40, about equally divided between men and women. Regular meetings are held on Monday nights for two hours throughout the year.

Funds are obtained from the numerous appearances in other communities and from the small admission fee charged on campus to make the organization self-supporting.

The circus features tumbling, apparatus work, aerial acts, circus band, clowns, and a circus queen.

Mar 19, 1952 (front page)

Elementary Major Reigns As Queen Miss Joan Allen, a sophomore in elementary education, was present Friday and Saturday nights as the ISNU Gamma Phi queen for the current year.

Elected a week ago by students of the school, Miss Allen had a group of five in her court, including Carol Hunsinger, Cel Cardosi, Beulah Smith, Lois Kafer, and Lawanda Fay Dillow.

A Circus in the Paper

Miss Allen is a resident of the new women's dormitory, and she has been active in the organization of the hall, serving during this year as a member of the Hall Council. Further, Joan has worked in Women's League events and is a member of the Elementary Education club. Her home is Chicago.

MISS JOAN ALLEN, sophomore elementary major, is shown above as she reigned Friday and Saturday as queen of the Gamma Phi circus.

Vidette Mar 19, 1952 (front page)

Mar 26, 1952 (page 4)
Gamma Phi Draws 3,010 to Circus; Plans Additional Show for 1953

Heavy attendance last Saturday brought the total Gamma Phi circus gate receipts to a new high this year.

The total attendance, as reported by circus chairman Arley Gillett, was 3,010, or 500 better than last year's 2,510 which was the previous high. Here is the record:

Friday: This year, 1325; last year, 1359.
Saturday: This, year, 1685; last year, 1151.

Because of the crowds attending both performances, Mr. Gillett
promised that there will definitely be an added show next year. This
may be done either lay setting aside another night or by featuring a
matinee. Ticket sales may also be limited to equalize the attendance.

Some people were refused tickets this year, he reported, because of
insufficient seating capacity; and others, seeking information about
seating by telephone, were discouraged. Interest in the performance
reached far beyond the campus, he continued, drawing many people
from Bloomington and the surrounding vicinity.

Two members of the circus received the Gamma Phi Service Pin
award. They are Patricia Meyer, senior in physical education from
Schiller Park, and George Youngren, senior in speech from Zion.

The Service Pin is annually awarded to a senior member or members
of Gamma Phi who "have at all times manifested a spirit of
willingness and helpfulness in carrying out the ideals of the
organization, who have participated in the activities of the
organization above and beyond the normal expectations of a
member."

Apr 2, 1952 (page 3)
Russell Steele, of the publicity office, gave a talk on offset printing
and showed a movie of the recent Gamma Phi circus.

Apr 2, 1952 (page 7)
Gamma Phi Circus In Off-Campus Benefit
The Gamma Phi circus, which recently put on its annual shows on
our campus, went to DeKalb last weekend, where the members put
on a benefit performance.

This Friday the group will take to the road again when the circus
performers and the circus band travel to Mendota, where the Lions
club will sponsor another benefit show.

According to early plans, the group intends to leave our campus at four o'clock Friday to allow students to attend all classes on the day of the trip.

1952 – 53 School Year

1953 Group Picture Gamma Phi Circus

Sept 24, 1952 (page 6)
Gamma Phi Gymnasts To Hold Tryout Monday

Tumbling and circus stunt enthusiasts, experienced or not, are invited to the Men's Gym Monday evening from 7 till 9 to see the opportunities for participation provided by Gamma Phi, according to Darwin Hany, president.

Gamma Phi members are already making plans for this year's activities. The dates for the annual circus have been set for March 13 and 14. After last season's successful off-campus trips to Mendota, Canton, DeKalb, and Jacksonville, members are now considering the choices of circus trips for next spring.

Arley Gillett, physical education instructor on campus, will again be the organization's sponsor. Other officers for the year are Dick Carr, vice-president; Eileen Schumaker, treasurer; and Imogene Lindberg, secretary.

Nov 5, 1952 (page 6)
Gamma Phi's Equipment Buy Incites Spring Circus Plans

Gamma Phi members are going sky-high in their preparations for the annual spring circus this year. One of the chief causes for this is the new trampoline which the organization recently purchased. The new tramp has an improved web-bed, consisting of interlaced strips of canvas, which enables the performer to venture higher than ever into the blue.

The club has also purchased a new web, and new costumes for the circus, which will take place during the last of March and the first part of April. Performers are already hard at work on their individual acts for the event.

Dec 17, 1952 (page 3)
Federal Bank Building Scene for Circus Party

The party room of the Federal Bank building in Bloomington was the scene of festivities for the Gamma Phi Christmas party. Over 30 members and pledges took part in the games and square dancing which were a major part of the program.

Club members exchanged gifts in the usual party grab-bag manner. Following the grab bag, a light supper was served in the way of refreshments. Sponsor of the club, Arley Gillett, was present at the meeting with his wife and two children.

Feb 11, 1953 (page 6)
Cardinals Even Conference Slate Against Western

...

The halftime show was presented by Gamma Phi and featured Nancy Quimby on the "web."

Campus Clubs to Nominate Gamma Phi Queen and Court
The circus is on its way!
Gamma Phi circus is coming to the ISNU campus for a two-night stand. McCormick gymnasium will serve as the big top on March 13 and 14 for the circus. The Grand entry will begin at 8 on both nights.

A new policy for the election of the circus queen is being featured. Traditionally, the students have elected the queen and the members of her court; but this year, in accordance with a recent rule change announced by Gamma Phi President Darwin Hany, all campus organizations are being asked to submit their nominations for the queen and her court. The student body will have an opportunity to elect the royal group on March 5 and 6 on the West Bridge.

This 17th annual circus will again go on tour. The entire show, including the circus band, will travel to Galesburg April 11 and to Clinton April 18. Prior to these engagements, the circus will appear at Mendota for the sixth consecutive year on March 20.

Because of capacity crowds, Gamma Phi is limiting ticket sales. Only 1500 tickets will be available for each night. Students and faculty will have an opportunity to purchase their tickets before they are released for the general public. An announcement pertaining to ticket sales will be made in the March 4 assembly. Tickets go on sale on March 5, the price of admission being 60 cents for adults and students and 30 cents for grade school children.

Gymnasts Plan Assembly
Gamma Phi will mentally transport its audience to McCormick gym during assemblies on Wednesday, March 4. "Down at the Gym," the spectators will see a typical circus practice session.

Imogene Lindberg, Gamma Ph secretary, said the gymnasts will open the assembly with a business meeting, at which all the candidates for circus queen will be introduced. Then, accompanied by the circus band under the baton of Wayne F. Sherrard, the members will give a plain clothes preview of several circus acts.

Included will be unicycle and balancing acts, demonstrations of skill on the low parallel bars, tumbling, the ever popular clowns, and many others.

Fraternity members who will take part in the assembly include Gene Cruze, Nancy Quimby, Dick Carr, Darwin Hany, Konstantin Morhan, Lydia Almquist, Celio Bongiani, Emma Flaminio, Dick Wuthrich, Merrill Kallenbach, Mrs. Arley Gillett, and Arley Gillett, sponsor.

Mar 4, 1953 (front page)
Gamma Phi Releases Club Nominees For Queen and Lists Acts of Circus
Nominees for queen of the 1952 Gamma Phi circus, to be held in McCormick gymnasium on March 13 and 14, at 8 p.m., have just been released by the gymnastic fraternity.

Mary Behling, senior from Elgin, is the choice of the Women's Physical Education club, while Joyce Brown, senior from Bloomington, will be sponsored by the Elementary club.

Other nominees and then sponsors include Kathleen Lyons junior from Odell, Home Economics club; Yvonne Garry, senior from Momence, Orchesis; and Carol Hunsinger, junior from Staunton, Industrial Arts club.

Still other nominations for the queen include Patricia Schmitt junior from Cissna Park, Art club; Elaine Eickmeyer, sophomore from Litchfield, Lutheran Club; Norma Little, senior from Springfield, Physical Science Club; Bonita Fitzpatrick, junior from Campus, Newman club; and Delores Lauf, senior from Belleville, Special Education club. The student body will vote on the several candidates tomorrow and Friday on the West Bridge.

Special features of the circus include Gene Cruze, junior, a circus newcomer of balance personified, walking the ball and riding the unicycle, while Nancy Quimby, senior, will again perform on the Web and the Foot Revolve.

Celio Bongiana, senior; Merrill Kallenback, sophomore; Dick Wuthrich, sophomore; Emma Flaminio, freshman; and Lydia Almquist, junior, will comprise the Tumbling Five. Darwin Hany, senior, will return as a featured performer on the trampoline and Eileen Shumaker, senior, will conclude the circus with the spectacular Cloud Swing.

Tickets, limited to 1500 for each night of the show, will go on sale on March 5. The price of admission is set at 60 cents for adults and 30 cents for grade school children.

Mar 4, 1953 (page 2)
Letter to the Editor
Dear Editor, The forthcoming election of a queen for the Gamma Phi circus has prompted this inquiry as to the value of electing so many queens for so many functions. Gamma Phi, the Homecoming committee, the sophomore class, and the recent addition of the University club sweetheart queen, all run the value of electing a queen into the ground.

It becomes a University race whereby the girl who knows the most people, who, in turn, have the most friends, can influence the most people to vote for the most POPULAR girl.

If the contest is to be based on popularity, I say that is a sad value for the election of a queen.

One organization reported that they were not nominating a candidate for the Gamma Phi queen because other larger organizations could easily sway the vote in another direction.

Consider the day when one girl claims that she was elected queen of love and beauty, while another girl, meeting her, proclaims her triumph as queen of every day. Then the purpose and value of electing a queen becomes rather silly, absurd, and commonplace.

Glenn Schuermann

Mar 11, 1953 (page 8)
'Circus Artists Invade Gym' Announces Gamma Phi

"Ladies and gentlemen!! Presenting for your entertainment ..."
The Gamma Phi Circus opens its seventeenth circus this Friday and Saturday night in McCormick gym. The three-ring spectacle commences at eight o'clock with the coronation of the Circus Queen by Darwin Hany, president of the organization.

Participating in the queen's court will be Bonita Fitzpatrick sponsored by the Newman club; Carol Hunsinger, sponsored by the Industrial Arts club; Dolores Lauf, sponsored by the Special Education club; Kathleen Lyons, sponsored by the Home Economics club; and Patricia Schmitt, sponsored by the Art club. The name of the queen will not be known until Friday night.

Twenty-five acts of acrobats, clowns, and other skilled performers presenting their acts on a variety of circus apparatus will comprise the program. Some of the outstanding acts that will be presented include the "Web Ballet," the "Swinging Perch Poles and Ladders," the "Flying Trapeze," and many others.

Tickets are now on sale on the West bridge. Adults admission is sixty cents and grade school children thirty cents.

DELORES LAUF, above, beams as Darwin Hany, president of Gamma Phi, dubs her queen of the 1953 Gamma Phi Circus.

Vidette Mar 18, 1953 (front page)

Delores Lauf Reigns Over Gymnastic Circus

Amid balloons, popcorn, trapeze artists, clowns, and the ISNU circus band, Delores Lauf, senior from Belleville, was crowned queen of the 1953 Gamma Phi circus.

Escorted to her throne by Darwin Hany, president of the gymnastic organization, the queen reigned last Friday and Saturday evenings. Her attendants were Bonita Fitzpatrick, junior in home economics; Carol Hunsinger, junior in elementary; Kathleen Lyons, junior in home economics; and Patricia Schmitt, senior in art.

At the circus, the Gamma Phi awards for outstanding participation in the functions of the club were presented to Eileen Schumaker, senior from Arlington Heights, and Darwin Hany, senior from Gridley.

PICTURED ABOVE are Gamma Phi barmen as they practiced for their annual circus, held last Friday and Saturday nights.

Vidette Mar 18, 1953 (page 2)

Mar 25, 1953 (page 8)
Delores Lauf Overcomes Handicap To Become Outstanding Student
By Norma Canham

Who is the girl who became Gamma Phi queen this year? Most of us know that her name is Dolores Lauf. Those who know her name only are missing the acquaintance of an outstanding personality on campus.

Dolores, known as "Del" to her friends, finished her undergraduate study in January this year and is now a graduate student in special education.

On to a M.D.

STUDENT TEACHES BRAILLE SYSTEM. Delores Lauf, a graduate student in special education, uses the skill she has developed in reading Braille to assist two youngsters in the special education building.

Included in her duties as a faculty assistant is teaching brail to two small blind girls in the special education building. Her assistantship will continue through this summer. At present "Del" intends to finish her studies for her master's degree at ISNU.

Hailing from Belleville, Illinois, Del received her high school education at the School for the Blind in Jacksonville, Illinois. There she learned to play the piano. Her teachers were the first to impress her with the idea of attending ISNU. Del has two brothers—one in the Air Corps, the other in high school—and one sister, nine years old.

Del lived in Fell Hall her freshman year. The following year she moved with some of the close friends she had at the dorm. Those girls have remained Del's closest friends through her years at ISNU.

Three rooming houses have been Del's home at different times since she moved from Fell Hall. Her present residence is at 308 West Locust street.

This semester Del is carrying 12 hours plus her teaching duties, which demand approximately 3 y 2 hours of her time each day. She has three night classes each week. She loves children and enjoys teaching very much.

Studies Come Easy
"I have been able to find something about every course that I really like," says Del. She hasn't found her studies particularly hard, when she has had the help of a reader. All of her electives have been music courses. She has found students and faculty very friendly.

Although she has served on many committees, Del says she has never held any offices. She is quite active in both the Special Education club and Bloomington chapter of the International Council for Exceptional Children. She was in the queen's court of her sophomore Cotillion and was elected Gamma Phi queen this year.

One of Del's favorite pastimes in college has been singing with a girls' quartette, which broke up last June when two of the girls graduated. The quartette sang for many meetings on campus as well as for some organizations off-campus. The girls won second place in the annual stunt show one year.

Piano Player, Too
Del plays the piano "by the hour." Her favorite music is that of Tchaikovsky, although she likes all kinds of music. Once in a while she likes to knit.

Being an avid fan of the St. Louis Browns, Del is very enthusiastic about sports. "I'm not very good at them myself," she says, but there are few football or baseball games at ISNU that Del does not attend. She also attends all the entertainment series as well as the other annual shows on campus, such as Blackfriars or Gamma Phi. She does not go home often, as it is a five-hour trip by bus.

Having an abundant sense of humor, Del chuckled as she recalled that she was a model for an art class for one semester during her junior year. She made 50 cents an hour at this job, and "it was fun" besides.

This summer will be the first summer in school for Del. She is looking forward very much to a teaching career after she finishes her studies.

May 6, 1953 (page 4)
Gamma Phi Receives Twenty-One Members
Gamma Phi gymnastic fraternity held its annual initiation meeting April 27. Twenty-one people became members.

They are: Ronald Beales, Elmer Busch, Robert Churchill, Gene Cruze, Margaret DuBois, Caroline Duvick, Emma Jean Flaminio, James Frye, Cynthia Harris, Roger King, Doris Richter, Shirley Romano, Hillard Roznowski, Beulah Smith, Glenn Swichtenberg, Kenneth White, Myron Wilcox, Nancy Williams, Patricia Williamson, and Willetta Wyatt.

Arthur Howard, equipment manager at the gym, was also initiated and given a service pin in appreciation of the club for the extra work he has done in helping Gamma Phi put on its circuses.

At this meeting the officers for next year were elected. Merrill Kallenback will be the new president. Also elected were Robert McKinley, vice-president; Imogene Lindberg, secretary; and Beulah Smith, treasurer. Arley Gillett was renamed as sponsor of the organization.

Other highlights of the meeting were the serving of refreshments and the showing of the movies taken at this year's circus.

1954 Group Picture Gamma Phi Circus

Nov 4, 1953 (front page)
Homecoming
Gamma Phi mobile float comes in 18th place and is awarded $2.50.

Nov 30, 1953 (page 7)
Gym Club Plans Open House for All Interested in Circus
Gamma Phi, the gymnastics club that annually produces the famed "Circus," will hold open house next Monday for all ISNU students—freshmen or upperclassmen—who want to take part in the circus activities. The meeting will begin in the Men's gym promptly at 7:00 p.m.

Students who join the co-ed club now will have an opportunity to develop an act before circus time. The circus fraternity will hold a training hour every Monday from 7 to 8 p.m.

Dec 16, 1953 (page 4)
Basketball game against Eureka
Halftime saw Richard Carr,. Konstatin Morhun, Dave Thomas, Richard Clarke, and Roger Cunningham of Gamma Phi perform on the parallel bars.

Feb 17, 1954 (page 2)
Gymnasts Make Early Start on Circus
Plans are already well under way for the Gamma Phi circus, according to club president, Bob McKinley The gymnastic display is scheduled for March 11, 12, and 13.

Besides the campus showings, the circus will also appear in Clinton and Mendota, under the sponsorship of local organizations. This year marks the 18th annual appearance of the circus.

Committee chairmen named for the event are Nancy Williams, sophomore in health and physical education, tickets; E. J. Flaminio, sophomore in elementary, queen candidates; Beulah Smith, junior in home economics, publicity; Romaine Zehr, senior in health and physical education, costumes; Cynthia Harris, sophomore in health and physical education, and Shirley Romano, sophomore in health and physical education, decorations; Ken Crochett, senior in elementary, and Gene Cruze, sophomore in industrial arts, assembly.

Each organization is asked to nominate one girl to run for queen of the circus. A queen and a court of four will be elected from those nominated, in an all school election.

Names of the queen candidates and information concerning ticket sales will be released at a later date, according to Beulah Smith, club secretary.

A Circus in the Paper

Gamma Phi Readies for Circus Opening Night
Sherrard Prepares Musical Atmosphere

With "opening night" only three weeks away, members of Gamma Phi have become increasingly busy putting finishing touches on their annual circus program.

This year a number of new stunts will appear among those made popular by the group in the past. The new acts include the "balance beam and juggling quartet," and the "roller skating duo."

Other gymnastic feats perfected by the members for the 1954 performance scheduled for March 12, 13, and 14, include the Gamettes, a number of acts such as the "cloud swing," the "web stunt," and "trapeze techniques," and the "Gilletts." The latter group is a familiar one to regular circus fans. Led by Arley Gillett, Gamma Phi sponsor, his children, Arlene and Jay Gillett, perform difficult acrobatic stunts. The three Gilletts have been a feature of the circus for a number of years.

Of the 60-odd Gamma Phi members, 45 will appear in the big show. Practice sessions began shortly after the opening of school, and were scheduled once a week until the Christmas holidays. Since then they have been held twice weekly.

But preparations for the circus have not been the work of Gamma Phi alone. Wayne F. Sherrard, director of the ISNU band, has compiled, with the aid of his musicians, a set of appropriate circus selections. The band will open the program with a short concert, and will provide music during and between the numbers.

Committees for the affair were named recently. Headed by co-chairmen Ken Crochett, senior in elementary, and Gene Cruze, sophomore in industrial arts, the assembly committee includes JunAnn Husir, junior in special education; Glenn Swichtenburg, sophomore in elementary; Cynthia Harris, sophomore in health and physical education; Bob McKinley, junior in industrial arts; and Kenneth White, freshman in industrial arts.

Beulah Smith, junior in home economics, chairman of the publicity committee, will be aided by Leona Colebar, freshman in English; and Al Larson, junior in special education.

Sarah Butler, sophomore in special education, and Barbara Boehm, junior in health and physical education, have been named to the queen committee. Costumes will be managed by Romaine Zehr, senior in health and physical education, and her assistants, JunAnn Husir, and Mary Ann Welge, freshman in speech.

Decorations, with Cynthia Harris and Shirley Ramano in charge, will be taken care of by Malinda Murphy, freshman in home economics; Barbara Lambdin, freshman in business education; Dean Freesmeyer, freshman in mathematics; Dawn Butler, sophomore in art; Dick Gifford, senior in elementary; Marilyn Salima, freshman in health and physical education; Janet Wakefield, freshman in special education; and Kay Short, freshman in business education.

Glenn Swichtenberg, sophomore in elementary; Esther Day, senior in elementary; Edward Elliott, freshman in biological science; and Nancy Williams, sophomore in health and physical education, are the members of the ticket committee.

Mar 3, 1954 (page 2)
Circus Shows Sneak Preview
Actors Share Stage With Ten Contestants
This morning's assembly programs were sparked with interest and anticipation when a group of Gamma Phi members presented a "sneak preview" of their forthcoming circus. The preview was complete with circus color, music, and stunts. A special feature of the program was the introduction of the 10 women now vying for the title of circus queen.

King Introduces Candidates
Introduced by Roger King, sophomore in health and physical education, who will act as master of ceremonies for the circus, the nominees and their sponsors are Rosemarie Baier, senior in

elementary, Industrial Arts club; Kay Burmeister, freshman in art, Lutheran club; Marjorie Doman, junior in Spanish, Foreign Language club; Becky Glassman, senior in elementary, Elementary Education club; Gloria Hickman, junior in biological science, Nature Study club; Camilla Holt, junior in special education, Women's League and Special Education club; Gloria Ketchmark, junior in English, English club; Evelyn Miller, freshman in elementary, freshman class; Margaret Patton, junior in home economics, Home Economics club; and Maryann Quigley, senior in health and physical education, Women's Health and Physical Education club.

The queen will be crowned during the circus, which is scheduled for March 11, 12, and 13.

Jugglers Perform
The remainder of the program consisted of a number of skilled stunts. Roger Cunningham, freshman in health and physical education; Richard Clarke, freshman in biological science; and Arley Gillett, sponsor of Gamma Phi, performed on the low parallel bars.

Janet Wakefield, freshman in special education; and Barbara Lambdin, freshman in business education, exhibited their proficiency in juggling. Gene Cruze, sophomore in industrial arts, held the attention of the audience with his stunts on the unicycle.

Clowns Get Laughs
One of the feature acts, the Gamettes, was presented, with Lydia Almquist, senior in health and physical education; E. J. Flaminio, sophomore in elementary; Ken Crotchett, senior in elementary; and Dick Wuthrich, junior in health and physical education, taking part.

Jerry Caruso, freshman in art, and Ken White, freshman in industrial arts, brought laughter as they went through clown antics.

Tickets for the annual event - will go on sale Monday, March 8, at 1 p.m. on West bridge. A limited number of tickets will be sold for each performance. There will be no reserved seats.

Mar 10, 1954 (front page)
Four Women to Grace Crown Wearer's Court
Five campus women have been selected as finalists in the Gamma Phi queen contest. Of these five, one will wear the crown during the annual circus, while the other contestants will serve as members of her court.

Margaret Patton, junior in home economics; Rose Marie Baier, senior in elementary; Jo Ann Murray, sophomore in elementary; Evelyn Miller, freshman in elementary; and Camilla Holt, junior in special education, were the winners of last week's election.

Arley Gillett, sponsor of Gamma Phi, reminds students to purchase their tickets for the performances, if they have not already done so. One third of the receipts of the three consecutive presentations, Thursday, Friday, and Saturday of this week, will go to the fund for a student union building on the campus.

On March 19, the circus will appear at Mendota high school. A second out-of-town performance at Clinton community high school, has been scheduled for April 3.

Mar 17, 1954 (page 3)
TV Station To Review Circus Acts Via Film
Bloomington's television station, WBLN, is making plans to show ISNU's first film program over that medium. The film, according to Russ Steele of the publicity department, is a review of the recent Gamma Phi circus held on campus.

Arley Gillett, sponsor and director of the gymnastic show, is the narrator of the 27-minute, synchronized tape show. The film includes shots of most of the acts in the circus, the processional and crowning of the circus queen, the clowns' antics, and the reaction of the crowd.

Russ Steele and Nelson Smith of the publicity department collaborated on shooting the movie, while Herbert Sanders of the music department was in charge of the sound recording.

Tomorrow night is the date scheduled for the film's TV showing, although developing difficulties might occur. Station WBLN will carry the show between 9 and 9:30 p.m.

Mar 31, 1954 (page 2)
Activities Rate Merit

...

Participants in the Gamma Phi circus are also deserving of merit at this time, even more so because their activities are not limited just to the campus. Outside tours are being conducted, and again part of the proceeds are being donated to the Student Union fund.

Mar 31, 1954 (page 5)
The Press Box
By Jack Martin

THE N CLUB'S financial project for the year will make it possible to improve the motion picture coverage of ISNU athletic events and other campus activities, according to president Gene Hoffman.

The lettermen voted this year to buy the motor, two magazines, and a case for a 16 mm camera owned by the University. In the past the club has purchased scoreboards, a whirlpool bath for treating sore muscles, a motion picture projector for the coaches, a telephoto lens, and a magazine motion picture camera.

As is the case for previous club projects, this will aid the University generally, as well as give a boost to athletics. Films of sports contests, the Gamma Phi circus, and the "Across the Campus" color film and others are used to $how alumni, school, and community groups various activities of ISNU. The publicity office staff takes these and a limited number of other films on a cost basis, with the various organizations paying only for the cost of the film and other supplies.

Gamma Phi Initiates 41 New Members; Elects 1954-55 Officers

At a recent meeting of Gamma Phi, 41 new members were initiated into the organization, and officers for 1954-55 were elected.

Dick Wuthrich, junior in health and physical education, was named president. Assisting him will be Glenn Swichtenberg, sophomore in elementary, vice president; Cynthia Harris, sophomore in health and physical education, secretary; and Shirley Romano, sophomore in health and physical education from La Salle, treasurer.

The group has planned a picnic at Lake Bloomington on Sunday, May 23, from 1 to 6 p.m. Transportation will be provided. The buses will leave from the parking lot behind Fell hall.

Members of the committees include the following: food, Gene Cruze, sophomore in industrial arts; Shirley Truitt, freshman in elementary; Sarah Butler, sophomore in special education; Beulah Smith, junior in home economics.

Bob Brandt, freshman in health and physical education, Glenn Swichtenberg, John Fender, junior in social science; and Barbara Boehm, junior in health and physical education, compose the. equipment committee.

1954 – 55 School Year

Gamma Phi

Spring marked the date of the biggest project of the Gamma Phi fraternity, the circus. The organization aimed to promote interest in the field of physical education and to encourage gymnastic excellence.

Dick Wuthrich, president, Glen Swichtenberg, vice-president, Cynthia Harris, secretary, and Shirley Romano, treasurer, worked with Arley F. Gillett, sponsor, to plan the trip for the circus troupe.

Cynthia Harris is the center of attention during a time-out conversation among Shirley Romano, Glen Swichtenberg, and Dick Wuthrich.

1955 Index (page 88)

Sept 22, 1954 (page 5)
Student Council, Gamma Phi Supply Funds for New Campus Markers

Incoming freshmen this year owe a great vote of thanks to the Student council and Gamma Phi organizations for the comparative ease with which they accomplished their registration. Those two organizations contributed the money for the erection of the information signs around campus that enabled new students to find their way around as old grads do.

For years the Public Relations committee of ISNU has wanted to have signs erected on campus but has lacked the funds to do so. Last year a subcommittee of the Public Relations committee headed by Dr. Harold Gibson, initiated plans by which construction could be undertaken by the industrial arts club. To see how student opinion was, the IAers made three large signs and put them up at strategic spots on campus. Students and faculty alike roared their approval and the Industrial Arts club went to work to make more signs.

University funds available for the project plus generous contributions by the student council and Gamma Phi enabled the IA men to construct signs for every building on campus except one and several larger signs on the margins of the campus. Dr. Ray Stombaugh, head of the industrial arts department, served as chairman of the subcommittee on signs and with the help of Robert Hammond, instructor of industrial arts, supervised the actual construction and erection of the signs.

Oct 13, 1954 (page 4)
"N" Club To Greet Alumni
Plans for the combined booth of Gamma Phi and the "N" club to receive alumni at Homecoming were made. Initiation of new members will be held the next meeting on November 6. Following the business meeting, movies of this year's game between Bradley and Normal were shown.

Nov 22, 1954 (page 4)
ISNU Gymnastics Fraternity Urges Interested Students To Perform in Annual Circus
Gamma Phi, honorary gymnastic fraternity, urges all students interested in performing in the annual ISNU gym circus to contact members of the fraternity.

Experience is unnecessary. The Gamma Phi members will train newcomers in any of the following areas: tumbling, trampoline, parallel bars, aerial acts, juggling, acrobatic dancing, roller skating, hand to hand, trapeze, clowning, horizontal bars, and unicycle techniques. Any other specialties or talents are welcomed.

Gamma Phi meetings are held every Monday evening from 7 to 9 p.m. in McCormick gym.

A Circus in the Paper

Feb 16, 1955 (front page)

Gamma Phi Tells 1955 Plans

Circus Scheduled For March 10,11,12

Although the production date is practically a month away, the Gamma Phi tumbling fraternity is making plans for its annual circus. The campus dates for the circus this year are March 10, 11, and 12.

Tryouts have just been completed and the squad will be announced soon. As usual, the sponsor is Arley Gillett. He is being assisted by graduate students Don Kinderfather and Charles Imig. Arden Vance will direct the band.

Make Nominations
One item which will be of immediate interest to students is the fact that organizations are to start considering candidates for queen. Petitions will be out soon, and nominations will have to come from an organization.

Gamma Phi will present an assembly program March 2. President Dick Wuthrick has also announced a series of three off-campus appearances by the group. The circus will travel to Leland March 18, to Lake Zurich March 26, and to Watseka April 1.

Reserved Seats
Included in the changes this year will be reserved seats. In previous years the McCormick gym seats were not on a reserve basis.

Officers for the fraternity, besides president Wuthrich, are vice-president Glen Swichtenberg, treasurer Shirley Romano, and secretary Cynthia Harris.

The officers have named committees to start the plans rolling. The program committee is made up of the officers themselves.

Committees
Roger Cunningham, a sophomore from Winnebago, will head the Queen committee. Assisting him will be Kay Gecar, Sue Faulkner, John Carlson, and Ron Tinsley.

Malinda McKinley, a sophomore in home economics from Normal, and Janet Wakefield, a sophomore in special education from Clinton, are co-chairmen of the costumes committee. Other members of that committee are Jessie Mae Warren and Rae Ann Austin.

Marilyn Salima, a health and physical education sophomore from Calumet, is chairman of the tickets committee. Her group consists of Louise Gwaltney, Phyllis Winkler, Beverly Reinhart, Shirley Kilburn, Ramona Doran, and Jacquie Cannon.

Doug Ploss, a sophomore in art, from Normal, and Shirley Truitt, a sophomore in elementary from Rockford, are co-chairmen of the decorations committee.

Bob McKinley, a senior in industrial arts from Normal, heads the publicity committee, with Ray Cluts and Sarah Butler assisting.

Feb 23, 1955 (page 2)
Riley Pittman Speaks To Assembly Goers On Brotherhood Week

Dr. Riley H. Pittman spoke at today's assemblies on the occasion of the annual Brotherhood week observance. Dr. Pittman also met with the Bloomington Normal Council on Human Relations on Tuesday, February 22, at 7:30 p.m. at the YWCA. As executive director of the Illinois Commission on Human Relations, Dr. Pittman is applying the principles he formerly taught as a professor of religion.

The third and fourth hour assemblies will thrill to the circus band of Gamma Phi Wednesday, March 2, as they present their annual assembly program. The circus clowns will also entertain the incoming students with their acts. Roger Cunningham, a sophomore in health and physical education, who is in charge of the queen election, will introduce the queen candidates.

Circus Preview
The assembly program will be a preview of the circus which will be presented March 10, 11, and 12. Portions of acts which can be performed on the stage will be presented. The acts will include

tumblers, juggling, balance beam and the unicycle.

Roger Cunningham, a sophomore in health and physical education, who is in charge of the queen election, will introduce the queen candidates. The election for the queen and her four attendants will be held March 3 in McCormick gym.

Arley Gillett, instructor in physical education and sponsor of Gamma Phi, said ticket sales would be conducted Thursday March 3, in McCormick gym. Students may vote for queen and purchase tickets at the same time. All seats will be reserved with students and adults tickets 75 cents and children's tickets 25 cents.

Feb 23, 1955 (page 2)
The Maze
By Jack Martin (opinion writer at the Vidette)
...
Barely has the Valentine queen passed into history, and the Gamma Phi tumbling fraternity is starting its annual campaign for Circus royalty. Ah yes, "The Queen is dead, long live the Queen."

Mar 2, 1955 (page 5)
"The Circus Comes to Town"
McCormick Gym Is Tent, March 10-12
Gamma Phi, the honorary gymnastic fraternity at ISNU, will present its 19th annual gym circus in McCormick gymnasium March 10, 11, 12 at 8 p.m.

Gamma Phi will "go on the road" with the circus for performances at three different locations. They will travel to Leland on March 18, to Lake Zurich March 26, and appear at Watseka April 1.

Ticket sales and voting for the queen will begin today in McCormick gym. For the first time all seats will be reserved. Adults and student tickets are 75 cents and' children's passes are 25 cents.

Horton Is Founder
Gamma Phi was founded at ISNU in 1929 by Dr. C. E. Horton,
present director of the Division of Health and Physical Education. It
was at first an all-men's organization, but in 1941 women were
admitted to membership and have since taken an active part in the
fraternity.

Arley F. Gillett, the present sponsor and coach, took over the
direction of the group in 1947. The circus has been presented on
campus every year since 1932, except for the war years. The first
campus queen was elected by Gamma Phi.

The 35-piece circus band, under the direction of Arden Vance,
instructor in music, plays appropriate accompaniment for all of the
acts and appears with the circus on all engagements.

The sixty members of Gamma Phi practice every Monday all year
and since Christmas they have been practicing an additional two
hours on Sunday.

The Gamma Phi circus will be opened by a concert by the ISNU
circus band, followed by the coronation of the queen and the various
acts.

Features "Whirl of Death"
A new act added this year is 'The Whirl of Death." It consists of two
rings so constructed that men are able to whirl in them. The new
piece of apparatus stands off the floor and the two rings come out of
an axle. Glenn Swichtenberg, a junior in elementary, and Ray Cluts,
a freshman in industrial arts, will participate in the act.

Another feature is called the "Disney fantasy," which is a humorous
take-off on "Snow White and the Seven Dwarfs." Doug Ploss will
portray the part of the charming, petite Snow White. The seven
dwarfs will be played by Marilyn Salima, Shirley Kilburn, Beverly
Reinhart, Louise Gwaltney, Phyllis Winkler, Ramona Donar, and
Jacquie Cannon.

"The Whirlo's" will also be featured in the circus. The act will be presented by Mary Carney and Russ Fitzgerald, a rollerskating team.

Gilletts To Appear
Every year the Gamma Phi circus presents "The Gilletts." This act includes the Gamma Ph sponsor, Arley Gillett, and hit two children, Jay and Arlene This year the Gilletts are keeping the act a surprise, but they promise something new and different.

Those participating in the web ballet are Barbara Boehm, a senior in health and physical education; Joanne Thieme, a sophomore in biology; Jessie Mae Warren, a freshman in health and physical education; and Malinda McKinley.

The tumbling and balancing act will include Richard Wuthrich, Robert McKinley, Charles Brubaker, Leo Benson, Charles Odell, Ray Cluts, Mardell Stegmaier, Mary Lynn Brown, Florence Grebner, Dawn Silvers, Nancy Hancock, and Sue Faulkner.

Other participants are Marilyn Leismeister, Kay Gecan, Judy Renfro, Joyce Gobush, Julie Ortgiesen, Nancy Melcher, and Flo Tooke.

Juggling, Trapeze Acts
Also featured is a juggling duet including Janet Wakefield and Don Blattner. On the horizontal bars are Richard Clarke, Ron Tinsley, Robert Loveridge, Roger Cunningham, Leo Benson, and Glenn Swichtenberg.

Jessie Mae Warren, Robert Brandt, and Cyril Chung will present trapeze thrills, while on the ground limberback acrobatics will be performed by Mary Ann Welge, Margaret Menne, and James Ping.

Other acts include such entertainment as the balance beam performance by Shirley Romano and Ardene White; a swinging ladder act by Rae Ann Austin, Sarah Butler, Nancy Gerold, Beulah Smith, Joanne Thieme, Lavaughn Cotterell, Audrey Gibson, and

Shirley Truitt; and a parallel bar act by Carol Hoffa, Richard Clarke, Roger Cunningham, Ron Tinsley, and Leo Benson.

Trampoline performers include Cynthia Harris, Clarence Patterson, Jerry Symons, Barbara Blish, Joyce Haemeker, Ginger Whalen, Ed Elliott, and John Carlson.

Soloists To Star
Two single acts will also be in the circus this year. The foot-revolve will be performed by Rae Ann Austin, and John Fender will perform with his ball and unicycle.

No circus would be complete without the clowns which include Doug Ploss, Harry Busch, Frank Seville, John Brinderhoff, and Al Gray.

The Gamma Phi circus ringmaster is Roger King.

The publicity committee includes Robert McKinley, chairman, assisted by Sarah Butler and Ray Cluts.

Roger Cunningham, a sophomore in health and physical education, is chairman of the queen committee. He is assisted by Kay Gecan, Sue Faulkner, John Carlson, and Ron Tinsley.

Doug Ploss, a sophomore in art, and Shirley Truitt, a freshman in elementary, are co-chair-men of the decorations committee.

The costumes co-chairmen are Malinda McKinley and Janet Wakefield. Assisting them are Jessie Mae Warren and Rae Ann Austin.

Marilyn Salima, a sophomore in health and physical education, is chairman of the ticket committee. Also on the committee are Louise Gwaltney, Phyllis Winkler, Beverly Reinhart, Shirley Kilburn, Ramona Donar, and Jacquie Cannon.

The program committee includes Richard Wuthrich, a senior in health and physical education; Shirley Romano, a junior in health and physical education; Glenn Swichtenberg, a junior in elementary; and Cynthia Harris, a junior in health and physical education.

QUEEN CANDIDATES — Front (top to bottom): Jo Wills, Toni Novak, Roberta Cutter, Lynn Thompson. Back (top to bottom: Donna Hodgson, Kathy Gallagher, Barbara Conder, Midge Stewart, and Barbara Norden. Pat Friedrich is not present.

Vidette Mar 2, 1955 (front page)

Mar 2, 1955 (page 4)

Gamma Phi Presents Preview of Circus In Assembly

Circus Music, Tumbling, Roller Skating, Acrobatics Thrill Morning Audiences

Today's assembly was entertained by Gamma Phi members as they gave their annual preview of their circus which will be held March 10, 11, and 12 in McCormick gym.

The circus band, directed by Arden Vance, instructor in music, played appropriate accompaniment for all of the acts.

Roger Cunningham, a sophomore in health and physical education, who is in charge of the queen election, introduced the queen candidates. The queen candidates are Joan Wills sponsored by English club, Barbara Norden sponsored by Elementary club, Toni Novak sponsored by Women's P.E. club, Lynn Thompson sponsored by N club, Kathy Gallagher sponsored by the Newman club, Midge Stewart sponsored by the Vidette and Lutheran club, Patricia Friedrich sponsored by the Home Economics club, Donna Hodgson sponsored by the Business Education club, Roberta Cutter sponsored by Women's League, and Barbara Conder sponsored by W.R.A.

The acts presented at the assembly were portions of ones which will be seen at the circus next Thursday, Friday, and Saturday. Only ones which could be performed on the stage were performed. These included tumbling, roller skating, balance beam, limberback acrobatics, and ball and unicycle.

Those performing in the tumbling acts were Leo Benson; Mardell Stegmaier, freshman in health and physical education; Sue Faulkner, freshman in home economics; Julie Ortgiesen, sophomore in special education; Marilyn Leismeister, sophomore in health and physical education; Flo Tooke, sophomore in home economics; Nola Crotchet, freshman in health and physical education; Judy Renfro, junior in elementary; and Nancy Melcher, sophomore in health and physical education.

The roller skating act was performed by Russ Fitzgerald and Mary Carney. Ardene White, freshman in special education, and Shirley Romano, junior in health and physical education, performed on the balance beam

The limberback acrobats were James Ping, freshman in music; Mary Ann Welge, sophomore in business education; and Margaret Menne, freshman in special education. The ball and unicycle act was performed by John Fender, senior in social science.

At the assembly it was announced that students could vote for queen and purchase tickets at the same time. This may be done March 3 in McCormick gym. All seats will be reserved, with students and adults tickets 75 cents and children's tickets 25 cents.

A Circus in the Paper

Gymnasts Ready Acts for Opening Night Performance

With the "big top" performance only one night away, Gamma Phi members are busy putting the finishing touches to their 19th annual circus. The program, featuring gymnastic stunts, tumbling, juggling and roller skating, will be staged in McCormick gymnasium Thursday, Friday and Saturday nights, beginning at 8 p.m.

DICK WUTHRICK SAILS THROUGH THE AIR with the greatest of ease as Mary Lynn Brown and Mardell Stegmaier do headstands. This is only one of the entertaining acts that will be presented at the annual Gamma Phi circus on March 10, 11, and 12. Tickets go on sale March 3. All ticket holders will have the right to vote for the Gamma Phi circus queen.

Vidette Mar 2, 1955 (page 4)

Highlighting the circus program will be a new act, the "Whirl of Death" to be performed by Glen Swichtenburg and Ray Cluts. The "Disney Fantasy" starring Doug Ploss as "Snow White" promises to be one of the most entertaining bits of the show.

Rollerskaters Mary Carney and Russ Fitzgerald, sponsor Arley Gillett and his two youngsters, Jay and Arlene, promise to be in top form for the annual circus.

Worthy of mention are the clowns, who gave the assembly audience a hint concerning forthcoming stunts. These fellows seldom have a planned routine for the event so surprises can be expected.

The web ballet, tumbling and balancing, juggling duet, and the horizontal bar acts, trapeze stunts, acrobatics and the unicycle, all traditional show-stoppers, are scheduled.

Prior to the performance on Thursday night, the Gamma Phi queen will be crowned. The identity of the winner of last week's campus election will not be disclosed until then.

Five campus women are eligible for this honored position, they being finalists from last week.

They are Midge Stewart, a freshman in elementary, from Midlothian, sponsored by the Vidette and Lutheran club; Lynn Thompson, sophomore in business from Melrose Park, sponsored by the "N" Club; Toni Novak, freshman in health and physical ed, sponsored by Women's P. E. Club; Donna Hodgson, freshman in business from Pekin, sponsored by Business club, and Barbara Conder, freshman in elementary from Highland Park, sponsored by WRA.

Mar 9, 1955 (front page)
The Maze

...
Only 534 students turned out to vote for the Gamma Phi queen. However, the tumbling fraternity is much to blame, since the polls, being located in the gym, were inconvenient to reach, and too much a break from the traditional west bridge.

NOTE:
The "west bridge" is a second-floor hallway connecting he
Old Main building to Edwards Hall. It was a common
area used for voting.

Mar 16, 1955 (page 2)
Vidette Offers Praise
Time out from issues at hand to say a few words to some of the ISNU students —

Congratulations are in order for Women's League, Gamma Phi, and Orchesis.

The first two organizations entertained campus men and women in high style recently, while the last group will follow suit this weekend. What is more important than the excellent programs presented is the fact that these student organizations are helping to build a firm foundation for better campus recreation through their contributions to the Student Union fund.

Profits from the recent activities of all three groups will be turned over in entirety to the Union committee. The committee needs some $9,000 more before construction on the new building can begin.

Most of the money must come from the campus, and must be raised by April 18, so that Union bonds can be issued. A total of $101,000 in cash must be on hand before construction can begin.

The contributions of these three ISNU groups will give the campaign for funds a big boost. Other University organizations can aid the "cause" by making their second Union pledge payment. Faculty members, 90 of them, can also help by making initial payments of their pledges, which total some $10,442. April 18 is about 30 days away. The Student Union Forward committee must have the remaining $9,000 by then.

Three University organizations—Women's League, Gamma Phi, and Orchesis—have done or are doing their part to reach the goal. Because of their response to the call for help from the committee, we feel a little applause and appreciation are in order.

Apr 17, 1955 (page 1)
Stunt Show Participants Play for Keeps This Year
The thirty-sixth annual Stunt show will go on stage this Friday night at 8:15 in Capen auditorium. Tickets for the Stunt show go on sale this afternoon and will be sold all day Thursday and Friday for the price of 75 cents each.

1955 – 56 School Year

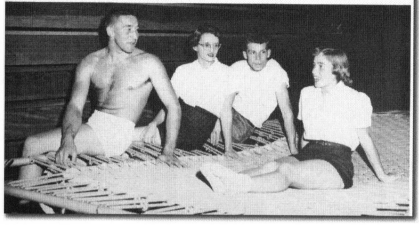

1956 Index (page 105)

Sept 28, 1955 (page 5)
Gamma Phi . . .

Gamma Phi, honorary gymnastics fraternity, elected officers at its initial meeting September 19.

Those elected are president, Pat Patterson, a junior in mathematics from Fithian; vice-president, Glenn Swichtenberg, a senior in elementary from Barrington; secretary, Cynthia Harris, a senior in health and physical education from Deerfield; treasurer, Mary Lynn Brown, a sophomore in health and physical education from Eureka.

It was stressed by Arley Gillett, sponsor of the organization that all students interested in joining the circus performers particularly freshmen, should come to the next meeting.

New students joining the Gamma Phi will be pledged on October 3. On that evening movies of last year's circus will be shown and refreshments will be served to all.

This year's circus will take place on March 8, 9, and 10.

Oct 26, 1955 (page 5)
Gamma Phi . . .

Fifty-two prospective members of Gamma Phi signed pledge cards at the fraternity's first meeting.

Arley Gillette, sponsor for the organization, has announced that people who are interested c in bouncing on trampolines, juggling, or being another Emmett Kelly should come to the regular Monday meetings from 7 to 9 p.m. in McCormick gymnasium to try out their talents.

New people are furnished with pledge cards and after signing them, they remain in pledge status until the time when they have fulfilled the requirements for becoming members of Gamma Phi. These requirements have recently been changed. Personal appearance, personality, and character are considered under general requirements and participation in the circus, regular attendance at the meetings and scheduled practices, serving on standing committees, and taking responsibility for helping with equipment for practice are considered under specific requirements by the Membership Committee.

Once the pledge has fulfilled all of the requirements for membership his application for admission to Gamma Phi must be voted upon by two-thirds of the active membership and must receive a favorable ballot from two-thirds of the voters. The date of initiation for new members is arranged by the Initiation Committee. The pledge then becomes a member of Gamma Phi.

Tryouts for this year's circus, March 8, 9, 10, will be held at Christmas time. Both members and pledges are eligible to be in the circus.

Nov 9, 1955 (page 6)
Gamma Phi Reveals Program
Gamma Phi, honorary gymnastic fraternity, has tentatively planned the off-campus presentation of the circus for March 17, April 13, and April 30, 1956.

Arley Gillett, sponsor of the organization, named the following schools as probable places to present the circus; Thornton Township High School in Harvey, Marquette High School in Ottawa and Mendota High School in Mendota.

A Christmas party at the home of Mr. and Mrs. Gillette is being planned.

Nov 23, 1955 (page 3)
Gamma Phi ...
Gamma Phi, gymnastic fraternity, will hold its Christmas party December 11 from 2 to 5 p.m. at the home of Mr. and Mrs. Arley Gillett. The open house will be for members and pledges only. Refreshments will be served.

On December 14 approximately 30 members of Gamma Phi will travel to Dimmick, Illinois, to present a few acts from its coming circus program in March.

Jan 16, 1956 (page 4)
Gamma Phi . . .
The circus troupe of Gamma Phi has begun preparations for their annual Spring Circus which will be held this year on March 14, 15, and 16. Tryouts for the various circus acts were held Sunday and Monday.

Friday night some of the acts will travel to the Dimick school in Dimick, Illinois, to present an evening performance for the public.

Among the acts participating are "The Whirls," a roller skating team, the unicycle act, tumblers, balance beams, hand to hand balancing act, "Balance Supreme," and the clowns.

Feb 8, 1956 (page 3)

Gamma Phi . . .

*Again this year, Gamma Phi is inviting each organization to
nominate one girl to run for queen of the circus. A queen and a court
of four will be elected from those nominated in an all-school election
to be held on March 1.*

*Nominations should be sent to Arley Gillett, sponsor of Gamma Phi,
via the University post office, by February 15. Each candidate will
be requested to supply a negative for publicity purposes.*

*Shirley Romano, senior in health and physical education, is the
chairman of the queen committee. Assisting her are Rae Ann Austin,
sophomore in home economics; Charles Odell, sophomore in health
and physical education; Florence Tooke, junior in home economics;
and Cyril Chung, graduate in social science.*

*Try-outs have been completed and squads will be chosen for the
annual Gamma Phi circus to be presented March 8, 9, and 10.*

*A queen and four attendants will be chosen from girls nominated by
organizations on the campus. Petitions must be returned before
February 15. The queen and her court will be presented the nights of
the circus performances.*

*On February 4 twenty members of Gamma Phi performed for the
Travelers Protective Association at Trinity Lutheran school in
Bloomington. The following acts were presented: trampoline,
balance beam, Limberbacks, parallel bars, roller skaters, balance
act, and tumbling.*

Feb 22, 1956 (page 4)

Organizations Nominate Eleven ISNU Women For Gamma Phi Queen

*Eleven Gamma Phi queen petitions have been received by Arley
Gillett, sponsor of the organization.*

Shirley Romano, senior in health and physical education, announces

A Circus in the Paper

that all campus voting for the queen will take place on Thursday, March 1, in West Bridge and in McCormick gymnasium.

The queen and her court of four attendants will be presented the nights of the Gamma Phi circus, March 8, 9, and 10. They will preside over the activities of the circus.

The queen candidates nominated are Jean Leemon, senior in business education, by the Business Education club; Marcia Cole, junior in business, by the N club; Nancy Gove, sophomore in home economics, by Home Economics club; Joyce De Ment, sophomore in special education, by Special Education club; and Jo Ellen Bidner, sophomore in elementary, by Elementary club.

Others are Adel Lemanski, senior in health and physical education, nominated by Women's Physical Education club; Barbara Cannell, freshman in English, by English club; Mary Lou Brucker, senior in math, by Kappa Nu Epsilon; Martha Gronemeier, junior in music, by Women's league; Clara Swenson, freshman in health and physical education, by WRA; and Jacquelyn McKay, junior in home economics, by Lutheran club.

Feb 29, 1956 (front page & page 3)
Polls Open Tomorrow For Circus Queen Vote
All campus voting for the Gamma Phi circus queen will take place on Thursday, March 1 from 8 to 12 a.m. and from 1 to 4 p.m. in West Bridge. The only requirement for voting is that students present their activity ticket.

The queen candidates will be introduced in the assembly on Wednesday, February 29.

Court Appears Nightly
The queen and her four attendants will be presented the nights of the Gamma Phi circus on March 8, 9, and 10 at 8:15 p.m. Senior men of the organization will serve as ushers. Pat Patterson, junior in mathematics, will crown the queen. Lynn Thompson, last year's queen, will be presented at the performances of March 9 and 10.

The varied program of the 20th annual gymnastic circus includes skillful and daring feats on the trampoline, trapeze, swinging ladders and perch poles. Precision and grace in balancing on the revolving ladder, the balance beam and the parallel bars are other acts. The clowns will add a note of comedy to lighten the program.

Gamma Phi History
Gamma Phi was founded at ISNU in 1928 by Dr. C. E. Horton, director of the division of health and physical education. It was at first an all men's organization that presented exhibitions of formal gymnastic work. In 1941 women were admitted to membership in the organization and have since taken an active part in the group.

Dr. Arley F. Gillett, the present sponsor and coach, was a member of the organization as an undergraduate student. He took over the direction of the circus in 1947. The circus has been presented on the campus every year since 1930, except for the war years.

The thirty piece circus band will play for all the acts and will appear with the circus at all performances. The band is directed by Arden Vance, assistant professor of music.

Committee Members
Various committee chairmen for the circus are: decorations, Robert Loveridge, junior in industrial arts; costumes, Mary Lynn Brown, sophomore in health and physical education, and Mrs. Arley Gillet, costume supervisor; equipment, Scott Blakeley, freshman in mathematics.

Other chairmen are: programs, Cynthia Harris, senior in health and physical education; publicity, Merrill Kallenbach, junior in elementary; queen, Shirley Romano, senior in health and physical education; and tickets, Ardene White, sophomore in special education.

Officers of Gamma Phi are: Pat Patterson, president; Glenn Swichtenberg, senior in elementary, vice-president; Cynthia Harris, secretary; and Mary Lynn Brown, treasurer.

Gamma Phi queen candidates are from left to right, front row, Marthat Gronemeier, Adel Leman-ski, Clara Swenson, Nancy Gove, Joyce DeMent, Marcia Cole, Mary Lou Brucker. In the second row are Jean Leemon, Jacke McKay, Barb Connell, and Jo Ellen Bidner. Voting will be in West Bridge from 8 to 12 and 1 to 4 tomorrow.

Vidette Feb 29, 1956 (page 1)

Feb 29, 1956 (page 2)
Circus Comes to Capen Next week's assembly will be a preview of the Gamma Phi circus, which will be presented March 7, 8, and 9. According to Pat Patterson, president of this organization, this year's circus promises to be something different, new, and humorous. He feels that this show will be more interesting than any Gamma Phi production of the past.

Mar 7, 1956 (front page & page 3)
Gamma Phi Brings '56 Circus to Town
The Gamma Phi queen, and her court will preside over the acrobatic antics of 50 performers at the circus this week.

The hour and one half long show opens tomorrow at 8:15 in McCormick gymnasium and will run through Saturday. The queen and court will be crowned at each performance.

Tickets to the circus are being sold in the lobby of McCormick gymnasium from 8 a.m. to 4:30 p.m. All seats are reserved. Tickets are 75 cents for adults' and 25 cents for children.

Beginning the program will be a "Salute to the Big Top overture" played by the ISNU Circus band under the direction of Arden L. Vance, assistant professor of music.

Among the featured acts is the giant whirl. Working on this equipment, which requires precision, skill and grace in balancing, will be Audrey Gibson and Rae Ann Austin. This is the first year that girls have worked on this apparatus.

Glenn Swichtenberg and Robert Libby will perform on the revolving ladder, a newly acquired piece of equipment which requires daring and extreme skill in balancing.

Monkey Shines
Carol Cleveland and June Alberty, working on unicycles, and Don Blattner, a juggler, will present "Monkey Shines." The Whirlo's, a roller skating act, will be performed by Mary Carney and Russ Fitzgerald.

Trapeze thrills will be given by Jessie Mae Warren, Carol DeRocker, Cyril Chung, and Dale Sutter. Presenting a ballet on the web will be Jessie Mae Warren, Rae Ann Austin, and Audrey Gibson.

Personifying poise on the balance team will be Ardene White and Shirley Romano. Nola Crotchett and Leo Benson will present an unusual act on the rings.

The tumbling squad consists of Mary Lynn Brown, Nancy Hancock, Dawn Silvers, Flo Grebner, Carole Kamp, Ruth Mondrzyk, Elsie Hasler, Merrill Kallenback, Charles Odell, and Don Hamilton.

Lady Aerial Artists
The aerial artists include Sarah Butler, Joyce Schulte, Judy Darby, Lavaughn Cotterell, Clarabel Sarff, Marilynn Lesmeister, Dodie Chandler, and Jacquie Cannon on the swinging ladders.

A Circus in the Paper

Sarah Butler, Rae Ann Austin, Audrey Gibson, John Hinds, and Jack Clifton will perform on the swinging perch poles. Exhibiting balance supreme will be Phyllis Winkler and Leo Benson.

Showing remarkable strength on the parallel bars will be Don Burda, Roger Cunningham, Ron Tinsley, Robert Loveridge, Carol Ann Roan, and Kay Stewart. Working on the horizontal bar will be Ron Tinsley, Robert Loveridge, and Roger Cunningham.

Providing feats on the trampoline will be Cynthia Harris, Nancy Hancock, Gloria Kaszynski, Pat Patterson, John Lowey, Jim Sheahan, and Dale Montgomery.

Flexibility Extraordinary
Margaret Menne and James Ping will present the "Flexibility Extraordinary," a unique tumbling act. Performing in a balancing trio will be Ron Tinsley, Don Burda, and Robert Loveridge.

Adding humor to the program will be these clowns: Frank Seville, Charles McDermand, Gary Widmer, John McKay, Gerle Gallion, and Edmund Simmons. John Fender will present an act, "The Globeman." Doug Ploss will serve as the ringmaster.

In addition to the three home performances, the circus will be presented at Harvey on March 16, Mendota on April 13, and Ottawa on April 20.

Mar 7, 1956 (page 2)
Students See Preview of Coming Attractions; Gamma Phi Performs Under Capen Big Top
Today ISNU students witnessed a sneak preview of the Gamma Phi circus which will be presented March 7, 8, and 9.

Pat Patterson, president of Gamma Phi, said that they presented two new acts that have never been presented in the assembly before.

One of these was a trampoline act starring Cynthia Harris, senior from Deerfield, Gloria Kasznski, freshman from Peru, and Pat Patterson, junior from Fithian.

The second was a parallel bar act presented by Dr. Arley Gillett, Don Burda, junior from Chicago, Bob Loveridge, junior from Tremont, and Ron Tinsley, sophomore from Pontiac.

Marge Meene. sophomore from Canton, and Jim Ping, sophomore from Alvin presented a limber back act.

Don Burda and Ron Tinsley gave a hand to hand act. Burda, Tinsley, and Loveridge performed a balance act.

Mar 21, 1956 (page 6)

The Gamma Phi performers returned from Thornton of Harvey last Friday, where they gave their show before approximately 4,000 people. Nothing was mentioned in the Vidette about the Normal program, and the pangs of conscience have conquered me, so that I must state something about the organization's performance. I am certain that most people will agree that Gamma Phi put on a polished, entertaining show. When you consider the fact that most of the participants learned and mastered their stunts with only one practice a week you realize what a wonderful job the group has done.

Queen Martha Gronemeier is escorted by Pat Patterson, Gamma Phi president.

Vidette Mar 14, 1956 (page 1)

1956 – 57 School Year

1957 Group Gamma Phi Picture, *Special Collections*

Aug 1, 1956 (page 4)
Lions Club Gives Gift To Scholarship Fund
Gamma Phi, honorary gymnastic group, recently received a $200 contribution from the Mendota Lions club. The entire Gamma Phi circus was presented at Mendota last spring under the sponsorship of the fraternal organization.

Arley Gillett, club sponsor, reports that the money will be added to the Gamma Phi scholarship fund. Roger Cunningham, a senior in health and physical education from Winnebago, will be the recipient of a Gamma Phi scholarship for the coming school year.

Oct 3, 1956 (page 5)
Gamma Phi . . .
Gamma Phi, gymnastic fraternity, accepted 40 pledges last Monday.

Movies of the 1956 circus were shown to members and pledges. Arley Gillett, sponsor, explained the circus organization and requirements for the following pledge year.

Any student interested in joining Gamma Phi may contact Mr. Gillett or one of the officers.

Officers are Pat Patterson, senior from Fithian, president; Ronald Tinsley, junior from Pontiac; vice president; Ardene White, junior from Waukegan, secretary; and Margaret Menne, junior from Canton, treasurer.

Oct 10, 1956 (page 6)
Gamma Phi ...

Gamma Phi, gymnastic fraternity, will be co-sponsor with the N Club of an open house for alumni and homecoming guests next Saturday. It will be held in F-O after the Homecoming parade until noon.

Oct 24, 1956 (page 7)
Two Gamma Phi Acts Head WRA Playday On Saturday

Two circus acts will provide the entertainment for the WRA Playday to be held in McCormick Gymnasium next Saturday. Eight white Gamma Phi letters were awarded last week to those seniors who have been active in two previous circuses.

Those receiving letters were Jacquie Cannon, elementary major from Lockport; Roger Cunningham, health and physical education major from Bloomington; Audrey Gibson, elementary major from Waverly; and Louise Gwaltney, health and physical education major from Grayslake. Others were Marilyn Lesmeister, elementary major from Calumet City; Bob Loveridge, industrial arts major from Tremont; Pat Patterson, a mathematics major from Fithian; and Phyllis Winkler, elementary major from Lockport.

The officers also received Gamma Phi emblems with the name of their office on them.

Dec 5, 1956 (page 6)
Men's PE Club Changes By-Laws; Gillett Relates Gamma Phi Functions

The Men's Physical Education Club changed their by-laws by a majority vote on November 29. instead of the monthly meeting the social life and organization board will call the meetings as necessary.

At this meeting, Dr. Arley Gillett related the functions of Gamma Phi and showed the Gamma Phi Circus film. He also encouraged health and physical education majors and minors to join the American Association for Health, Physical Education, and Recreation, which is a national professional association.

At the November meeting, new Officers were elected. They are president, Ron Slack, senior from Moline; vice-president, Ron Riek, senior from Pekin; secretary, Charles Odell, junior from Galesburg; and treasurer, Norman Seeley, freshman from Des Plaines.

The class representatives are Jerry Meidel, senior from Springfield; Ed Koch, junior from Trenton; Pat Grant, sophomore from Pekin; and Jim Hafner, freshman from Highland Park.

Dec 12, 1956 (page 5)
Gamma Phi. . .

Gamma Phi will hold their annual Christmas party for members and guests Friday night at 8 p.m. in the Student Union ballroom.

Margaret Nenne, junior in special education, is chairman of the social committee planning the party.

Entertainment will include music by some of the members, games, and dancing. Refreshments will be served.

Feb 27, 1957 (front page)
Gamma Phi Circus Goes Into Action
According to president Pat Patterson, the Gamma Phi queen nominations by the various clubs must be turned in by Thursday, February 28.

Tickets for the circus go on sale Friday, March 8, at 8 a.m. to 4:30 p.m. in McCormick Gymnasium and will be sold Monday through Friday, March 11-15.

Five new acts are being featured in this year's circus: baton twirlers, the cloud swing, the cradle, uneven parallel bars, and the trampoline. Many of the of acts are being revised.

Mar 6, 1957 (front page)
Gamma Phi Holds Queen Election Tomorrow
Queen, Four Attendants To Preside Over Circus
The all-school election for the Gamma Phi queen will take place tomorrow, March 7, from 8 a.m. to 4:30 p.m. in the Student Union and McCormick Gymnasium. In order to vote, students must present their activity tickets.

Those girls sponsored by various campus organizations include Lenore Renner, senior, Home Economic Club; Pauleen Dombrosky, junior, Women's League; Dorothy Dziadula, freshman, Newman Club; Joy Kimmel, freshman, Lutheran Club; Shirley Rose, junior, Special Education Club; Joyce Sand, sophomore, Elementary Club; and Frances Novak, sophomore, Kappa Mu Epsilon.

Others are Eleanor Mitchell, junior, Social Science Club; Pat Florent, freshman, Business Education Club; Shirley Jacob, sophomore, N Club; June Crowell, sophomore, Women's Physical Education Club; Judy Howard, sophomore, Jesters; Jane Green, junior, Kappa Delta Epsilon; and Bettye Howard, freshman, NAACP.

The queen will be crowned by Pat Patterson, president of Gamma Phi, and with her court of four attendants Will reign over the circus performances on March 14, 15, and 16.

'Greatest Show On Earth' Comes to Campus

Gamma Phi, honorary gymnastic fraternity, presents its 21st annual circus next weekend on March 14, 15, and 16, at 8 p. m. in McCormick gym. A circus troupe of over 50 performers will be accompanied by the band under the direction of Professor Arden Vance.

Tickets go on sale for all three performances Friday, from 8 a. m. to 4:30 p.m. in the gym, and will be sold Monday through Friday, March 11-15. The cost will be 75 cents for adults and 50 cents for children.

Various acts featured ate the baton twirlers, the cloud swing the cradle, uneven parallel bars swinging ladders, trapeze, and the trampoline.

Other acts include tumbling, knife throwing, unicycles, an animal act, web ballet, rings, and the "Whirlo's."

The coronation of the Gamma Phi Circus Queen will take place following the opening overture. Clowns will perform their antics throughout the rest of the program.

Chairman of the Queen committee is Ardene White, junior in special education; publicity, John Lowey, sophomore in business; tickets, Ron Tinsley, junior in biology; and decorations, Carol DeRocher, sophomore in health and physical education.

Other committees include costumes, Joyce Schulte, sophomore in English; equipment, Gene Gallion, senior in geography; Cleanup, Dale Montgomery, sophomore in agriculture; and program, Phyl Winkler, senior in elementary.

Mar 13, 1957 (page 8)
ISNU Gamma Phi Circus Opens Tomorrow
Circus Queen Takes Center Ring Surrounded By Court, Acts,
Band

UP IN THE AIR, JUNIOR BIRDSMAN!

Gladys Goodhart, freshman in English, previews a cloud swing, one of the acts in this year's circus.

Vidette Mar 6, 1957 (page 4)

By an all-school vote of 740, five girls were chosen to make up the court of the Gamma Phi Circus. The queen, one of these five, will be crowned tomorrow light to reign over the three performances.

The court is comprised of Pauline Dombrosky, junior, Women's League; Shirley Jacobs, sophomore, N Club; Joy Kimmel, freshman, Lutheran Club; Fran Novak, sophomore, Kappa Mu Epsilon; and Joyce Sand, sophomore, Elementary Club.

The 21st annual circus will begin tomorrow evening at 8 p.m. in McCormick Gym. Performances will also be held on Friday and Saturday nights. Tickets are now on sale in the gym for 75 cents for adults and 50 cents for children.

Ron Tinsley, top, Bob Loveridge, and Don Burda display balancing abilities above. Other acts at the Circus will include baton twirlers, the cloud swing, cradle, uneven parallel bars, swinging ladders, trapeze and trampoline. Also to be seen at the gym tomorrow, Friday, and Saturday will be tumbling, knife throwing, unicycle riding, an animal act, web ballet, rings, and the "Whirlos." The circus band, under the direction of Mr. A. Vance, will accompany the acts.

Vidette Mar 13, 1957 (page 8)

And Away We Go

Leo Benson balances Phyllis Winkler in a preview of the many feats to be seen this weekend. They are a part of a troupe of 50 members who will entertain ISNU students at the 21st annual Gamma Phi Circus. The circus queen and her court will start their reign over the festivities following the coronation tomorrow evening. The show begins at 8 p.m., and will feature clowns as well as various acts throughout the three performances.

Gamma Phi Circus Troupe Schedules Tour; To Perform Before Four Area High Schools

The 21st Gamma Phi Circus, its three big on-campus performances behind it, is preparing for the road trip on March 29.

High schools in Sidell, Mendota, and Lexington and Elmwood School will be included in this year's tour of the show which, except for the war years, has been held continuously since 1930 under the auspices of the only college gymnastic fraternity in the United States.

Women Receive Equal Rights
Organized by Dr. C. E. Horton in 1928, Gamma Phi was originally an all-male organization. However, in 1941 the war took so many of its male performers that women were allowed to join.

The circus troupe includes both members and pledges. Pledging is simple. Anyone interested can begin working out on apparatus for the first three weeks at the beginning of the year. If, at the end of this period, the person decides he wants to become a member, he becomes a pledge and remains so for the rest of the year.

However, to qualify for membership, he has to become a part of the circus troupe. A pledge night and a formal initiation ceremony are conducted in May. All who thus become members always remain so, whether or not they stay active. At present, the active members number about 80.

Oh, Their Aching Backs
Hard work is the secret of success in the circus. Performers practice every Monday night, usually for at least 90 minutes. January marks the beginning oi actual circus practices, which are held on Mondays and also on Sunday afternoons.

Requests for performances come annually from many high schools. From these, the group decides which ones to accept Each school so favored must agree to provide two meals for the troupe and pay all traveling expenses. A truck carries the equipment, all of which is portable, while three buses transport the performers and circus' band members.

Profits Form Scholarship Fund
The circus is essentially a nonprofit affair. Returns from its several
performances usually go to a benefit of some sort promoted by the
host school. Any money that is received for a performance goes in a
special Gamma Phi scholarship fund. At present the group gives two
scholarships annually.

Officers are Pat Patterson, senior from Fithian, president; Ron
Tinsley, junior from Pontiac, vice-president; Ardene White, junior
from Waukegan, secretary; and Margaret Menne, junior from
Canton, treasurer.

Dr. Arley Gillett is the present sponsor of Gamma Phi, and Mrs.
Gillett is circus costume supervisor. For many years both Dr. and
Mrs. Gillett and their two children, Arlene and Jay, performed in the
circus. Today, however, all four have withdrawn to the sidelines.

July 10, 1957 (page 4)
Truex, Harris Join ISNU PE Staff

...

Truex hails from Bloomington,
Indiana, where he has just
finished work on his Master's
Degree. He also did his
undergraduate work at Indiana
University. Truex will teach PE
classes, specializing in
gymnastics, and assist Dr. Arley
Gillette with Gamma Phi and
other activities. In the event that
ISNU puts gymnastics on a
competitive intercollegiate
basis, Truex will be the coach.

Wayne Truex

Clarence (Pat) Patterson, graduate student from Fithian, and winner of the Redbird Award, is being congratulated by ISNU President Robert Bone. Patterson was notified of the honor at the "N" Club dinner-dance last spring. He was a diver on the Normal swimming team for the past three seasons and was also active in the various Gamma Phi productions. The award is given annually to the athlete with good scholastic as well as athletic prowess.

Vidette July 31, 1957 (page 5)

1957 – 58 School Year

Ron Tinsley becomes the first African-American President of Gamma Phi.

Wayne Truex becomes Assistant Director, a position he holds until 1965, after which he becomes the third Gamma Phi Director

When Normalites think of the color of the circus big-top, they immediately look forward to the annual Gamma Phi circus. Each Monday throughout the year both experienced performers and pledges of this gymnastic fraternity work out on all sorts of flying ladders, roller skates, and balance beams. Members of the circus troop then choose one or two pieces of apparatus for their special efforts. The polished circus success is their ultimate satisfaction.

Gamma Phi

Informal attire sets the mood for the Monday night workout of Gamma Phi officers, Ardene White, June Alberty, Dody Chandler, Coach Wayne Truex, Dale Montgomery, John Hinds, Ron Tinsley, and Sponsor Arley Gillett.

1958 Index (page 96)

A Circus in the Paper

Gamma Phi Orients Pledges, Concentrates On Homecoming

Gamma Phi, honorary gymnastic fraternity, has selected Monday, September 30, as pledge night for those interested in joining the organization.

During this pledge night, which begins at 7 p.m. in McCormick Gymnasium, the pledges will be assigned groups and group leaders, and for each consecutive meeting they will be required to report to their group leader.

A committee to plan Homecoming activities has been chosen with Chuck Odell, junior from Galesburg, and Dale Montgomery. junior from Washington, as co-chairmen.

Others on the committee are:
June Alberty, junior from Rockford; Barbara Nickoley, junior from Libertyville; Sheila Pitchford, junior from Danville; Marge Menne, senior from Canton; Hank Nowers, senior from Annawan; Janet Feirn, sophomore from Rock Island; Gladys Goodhart, sophomore from Cordova; John Lowey, junior from Bradley; and Irene Pagel, sophomore from Evanston.

At the first meeting last Monday night, Ron Tinsley, this year's president, gave the prospective pledges the requirements for membership. Arley Gillett, the sponsor, gave a brief history of Gamma Phi at ISNU and introduced to the group Wayne Truex, a new assistant.

Other officers for this year are: vice-president, Dale Montgomery; secretary, Ardene White, senior from Waukegan; treasurer, Dodie Chandler, junior from Kankakee; social chairmen, John Hinds, junior from Maywood, and June Alberty.

Oct 17, 1957 (page 4)
Gamma Phi . . .

Gamma Phi, honorary gymnastics fraternity, in cooperation with the "N" Club, will sponsor a coffee hour for alumni and other Homecoming visitors beginning at 10:30 a.m. in the Federal "O" Building.

Gamma Phi members volunteering their services to serve coffee and donuts at the reception are John Hinds, junior from Maywood; Sheila Pitchford, junior from Danville; Dick Walker, sophomore from Highland Park; and Leo Desch, sophomore from Riverton.

Work on the Homecoming float began Monday afternoon and will continue every night this week. President Ron Tinsley urges members and pledges to help with the float whenever possible; the float is being kept at the Normal Sanitary Dairy.

Any student wishing to pledge Gamma Phi may still do so. Meetings are held every Monday night at 7 p.m. in McCormick Gymnasium.

Oct 23, 1957 (page 3)
Homecoming...

...
Innumerable breakfasts, receptions and coffee hours kept the hours busy Saturday, in between the parade, game, and dance. Women's League walked away with first prize in the parade float judging. It was followed by Lowell Mason and Gamma Phi contributions. According to authority, "The floats were better than ever this year," which made the judging most difficult.

Oct 30, 1957 (page 6)
Mr. Truex, one of Gamma Phi sponsors, reports men are needed to participate in the gymnastic circus. Any male interested should contact Mr. Truex or Dr. Arley Gillett in McCormick Gymnasium.

Oct 30, 1957 (page 7)

Rules For Gamma Phi

President Ron Tinsley announces that Gamma Phi pledges are to be at practice by 7 each Monday evening in the gymnasium and must report to their assigned pledge squad leaders for attendance and warm-up exercises.

Pledge squad leaders are seniors, Mary Lynn Brown from Eureka, Marg Menne from Canton, Leo Benson from Zion, Nola Crotchet from Kankakee, and Ron Tinsley from Pontiac.

Other leaders include juniors, Dale Montgomery from Washington, Dodie Chandler from Kankakee, Chuck O'Dell from Galesburg, and sophomores, Gladys Goodhart from Cordova and Dick Walker from Highland Park.

Pledge workouts are from 7 to 8 and members work out from 8 to 9 p.m.

Dec 11, 1957 (page 5)

Gymnasts' Party Includes Caroling, Games, Dancing

"They're gonna dance, they're gonna sing, they're gonna make the rafters ring" at the Gamma Phi Christmas party where there will be caroling, balloon dances, the hokey pokey, and social dancing.

This informal party for members, pledges, and their guests will begin at 7 p.m. Monday, December 16, in the Student Union Ballroom.

In charge of the party are John Hinds, June Alberty, Marg Menne, Mary Carney, John Lowry, and Sheila Pitchford.

Five Gamma Phi members — Ron Tinsley, Dick Walker, Dale Montgomery, Pat Grant, and Will Nunnally — participated in an open gymnastic meet at Indianapolis Saturday, Dec. 7. Coach Wayne Truex furnished the transportation.

Dec 18, 1957 (page 6)

Truex, Five Men Attend Open Gymnastic Meet

Coach Wayne Truex, assistant adviser of Gamma Phi, took five of his men to an open gymnastic meet at the Indianapolis Athenaeum Turners Gymnasium last Saturday.

ISNU's representatives included Pat Grant, Dale Montgomery, Dick Walker, Ron Tinsley, and Will Nunnally. Four of the five men competed in the meet which included teams from Canada, Ohio, Indiana, Michigan and Illinois. Ron Tinsley gained Normal's only honor by copping a fourth place on the high bar.

Jan 15, 1958 (page 5)

Gamma Phi Journeys To Champaign; Views Gymnasts of Germany

A trip to the University of Illinois Thursday, January 16, will provide an opportunity for Gamma Phi members to view outstanding feats performed by the West Germany Gymnastic team, which has been touring the United States.

Assistant Coach Wayne Truex and sponsors Mr. and Mrs. Arley Gillett will accompany the group who will leave by bus late that afternoon.

Tryouts for the spring circus were held Sunday afternoon at 1:30 and Monday evening at 7. The circus squad will now be practicing on Sunday afternoons as well as on Monday nights.

Feb 12, 1958 (page 5)

Gymnasts Travel To Minonk
Dr. Gillett To Speak Before PTA Meeting

Tumblers Ron Tinsley and Will Nunnally and trampoline artists Pat Grant, Dale Montgomery, and Jay Gillett will travel to Minonk tomorrow to perform at 7:30 pan. for a TTA meeting at the Minonk Grade School.

Gamma Phi sponsor, Dr. Arley Gillett, will speak at this meeting on
"Elementary School Physical Education."

With circus time one month away, queen committee chairman
Sandra Nardin has asked each campus organization to select one of
their members as a queen candidate. She plans to inform them as to
when the petitions are due and when the election will be held.

Other committee chairmen are Dick Walker, program; Dale
Montgomery, tickets; Gladys Goodhart, publicity; Sheila Pitchford,
costumes; Hank Nowers, decorations; Ardene White, music and
arrangements; and Russ Fitzgerald, equipment.

Feb 12, 1958 (page 6)
Gymnastic Coach Wayne Truex would like it announced that Gamma
Phi will put on its annual gymnastic circus March 13, 14, 15 in
McCormick gym. The gymnasts have been working intensively every
Sunday afternoon and Monday evening in preparation for the circus.
This year's attraction should be better than ever with Coaches
Gillett and Truex working together.

Feb 19, 1958 (page 5)
Circus Searches For Queen
Gymnasts Perform In Half-Time Shows
Queen chairman Sandra Nardin announces that petitions for Gamma
Phi queen candidates must be turned in to her by February 27 at Fell
Hall, box 135. Elections will be held March 5.

This year each candidate will provide her own pictures for publicity
and Gamma Phi will take charge of arranging and exhibiting
posters.

WL Readies Midway For Carnival

Roscoe Spechts looks unworried at attempts of Terry Flatt, Jim Crotchett, and Bill Wilson to fire a lethal-looking cannon at him. The four will perform their capers at the annual Women's League Carnival March 8. A fifth clown, John Lowry, is not pictured but will also be among those cavorting at the event.

Feb 19, 1958 (page 8)

Two weeks from Saturday, March 8, is the date for Carnival Night. The carnival, annually sponsored by Women's League, will put down stakes and open its booths at 8:30 that night and pack up at 11:30.

...

Gamma Phi, whose circus will be held the week following the Carnival, will supply five clowns for the evening. The five include Terry Flatt, sophomore in agriculture; John Lowry, Junior in business; Bill Wilson, sophomore in English; Jim Crotchett, freshman in health and physical education; and Roscoe Specht, freshman in health and physical education.

...

289   A Circus in the Paper

Gamma Phi Pounds Stakes For March 13 Opening Date

If you've never seen a trick bicycle in action, you won't want to miss opening night of Gamma Phi circus two weeks from tomorrow night. This unique vehicle will be used with the three unicycles to produce "something new and different" in circus acts.

Creating this new act are June Alberty, Barb Nickoley, June Crowell, Jan Welsh, Carol DeRocker, Jim Forneris, and Neil Rine, who met with Arley Gillett for extra practice last week in Metcalf Gymnasium.

Sandra Nardin, queen chairman, requests that all campus organizations turn in their queen nominations to her in Fell Hall, box 135, by tomorrow. Candidates will be notified of the time and place for a group picture.

"The Whirlos," this year's roller skating act, will highlight half-time at the Wesleyan-Normal game tonight in McCormick Gymnasium. Composed of Mary Carney, Lanida Jacobs, Judy Damotte, Marg Swalec, Russ Fitzgerald, and Duane Hughes, "The Whirlos" will give a sneak-preview of their act.

With the greatest of ease . . .

Tumblers Will Nunnally, Ron Tinsley, Pat Grant, Chuck O'Dell, Paul Purnell, Jan Greenwald, Roylene Gruever, Joann Ford, and Sue Wolfinbarger will demonstrate their agility during halftime at the Western-Normal game held on the home court Friday, February 28.

Dr. and Mrs. Gillett, sponsors, and coach Wayne Truex Journeyed to Chicago last Friday for new circus costumes. They selected leotards, special costumes, sequins, feathers, and other trimmings for the costumes from such clothing stores as Leo's and Lester's.

Mar 5, 1958 (page 8)

Gamma Phi's 3-Night Stand Brings Set of New Gymnastic Troupe Arts

March 13, 14, and 15 at 8 p.m. in McCormick Gymnasium will be Gamma Phi's three-night stand to show the results of a year's work in gymnastics. Arley Gillett and coach Wayne Truex have worked diligently with the members to comprise many new acts for the 1958 circus.

"Salute to the Fire Gods" is one of the new acts, with Marilyn Weith dancing Indian style with a hoop of fire. Accompanied by Sandra Nardin and Ann Rehn, who will twirl flaming batons, this group will add a dangerously exciting and fiery bit to this year's performance.

Another new act is the revolving ladder featuring John Hinds and Dale Montgomery, who will take opposite ends to perform such intricate feats as shoulder stands while balancing. This act is being used for the first time in several years.

"THE BIG WHEEL," one of the new circus acts, will feature Clarabel Sarff and Bernie Shumaker, who will be fastened onto each wheel and revolve with breath-taking speed. This apparatus is an invention of one of Barnum & Bailey's old-time performances.

291   A Circus in the Paper

A swinging perch pole will show timing and precision at its height when Bob O'Dell and Gladys Goodhart combine efforts to produce a web routine in unison on this flying apparatus.

Mass free exercise will be demonstrated for the first time at ISNU when "Gymnasts in Rhythm," composed of a selected group of the circus troupe, will unite tumbling feats with graceful ballet-like movements.

Mar 12, 1958 (front page)
Annual Gamma Phi Show Opens Tomorrow
Gymnasts Provide Thrills at Circus
By GLADYS GOODHART
Circus thrills and chills will raise the roof in McCormick Gymnasium tomorrow night when Gamma Phi's troupe invades for a three-night stand at 8 p.m. on March 13, 14, and 15.

One of the five girls selected last week will reign as queen during each night's performance. Those seeking the title are Sheila Anderson, nominated by University Club; Gert Haas, Student Council; Paulette Hase, Home Economics Club; Joey Hoffman Women's League and Elementary Club; and Judy Romary, N Club

The queen will be announced tomorrow night and will be escorted to her throne by Gamma Phi president Ron Tinsley.

With a troupe of over 50 performers, the 22nd Annual Gymnastic circus will open its hour-and-a-half-long show with the Cloud Swing, a high-flying act featuring Gladys Goodhart.

Alley-oop
Tumblers Nancy Carstensen, Jan Greenwald, JoAnn Ford, Roylene Gruever, Sue Wolfinbarger, Pat Grant, Will Nunnally, Ron Tinsley, Charles Odell, and Paul Purnell will put on an exhibition of hand-springs, back flips, and mid-air feats.

The Balancing Ball, one of this year's new attractions, require balance and coordination from DeVee DeRocker, whose entire act is done while rolling on the ball.

Even Parallel Bars and the Side Horse combine male and female talent when Carolyn Hanson, Renate Decker, Ron Tinsley, Will Nunnally, Tom Walthouse, and Dale Montgomery demonstrate their routine requiring strength and balance.

Look, Ma, No Hands
Swinging Ladders team consists of Clarabel Sarff, Dodie Chandler, Judy Darby, Joyce Sand, Norma Jones, and Sally Albright. "The Whirlos," a memorable act from last year, has a topnotch squad of roller skaters with Mary Carney, Lanida Jacobs, Judy Damotte, Duane Hughes, and Russell Fitzgerald.

Still and flying rings will feature Nola Crotchet, Gladys Goodhart, Ron Tinsley, and Dick Walker, who will combine strength and timing for dislocates, inlocates, shoulder stands and cut-offs.

Springing to Fame?
Trampoline artists Nancy Hancock, Gloria Kasznski, Irene Pagel, Dale Montgomery, and Pat Grant will provide on exhibition on one of a circus' favorite pieces of apparatus.

Flying through the air with the "greatest of ease" will be Nancy Peter, Donna Weller, John Hinds, and Leo Desch on the trapeze.

Tickets-for the circus may still be obtained at McCormick Gymnasium. Prices are 75 cents for adults and 25 cents for children.

Clowns Terry Flatt, John Lowey, Bill Wilson, Jimmy Crotchett, Roscoe Specht will add comedy with their antics. Don Blattner will serve as ringmaster.

Equipment men will be Henry Nowers, Dave Murphy, Phil Henebry, Paul Kronstead, and Roger Eckstein.

Seated left to right are the Gamma Phi Court contenders for the final crown: Gert Haas, Paulette Hase, Joey Hoffman, Sheila Anderson, and Judy Romary. Tomorrow night tells the tale!

Perched precariously on the bicycle of Neil Rine are left, June Alberty, and right, Jan Welch. Trick bike stunts are only a part of the many acts the Gamma Phi Circus offers.

Mar 19, 1958 (page 6)
RON'S ROUNDUP
...

Before closing the column, special praise should be acknowledged to the Gamma Phi group for the fine performance they displayed last weekend. Coaches Arley Gillett and Wayne Truex are to be congratulated along with all the performers who worked diligently all year long in preparation for this once-a-year affair.

Apr 16, 1958 (page 7)
Gamma Phi Hits Road; Performs Out of Town
Gamma Phi's circus squad will perform at Sidell High School 8 p.m. Friday. The troupe, accompanied by the circus band, will leave at 3 p.m. from McCormick Gymnasium.

Sponsor Dr. Arley Gillett and Coach Wayne Truex will leave earlier to set up equipment for the show. After the performance, the troupe and band will be treated to a dinner.

Last Friday evening the squad journeyed to Eureka for their first out-of-town performance.

Apr 30, 1958 (page 6)
The Gamma Phi performers returned from Warrensburg grade school Friday, having performed before a packed gymnasium of circus enthusiasts. Nothing has been mentioned about the troupe, who have been entertaining various grade and high schools with the ease and perfection of polished performers.

May 14, 1958 (page 6)
RON'S ROUNDUP
...

Gamma Phi also had an election of officers at their final meeting of the year. Dale Montgomery, junior in Social Science, was elected president of the gymnastic club; John Hinds, vice president; Joyce Sand, secretary; and Pat Grant, treasurer.

May 28, 1958 (page 11)

Course Prepares Gymnasts

For those who are interested in learning gymnastic feats without joining the ISNU gymnastic team or Gamma Phi, the Physical Education Department is offering gymnastic course 111 next fall to both men and women.

This course consists of basic training on the trampoline, parallel bars, horizontal bar, side horse, rings, and in tumbling. It will be offered for the first nine weeks and is worth one half credit. No previous experience in gymnastics is necessary.

During the second nine weeks, course 112 will be given with more advanced training on the various apparatus. One half credit is gained from this course also. Course 111 is prerequisite.

Mr. Wayne Truex, ISNU's gymnastic coach, will teach 111 and 112, assisted by Ron Tinsley.

1958 – 59 School Year

First Row: *Lanida Jacobs, Judy DeMotte, Dixie DeRocker, Marilyn Weith*. Second Row: *Dr. Gillett, Sponsor; Leo Deneh, Joyce Saml, Secretary; Dale Montgomery, President; John Hinds, Vice-President; Nancy Petes, Pat Gcount, Treasurer; Mr. Teaea, Assistant Sponsor*. Third Row: *Will Nunnally, Ann Rehn, Sandra Nardin, Dodie Chavalier, Neil Rime, John Lowey, Carol DeRocker, Bern's Shumaker, Lucy Underwood, Paul Parnell.*

Sept 17, 1958 (page 3)
Gamma Phi . . .
For all those interested in joining Gamma Phi, honorary gymnastic fraternity, meetings are held at 7 p.m. each Monday in the men's gymnasium.

Some of the various acts included in Gamma Phi are rings tumbling, bicycling, roller skating, and bars.

Tryouts for the annual circus in the spring will not be held until December, but everyone who has a gymnastic talent or wishes to develop one is urged to attend the meetings.

Oct 1, 1958 (page 6)
Just a brief bit from Gamma Phi. Dr. Arley Gillett announces that the Gamma Phi organization, in cooperation with Women's Physical Education Club, will sponsor the Danish Olympic Gymnastics team here on November 22.

Gamma Phi Gymnasts Receive Letters

Thirteen members of the Gamma Phi gymnastics team were given white letters, a special recognition for seniors only. Those receiving the award were John Hinds, biology major, Maywood; Leo Desch, biological science major, Riverton; Nancy Peter, elementary major, Belleville; Joyce Sand, elementary major, Galesburg; Carol De-Rocker, health and physical education major, Coal Valley; rom Walthouse, health and physical education major, Normal; and Dale Montgomery, social science major, Washington.

Other recipients are Pat' Grant, health and physical education major, from Pekin; Dodie Chandler, elementary major, Kankakee; Neil Rine, business major, Normal; Bob O'Dell, physical science major, East St. Louis; June Alberty, elementary major, Rockford; and Barb Nickoley, special education major, Libertyville.

Danish Gymnasts Slate Performance

The Danish Gymnastic Team will perform in McCormick Gymnasium at 8 p.m., Friday, November 21.

Advance tickets for the show are now being sold in the lobby of McCormick Gym and will be on sale until November 14. Prices are 50 cents for grade and high school students and 75 cents for college students and adults.

Tickets will also be sold at the door on the night of the performance for 75 and 90 cents.

Gamma Phi, honorary gymnastics fraternity, and Women's Physical Education Club are the joint sponsors of the exhibition.

The two-hour long show given by these champion gymnasts will include costumed folk dances and rhythmical gymnastics as well as the type displayed by Gamma Phi.

Giving three and four performances each week and practicing in their spare hours have taken up most of the team's time since they arrived in the United States over two months ago.

The team has given performances all over the east coast. Their talents have been displayed in Chicago's Soldiers Field, in New York's Madison Square Garden, and on Ed Sullivan's television program.

Nov 19, 1958 (page 2)
Danish Gymnasts Demonstrate Techniques
Twenty-eight Danish gymnastic champions, touring the United States for the third time, will demonstrate their athletic abilities in McCormick Gymnasium, Friday at 8 p.m.

Gamma Phi and the Women's Physical Education Club are sponsoring the two and one-half hour program which will feature fundamental gymnastics for men and women, dual tumbling, courtesy dances of olden days, Danish folk dances, apparatus and tumbling exercises, and other acts.

Tickets may be purchased at the door the evening of the performance: 75 cents for grade and high school students and 90 cents for college students and adults.

Members of the troupe are all amateurs. Many are gymnastics instructors and past Olympic champions. Their tour is designed to present the ultimate in Danish physical education to the people of America.

The Danish government is sponsoring the group on their tour.

Dec 3, 1958 (page 3)
Gamma Phi . . .
Gamma Phi, honorary gymnastic fraternity, will hold its annual Christmas party December 8, in the Student Union from 7:30 to 9:30 p.m.

Social chairmen for the event are Leo Desch, Riverton junior in biological science, and Nancy Peter, Belleville senior in elementary.

Feb 1, 1959 (page 9)
Gamma Phi Announces 1959 Queen Contest

June Alberty, chairman of the Queen committee of Gamma Phi Circus, announces that letters have been sent to the various organizations on campus asking them to nominate an entry for the Queen contest.

A campus-wide election will be held the week before the Circus to determine who will reign as Queen Friday and Saturday, March 13 and 14.

June also said that the circus squad has been chosen. Individuals have tried out for the event that most interests them, and all are busy working up their acts at the regular meeting on Monday evenings and the special Sunday afternoon sessions.

Feb 25, 1959 (page 3)
'59 Gamma Phi Circus Comes To McCormick Gym March 12
17-Act Show Sees New Students Added

McCormick gymnasium will serve as the "big top" March 12, 13, and 14, for the Gamma Phi Circus. The opening parade will commence at 8 p.m.

Voting for the Queen will take place in the gym Wednesday, March 4. Joyce Sand, publicity chairman, said "Voting is open to all ISNU students upon presentation of activity tickets."

The various committee chairmen have been announced. Joyce Sand, senior from Galesburg, is publicity chairman. Joyce Peter, senior from Belleville, is in charge of costumes.

Other chairmen are: John Hinds, senior in biology, decorations Jan Miller, freshman from Stanford, programs; Russel Fitzgerald, mailing service supervisor, equipment; Marilyn Weith, junior from Elmhurst, tickets; and June Alberty, senior from Rockford, queen committee.

Devee DeRocker, sophomore from Downey, is in charge of music and musical arrangements.

New equipment has been purchased this year to add new acts and thrills to the circus. Among the new acts will be a trick bicycle act, a high trapeze act, and vaulting. Acrobatic dancing will also be featured in the 17-act 1959 Gamma Phi Circus.

ONE WILL BE CROWNED . . .

Pictured above are eleven of the candidates for 1959 Gamma Phi Queen. Standing are Armstrong, Carmichael, E. Lindsey, S. Lindsey, Roby, and Matsuda. Seated are Moore, Douglas, Buckman, Murphy, and Woodyah. Several candidates are not pictured.

Vidette Mar 4, 1959 (page 8)

Select Gamma Phi Queen Friday
Candidates Vie For Title When Polls Open At Schroeder, Union

Friday, March 6, at 8 a.m. marks the opening time of the polls for electing Queen of the Gamma Phi Circus. Election booths will be available in Schroeder Hall and the Student Union Building and will be open from 8 a.m. to 4 p.m. with the exception of lunch hour, during which time they will be closed.

This is an "all-campus election" with voting privileges being given to all ISNU students upon presentation of their activity tickets. Photographic displays of the candidates can be found on posters located in McCormick Gymnasium, Student Union Building, Schroeder Hall, the Co-op, and possibly in the dormitories.

This year's list of candidates seeking the queenhood include five sophomores, five juniors, and two seniors. Sophomore candidates are as follows: Kay Woodyah, elementary major from Sterling; Sally Buckley, a business major; Marilyn Armstrong, home economics major from Clinton; special education major, Sheryl Lessen from Lincoln; and health and physical education major, Judy Jackson from Lake Forest.

Junior candidates include Sally Roby, mathematics major from Brookfield; elementary major Carol Moore from Robinson; special education major Lois Buckman; Doris Carmichael, Decatur elementary major; and Joanne Cottingham, health and physical education major from Elm Grove, Wisconsin. The two remaining candidates are seniors Sandy O'Brien and Kay Murphy, both special education majors from Canton.

The queen and her court of four will be presented just prior to the opening of the Gamma Phi Circus and will reign throughout its duration. June Alberty, chairman of the queen committee, urges everyone to use his voting privileges to help elect a queen.

Big Top Goes Up For Circus; 50 Performers Head Yearly Show

By MARTHA CHILDERS

Thrills, with sighs of breathtaking fascination, will sweep over McCormick Gymnasium this Thursday, Friday and Saturday as Gamma Phi stages its twenty-third annual circus.

Presenting over 50 performers in a fast-moving program, the gymnasts will be accompanied by the 36-piece ISNU Circus Band under the direction of Arden L. Vance, assistant professor of music.

Preceding the performances will be the presentation of the Gamma Phi Queen and her court, who will then reign for the duration of the program.

Making up the court, one of whom will be crowned Queen, are Doris Carmichael, Decatur junior in elementary; Jo Cottingham, Elm Grove junior in health and physical education; Karlene Douglass, Le Roy sophomore in home economics; Elmarie Lindsey, Ottawa junior in English; and Carol Moore, Robinson junior in elementary.

The circus will present a variety of performances. Providing the evening with a real-time circus atmosphere will be trampoline, trapeze, swinging ladder and perch pole acts, as well as exhibitions on revolving ladders, balance beams, and parallel bars.

On the swinging ladders will be Dodie Chandler, Maty Doenitz, Joyce Sand, Jan Miller, and Judy Boaden.

Adding a light touch to the performances will be the Acrobatic Dance with Janice Howarter, Jan Moberg and Bessie Bourn, and the Trampoline with Pat Grant, Dale Montgomery, and Patricia Werner.

Exhibiting great skill and ease, Nancy Peter, Mary Anderson and John Hinds will perform on the Flying Trapeze. Tom Walthouse, Pat Grant, and Bob Stoner will perform on the Horizontal Bar, followed by Jacinta Lyon, Joyce Sand, and Lucy Underwood doing the Spanish Webs.

Two other performances featured in the program will be "The Whirlo's" by Judy Damotte, Duane Hughes, and Russ Fitzgerald, and Marilyn Weith, Sandra Nardin and Ann Rehn doing fire dancing and twirling.

Clowns John Lowey, Jim Hopp, Dave Murphy, Jim Topliff and Dave Sigler will add a note of comedy to the circus.

Tickets, priced 75 cents for adults and 25 cents for children, will be on sale from 8 a.m. to 4 p.m. through this Friday. All tickets will be for reserved seats.

Performances are scheduled to begin at 8 p.m. each night of the circus.

Tickets Sold at Door

Mar 11, 1959 (page 4)
Dance Will Climax Annual Gamma Phi Circus Production
"Big-Top Bounce" is the name given to the record dance to be held in the Student Union Ballroom after the Gamma Phi Circus Friday, March 13.

The dance, which is sponsored by the Student Union Board, will get under way at 8:30 and will end at 11:30. Price of admission is 50 cents per couple or 35 cents stag.

According to Pat Florent, Student Union Board dance chairman, a special feature of the "Big-Top Bounce" will be a dance contest which will include the cha-cha, jitterbug, and fox trot. The three co-chairmen of the dance are Bonnie Carpenter, freshman in elementary from Waukegan.

Doris Carmichael, Decatur elementary junior, is shown as she reigned last weekend as Queen of the Gamma Phi Circus. Her escort is Gamma Phi president Dale Montgomery, social science senior from Washington.

Apr 22, 1959 (page 8)
Students, Faculty Select Four Stunts For Annual University Club Show
Officers, Chairmen Work With New Members To Plan '59 - '60 Program, Schedule Stunts submitted by Barton Hall, Fell Hall, Jesters, and Gamma Phi have been chosen by the University Club Stunt Show Committee for the Stunt Show May 1.

The acts, which were selected on the basis of originality, cleverness, smoothness of production, and appropriateness of staging and costume, are based on campus situations.

Apr 29, 1959 (page 4)
Gamma Phi To Hold Election
Monday, May 4, Gamma Phi members will elect their next year's officers. The meeting will be held at 8 p.m. in McCormick Gymnasium.

1959 – 60 School Year

First Row: Bess Desch, Dever DeRocker, Louise Manelia, Jan Miller. Second Row: Dr. Arley Gillett, Sponsor; Marilyn Weith, Secretary; Leo Desch, Vice-president; John Hinds, President; Bernie Schumaker, Treasurer; Lucy Underwood, Social chairman; Mr. Wayne Truex, Assistant sponsor. Third Row: Arlene Sabador, Ann Rehn, Mary Anderson, Mary Doenitz, Murray Rounds, Beatrice Urquiza, Jan Moberg, Jan Howater, Sharon Schillinger, Martha Staab.

1960 Index (page 55)

Sept 20, 1959 (page 4)
Gamma Phi Needs Pledges; Starts Homecoming Project

Gamma Phi members will be busy working on the Homecoming float for the next several weeks at McCormick gym Monday nights from 7 to 9 p.m. Pledge applications are still available for students interested in becoming members.

Serving as officers this year are John Hinds, president, from Maywood; Leo Desch, vice-president, from Normal; Marilyn Weith, secretary from Elmhurst; Bernie Shumacker, treasurer from Arlington Heights; and Lucy Underwood, social chairman from Kewanee, all who were elected last spring.

Sponsors are Dr. Arley Gillett, associate professor of health and physical education, assisted by Mrs. Gillett, in charge of costumes, and Mr. Wayne Truex, instructor of health and physical education.

A Circus in the Paper

Oct 21, 1959 (page 5)

Gamma Phi Plans Open House

Gamma Phi's open house for alumni will be held in the intra mural building immediately following the Homecoming parade.

At the Gamma Phi meeting October 5, president John Hinds presented the Gamma Phi emblem to senior members. Those who received the emblem were: Judy Damotte, Renate Decker, Leo Desch, Carolyn Hanson, Jim Hopp, Lanida Jacobs, Dave Murphy, Sandy Nardin, Ann Rehn, Diane Rothenberg, Bob Stoner, Jim Topliff, Lucy Underwood, and Marilyn Weith.

Oct 21, 1959 (page 7)

STEP RIGHT UP LADIES, GENTS ...

Big Top Comes To Campus Library
By Bev Borovausky

The Big Top has come to ISNU! A rare collection of circus materials consisting of books, circus magazines, newspaper clippings, as well as many photographs and camera shots of circus personalities, route books, souvenir programs, letters and posters is now being assembled at Milner Library.

Many of the items have been gifts to the library from famous circus performers who originated acts from our twin-sister city, Bloomington.

They include such teams as the Great Russian Athletics, the Fisher Brothers, and the Fly Thrillers.

Some of the contributing personalities are Mrs. Clyde Nobk, known as La Petite Emile, her husband, Arnold Riegger, formerly a member of a flying act, and Harold Ramage, a member of the Circus Fans Association.

"It was in Bloomington," said Dr. Hertel, new director of libraries, "that many circus aerialists practiced their flying acts in the old Ward Barn and the Bloomington YMCA during their winter stay."

These performances, needless to say, attracted many crowds of youngsters who had never before seen a circus. Many of these youths caught the familiar feeling of sawdust and spangles and they began to organize their own acts.

Much Data
Some of the more important items in the rare collection are the circus poster showing the five Ringling Brothers, Barnum and Bailey, the Blue Book showing pictures and giving information of the important people in the Circus, and the recent contributions of John A. Anderson, now living in Bloomington and better known as veteran acrobatic clown, Art Monette.

"Mr. Anderson is one of many retired performers living in the Bloomington areas," commented Dr. Hertel. "Another famous circus man Mr. Bert Doss, and his wife Agnes, who now own the Circus Roller Rink in Bloomington, were at one time two members of the Flying Wards."

Available to the Interested Some of the books in the collection have been placed on the stacks and may be checked out; other items are available for research purposes only. All materials in the collection will be kept in fireproof storage until arranged for permanent exhibition.

The library believes this collection will also expand the widespread interest in Gamma Phi, the University organization which annually produces a superior amateur circus and gives the performers ideas of the types of costumes and acts used some fifty-five years ago.

Oct 28, 1959 (page 8)
Queen Sharon Palmer Reigns At Weekend's Homecoming Activities
The 1959 Homecoming Queen at Illinois State Normal University is Sharon Palmer."
...
The new queen is a senior elementary major from Clinton. A resident of Barton Hall, Miss Palmer is an "A" squad cheerleader and a

Gamma Phi pledge. She was previously a member of the physical education club.

Nov 11, 1959 (page 4)
Gamma Phi Holds Tryouts
Preliminary tryouts for Gamma Phi pledge applicants are scheduled for November 15, from 2 to 4 p.m. and November 16, from 7 to 9 p.m. The purpose of the tryouts is to select a basic circus troupe. Individual act tryouts will be in January.

Dec 2, 1959 (page 3)
Gamma Phi Has Tryouts; Plans Workout Period, Annual Christmas Party
On November 15 and 16, Gamma Phi held tryouts for its selection of a tentative circus squad. Thirty out of sixty-nine were accepted as tentative pledges.

Those chosen are:
Diane Alt, Marilyn Armstrong, Nancy Bair, Bill Ballister, John Baltes, Dean Behnke, Janet Buxton, Kay Chapman, Jack Dearth, Bill FranCoeur, David Frye, Louise Glass, Darrell Harvey, William Hunt, Phyllis Hunt; Sandi Kinney, Martha Klinefelter, Carl Larson, Allan Martling, Karen Nally, Janet Nardin, Sharon Peters, Ron Rake, Sandra Rapps, Janice Severns, Evelyn Solberg, George Solomon, Marijane Unsicker, Darlene Westman, and Jerry Wright.

The annual Christmas party will be held on December 14 after a workout period in McCormick gym. The party will be closed to all but members and pledges.

Jan 20, 1960 (page 4)
Gamma Phi
There will be no practice on January 25, due to the basketball tournament. Tryouts - for the Gamma Phi circus squad were held Sunday, January 17, from 1:30 to 3 and Monday, January 18, from 7 to 9 in McCormick gym.

Feb 17, 1960 (page 4)
Gamma Phi. . .
Gamma Phi members are in demand!

Small groups of performers will be entertaining in the Bloomington area this month.

On February 23, performers will go to the Washington School in Bloomington. Another group will be entertaining at the annual Banquet of the Fraternal Organization of Bloomington on February 29.

Mar 2, 1960 (page 4)
Gamma Phi Stages Circus March 17,18,19
McCormick Gymnasium will soon be turned into a circus arena when members of Gamma Phi stage their 24th annual gymnastic Circus on March 17, 18, and 19.

Tickets for the three 8:00 p.m. performances will go on sale March 11, in the lobby of McCormick Gymnasium. All seats will be reserved.

Nineteen acts will be included in this year's billing. Arden Vance, directing the circus band, and a multitude of clowns will round out the fabulous show.

The performances, under the supervision of Dr. Arley Gillet and Wayne Truex, will feature both old and new faces, and old and new acts. Tumbling, trapeze routines, bicycles, trampoline, and vaulting will be featured.

Highlighting this year's circus of 1960 will be five new acts. These include a cloud swing exhibition by Nancy Bair and Darlene Westman, and a swing perch pole act by Janet Nardin, Judy Boaden, Arlene Sabador, Darlene Westman, Jan Howarter, and Mary Doenitz.

A Circus in the Paper

Two other new acts feature Dave Frye, Bill Hunt, Phyllis Hunt, am Janet Buxton juggling, rope twirling, and whip lashing.

The fifth act is a graceful display of coordination on the uneven parallel bars by Sharon Schillinger, Martha Staab, Lucy Underwood, DeVee DeRocker, and Diane Alt.

The entire circus troupe will combine efforts and talents to produce a grand finale comprised of intricate pyramid.

Mar 9, 1960 (front page)
Carnival Night Arrives on Saturday; Booths Represent 28 Organizations
...
Adding to entertainment will be the music of the Blackfriar's German band, and the antics of Gamma Phi clowns.
...

Martha Klinefelter and Al Martling as they will appear in the forthcoming Gamma Phi Circus at ISNU on March 17, 18, 19.

Vidette Mar 9, 1960 (page 5)

Mar 16, 1960 (front page)

Gamma Phi Presents Circus in McCormick

With circus time only one night away, members of Gamma Phi are busy putting finishing touches to their 24th annual circus.

The program will be staged in McCormick Gym this Thursday, Friday, and Saturday beginning at 8 p.m.

All seats are reserved. Tickets are on sale in the lobby of McCormick Gym from 8:00 a.m. to 4:00 p.m. Ticket prices are 75 cents for adults on Thursday night and $1 for Friday and Saturday. Children's tickets are 25 cents for every performance.

BIG TOP TIME . . .

Diane Alt, DeVee DeRocker, and Sharon Schillinger display their balancing skill as they practice for the Gamma Phi Circus that opens tomorrow night.

Vidette Mar 16, 1960 (front page)

The performances will begin this year when Sandy Nardin and Ann Rehn, twirling their batons, salute the 1960 Queen and her court. Following will be the cloud swing, which was last performed three years ago by Gladys Goodheart, now featuring Nancy Bair and Darlene Westman on alternating nights.

Other acts will include trapeze and ring thrills, poise on the balance beam, skill on the trampoline and sidehorse, beauty on the webs, and agility in tumbling routines. The popular vaulting routine from last year's show will also be repeated again this year.

What would any circus, including the Gamma Phi Circus, be without clowns? This year Dave Murphy. Dave Sigler, Carl Larson, Jim Topliff, and Darrell Harvey will furnish laughs for everyone from one to one-hundred. Leo Desch will serve as ringmaster.

Before the performance begins on Thursday night, the Gamma Ph: Queen will be crowned. Her identity will be kept a secret until then The five hopefuls from Iasi week's election will know just before show time. They are Jeanne Litton, sponsored by Industrial Art Club; Carolyn Mitchell, sponsored by Home Economics Club; Judy Nordberg, sponsored by the Women's League; Sharon Reedy, sponsored by Newman Club; and Zorine Teofan, sponsored by Orchesis.

(Note: The Circus Queen elections did have some issues going back into the 1930's. In 1938, Gamma Phi actually removed the Queen portion of the circus because of a controversy in 1937.)

Mar 16, 1960 (page 2)
Campus Elections, Student Senate Actions Attract Interest
Madam Editor:
We should like to know if there are any academic standards governing the candidates for campus elections We had assumed that a C average was required for such candidates. If this is the case, we should like to make known the fact that one of the outstandingly publicized candidates in the recent Gamma Phi election is on probation with an average 13-14 honor points below a C.

If our assumptions are correct, we hope that this situation will be corrected either for this current election or for future elections. If we are mistaken, we should like a small notice in the Vidette to the effect that there are no specific academic qualifications for such elections.

Interested Voters
...

Dear Editor,
I'm fed up—along with plenty of other people around here. This Gamma Phi election has finally been the "straw that broke the camel's back."

Elections around here are about as fixed as they can get. Any candidate favored by Nelson Smith and his crew seems to feel that certain rules can be broken to her advantage. To cite a brief example: The candidates for Gamma Phi Queen were explicitly told that the only publicity allowed were the six posters made by the Queen's committee. Twenty-one of the candidates observed these rules. One candidate took it upon herself to have signs made to be worn, hung, and strewn all over the campus. This is fair??????

This isn't the first time that this has happened. Mr. Smith has used "our" money and "our" publicity office to back certain candidates in other elections. (In fact, two major elections this year!)

Something should be done IMMEDIATELY!

Sincerely, Sally Shorthair

...

Dear Editor,
Was there only one club who cared enough to back their candidate in the Gamma Phi Election?

To those who don't know the facts, this was the way it appeared.

At a meeting previous to the election, each of the twenty-two candidates was told by the head of the Queen committee that absolutely no publicity was to be used.

The Industrial Arts club, however, took special privileges in erecting a wheel of revolving pictures of their candidate. Where did the pictures come from? The ISNU Publicity office made up many pictures and distributed them around the campus to Dunn Hall mailboxes and to other areas via the Industrial Arts candidate and the publicity office.

315   A Circus in the Paper

Other candidates would have had posters made and pictures distributed if it were possible and according to the rules.

Should candidates be allowed to remain on the Queen Court if this poor sportsmanship is discovered? Evidently so, because this matter was taken to authorities in charge and ignored. Why even set up rules if they can be violated with a smile?
Fair Play

Mar 23, 1960 (page 2)
Election. Outstanding Senior Selection Retain Limelight
Dear Sally Shorthair, Fair Play, and other interested persons,
Concerning your trite letters to the editor in last week's Vidette, the Industrial Arts Club sponsored the candidate—not Mr. Nelson Smith or the candidate herself. If there are any derogatory remarks to be made, they should be submitted to the sponsor of the candidate, the Industrial Arts Club. The club takes full responsibility for all or any part of the campaign.

Our committee in charge of publicity for the queen election went to the sponsor of Gamma Phi before any plans were made for the campaign. They asked him if additional publicity would be permissible and ethical. He replied that publicity rules for the campaign were very vague. The letter received by the Industrial Arts Club stated: "Please send your nomination accompanied by 6 wallet size pictures that we will use for publicity purposes . . . Since Gamma Phi will exhibit several posters of all candidates we are requesting that individual posters be eliminated." As for other publicity, nothing was mentioned to the club or its candidate.

What is the purpose of campus organizations sponsoring queen candidates if they cannot give them every possible support within their power?

Regarding Mr. Smith using your money and your publicity office to back the candidate, this is a complete falsehood. In the first place, the Industrial Arts Club is financially stable and has absorbed all financial expenditures for the campaign. Also, the original prints of our candidate were for use by the University for publicity purposes. The pictures used in the campaign were printed by members of the Industrial Arts Club in their free time on paper paid for by the club. The proofs obtained from Mr. Smith were not originally taken in anticipation of promoting our queen candidate in the Gamma Phi contest. Distribution of pictures was done by the Industrial Arts Club and not by the candidate.

Concerning your letter (Sally Shorthair and Fair Play), we feel that before you write derogatory remarks to the Vidette editor, you should examine the "true" facts and then express your opinion. Your remarks give the feeling to us that your so-called "facts" were based on personal prejudice and a great deal of petty bickering. Seeking the "true" facts before writing such a letter should eliminate future unjust criticism due to a lack of understanding. Probably if the Industrial Arts Club had not publicized its candidate, the entire campaign would NOT have been known to many of the students on campus. We believe also that our campaigning actually helped the other candidates by bringing more attention to the election.

We would like to take this opportunity to express our sincere apologies to Jeanne Litton and Mr. Nelson Smith for the rudeness that they were subjected to due to this "misunderstanding," which appeared in last week's Vidette. All of these unjust, threadbare accusations should have been submitted to us rather than to the editor of the Vidette. If a person is going to write a letter to the editor of the Vidette containing derogatory remarks on personalities, they should at least have the decency to sign their own name to the article. If an individual or individuals are not willing to sign their name to a letter worthy of printing in the Vidette, then the reader must believe that something is going on that does not meet one's eye.

We hope that this letter will clear up some of the misunderstandings that have developed from the Industrial Arts Club's campaign for our candidate. As we stated before, please come and talk to one of our officers if you feel that our campaign was unethical, but please do not blame our candidate. The campaign was conducted by the Industrial Arts Club, NOT by our candidate.

Respectfully submitted, The Industrial Arts Club Ron Cumming
President

(Editor's note: The Vidette wishes to clear up a problem arising from letters that dealt with the Gamma Phi queen election of March 16. The paper wishes to clear Mr. Nelson Smith of the Publicity Department of the statements made by the authors of these letters. An incorrect assumption was made by the authors. The attack on the campus organization who backed the candidate involved in the controversy has also been dissolved and settled.)

May 18, 1960 (page 4)
GAMMA PHI . . .

Gamma Phi members elected their officers to serve for the 1960-61 school year. Skip Rounds, a health and physical education major from Rockford, will serve as president.

Others include Jerry Wright, industrial arts major from Farmington, vice president; Marty Staab, business major from Peoria, secretary; Bea Urquiza, business major from Kewanee, treasurer; and Carol Dueringer, home economics major, social chairman.

At a recent meeting, the pledges were officially activated.

May 25, 1960 (page 4)
Gamma Phi . . .

Gamma Phi will close their active year with a picnic at Lake-of-the Woods on May 29. The group will leave campus at 9 o'clock a.m., and return at approximately 5 o'clock p.m.

1960 – 61 School Year

GAMMA PHI—*Front Row:* Mr. Wayne Truex, adviser; Richard Walker, Martha Staab, secretary; Murray Rounds, president; Jerry Wright, vice-president, Carol Doeringer, social chairman; Devee DeRocker, Mr. Arley Gillett, adviser. *Second Row:* Gladys Goodhart, Marjorie Unseiker, Louise Masolia, Sharon Schillinger, Arlene Saboder, Evelyn Solberg, Marilyn Armstrong. *Back Row:* Sharon Peters, Mary Doenitz, Al Martling, Ron Bake, Dave Sigler, Diane Alt, Louise Glass. *Not Pictured:* Beatrice Urquiza, treasurer.

1961 Index (page 50)

Sept 21, 1960 (page 8)
Campus Graduates Perform In New "Teachers Of Tomorrow" Color Film

...

An English major, she served as literary editor of the INDEX, student yearbook. Her teaching at University High School as well as her "Fire-Dance" in the Gamma Phi Circus and counselling in a residence hall are all featured.

Feb 15, 1961 (page 4)

GAMMA PHI, gymnastics organization, will present its annual circus in McCormick Gymnasium on March 16, 17, and 18.

Following their presentation at ISNU, the group will appear in three off-campus locations in Illinois—Eureka, on April 7; Beardstown, on April 14; and Kewanee, on April 21.

Dr. Arley Gillett, associate professor of health and physical education, stated -that each organization on campus is allowed to sponsor one girl as its candidate for the GAMMA PHI Queen.

Petitions for queen candidates will be due February 28, and the election of the queen and her four attendants will be held on March 9.

Letters giving additional details are being sent to the various organizations.

Feb 22, 1961 (page 3)
Gillett Accepts Names
Petitions for GAMMA PHI circus queen are due by February 28. Dr. Arley Gillett, professor of health and physical education, will accept the petitions until 4 p.m.

A queen and her four attendants will be elected from the candidates on March 9. The name of the queen will not be disclosed until the opening night of the circus on March 16.

Mar 1, 1961 (page 8)
Gamma Phi Prepares Show
Gamma Phi's silver anniversary performance will be presented in McCormick Gymnasium March 16, 17, and 18 at 8 p.m.

The circus troupe of more than 50 performers, under the sponsorship of Dr. Arley Gillett, professor of health and physical education, will present their program to the accompaniment of the Circus Band which is directed by Mr. George Foeller, instructor in music.

Regular weekly practices' are held throughout the year, and in January tryouts were held for the selection of the circus squad. In addition to their performances on campus, the members of the circus squad appear before local civic groups and area schools. A number of tours are scheduled for off-campus locations.

The annual circus has been presented at ISNU each year since 1930 with the exception of the war years.

Committee Chairmen
Committee chairmen appointed for this year's circus are as follows:

costumes, Janet Nardin, sophomore home economics major from Normal; equipment, Dean Sanders, freshman mathematics major from Rock Island; and program, Diana Blackford, freshman elementary major from Peoria.

Others are queen, Carol Dueringer, senior home economics major from Meloin: publicity. Mary Doenitz, junior elementary major from Bloomington; and decorations, Janet Miller, sophomore music major from Neponset.

Still others are music and arrangements, DeVee DeRocker, senior music major from Orion; and tickets, Jerry Wright, senior industrial arts major from Farmington.

The election for the Gamma Phi queen and her court will be held on March 9.

Mar 8, 1961 (page 5)
Gamma Phi Presents Circus, Elects Queen
Gamma Phi, honorary gymnastic fraternity which was organized in 1928, will present its annual circus in McCormick Gymnasium on March 16, 17, and 18 at 8 p.m.

The first group, organized by Dr. C. E. Horton, head of the health and physical education department at that time, was an all men's organization that presented exhibitions of formal gymnastic work.

Circus acts were gradually introduced into the program, and in 1941 women were admitted to membership in the organization.

The self-supporting group is sponsored by Dr. Arley Gillett, professor of health and physical education, and Mr. Wayne Truex, instructor in health and physical education.

Off-Campus Performances
Off-campus performances, including the entire circus troupe and the circus band, will be at Eureka on April 7, Beardstown on April 14, and Kewanee on April 21. Tickets go on sale in McCormick

Gymnasium from 8 a.m. to 4 p.m. on March 9 until performance days. All seats are reserved.

Persons who are unable to get tickets from the gym should write to Dr. Arley Gillett.

Ticket prices are 75 cents on Thursday night for adults, one dollar on Friday and Saturday nights for adults, and 25 cents on all nights for children of elementary school age or under.

Elections for Gamma Phi Circus queen will be held tomorrow, March 9, from 8 a.m. to 4 p.m. Polls will be in Schroeder Hall and McCormick Gymnasium.

Members of the Gamma Phi Court are (top) Marie Chmielewski, Sue Stock (bottom) Jan Beardsley, Marti Laird, and Pat Miles

Vidette Mar 15, 1961 (front page)

Mar 15, 1961 (front page)

Gamma Phi To Crown Queen

One of five girls will be crowned Gamma Phi queen during the opening night performance of the silver anniversary circus.

The five girls who were selected from a list of 20 nominations are Janet Beardsley, junior mathematics major from Springfield; Marie Chmielewski, sophomore health and physical education major from Chicago; Martha Laird, senior music major from Watseka; Patricia Miles, junior home economics major from Danville; and Susan Stock, sophomore special education major from Maywood.

The circus troupe will present its performances in McCormick Gymnasium March 16, 17, and 18 at 8 p.m.

Variety of Acts
The program of 16 acts includes "skillful and daring feats on the trapeze, swinging ladders, and the "big wheel," as well as novelty acts on the unicycles and trick bicycles.

Furthermore, there are appearances on the trampoline, parallel bars, skates, rings and horizontal bars, balance beam, and webs.

Clowns add a note of enlightenment to the program and provide entertainment and enjoyment for all age levels.

Special Features
Special features for this year's performances include the "big wheel," swinging ladders, and the balancing ball.

The performance on the "big wheel" is done on an original piece of equipment created by one of Barnum and Bailey's star performers.

The swinging ladders act, one of ISNU's oldest circus acts, is being revived this year with several new innovations in the routine.

The ball used in the balancing ball act is over 50 years old. It was originally used in the Ringling Brothers Circus by the late Gene Enos of Bloomington.

The activities of Gamma Phi are under the direction of student officers and are sponsored by Dr. Arley Gillett, professor of health and physical education, and Mr. Wayne Truex, instructor in health and physical education. Mrs. Arley Gillett serves as costume supervisor.

Skip Rounds escorted Sue Stock at the Gamma Phi Circus last week-end. Members of the court were Janet Beardsley, Marie Chmielewski, Marti Laird, and Patricia Miles.

Vidette Mar 26, 1961
(page 8)

Vidette Mar 26, 1961 (page 8)

Devee De Rocker performs in a balancing ball act at the Gamma Phi Circus. Beside her is a Gamma Phi Clown, Carl "Moose" Larson.

Janet Buxton balancing on swinging ladder in Circus. Also in act were Mary Doenitz, Janet Hardin, Marilyn Armstrong, and Charlotte Daniel.

Vidette Mar 26, 1961 (page 8)

Apr 29, 1961 (page 3)
Reporter Features Non-Academic Employees
By ANN KELLY

...

Another employee is Duane Hughes, better known to the student body as "Sonny." Many students may know him as the roller skater in the Gamma Phi Circus. He is also a trapeze artist. "Sonny," an ISNU bus driver since 1955, enjoys playing the organ as a hobby.

May 10, 1961 (page 6)
'Pop' Horton Retires After 38 Years
By FRITZ KAEMPFER

Fritz Kaempfer listens to "Pop" Horton as he reminisces about his 38 years of service to ISNU as head of the department of health and physical education for men.

Vidette May 10, 1961 (page

No wonder a handicapped child calls "Pop" Horton his friend, and 340 men and women came from all over the USA to attend a testimonial banquet for him on April 30.

For Dr. Clifford E. Horton, the retiring head of the department of health and physical education for men at ISNU, has been interested in young people for almost all his life.

As a young man in Spokane, Washington, he belonged to the Leaders' Corps of the YMCA. It was his respect for the directors of this group which made him choose to go to Springfield YMCA College in Massachusetts, from which he received his bachelors.

He was on the gymnastics team there and his interest in and enjoyment of sports and recreation then has never dwindled.

After receiving his masters from Clark University in Worcester, Massachusetts in the spring, Dr. Horton came to ISNU in the fall of 1923.

He was for two years the only full-time teacher of physical education and became the head of his department when it was established in 1925—a job he has held ever since. He was director of athletics here from 1923 to 1931, and has been a coach of football, basketball, and baseball.

In 1927 Dr. Horton became a member of the eligibility committee of, the HAC when it was composed of 24 liberal arts and teachers colleges, and has since served as commissioner of the conference. He was also a charter member of the Illinois physical education association and has served as its president.

Develops Program
A four-year program for coaches and physical education teachers was developed by Dr. Horton in 1931. He helped to organize the "N" Club in 1926 and Gamma Phi in 1932, sponsoring the latter organization until 1947.

In 1939 he helped to establish the East Bay Camp at Lake Bloomington which offered physical education students from ISNU nine semester hours' credit in recreational leadership.

During World War n Dr. Horton made his contribution to the war effort by teaching courses in swimming and first aid in conjunction with the American Red Cross. The V-12 unit at ISNU received swimming instruction from Dr. Horton. In 1942 he received his doctorate from Indiana University.

Directs Camp
In 1950, the McLean County chapter of the Illinois Association for the Crippled, the local Easter Seal organization, had money available for a special program. A summer camp for handicapped children was established at the Boy Scout camp on Lake Bloomington.

ISNU physical and special education students earn university credit acting as counselors and instructors, under the direction of Dr. Horton and other staff members.

This camp experience provides for the college students excellent training in working with handicapped children because, as Dr. Horton says, "The children are out there to learn to do the things they want to do."

Two hundred fifty-five different children have attended the camp and "Pop" Horton has became a friend to each of them. They come from McLean and nearby counties and costs are covered by the Illinois Association for the Crippled.

After 38 years on the faculty of ISNU, Dr. Horton is retiring August 31. One of his last achievements before leaving has been the planning of the new gymnasium and field house.

He feels that the men of his department have done an excellent job with the cramped quarters and limited facilities now available. But with these new facilities, now approved by the Teachers College Board, Dr. Horton believes that the new department head, Dr. Burton L. O'Connor, now director of athletics at U-High, and his staff will be able to extend the services of ISNU and take a great step forward in preparing physical education teachers.

Honored at Banquet
A Clifford Horton Testimonial Banquet was held at the University Union recently, sponsored by the "N" Club and Gamma Phi. All former members of both groups which Dr. Horton established, as well as all health and physical education majors who could be located, were invited.

Some came from as far away as Alabama, New York, and Texas to honor "Pop" Horton. Also invited were representatives of the Red Cross, the Association for the Crippled, the Boy Scouts, the ISNU Outdoor Education Committee, the Illinois Association for Health, Physical Education and Recreation, and the ISNU faculty.

After his retirement Dr. Horton and his wife plan to stay in Normal, for Mrs. Horton was recently elected president of the Bloomington-Normal Women's Club.

Dr. Horton plans to continue his work with the Boy Scouts, the camp for handicapped children, (as the representative of the McLean County chapter of the Illinois Association for the Crippled), and the IIAC.

Dr. Horton says that in working with young people, he tends to feel their age. Thus it is understandable that he would want to remain active in these groups which are dedicated to health and recreation for young people.

1961 – 62 School Year

GAMMA PHI CIRCUS
1962
ILLINOIS STATE NORMAL UNIVERSITY
NORMAL, ILLINOIS
Row One: Mrs. Arley Gillett, John Baites, Vice President; Sharon Schillinger, Treasurer; Marijane Unsicker, Secretary; Bill Hunt, President; Mr. Truex, Assistant Sponsor. Row Two: Bob Stoner, Diane Blackford, Judy Anderson, Judy Verhunce, Nancy Opperman, Jill Marser, Barl Gillett, Carol Butler, Ginny Rieger, Sharon Peters, Alan Weith, Paul Zert. Row Three: Niel Barton, Linda Girard, Diane Gasper, Sally Jessaman, Nancy Glover, Sharon Duerinzer, Janis Mareeak, Sandi Kenny, Nancy DeRocker, Karen Park, Margaret Volk, Dan Malloy. Row Four: Ryan Smith, Dale Manning, John Fussner, Barb Messman, Tom Kordewick, Charlotte Daniel, John Read, Nat Hubbard, Dick Rounds, Dick George, Jim Furrow, Arley Gillett, Not Pictured.

1962 Group Gamma Phi Picture, *Special Collections*

Nov 8, 1961 (page 4)
Gamma Phi

It's still not too late to join Gamma Phi! Gamma Phi meets each Monday evening from 7-9 at McCormick Gym. Anyone who has a new trick or different act is urged to come and try out.

Nov 15, 1961 (page 4)
Gamma Phi ...

Although the "man on the flying trapeze" doesn't quite fit into the Gamma Phi act at the Ninth Annual Convention of the Illinois Association for Health, Physical Education, and Recreation, the program will undoubtedly be nearly as exciting as that of the annual Circus.

By combining their efforts, the ISNU Gamma Phi and gymnastic team and the Thornton Township High School gymnastics team will perform in "Gymnastics for All" held in Spaulding Gymnasium at Peoria tomorrow.

The ISNU group of 32 will be sponsored by Dr. and Mrs. Arley Gillett and Mr. Wayne O. Truex.

Clifford 'Pop' Horton

Vidette Dec 15, 1961 (front page)

Dec 15, 1961 (front page)
Horton Turns Spade For Field House
The groundbreaking ceremony for the 3 1/4 million dollar building which will house physical education for men took place at 3 p.m. yesterday.

Thanks to the foresight of the grounds crew, the frozen earth was prepared to enable Clifford E. Horton, retired head of the department of physical education for men, to turn the first spadeful of sod. Mr. Horton was a member of the staff of the University for 38 years.

Dr. Arthur H. Larsen, vice president of ISNU and dean of the faculty, presided over the activities. The invocation was given by Clarence Ropp, secretary of The Teachers College Board, and was followed by remarks from Dr. Robert G. Bone, president of ISNU.

Those persons who followed Mr. Horton in the earth turning were Dr. F. H. McKelvey, executive officer of the Teachers College Board; Carl Dunbar, chairman of the building committee on the Teachers College Board; Clarence Ropp; President Bone! Dr. Larsen; Howard Hancock; director of athletics; Preston Ensign, business manager of the University; John Wroan, representative of J. L. Wroan and Sons, Inc., general contractors; and James Terry, representative of Lankton-Ziegele-Terry and Associates, architects.

Those who planned the ceremony will remain as a committee to plan the cornerstone laying of the building which will be held during early June of 1961. A number of the members were selected because of their association with the Universities bond issue campaign of 1960. This building represents the first construction on this campus utilizing funds from the bond issue.

Dec 15, 1961 (front page)
P E Plant To Bear Horton's Name
Dr. Clifford E. Horton, who directed the men's health and physical education department at Illinois State Normal University for 38 years learned yesterday that the new $3,475,000 physical education building and field house will bear his name.

Teachers College Board and University officials, as well as students, took part in the ground-breaking ceremony for the new structures at which public announcement of the name was made by ISNU President Robert G. Bone. The project, to be completed by the summer of 1963, will be known as the Clifford E. Horton Physical Education Building.

Dr. Horton, known to all as "Pops", officially retired in August but recently returned to the staff in order to help with the development of a graduate program leading to the doctorate by the men's department.

Dr. Horton is credited with helping found the honorary Gamma Phi gymnastics fraternity, the Illinois Association for Health, Physical Education and Recreation, and the McLean County Camp for Crippled Children. He has been an Interstate Intercollegiate Athletic Conference commissioner since 1950.

In 1925 Dr. Horton helped to plan the McCormick Gymnasium for ISNU, soon to be turned over to University women. For the past few years he has been on the central planning group for the new physical education project.

Feb 8, 1962 (page 2)
GAMMA PHI QUEEN

Gamma Phi is now accepting petitions from organizations' nominating campus women for queen of the coming Gamma Phi Circus.

According to Diane Alt, junior in vocal music from Morton and chairman of the Queen Committee, this year's circus will be held March 22, 23, and 24, with a queen and her court of four to be chosen in an all school election March 15.

Nominations should be accompanied by six wallet size pictures and sent to Dr. Arley F. Gillett, sponsor of Gamma Phi, by March 22.

Gamma Phi will exhibit several posters of all candidates. All organizations are requested to limit their publicity to tags and badges without pictures.

Feb 22, 1962 (page 4)
GAMMA PHI PRACTICING

In preparation for their annual circus, Gamma Phi members will be practicing both Sunday at 3 p.m. and Monday at 7 p.m. in McCormick Gymnasium. The regular business meeting will be at 8 p.m. on Monday.

Gamma Phi Queen Contest applications which were sent to each *organization on campus are to be returned to Dr. Gillette before March 2. The queen will reign during the Gamma Phi Circus to be held March 22, 23, and 24 at McCormick Gymnasium.*

Mar 1, 1962 (page 3)
Gamma Phi Selects New Club Members
Gamma Phi officers are proud to announce their new pledges who were selected after surviving highly competitive tryouts last week in McCormick Gymnasium.

The twenty-three pledges who will be performing with the other thirty-two members in the Gamma Phi annual circus on March 22, 23, and 24 are Paul Ziert, Creve Coeur; Tom Kordewick, Park Forest; Judy Verhunce, Morton Grove; Sharon Dueringer, Melvin; Jill Morser, Chicago; Bari Gillett, Rockford; Susan Rowe, Bloomington; Ginny Rieger, Oak Park; Dan Malloy, Prospect Heights; Barb Messman, Homer; Sandi Kinney, Washington; John Read, Danforth.

Others are Ron Thompson, Chicago; John Fussner, Millstadt; Ray Dalton, Chicago; Karon Park, Belvidere; Jim Furrow, Towanda; Carole Butler, Decatur; Margaret Volk, Washington; Neil Barton, Chicago; Nate Hubbard, Rockford; Nancy Glover, North Aurora; and Dick Rounds, Rockford.

Officers of Gamma Phi are president, Bill Hunt of Normal; vice president, John Baltes of Crete; secretary, Marijane Unsicker of Tremont; treasurer, Sharon Schillinger of Coal Valley; and social chairman, Diane Alt of Morton.

Mar 8, 1962 (front page)
'Open House' Releases Broadcast Schedule
ISNU's "Open House" which is broadcast over WJBC every Sunday at 12:15 has released its schedule for the remainder of March.
...
March 18, an interview with William Hunt, president of Gamma Phi, on the coming circus production.

Ziert Drifts From Tap Dancing To Gymnastics
By GUY CARDARELLI

Illinois State has been blessed with some outstanding freshmen in the field of athletics this year. Bert Popejoy, Fred Horn, Preston Jordan, Bill Ridings, and Dick Russell are just a few who have given us hope for the future.

Another of these young giants is Paul Ziert, who is currently a member of the gymnastics team coached by Wayne O. Truex.

IIAC Gymnastics Competition
Entering 3 events is work enough but for the performer to win first in all 3 and score a total of 18 out of a possible 18 points is magnificent.

This remarkable feat Paul succeeded in doing against the University of Chicago in the final dual gymnastics meet of the season. He scored firsts in free exercise, tumbling, and on the trampoline.

Earlier he scored 32 points in a double dual meet with Ball State and Central Michigan. Unofficially, Ziert has scored 120 points for the Redbirds in gymnastics competition this season.

In the annual IIAC gymnastics tournament held here in McCormick Gym this past weekend Paul scored 28 points to lead all other team members, and scored the third highest number of points for an individual performer in the meet.

Southern Illinois took first place in all other events except tumbling in which Ziert placed first. Paul was the only gymnast to take first place from a school other than Southern. Ziert picked up his 28 points by placing third on the trampoline, second in free exercise, and first in tumbling.

Although Paul Ziert was ranked third nationally by the National Gymnastics Coaches Association in free exercise earlier this year, his talents do not end here.

He has scored well on the trampoline, and in tumbling. According to Coach Truex, "Next year he should be able to add a doubleback flip to his tumbling routine and be ready for national competition."

How He Got His Start

As happens in many instances Paul began his career in athletics through another medium, At an early age Paul was induced to take tap dance lessons. During these lessons there were breaks when the students performed tumbling exercises. Because Paul began to excel in these workouts his interest drifted from dancing to tumbling.

About the time Paul was 12 years old a Mr. Rozanas came to the Peoria YMCA from Chicago to demonstrate tumbling. It was at this point in his young life that Paul decided to devote his talents to gymnastics.

Paul is a graduate of East Peoria High School where he was a member of the debate team, student government, student senate in his junior and senior years, and also a member of the National Honor Society.

Academically speaking Paul was not completely occupied. For two years he competed in the National Novice Meet in gymnastics. Both years he won two firsts, free exercise and tumbling, and two thirds in trampoline competition.

While in his junior year he traveled to West Point, New York to compete in the National AAU Meet. The year was 1960 when Olympic trials were being held, a distinct incentive for any performer in athletics that year.

As the end result proved, a new top level gymnastics performer reached the national scene. Paul was rated between 4-15 in the nation in free exercise, and in the top ten in tumbling. (The exact positions were not made known.)

All Around Performer

Not only has his ability been proven in gymnastics, but in the classroom as well. Paul is sporting a 3.7 average academically. He is a major in mathematics and a minor in social science.

Although many believe that education and sports do not go hand in hand, Paul himself states, "If a person budgets his time properly, he should not have any trouble keeping up with his studies."

As a truly fine athlete and a modest gentleman Paul realizes the need of constant learning and practice. He does not feel that he knows all there is about gymnastics, and said so in a statement made to me about Coach Truex. "Coach Truex is an excellent coach, and I have learned a great deal from him in the short time I have been at Illinois State."

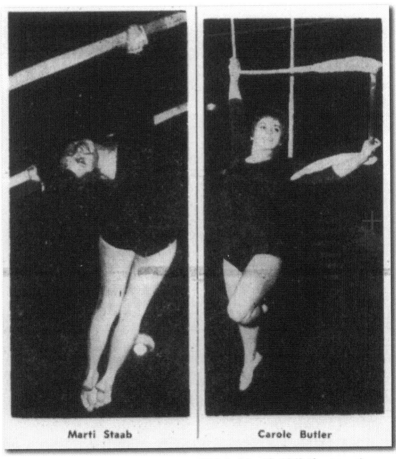

Marti Staab   Carole Butler

Vidette Mar 13, 1962 (front page)

Mar 13, 1962 (front Page)

Annual Circus To Highlight New Show Acts

Gamma Phi's Annual Circus is only one week away, (March 22, 23, and 24). Tickets will go on sale beginning Friday in the lobby of McCormick Gymnasium from 8am until 4pm They may also be purchased on May 19, 20, 21, 22, and 23, as well as at the box office on the Thursday night performance.

All Friday and Saturday night seats will be reserved. Adult admission will be 75c for Thursday evening and $1 for the Friday and Saturday performances. Children's tickets will be 25c every evening.

This season's circus will feature several new acts which promise to be the highlights of the show. One will be the revolving ladder, a typical circus act which tests balance, coordination, and confidence.

The tight wire, designed and built by the father of one of the gymnasts, is an act created for determination and ingenuity. A vicarious experience is in store for the audience when the performer whirls around high in the air in the foot revolve, an act of skill and daring. Those and many other acts will thrill the audiences.

The following program of events has been released by the Gamma Phi publicity staff:

Overture - George Foeller, Band Director
Coronation of the Queen - Circus Troupe
Revolving Ladder - Dale Manning and William Hunt
Uneven Parallel Bars - Diane Alt, Diane Gasper, Janis Marecsak, Martha Staab, Sharon Shillinger
Swinging Ladders Charlotte Daniel, Janet Nardin, Judy Verhunce, Sharon Dueringer, Jill Morser, Bari Gillett
Trampoline - John Baltes, Tom Kordewick, Paul Ziert
Unicycles - Nancy DeRocker, Sharon Peters, Bill Hunt, Nate Hubbard
Trapeze - Virginia Rieger, Louise Glass, Carole Butler, Margaret Volk, Ryan Smith, Neil Barton
Tumbling and Trampolett - Charlotte Daniel, Marijane

Unsicker, John Baltes, Paul Ziert, Dale Manning, Bill Hunt, Tom Kordewick

"The Whirlos" - Janet Miller, Sandi Kinney, Shirley Fitzgerald, Duane Hughes, Russ Fitzgerald

High Trapeze - Linda Girard, Carole Butler, Dale Manning.

Balance Beam - Wanda Clark, Karen Hill, Susan Rowe, Nancy Opperman, Bea Urquiza, Martha Staab

Tight Wire, Ball Juggling - Diane Alt, Barbara Messman, Jim Furrwo, Bill Hunt

Webs - Linda Girard, Janet Nardin, Diana Blackford, Barbara Messman, Jill Morser, Bari Gillett

Parallels - Bill Hunt, Bob Stoner, Dale Manning, Tom Kordewick

Rings - Diane Gasper, Sally Jessman, Virginia Rieger, Connie Schroederus, John Baltes, Dan Malloy, Al Weith

Vaulting - Sandi Kenney, Sharon Schillinger, Judy Anderson, Marijane Unsicker, Karen Park, Charlotte Daniel, Ray Dalton, John Read, John Fussner, Ron Thompson, Paul Ziert, Jim Furrow

Foot Revolve - Judy Verhunce, Barbara Messman

Finale - Circus Troupe

Clowns - Al Martling, Dick Rounds, Dick George

Ringmaster - Byron Roderick

Gamma Phi, a coeducational gymnastics fraternity, draws its members from interested students, faculty, and staff from all departments of Illinois State. Its activities are under the direction of student officers. Its sponsors are Dr. Arley F. Gillett and Wayne O. Truex. Mrs. Gillett serves as costume supervisor.

The organization is self-supporting and owns most of the gymnastic equipment and all of the costumes used in the circus.

Mar 13, 1962 (front page)
Students To Select Gamma Phi Queen

A Queen for the Gamma Phi circus will be chosen Thursday, March 15, at an all school election. The polls will be Open between 8 a.m. and 4 p.m. in the University Union and McCormick Gym.

The all-school vote will choose one of the following girls as queen:
Ruth Ann Rainford, sophomore in home economics: Rosemary
Polivka, sophomore in elementary; Sharon Spitery, sophomore in
geography: Judy Kennedy, senior in special education or Bonnie Lee
Sumner, junior in home economics. Marie Anna Bazik, senior in
elementary; Phyllis Patton, junior in business: Donna Johnson,
junior in special education; Bonnie Gentry, sophomore in
elementary; Sharon Rapp, sophomore in elementary; or Marie
Ragans, junior in elementary may be one of the students chosen to
reign over the circus.

Others who might be elected are Marian Pilarski, junior in Health
and P.E.; Linda Fortna, junior in elementary; Janet Ptasnik, junior
in Health and P.E.; Mary Johnson, junior in music; Barbara La
Bedz, junior in elementary; Carol Berthold, sophomore in speech;
Diana Taylor, sophomore in speech; or Virginia Roth, junior in
business.

Mar 15, 1962 (front page)
Circus Lists Chairmen
Between workouts, the gymnasts of Gamma Phi have appointed
committees for the fast approaching Gamma Phi Circus to be
presented on the 22, 23, and 24 of this month.

Chairman of costumes is Linda Girard of Cornell. The queen contest
is in charge of Diane Alt of Morton. Publicity is the responsibility of
Marijane Unsicker of Tremont while the programs are being
organized by Sharon Schillinger of Coal Valley. Dale Manning of
Springfield is handling the equipment, and Sharon Peters of Round
Lake is planning the decorations.

The committees will include all members and pledges of the club.

Mar 20, 1962 (front page)
School Picks Court
Following the tradition which dates back to 1932 Gamma Phi will
once again crown its Circus Queen who, with her court, will reign
throughout the three performances of the circus.

After last Thursday's vote the five finalists have been announced. They are Linda Fortna Marian Pilarski, Janet Ptasnik, Sharon Rapp, and Diana Taylor.

The finalists represent various clubs which are active on the Illinois State campus. From Women's League is Linda Fortna a junior in elementary education from Pontiac. Marian Pilarski a junior in health and physical education from Elmhurst is representing the Women's Physical Education Club. The WRA candidate is Janet Ptasnik a junior in health and physical education from Kewanee.

Sharon Rapp a sophomore in elementary education from Bloomington was chosen as the Industrial Arts Club representative. Diana Taylor a sophomore in speech from Granite City is the contestant from the Jesters.

Bill Hunt Gamma Phi president will crown the queen at the coronation ceremony to be held in McCormick Gymnasium previous to the Thursday evening performance.

Mar 22, 1962 (front page)
Gamma Phi To Start Three-Day Run
Tonight at 8 p.m. the 26th annual Gamma Phi Circus will begin its three-night run in McCormick Gymnasium. The co-educational gymnastic fraternity will present over 50 performers in 19 fast-moving acts of skill on the trapeze swinging ladders, parallel bars, tight wire, and other gymnastic equipment.

Novelty acts on unicycles and trick bicycles, as well as clowns to add a note of comedy, will provide entertainment for all age levels.

Performances by the gymnasts will be accompanied by the Illinois State's Stage Band under the direction of Mr. George Foeller, assistant director of university bands.

The Stage Band is a special group organized by the music department which accompanies Gamma Phi on all campus and off-campus performances.

Band members are Robert Baskovic of Brookfield, John La Motte of Springfield, Kenneth Kistner of Olney, Richard Davis of Wheeling, and Carleen Forth of Mendota on saxophones; Allan Harris of Earlville, Al Chuckman of Elmhurst, Bette Jane Irwin of Chatsworth, John Huber of Carlock, and John Winkler of Varna playing trumpets.

Others are Gabriel Baumgardner of Peoria, Thomas Miles of Lewistown, and Bruce Otto of Bloomington on trombones; Helen Hoblit of Atlanta as the pianist; Ronald Anson of Normal playing the string bass; George Southgate of Normal on the drums; and Harland Snodgrass of Bloomington playing the Latin drums.

Several committees have been diligently working to make this year's circus as successful as previous ones. Those committees are costumes, headed by Linda Gerard and Carole Butler, Virginia Rieger, Janis Marecsak, Bari Gillett, Jill Morser, Diana Blackford, Jo Ann Hopper, and Phyllis Hunt.

The decorations committee consists of Sharon Peters, chairman, Diana Blackford, Phyllis Hunt, Bill Hunt, Paul Ziert, Tom Kordewick, Dick George, Dick Rounds, and Ryan Smith. Handling equipment are Dale Manning, chairman, Dick Rounds, Bill Hunt, and Sharon Schillinger. The program was arranged by Sharon Schillinger, chairman, Diana Blackford, Nancy Opperman, and Bill Hunt.

Publicity is in charge of Marijane Unsicker, chairman, Margaret Volk, Sharon Dueringer, Louise Glass, Judy Anderson, Janet Miller, and Ryan Smith. The Queen Contest was promoted by Diane Alt, chairman, Janet Nardin, Ray Dalton, Ronald Thompson, Jim Furrow, and Tom Kordewick.

Music was decided by Nancy DeRocker, chairman, Wanda Clark, Karen Hill, John Read, and Diane Alt. The ticket committee includes John Baltes, chairman, Diane Gasper, Susan Rowe, Judy Verhunce, Nancy Glover, Sally Jessman, Connie Schroederus, Sandi Kinney, Charlotte Daniel, Dan Malloy, Al Weith, Barbara Messman, Paul Ziert, and Bill Hunt.

If you haven't purchased your tickets yet, they may be obtained today and tomorrow from 8 a.m. until 4 p.m. in McCormick Gymnasium, and also at the box office for tonight's performance.

Mar 22, 1962 (page 2)
Red Cross Mobile To Visit ISU
The Red Cross Bloodmobile, which is coming to Illinois State on March 27 and 28, is one week late this year so as not to fall on the same week as the Gamma Phi Circus.

It has been thought that because the Bloodmobile competed with the Circus last year many possible blood donors were lost.

Mar 27, 1962 (page 8)
Reporter Appraises Gamma Phi Performance
The performers were professional, the queen was radiant, and the music was perfect for this year's Gamma Phi Circus. A standing-room-only-crowd filled McCormick Gymnasium last Thursday, Friday, and Saturday evenings to witness the Queen's Coronation, and to watch the feats of skill and precision displayed in every event.

The Queen, brunette Sharon Rapp, the Industrial Arts Club candidate, and a sophomore in elementary education from Bloomington, was attractive in a white chiffon formal complemented by a pink beaded bodice. She carried a bouquet of long-stemmed American Beauty roses and was crowned each night by Bill Hunt, Gamma Phi president, with a traditional tiarra.

Members of the queen's court were lovely. Each girl carried a bouquet of daffodils. Composing the court were Janet Ptasnik, Kewanee junior; Diana Taylor, Granite City sophomore; Linda Fortna, junior from Pontiac; and Marian Pilarski, junior from Elmhurst.

At the queen's command, 26th annual Gamma Phi Circus began. The acts ranged from dangerous to graceful. Two such dangerous acts were the revolving ladder and the foot revolve, both acts requiring great courage.

Attendants Linda Fortna, Janet Ptasnik, Marian Pilarski, and Diana Taylor and Queen Sharon Rapp watch the Gamma performance.

Vidette Mar 27, 1962

Bill, Hunt and Dale Manning perform on the revolving ladder.

Vidette Mar 27, 1962 (page 8)

Many acts such as the uneven and even parallel bars, unicycles and bicycles, balance beam, tight wire, and the ball required skill in balance. Acrobatic abilities were best used on the trampoline and trampolet, and in tumbling and vaulting, while "The Whirlos," a roller skating group, depended on skillful precision.

Grace and stamina were exhibited on swinging ladders, the trapeze and high trapeze, the webs, and the rings, an act which dates back to the first circus which was presented in 1932.

Throughout the program three clowns entertained the audience with their humorous antics.

The Illinois State Stage Band, directed by Mr. George Foeller, added much to the suspense and excitement of the circus.

Although they weren't as elaborate, the costumes were typical of professional circus garb with ruffled and sequined leotards. Multicolored costumes highlighted many acts.

During a brief intermission, the; 1962 Service Awards were presented by Bill Hunt to Martha Staab, a senior in business from Peoria, and Sharon Schillinger, a senior in health and physical education from Coal Valley. These awards are annually awarded to outstanding Senior members of Gamma Phi, who have at all times manifested a spirit of willingness and helpfulness in carrying out the ideals of the organization.

The troupe presented gifts of appreciation to Dr. and Mrs. Arley F. Gillette, and Mr. and Mrs. Wayne O. Truex for their untiring supervision, support and encouragement.

May 22, 1962 (page 4)
GAMMA PHI
One of the busiest clubs on campus, Gamma Phi, recently held elections for the 1962-63 school year.

Bill Hunt, a junior in health and p.e. from Normal, was re-elected president; Dale Manning, a sophomore in business from Springfield, was elected to the vice-presidency; Mari jane Unsicker, a junior in elementary from Tremont, was re-elected as secretary; Diane Alt, a junior in vocal music from Morton, has been elected treasurer; Diane Gasper, a sophomore in French from Oak Park, has been elected as social chairman for next year.

Recently the officers presented a revision of the Gamma Phi constitution to the members, and the revision was adopted by the group.

All members are cordially invited to join in the festivities of the
Gamma Phi picnic at Weldon Springs on Memorial Day.

Gamma Phi club members who go on the annual picnic will leave
campus by bus and spend the entire day picnicking and socializing.

Keeping an eye on things will be Wayne Truex, Gamma Phi faculty
advisor.

June 27, 1962 (front page)
Dr. Gillett Obtains New PE Position
Dr. Arley F. Gillett, professor of health and physical education, has
been appointed temporary state supervisor of health and physical
education, according to George T. Wilkins, State Superintendent of
Public Instruction.

The appointment was approved by the Teachers College Board at a
recent meeting in DeKalb. Before leaving for Europe Dr. Bone
requested confirmation of the appointment.

Dr. Gillett will replace Dr. O. N. Hunter, who will become dean of
the College of Physical Education at Utah University.

As state supervisor Mr. Gillett will head a staff responsible for
instruction in driver training and recreation and safety as well as
health and physical education.

During the summer Mr. Gillett will work full time in Springfield.
Through the first semester of the 1962-63 school year he will divide
his time between the state office and the University.

An Illinois State alumnus, the new state supervisor has been on the
staff of his alma mater since 1944. He received his master's from
New York University and his doctorate from Indiana University. Mr.
Gillett was a district supervisor for the Illinois Department of
Welfare in 1943-44. He is also faculty sponsor of the Gamma Phi
Circus.

1962 – 63 School Year

GAMMA PHI—*Front Row:* John Fussner, Jill Morser, Bari Gillett, Diane Gasper, Dale Manning, vice-president; William Hunt, president; Marijane Unsicker, secretary; Margaret Volk, Virginia Rieger, Sandi Kinney. *Second Row:* Dr. Arley Gillett, adviser, Karen Park, Ryan Smith, Alan Weith, John Read, Neil Barton, Paul Ziert, Barbara Messmar, Diana Blackford. *Back Row:* Nancy DeRocker, Charlotte Daniel, Ronald Thompson, Raymond Dalton, Susan Rowe, Jim Furrow, Tom Kordewick, Judy Anderson, Sally Jessman, Nancy Glover, Nathaniel Hubbard. *Not Pictured:* John Baltes, Karen Hill, Diane Alt, Jan Marescak, Dick Rounds, Dick George, Mr. Wayne Truex, adviser.

1963 Gamma Phi Group Picture, *ISU Special Collections*

Sept 20, 1962 (page 4)
GAMMA PHI

Anyone interested in gymnastics or working out on circus equipment is invited to the second meeting of Gamma Phi. No former experience is necessary for an informal workout on all apparatus.

This meeting will be held at 7 p.m., next Monday in McCormick Gymnasium. Dr. Arley F. Gillett, professor of health and physical education, and Mr. Wayne O. Truex.

Oct 18, 1962 *(front page)*
Weekend's Festivities Feature Play, Parade, Game, Dance

...
Sunday afternoon at 2 p.m.. Gamma Phi will present a circus to honor returning alums. (McCormick Gym)

Nov 13, 1962 (front page)
Red Door Sponsors 'Roaring Twenties'
Vaudeville billboards, "Roaring 20's" theme, jazz singer Sarah Harris, Redmen Quartet, Dick Hanus's 'uke," slapstick comedy,

Charleston Flappers, barbershop harmony, jugglers, pianist Margo Knepp—all are scheduled for the "Horace Hyde's Amateur Hour" sponsored by Horace Hyde Coffee.

...

Bill Hunt, a member of Gamma Phi, will be the featured juggler.

Feb 7, 1963 (page 8)
Gamma Phi Selects 28 Pledges
Recent pledge tryouts for Gamma Phi, gymnastics fraternity, have been completed. In order to become full-fledged members, the pledges will also compete with the regular members for positions on the circus squad at the end of January.

Although the circus is the highlight of the year for Gamma Phi, some of the floor acts have performed at the State Farm Children's Show and at the Illinois Hotel for Lucy R. Morgan and Booker T. Washington children.

Those who made the pledge squad are Milt Neuman, Neil Whittington, Lee Davis, Gordon Winkleman, Dick Krase, Glenn Brownewell, Don Richter, Rich Linder, Carol Herman, and Bobbi Goulet.

Also on the squad are Dorothy Nesbit, Cheryl Dreyer, Anne Lehmann, Dixie Young, Pat Preno, Judy Preno, Pam Schovin, Dottie Voisen, Penny Berning, Jean Burpee, JoAnn Hopper, Betty Daggitt, Joanne Hrvatin, Ruth Jones, Carol Herndon, Nancy Anderson, Kathy Schuller, and Jerry Beesley.

Dr. Arley Gillett, sponsor, and Mr. Wayne Truex, his assistant, and members of the circus troop are expecting this year's circus to be one of the best shows performed by Gamma Phi. Bill Hunt, Gamma Phi president, says, "I am encouraged by the enthusiasm of those working out this year, and I have seen some really new and interesting talent."

Feb 21, 1963 Vidette (page 7)

Ziert Wins 'Athlete of Week' Honors
By ED CERES

Plato once said "A good education consists of giving to the body and the soul all the beauty and perfection of which it is capable." In saying this, Plato could very well have been speaking of our athlete of the week, Paul Ziert.

Paul, a sophomore, added three more awards to his already overflowing trophy case by placing first in tumbling and free exercise and third in trampoline in the IIAC conference meet.

It is impossible to describe the ability of this modest young athlete in words which would do his performance justice. Seeing is believing; only in Paul's case it's hard to believe your own observation.

Only those who have witnessed Paul's performances can visualize his grace and poise as he performs his specialties in tumbling, free exercise and trampoline.

One would think that Paul's accomplishments would be enough for anyone, but when asked for a high point in his career, Paul stated "Just -being on the team is enough, I hope the high point is still to come."

When one is the best in the conference, what could possibly be next? The answer will come in March when Paul will compete in NCAA national competition. Speaking of the nationals Paul says "It should be a real experience," and then upon thinking about it some more added "my highest goal of all is to make a good showing at the nationals."

Paul, a team man in every sense of the word, credits much of his success to coach Wayne Truex. "Mr. Truex is an outstanding coach," states Paul, "he has helped the entire squad to develop their routines to the highest of their abilities."

In continuing, Paul chose to talk more about the team, describing the gymnasts fast start and slow finish as something quite "unusual,"

349   A Circus in the Paper

adding "we should be real strong next year; we could use some younger members to build. However, with many experienced men returning and the new gymnastics facilities, our chances of improvement over this year's record is good."

Finally getting Paul back to talking about himself, something which is not very easily accomplished, one learns that Paul's activities go beyond gymnastics.

When not practicing for Gamma Phi, Paul can be seen serving on the Big Four Committee and exchanging political ideas. He is also president of the sophomore class. Somewhere in between activities Paul has managed to have an accumulative grade average of 3.7.

After a brilliant past, what lies ahead for Paul? In gymnastics, more competition, including a meet this week against Hal Holmes of the University of Illinois.

In speaking of Holmes Paul says, "Holmes is the greatest tumbler I've ever seen, he's one guy it's a pleasure to finish second to."

What lies ahead for Paul Ziert can be summarized in one word "success" in whatever he chooses to try.

Gamma Phi unicyclists, shown here performing at a basketball halftime intermission, are members of one of the acts which are now perfecting routines for the organization's annual circus.

Vidette Feb 21, 1963 (page 7)

Feb 28, 1963 (front page)

Annual Spring Carnival Promises Gala Festival
By MARSHA LYONS

To offer typical carnival excitement through the antics of Gamma Phi clowns, unique carnival booths, the aroma of sizzling hot dogs and freshly-made cotton candy has become the goal of the Central Board of the Association of Women Students as it presents its annual spring carnival on Saturday, March 16, in McCormick Gymnasium from 8 to 11 p.m.

...

Feb 28, 1963 (page 8)

Everyone Loves Gamma Phi Circus!
Hard work, Patience Make Polished Show
By JEANINE YEAST

Everybody loves a circus. Perhaps this is why the annual Gamma Phi circus is one of the most awaited events of the year at Illinois State.

During the performances the audience watches—mouths agape and awe-stricken — the intricate and dangerous stunts and acts being performed. They watch the man on the flying trapeze, high above the floor with no net to catch him. They fear for the pretty girl hanging by her wrist on the web. They thrill at the tumbling; hold their breath while the vaulters clear the vaulting box.

These acts, and many more, will be featured at the coming Gamma Phi Circus, April 21, 22, and 23.

Stunts Grow Up
While we all like to watch the acts at the circus, we tend to think they were born the way we see them. Actually, few of us realize that the Gamma Phi performers have been practicing since before Thanksgiving. These acts, although some of them may have been performed before, are done by different people, who must learn it from the beginning.

In the course of watching a practice session last week, I talked with

351   A Circus in the Paper

Bill Hunt, junior in physical education and president of Gamma Phi and Neil Barton, junior in social science, publicity chairman of the organization. Several things impressed me as I watched the various acts.

The greatest of these was, "what keeps the performers from getting hurt?" The two men explained that each stunt is learned one step at a time, and only with a spotter assisting. No new steps are attempted until the performer is thoroughly proficient with the preceding steps of that stunt. Bill proudly (and somewhat sheepishly) told me that the most serious accident they have had this season was when his baby boy fell out of his stroller while watching the practice performances.

The second thing that impressed me was the kind of people who are in the organization. They are not, as I had thought, mostly from physical education. The dominating group is gymnasts, but the rest come from various majors and minors, and some are not even students.

A Cheerful Bunch
The third point that impressed me was the group itself. They're a cheerful bunch, always ready to try something new. And patient. I looked on as Barb Messman, junior in math from Homer, patiently spotted Milt Newman, freshman, while he, with the patience of a saint, tackled the problem of juggling balls while walking on a large ball up and down what looked to me to be a teeter-totter.

I saw Neil Barton coaching Ginny Reiger, freshman, in a technical aspect of her trapeze act.

The 31-year-old organization will perform in Jacksonville on March 29, and in Mendota on April The various acts will consist of trapeze, rings, ladders, uneven parallels, balance beam, webs, ball, ropes and whips, trampoline, high bar, parallels, unicycles, bikes, skaters, tumbling, trampolett, vaulting, revolving ladders, and of course, the clowns.

All these add up to plenty of thrills when the circus comes to Illinois State!

Circus Creates Suspense, Sensation

By JEANINE YEAST

A long rope with a loop at the top—a Spanish Web. A girl climbs the rope, and slips her ankle through the loop and arches gracefully toward the audience. A hush falls over the onlookers. Slowly, then faster and faster, the rope is spun around and around. The Spanish Web is an old circus act that has been thrilling circus-going people for many years. Likewise, it thrills the audience of the Gamma Phi circus each year.

The act will be performed by Barbara Messman, junior, Bobbi Goulet, freshman, Jill Morser, sophomore, Bari Gillett, freshman, Diana Blackford, junior, 'and Carol Herman, freshman.

The Bicycle for Two, featuring Nancy Glover, junior and Nate Hubbard, sophomore promises to be a well-polished act this year. Nancy and Nate had the act last year and have been working together since then developing new tricks.

Who of us, when we were small, didn't enjoy jumping up and down on our beds, much to our mother's dismay? Perhaps this is why we all get a thrill out of watching a trampoline act. This year, the trampoline lays claim to Paul Ziert, sophomore, Jerry Beesley, freshman, and Tom Kordewick, sophomore. The two guys and the gal have been developing new tricks and taking some of the gymnastics out of the act to make it strictly circus.

The Horizontal Bar and Rings is one of the more popular acts. It is basically a gymnastic apparatus and a difficult one to work. Al Weith, junior, Dale Manning, junior, Sally Jessman, junior, Diane Gasper, junior, Ginny Rieger, freshman, JoAnn Hopper, senior Ryan Smith, junior, and Jim Furrow, sophomore are putting much originality into the act.

The balance Beam is quickly becoming one of the most popular acts of the Gamma Phi Circus. It is an all girl act featuring Susan Rowe, sophomore, Karen Hill, junior, Judy Preno, junior, Anne Lehmann, sophomore, Carol Herndon, sophomore, and Patricia Preno, senior.

The girls make the act look so easy that an onlooker begins to think that even he could do it. When it comes to trying it, that's a different story.

The beam is about 4 inches by 18 feet, and after trying to balance himself on the apparatus, Neil Barton, junior, reported that he wouldn't try the stunts they do on that thing on the floor, let alone on it.

Another all girl act is the uneven parallel bars. This is a very versatile apparatus promising unending possibilities of tricks, Diane Gasper, junior, Dixie Young, sophomore, Jan Marecsak, senior, Kathy Schuller, sophomore, Karen Park, sophomore, and JoAnn Hopper have devoted skill, work, and time to the act. They do tricks that even the men admit they wouldn't attempt. The audience loves it.

Gamma Phi will present its circus to the public on March 21, 22, and 23, and not on April 21, 22, and 23 as stated in last week's Vidette.

Mar 12, 1963 (front page)
17 COEDS VIE FOR CROWN . . .
Students To Select Circus Queen
Five girls will be chosen for the court of Gamma Phi Queen March 14. Voting will take place between 8 a.m. and 4 p.m. at the gym and in the dorms.

Each year, clubs and organizations submit candidates to run for the supreme title. The student body then votes for the queen and her court.

The seventeen girls who are contending for the crown and their supporting clubs are: Jackie Pfeiffer, junior, elementary club; Sue Landgraf, sophomore, N club; Patti Gartner, junior, Newman club; Rita Rakers, junior, Young Democrats; Nancy Walters, sophomore, Cloverleaf Collegiates 4-H Club; Bonnie Carter, junior, Industrial Arts Club; Kathy Stoneburner, sophomore, Womens' League; Carol Ann O'Mohundro, sophomore, Mathematics Club; Jean Miller, junior, Home Economics Club; Sue Scharlau, sophomore, Lutheran

Club; Sheila Smith, junior, Lowell Mason Club; Kathy Proehl,
sophomore, Jesters; Linda Murray, junior, Kappa Delta Epsilon;
Judy Simpson, sophomore, PEM Club; Sandy Dunham, junior, WRA.

The rearrangements of the fire exits in the gym are causing some
change in the location of the royal throne. Her Highness will rule
over her subjects from the south end of the gym instead of the north
end, as a result of those changes.

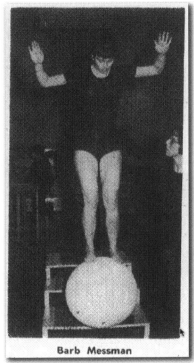

Barb Messman

Vidette Mar 14, 1963 (front page)

Neil Barton

Vidette Mar 14, 1963 (front page)

Mar 14, 1963 (page 4)
Circus Begins Ticket Sale Tomorrow
By JEANINE YEAST

"You're up on a ladder swinging high above the floor. You look to the audience. First they are close to you, then far away. You look at the floor. You see it coming up to meet you, then falling far below you. You get the sensation that the audience and the floor are moving, not you." This was the way the girls who perform on the Swinging Ladders in the Gamma Phi circus described their feelings while they perform.

These girls Bobbi Goulet, Carol Herman, Bari Gillett, Dottie Vosen, Susan Rowe, Judy Anderson and Penny Berning have developed an act that calls for timing, coordination, balance, and arm strength.

Since Gamma Phi puts on a circus that is a circus, they naturally provide a clown act. *"Un-coordination is the basic qualification to be a clown"* declares old clown Ran Smith who will be working with two new clowns, Larry Pennie, and Dale Finfrock.

One of the favorite gymnastics acts is the Parallel Bars employing strength, swing, and balance. It features Deil Whittington, Tom Kordewick, Dale Manning, Sally Jessman, and Al Weith.

"The Balancing Ball looks easier than it is" claims Milt Newman. *"Going down stairs is the hardest part of the act. It should be made into a clown act because we goof so much on it."* That remains to be seen at the circus.

Barb Messman, the other half of the act, will jump rope on the ball and twirl a lariat while balancing on top of it.

Traditional backflips and aerial tricks will be one segment of the tumbling and trampoline act. This act features Cheryl Dreyer, Jeanne Burpee, Paul Ziert, Tom Kordewick, John Fussner, Dale Manning, Marijane Unsucker, and Bill Hunt.

The fast moving vaulting act has developed new jumps, making the act faster and more competitive, endeavoring to employ some of the Danish tricks into the performance.

Vaulting team members are: Barb Messman Cheryl Dreyer, Jeanne Burpee, Betty Daggitt, Don Richter, and Gordon Winkleman, Karen Park, Susan Rowe, Paul Ziert, John Fussner, Ron Thompson, Tom Kordewick, Jim Furrow, Glenn Brownewell, Judy Anderson, Marijane Unsicker and John Read.

Tickets for the Circus will go on sale tomorrow in the gym lobby. Thursday performances are general seats, $.75 for adults, $.25 for children 12 years and under. Reserved seats for Friday and Saturday nights are $1 for adults and $.25 for children 12 years and under.

Mar 14, 1963 (page 8)
WIOK Presents ...

The Gamma Phi Circus will be in the spotlight Saturday afternoon at 2:45 on Dateline: ISNU over WIOK.

Dr. Arley Gillett, director of this year's circus, will offer a preview of the coming Gamma Phi spectacular. He will also relate the unique history of the troupe of circus performers.

The circus will be held March 21, 22, and 23 in McCormick Gymnasium.

Mar 19, 1963 (front page)
Gamma Phi Circus Features Aerialists. Cyclists, Jugglers
By JEANINE YEAST

"Jet Set" on Wheels is the name the unicyclists have given themselves. The performers preparing for Gamma Phi Circus are Nancy DeBosker, Sharon Peters, Dorothy Nesbit, Bill Hunt, Nate Hubbard, Dick Krase, Mike Schmitgall, and Lee Davis.

Lee, an ex-army man, has incorporated some army drills into the act, and Nate will do the twist on the high unicycle for one of the special features of the act.

Juggling and Rope Spinning features Bill Hunt, Milt Neuman, Jill Morser, and Larry Pennie.

Bill and Milt are enthusiasts over juggling and claim it is a thrill to meet the challenge of using more balls. Milt can juggle 3, and Bill has progressed to 4 balls. Bill claims he is working for the day when he can juggle 7 balls at a time, like his mentor, Paul Backman.

Bill's wife, Phyllis Hunt, is director of the rope spinning. "Swivel Wrist" Larry made some of the rope that he and Jill will be. using in the act.

One of the circus' favorite acts is the "Whirlos," starring Janet Miller, Sandi Kinney, Shirley Fitzgerald, Russ Fitzgerald, and Duane Hughes. This will be the second year that this particular group will have skated together. You will recognize Sonny Hughes from the biology department, and Ritz from the Mailroom.

Meg Volk, Ginny Rieger, and Neil Barton will provide the trapeze thrills for the Gamma Phi circus. Meg and Ginny will work together and Neil will work alone. Neil will use his own trapeze which he designed himself. He will also be using his own original "drop-outs" off the trapeze during his performance.

I will close my summary of the acts of the circus with the act which will open it, the Revolving Ladder starring Dale Manning and Bill Hunt. When I asked the men what they thought about while performing, Dale replied that he's always afraid that Bill will fall off. Fear for his fellow man? Not at all! If Bill falls, where does that leave Dale?

Tickets will remain on sale through Friday in the gym lobby. Thursday's prices are $.75 for adults, $.25 for children.

Mar 21, 1963 (front page)
Circus Crowns Queen at Annual Fling

Tonight at 8 p.m. a queen will be crowned and 35 women, 24 men, and two civil service employees— her loyal subjects—will scramble up ropes, ladders, trapezes, bars, balls, rings, and beams, juggle balls and spin ropes. They will turn somersaults, balance on balls, ride bicycles and unicycles, vault over boxes, bounce on trampolines, and clown around to please her majesty's whim and to carry out her first command—perform a circus.

The circus will also perform tomorrow, and Saturday at 8 p.m. in the gym. Tickets are on sale in the gym lobby.

The queen will be one of five girls chosen by the student body during the past week, and her subjects are the 61 performers of the Gamma Phi circus.

Gamma Phi, a self-supporting organization, is directed by student officers. It is sponsored by Dr. Arley F. Gillett and Wayne O. Truex, with Mrs. Arley F. Gillett as the costume supervisor. Gamma Phi owns most of the gymnastic equipment it uses, and all of the costumes worn in its performances.

The Illinois State Stage Band, under the direction of George Foeller, accompanies Gamma Phi during all its performances. The circus is composed of interested students, faculty, and staff from all departments of the University. The performers practice and work on their acts throughout the entire year.

The troupe makes numerous appearances besides the annual performances on campus, and certain acts from the circus represent the organization by special performances before local clubs and area schools.

One of the highlights of the circus is the presentation of the service awards to the outstanding senior members of the organization. These awards are voted upon by the senior members and are awarded on the basis of "manifested spirit of willingness and helpfulness in carrying out the ideals of the organization; and participation in the activities of the organization above and beyond the normal expectations of a member.

One of these coeds will be crowned tonight at the premier of the Gamma Phi Circus in McCormick Gymnasium. From l. to r.—Jackie Pfeiffer, Bonnie Carter, Patti Gartner, Sue Landgraf, and Judy Simpson.

Videte Mar 21, 1963 (front

May 9, 1963 (page 7)

Union Board Hosts Students at Roman Banquet

In a Roman setting with all people present wearing togas, sandals, and vine garland headpieces, University Union Board will shove off the annual Roman Banquet tomorrow at 6 p.m. in the Union Ballroom.

This is a service awards banquet at which 70 campus students who have worked 10 hours or more on Union Board activities, will be presented awards of merit by Bruce T. Kaiser, director of the University Union.
...
A Shakespearean play by a campus drama group, and a presentation by Gamma Phi and Orchesis will be featured.
...

May 16, 1963 (page 4)

John Carroll Speaks To Sixty At UU Annual Roman Banquet

...
Entertainment was provided by a campus drama class, members of Orchesis, and members of Gamma Phi Circus group.
...

May 23, 1963 (page 8)
Stage Band To Present Jazz Concert

...

The group gained experience with appearances at the APO Review, the name change program, Gamma Phi circus, and at the Pantagraph banquet.

...

May 28, 1963 (front page)
Board Slashes Vidette '63-'64 Budget

...

Follow-up stories and interviews of personages visiting the campus will undoubtedly be slashed along with', full coverage offered campus activities such as University theater, AWS Carnival, Gamma Phi Circus, Homecoming, and Entertainment Series.

...

May 28, 1963 (front page)
Campus Impresses Finnish Educator
By LYNN CAINS

"This University is so old, but yet it's so young," stated Paavo Kuosmanen, director of adult education for the Ministry of Education in Helsinki, Finland.

...

The Kuosmanens attended the Gamma Phi Circus and Blood Wedding. The Gamma Phi Circus was of particular interest to Mr. Kuosmanen, a former athlete, because physical education is stressed greatly in Finland. He noted that Paul Ziert and Neil Barton could be classified in the "master's class."

1963 – 64 School Year

The Gamma Phi Circus moves from McCormick Gym to the new Horton Field House—named, of course, after Pop Horton. The move allows for larger audiences and more circus/gymnastic equipment to be set up.

Along with the move for the new circus performance area, practices are moved from McCormick Gym to South Gym in the Horton building.

Front Row: Jean Hovde, Erika Idzelis, Kathy Vignocchi, Paul Ziert, Dale Manning, Diane Gasper, Ryan Smith, John Fussner, Virginia Rieger, Mrs. Gillett, Arley Gillett; adviser. Second Row: Carol Snodgrass, Annemarie Liberti, Carol Herndon, Cheryl Dreyer, Dixie Young, Jill Manning, Gordon Winkelman, Karen Park, Sue Rowe, Toni Kordewick, Wayne Truex; adviser. Third Row: Peggy Stern, Dinah Mohus, Carol Herman, Larry Penny, Paula Polechla, Jean Burpee, Sandee Chilton, Karl Heien, Jerri Beesley. Fourth Row: Milt Neuman, Betty Daggitt, Gail Sherer, Sandy Brunneman, Dale Kuhn, Jim Furrow, Neil Whittington, Dan Heagstedt. Back Row: Nick Ellis, Lee Davis, Terry Tamblyn, Dick Krase, Dorothy Nesbit, Richard Schuler, Ed Ceres.

1964 Index (page 43)

Dec 10, 1963 (page 4)
Whirlo's Perform On Amateur Hour

Russell Fitzgerald, supervisor of the mail room at Illinois State, and his daughter, will appear on the Ted Mack Amateur Hour over CBS television Sunday, Dec. 15. The Fitzgeralds, known as the "Whirlo's," perform a skating act that has been an annual feature of the Gamma Phi Circus at Illinois State each spring.

The show was taped in Chicago Nov. 20 before a live audience in the WBBM-TV studios. It will be seen locally over WCIA, channel 3, Champaign and WMBD, channel 31, Peoria at 4:30 p.m. Sunday.

Fitzgerald formed the act in 1959, and since then the Whirlo's have appeared at county numerous PTA functions, and at the annual polio benefit of McLean County.

Fitzgerald's daughter Shirley is an eighth grade student at Holy Trinity Grade School and learning a trapeze act for use in the Gamma Phi Circus.

Mar 17, 1964 (front page)
Clubs Nominate Twenty Coeds For Gamma Phi Circus Queen

Students will go to the polls Thursday to vote in the all-school election for Gamma Phi Queen.

The polls will be open from 8 a.m. to 4 p.m. in the Union, at the west entrance to Horton Fieldhouse and in Schroeder Hall.

Twenty coeds have been chosen to represent various clubs campus in the election. One girl will be elected to reign over the Gamma Phi Circus April 10 and 11.

The girls who have nominated and their club sponsors are Marcy Stine, Home Economics Club: Sandy Marquiss, Blackfriars; Jane Adams, Jesters; Sandy Shaner, Kappa Mu Epsilon.

Sally Sawyer, Theta Alpha Tau; Sandy Zaccagni, Kappa Epsilon: Carmelita Edgerton, AWS: Janet Drew, Industrial Arts Club: Marsha Sloan, Coryphees; and Carolyn Dwyer, Lowell Mason Club.

Holly Alexander, Senate; Kaye Johnson, Lettermen's Club; Pat Kuybida, Newman Club; Sharon Curley, Geography Club; Jan Axelson, Women's P.E. Club.

Lorraine Kracmer, Lutheran Club; Lynn Pedigo, Education Club; Bonnie Scents, A.C.E.; Diane Dal Pra, WRA; and Linda Rivers, English Club.

PERFECT BALANCE—Bobbie Goulet, sophomore in art from Springfield, is shown above as she prepares her act as part of Illinois State's annual Gamma Phi Circus. Bobbie is a veteran Gamma Phi member who is skilled in the art of perfect balance on both the ball and the webs.

Vidette Mar 17, 1964 (page 4)

Gamma Phi Performs Circus In Horton Gym

"Pop" Horton won't really "pop," nor will he be unhappy when he hears that Gamma Phi is making a "circus" out of Horton Gymnasium April 10-11.

With the help of several faculty members fifty of Illinois State's students will comprise the circus which has been a highlight of campus activity since 1930. The math, English, elementary and physical education departments are in greatest representation.

With tryouts for the circus squad out of the way, the troupe can now concentrate its energies on the presentation of the circus.

The home of Gamma Phi has changed from "Mother" McCormick to "Haughty" Horton and many problems are involved. First of all, the ceiling of the Fieldhouse has to be "lowered" for the aerial acts such as the trapeze, still rings and Spanish webs.

Also, the immensity of the Fieldhouse lessens the opportunity for interaction of the performers and the audience. But a spontaneous spirit of "family-ness" is generated by the troupe which counteracts any coldness of the gym.

Although the members of the circus squad are picked for their excellence in the gymnastics field, several of the members have had no previous experience other than that gained in Gamma Phi.

New members of the squad are Jean Bradshaw, Sandy Brenneman, Carol Capponi, Sandy Chilton, Jan Hartung, Dan Heagstedt, Ricki Idzelis, Dale Kuhn, Anne Marie Liberti, Dinah Mobus, Gail Sherer, Carol Snodgrass, Peg Stearns and Kathy Vignocchi.

Gamma Phi holds regular weekly practices throughout the year and conducts tryouts for the Circus squad in February. organization is self-supporting and owns most of the gymnastic equipment and all of the costumes used in the circus.

In addition to the annual circus, small groups of the squad make numerous appearances before local clubs and area schools. The entire group will give three off-campus performances in Fairbury, Dwight and Mendota.

SPANISH WHIPS—Two members of the Gamma Phi Troupe, Sandy Brenneman and Gail Sherer, seem to be extended into mid air as they practice routines for this year's circus.

March 19, 1964 (page 4)

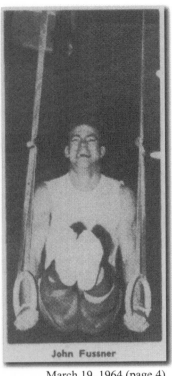

John Fussner

March 19, 1964 (page 4)

Kathy Vignocchi

March 19, 1964 (page 4)

Carol Herndon

March 19, 1964 (page 4)

367   A Circus in the Paper

Gamma Phi Displays Bright Colors, Pageantry; Clowns, Tumblers Thrill Audience With Daring

Everybody loves a Children's eyes are caught by the bright colors and the funny stunts of the clowns. The daring feats of performers attract "young adults," and older adults enjoy the general excitement pervading all.

Gamma Phi presents all of these aspects in its annual circus at 8 p.m. on Friday and Saturday in Horton Fieldhouse.

Circus-goers will be greeted by gay music and bright streamers and flags forming a big top in entrance. The gym itself will dominated by red, white and blue panels and large, merry clowns.

After the general excitement is relaxed and everyone has found his seat, ringmaster Ed Ceres announce the queen and her court who will reign over the proceedings. Then the entrance of Circus Troupe and the circus will get underway.

Acts of the circus include the parallel bars, trapeze, balance beam, trampoline, uneven parallels, rope spinning, unicycle, rings, tumbling, ball, and vaulting.

There are also several new acts. Free exercise consisting tumbling and balance moves will be performed by a group of 15 men and women in unison precision timing, grace coordination.

The Big Wheel is two circles connected in the form of a figure eight. while circling around each other two girls do balance moves.

The most astonishing act performed by the clowns. They have perfected skilled ways of throwing sharp, man-killing objects that will not injure men — at least not very much.

While you sleep tonight bakers will be baking bread — and circus performers will be dreaming of their routines and putting the last minute touches on them.

Tickets are still available for both performances and may be purchased in the Student Union from 8 a.m. to 4 p.m. today tomorrow. The remainder of tickets will be sold at the door. Prices are $1 for adults and 30 cents elementary school students. All seats are general admission.

Apr 9, 1964 (page 6)
Annual ISU Sports Banquet Features Northwestern Director Stu Holcomb As Main Speaker For I Men, Guests

...

A new award, the Horton award for the outstanding gymnast of the year, is being sponsored by Gamma Phi and will be presented to Paul Ziert, Creve Coeur, by Coach Wayne O. Truex.

ROSES—Gamma Phi Queen Janet Drew, holding a nest of red roses, is crowned by Dale Manning in Friday evening ceremonies preceding the Gamma Phi Circus performance.

April 14, 1964 (front page)

May 12, 1964 (front page)

Union Honors Seventy ISU Students At Annual Roman Banquet Wednesday

...

At this banquet, people will sit on pillows and eat the meal with their fingers from two feet high tables arranged in a During the meal, Latin Club and Gamma Phi will entertainment in the center of this square.

1964 – 65 School Year

Front Row: Jean Hovde, Erika Idzebs, Kathy Vignocchi, Paul Ziert, Dale Manning, Diane Gasper, Ryan Smith, John Fussner, Virginia Rieger, Mrs. Gillett, Arley Gillett, adviser. Second Row: Carol Snodgrass, Annemarie Liberti, Carol Herndon, Cheryl Dreyer, Dixie Young, Jill Manning, Gordon Winkelman, Karen Park, Sue Rowe, Tom Kordewick, Wayne Trues, adviser. Third Row: Peggy Stern, Dinah Mobus, Carol Herman, Larry Penny, Paula Polechla, Jean Burpee, Sandee Chilton, Karl Heien, Jerri Beesley. Fourth Row: Milt Nenman, Betty Daggitt, Gail Sherer, Sandy Brenneman, Dale Kuhn, Jim Furrow, Neil Whittington, Dan Heagstedt. Back Row: Nick Ellis, Lee Davis, Terry Tamblyn, Dick Krase, Dorothy Nesbit, Richard Schaber, Ed Ceres.

1965 Index (page 92)

Oct 29, 1964 (page 4)
Organizations Join In Parade Saturday
...

The ISU club organizations shall add their contributions to festivity with 26 floats displaying this year's Homecoming "Halloween Holiday." The Industrial Arts Club escort the 1963-64 Gamma Phi Queen, while the Gamma Phi organization will enter with "A Grave Defeat."

The Lutheran Club will enter a float, the Student Senate will ride in a 1965 convertible and Industrial Arts Club will escort Miss Gamma Phi Queen of 1933-34 in a 1934 Chevrolet Coryse.

Feb 25, 1965 (page 3)
Sign Warns Residents Of Peddling Unicyclist
A sign taped to the doorway of third floor Hamilton Hall tells the story: "Beware of the Unicycle." Any time of the night or day, an inexperienced rider is apt to come awkwardly peddling down a narrow hallway on her one-wheeled vehicle.

How did it all start? Hansen, sophomore in education, had to give a visual aids speech, and she wanted to do something really different. "I've always wanted to learn to ride a unicycle," she said, "and now I have a good reason."

She borrowed a unicycle from Rich Schuler, a Gamma Phi rider, and the next thing the third floor knew, Judi was slowly painstakingly making her way up and down the hall.

At first it was necessary to mount the cycle by using doorway of a room. With a sudden push, Judi would pedal her way down the hall, using her hands against the wall for balance.

Asked if she'd had any accidents, Judi looked at her colorful knees and grimaced, "I've got bruises all over from falling."

Now, other girls on the floor are riding the unicycle whenever Judi isn't practicing. They've become so attached to it, in fact, that they are thinking of taking up collection of $1.10 each to buy their own vehicle!

Judi's big day came Tuesday. Sitting on the unicycle hanging on to the blackboard, she gave her speech. Her instructor gave her the traditional "A for effort."

Mar 11, 1965 (front page)
Gymnasts Perform Acrobatic Feats At 29th Annual Gamma Phi Circus

Gamma Phi, honorary gymnastic fraternity, will present their 29th annual circus at 8 p.m. on March 26 and 27 in the Horton Fieldhouse. "There are no lions or tigers in the literal sense, or anything like that," stated Paula Polechla, head of publicity. "And it's not circus either. It's a combination of circus and gymnastic acts."

There are about 50 students in Gamma Phi, which was organized in 1928. Sponsors are Dr. Arley Gillett, professor of health and physical education, and Wayne Truex, assistant professor of health and physical education.

—Photo by Karen Vasos

THROUGH TRAFFIC—Judi Hansen is given the right-of-way as she rides her unicycle through the halls on third floor Hamilton.

Feb 25, 1965 (page 3)

The first act will feature the ISU Stage Band under the direction of George Foeller, instructor in music, followed by the queen's coronation.

Perform On Rings
Tod Fassbender, Joe Long and Paul Ziert will be featured on the horizontal bar. Gloria Brown, Carol Herman, Carol Herndon, Ricki Idzelis, Dinah Mobus and Judy Preno will comprise the balance beam. On the trapeze will be Betty Daggitt and Bob Herndon.

Rings performers are Miss Brown, Rhea Chouinard, Herman, Annamarie Liberti, Nancy Schermeizhorn,, Leslie Sheets, Kathy Vignocchi, Fassbender, Jim Furrow, Long, Dan Malloy and Willy Vrba.

Unicycles will be ridden by Lee Davis, Carol Fortney, Phil Harms, Dan Heagstedt, Bob Herndon, Dick Krase, Dorothy Nesbit, Dave Nesbit and Rich Schuler.

Clown At Circus
Free exercises will be done by Jeannie Burpee, Miss Daggitt, Pam Hahn, Diane Hermer, Herman, Miss Idzelis, Miss Mobus, Karen Pinney, Jane Sellers, Kathy Schuller, Miss Vignocchi and Joyce Zetterlind.

Dan Heagstedt, Dale Kuhn, Karl Heien, Larry Pennie and Gary Stevens will be the circus clowns, and Miss Burpee, Miss Sheets, Kathy Schuller and Dixie Young will perform on the parallels.

Milt Neuman will center his act around a ball, and Peggy Stearns, Miss Vignocchi, Neal Whittington, Furrow, Long, Tom Kordewick and Ziert will appear on the parallel bar and the parallels.

Perform on Trampolets
Trampoline artists will be Sandee Chilton, Tom Kordewick, Stevens and Ziert. On the webs, will be Sandy Brenneman, Miss Brown, Miss Herman, Karon Park, Miss Polechla and Miss Schermerhorn.

The tumbling and trampolet acts will feature John Kordewick, Jane Sellers, Miss Zetterlind, Ziert, Diane Harmer and Karen Pinney.

Lee Davis, Furrow, Fussner, Karl Heien, Kordewick, Dan Malloy, Whittington, Gordon Winkleman, Ziert, Miss Burpee, Miss Herman, Miss Harmer, Miss Park, Miss Pinney and Leslie Sheets will do vaulting.

Head Queen Committee
Chairman of the committee is Miss Chilton. Equipment co-chairmen are Dan Malloy and Long. In charge of publicity are Miss Polechla and Miss Daggitt, co-chairmen.

Social chairman is Miss Herman, and Miss Mobus and Miss Herndon are music co-chairmen. In charge of decorations are Miss Idzelis and Miss Burpee. Dan Heagstedt is in charge of the program.

Heading the queen committee is Miss Park. Ticket chairman is Kordewick, and Miss Brenneman is head of lighting.

The Gamma Phi Circus will also be presented in Beardstown, and parts of the show will be performed at Thornton Fractional and LaSalle-Peru High Schools.

Tickets for the circus will be sold March 22 through 26 at the University Union. They will also be available at the door the nights of performance.

Cost of the tickets is $1 for adults, and 50 cents for children eighth grade and under. There will be no reserved seats.

March 16, 1965 (page 2)

March 16, 1965 (front page)

Mar 18, 1965 (front page)
Calypso Music ...

Circus Performers Rehearse For Annual Gamma Phi Show
*Strains of calypso music echo in Horton Fieldhouse as Gamma Phi
performers rehearse their acts for the coming Gamma Phi circus, at
8 p.m. March 26 and 27.*

*On uneven parallel bars, Leslie Sheets, freshman in economics,
demonstrates specialty, an act in which she swings from one bar to
another in an intricate series of maneuvers from one height to
another. In another area, Betty Daggitt, junior in English, attaches
herself to a suspended bar with a sling around her neck. At an
increasing speed, she rotates herself through the air.*

The rehearsal stops when Gloria Brown, a special student business, catches her foot hanging from the webs 20 feet above the floor. After agonizing minutes with a large portion of the circus members focusing their attention on her, she frees herself and shrugs off her predicament, "I was more scared than anything." Back up she goes.

Other rehearsals have perfected various routines: a foot revolve, in which a woman on a trapeze swing in complete revolutions around a stationary bar; a revolving ladder act, consisting of two performing stunts of agility balance at the ends of a revolving ladder and free exercise, a unison performance of tumbling balancing acts for 12 women.

With the exception of the war years, Gamma Phi has produced an annual circus since 1930.

Mar 18, 1965 (page 4)
Head Coach Truex, Six Squad Members Depart For NAIA National Gymnastics Meet In Kansas
Illinois State gymnastics coach Wayne O. Truex and six members of his gym team left yesterday for Hayes, Kan., compete in the NAIA gymnastics meet at Fort Hayes Kansas State College today and tomorrow.

State's veteran squad finished a strong second at Eastern Illinois University March 5-6 in Interstate Intercollegiate Conference meet.

The six man team which will represent ISU in their quest for national honors includes Paul Ziert, Tom Kordewick, Neil Whittington, Dan Malloy, Jim Furrow and John Fussner.

Ziert, voted the Outstanding Gymnast" award at the recent IIAC meet at EIU will compete in all-around competition along with Furrow and Whittington. The slim-built senior captain placed in six events at Eastern, winning the tumbling, free exercise and long-horse vaulting event while placing second in trampoline, third in all around and fifth in competition.

377   A Circus in the Paper

Senior lettermen Kordewick, who finished third in trampoline, eighth in free exercise and sixth in tumbling, will compete in these three events and long vaulting at Kansas State.

Fussner is scheduled for duty on the side horse and trampoline at Kansas, while Malloy specialize on the still rings.

Mar 23, 1965 (page 4)

Strains of calypso music echo in Horton Fieldhouse as Gamma Phi performers rehearse their acts for the coming Gamma Phi circus, at 8 p.m. March 26 and 27.

Rehearsals have perfected various routines: a foot revolve, in which a woman on a trapeze swings in complete revolutions around stationary bar; a revolving ladder act, consisting of two men performing stunts of agility and balance at the ends of a revolving ladder and free exercise, a performance of tumbling and balancing acts for 12 women.

The co-educational gymnastics fraternity, organized in 1928, draws its members interested students, from all departments of the University. In the troupe this year are over 50 performers who will present 15 fast-moving acts of skill on the parallel bars, balancing ball, and other gymnastic equipment. Novelty acts on unicycles, antics of clowns and the coronation ceremony for the Gamma Phi queen are among the many features which entertainment for all age groups.

Tickets for shows on campus may be purchased at the door on performance nights. There will be 3,000 spectator seats available each night and only general admission tickets are required. No seats are to be reserved. Anyone wishing to purchase tickets in advance may do so by contacting Dr. Arley F. Gillett at ISU.

Mar 25, 1965 (front page)

Gamma Phi Show Starts Friday

Annual Circus Features Variety, Queen, Clowns

Circus thrills will abound on the Illinois State campus beginning at 8 p.m. tomorrow and Saturday evenings as Gamma Phi, honorary gymnastics fraternity, will present their 29th annual circus in Horton Fieldhouse. Under the direction of student officers and co-sponsors Dr. Arley F. Gillett and Wayne O. Truex, Gamma Phi will present a variety of circus and gymnastics acts.

There are about 50 students in Gamma Phi, which was organized by Dr. Gillett In 1928. The circus has been a traditional part of every school year, performing in McCormick Gymnasium until last year when they moved into the new fieldhouse.

Presents Queen
The first act of the evening will feature the ISU Stage Band under the direction of George Foeller, instructor in music. The stage band will play for both home shows in addition to traveling with the circus squad on performances.

Following the overture by the band, ringmaster Steve Craig will present the queen and her court. The circus acts begin with the royal command of the Gamma Phi Circus queen.

Making up the royalty are Karen Bock, senior in elementary who represents ACE; Donna Doetch, junior in special education who was nominated by Industrial Arts Club; Margie Herman, sophomore in elementary who was sponsored by WRA; Gloria Thomas, junior in geography who. was Newman Club's candidate and Barb sophomore in health and education who was selected as the IClub candidate.

Ride Unicycles
Tod Fassbender, Joe Long and Paul Ziert will be featured on the horizontal bar. Gloria Carol Herman, Carol Herndon, Ricki Idzelis, Dinah Mobus and Judy Preno will comprise the balance beam, while thrills and chills will be provided by Betty Daggitt and Bob Herndon on the trapeze.

Performing on the rings will be Gloria Brown, Rhea Chouinard, Miss Herman, Annemarie Liberti, Nancy Schermerhorn, Leslie Sheets, Kathy Fassbender, Jim Furrow, Long, Dan Malloy and Willy Vrba.

Riding the one wheel bicycle will be unicycle specialists Lee Davis, Carol Fortney, Phil Harms, Dan Heagstedt, Bob Herndon, Dick Krase, Dorothy Nesbit, Dave Nesbit and Rich Schuler.

A new routine in free exercise will feature an all performance by Jeannie Burpee, Daggitt, Pam Hahn, Diane Hermer, Miss Herman, Miss Idzelis, Miss Mobus, Karen Pinney, Jane Sellers, Kathy Schuller, Miss Vignocchi and Joyce Zetterlind.

Turn Attention Upward
Providing laughs before during the circus will be circus clowns Dan Heagstedt, Dale Kuhn, Karl Heien, Larry Pennie and Gary Stevens. Performing on uneven parallel bars will be Miss Burpee, Miss Sheets, Schuller and Dixie Young.

Trampoline artists include Sandee Chilton, John Fussner, Kordewick, Stevens and Ziert. Turning audience attention to the regions of Horton will performers on the webs, Sandy Brenneman, Miss Brown, Miss Herman, Karon Park, Miss Polechla and Miss Schermeizhorn.

The tumbling and trampolet acts will feature John Fussner, Kordewick, Jane Sellers, Miss Zetterlind, Ziert, Diana Harmer and Karen Pinney.

Cancel Appearance
Lee Davis, Furrow, Fussner, Karl Heien, Kordewick, Malloy, Neil Whittington, Gordon Winkleman. Ziert, Miss Burpee, Miss Herman, Miss Harmer, Miss Park, Pinney and Leslie Sheets will do vaulting. In addition to their performances Gamma Phi will travel to Beardstown on April 23 and LaSalle-Peru on April 30. The circus squad was to have performed at Thornton Township High School in Harvey, Tuesday, but the show was postponed by the bad weather.

March 23, 1965 (page 4)

A Circus in the Paper

Tickets for the circus are $1 for adults and 50 cents for children, 8th grade and under. The tickets are presently being sold in the University Union and will be available at the door. There are no reserved seats.

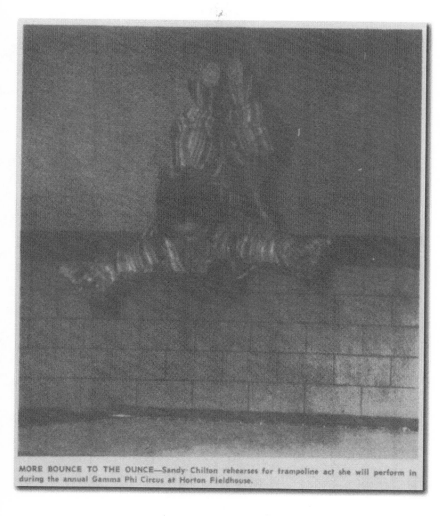

MORE BOUNCE TO THE OUNCE—Sandy Chilton rehearses for trampoline act she will perform in during the annual Gamma Phi Circus at Horton Fieldhouse.

March 25, 1965 (front page)

1964 - 65 School Year   382

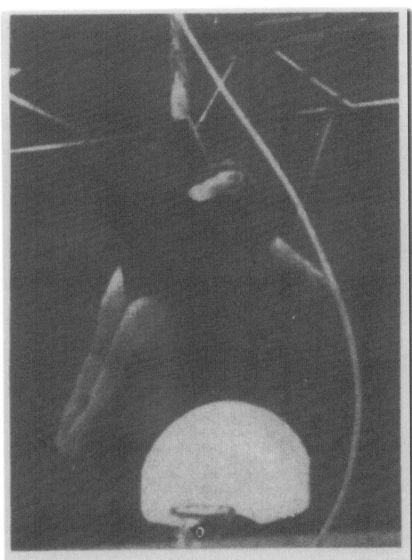

'ROUND AND 'ROUND WE GO—Gamma Phi circus performer runs through final practice on the webs before show opening Friday evening.

March 25, 1965 (front page)

383   A Circus in the Paper

ROYALTY REIGNS—Barb White, sophomore in p.e., reigned Friday and Saturday as Gamma Phi Queen. After being crowned by Paul Ziert, Gamma Phi president, she commanded that the performance begin.

March 30, 1965 (page 3)

May 13, 1965 (page 4)
Ziert Concludes Memorable Career
Leading Gymnast Ends Reign; Hits Academic, Athletic Highs
By JOE CIPFL

A phenomenal athlete and an ideal student is merely a minor description of probably one of the top students who has ever attended Illinois State University.

Who fulfills this description? I believe that an answer to the question is not even necessary — none other than Paul Ziert.

The mild-mannered, quick-talking gymnast has proven himself a topflight student by maintaining a 3.406 grade point average in seven semesters here at ISU. He is now completing his final semester.

Gymnastics is not his extracurricular activity. If one examines a list of what this student-athlete has done plus looking at his grade point, one might feel a bit ashamed of himself.

Awarded School Monogram
In his first year of attendance at Illinois State, Ziert became a member of Gamma Phi. completing a full season of competition with the gym team, he was awarded the school monogram.

Participating in all-conference gymnastic meet during this same year, Paul chalked up a first in tumbling, a second in exercise, and a third on the trampoline. Quite an accomplishment for a freshman!

At the honors day convocation at the end of his freshman year. Ziert received honors, as he ranked in the top three per cent of his class.

Still finding free time during his beginning sophomore days, Paul became a member of the Big Four Committee, along with continuing his Gamma Phi membership.

Enters Math Honorary
During this same year, he also qualified for entry into Kappa Mu Epsilon, the honorary math fraternity, and, naturally, he entered.

Attaining his second award in gymnastics, Paul participated in the all-conference meet once again. That year he copped a first in both tumbling and in free exercise, in addition to taking a second on the trampoline.

Gaining two firsts and the one second enabled him to enter the NCAA national tournament at Pittsburg. Competing outstanding athletes from practically every college in the nation, Ziert tied for fifth place honors tumbling and took thirteenth in free exercise.

Being just a member of organizations was not enough for Paul Ziert; he had to become an officer in them. In his junior year, Ziert was elected co-chairman of the Big Four Committee and social chairman of Gamma Phi - both positions taking many long tiresome hours of work.

Besides being a member of the math fraternity, Paul qualified for membership in Pi Gamma Mu, the honorary social science fraternity -- once again he entered.

Gains Horton Award
In the spring of that year Ziert was awarded the Horton Award, an annual honor which goes to the outstanding athlete at ISU.

Again capturing a letter gymnastics, he entered the conference meet. He made a repeat of his sophomore year and took first in tumbling and free exercise and a second on the trampoline.

He went to the NCAA finals at Los Angeles and was awarded a fifth in tumbling and an eleventh in free exercise.

Then Paul entered his final year, a year which he is now completing. He repeated as co-chairman of the Big Four Committee, but became president of Gamma Phi.

He was recognized as one of the outstanding seniors this year at Illinois State. However, his real honor came when he was selected by "Who's Who," a publication honoring those upperclassmen rendering outstanding services to their universities.

Wins Fourth Letter
Being awarded his fourth letter, thus making him a four-year letterman, Paul made his appearance at the all-conference meet - an appearance which will long be remembered.

In the competition, Ziert captured a first in free exercise, a first in tumbling, a first in long horse vaulting and a second on the trampoline. For that activities, Ziert was awarded a trophy for the outstanding athlete of the entire meet.

Because he had participated in gymnastics as a varsity member since his freshman year, Ziert was not allowed to enter NCAA competition.

He and the rest of the gymnastic squad went to the tournament. Once again, he captured a first in free exercise, a first in tumbling and a second on the trampoline.

At the all sports banquet which was held last month, Ziert received the Richard G. Brown Award. This award goes to the junior or senior athlete who has maintained the highest grade point average in the University.

Paul Ziert is definitely both an outstanding athlete and an outstanding student. Hats off to Paul Ziert!

1965 – 66 School Year

GAMMA PHI. Front Row: Alan Weith, assistant adviser; Paula Palechia, Jeanie Burpee, secretary; Gordon Winkelman, president; Larry Pennie, vice-president; Carol Herman, treasurer; Dr. Arley F. Gillett, adviser. Second Row: Bobbi Goulet, Cindy Haynie, Kathy Mulligan, Dan Heagstedt, Joyce Zetterlind, Bill Stark, Cheri Moore, Betsy Komaienc, Tom Hons, Ted Fassbender, Sue Weast. Third Row: Judy Brown, Becky Stone, Mary Krause, April Peterson, Dinah Mobus, Karen Pinney, Diana Harmer, Karl Helen, Lesley Sheets, Joe Long, Jerry Jones. Back Row: Rich Schuler, Sandy Brenneman, Dorothy Nebit, Dave Nesbit, Bill Dueringer, Bob Court, Dale Finfrock, Nancy Schermerhorn, Willy Vrba, Eric Keipper, Mel Wheeler.

Oct 7, 1965 (page 4)
Gamma Phi Works Out
Gamma Phi will hold a workout session every Monday from 7 to 9 p.m. in the South Gym, Horton Field House. Those interested are invited to attend.

Oct 21, 1965 (front page)
Dignitaries, Camel, Floats Highlight Saturday Parade
...
Varied Float Themes
...
Gamma Phi portrays "After a Night's Victory."
...

Oct 21, 1965 (page 11)
Homecoming Calendar
Saturday, October 23
...
After Parade - Gamma Phi and "I" Club Open House, Concession Area West of Horton

Jan 11, 1966 (page 4)
ISU Sets Scoring Record; Defense Lags In NIU Loss
...
Birdies Take Lead Every time Carthage started building a big lead, the Redbirds came on strong until the Birdies streaked ahead to take a 58-54 lead at halftime. The entertainment was provided by cyclists from Gamma Phi led by Sandy Brenneman and Judy Janecke.

Feb 24, 1966 (page 4)
Gillett Named ISU Athletic Director
Appointment of Dr. Arley Gillett, 50, to succeed Dr. Burton L. O'Connor as head of Department of Health and Education for Men and director of Athletics at Illinois University was announced today by ISU President Robert G. Bone.

Effective Sept. 1, 1966, promotion of Gillett to head department, of which he has been a member for 22 years, was made by President Bone following recommendation of a selection committee.

The committee recommended that Dr. Gillett be following a survey of the members of the health and education department which revealed a very large majority in favor of the appointment.

Announcement came six weeks after Dr. O'Connor, head of the department for five years athletic director for three, asked to be relieved of his administrative duties effective Sept. 1 because of health reasons.

Dr. O'Connor is recuperating from a series of two eye operations which have necessary within the past five months.

No Changes Yet
Dr. Gillett has indicated that the department will continue to be organized in three basic areas physical education, athletics, and intramurals, with the possibility of adding other areas as University program is expanded.

He said that it is likely that a person will be named to assist with the direction of the athletic program at a future date.

An ISU staff member since 1944, Dr. Gillett is now serving coordinator of the health physical education program on campus.

He has held this position for three years, following a year as State Director of Health, Physical Education, Safety, Education, and Outdoor Recreation for the Office of the Superintendent of Public Instruction, Springfield.

Prior to this Dr. Gillett Director of Physical Education for the Metcalf School, elementary school, and for a number of years, supervised student teaching both on and off the campus. He also taught University classes on both the undergraduate and graduate level.

Former Wrestler and Gymnast
Active in wrestling gymnastics as an undergraduate at ISU, he has coached wrestling University High School and has served as sponsor and coach of Gamma Phi, honorary fraternity, since 1947.

Widely known as a speaker and writer in his field, Dr. Gillett holds membership in Phi Delta Kappa; the NEA and IEA; the American and the Illinois Associations for Recreational; the National College Physical Education Association; and the Normal Rotary Club.

He has held editorial and other posts in state, regional, national organizations, and currently serving as editor of Illinois News — the official publication of the IAHPER.

Just completing two terms on the University Council, elected campus-wide advisory Gillett has also served on University Budget

Committee and as coordinator of committees in curriculum development.

After earning a degree from ISU in 1938, he completed the requirements for his M.A. at New York University in 1942 and a doctorate from University in 1954.

Dr. Gillett started his teaching career as an instructor elementary education in Peru, Illinois public schools in 1938-43, district supervisor for the Department of Welfare from 1943-44, and served with the U.S. Army in 1945-46.

Mar 24, 1966 (front page)
Carnival Mood Prevails At AWS 'Midterm Midway'

...

The Carnival has many things to offer this year. First of all, there will be several original booths sponsored by organizations. Second entertainment will consist of Gamma Phi with gymnastics acts, "The Three of Us" with folk singing, and the Lloyd Shaw Dancers with square dancing. Refreshments, cotton candy, clowns, and fun will add to the atmosphere. Purpose of the carnival is to unite the efforts of organizations in raising funds for the Mental Health Center.

...

Mar 29, 1966 (front page)
Acrobatics, Clowns Enliven Gamma Phi Circus

Gamma Phi Circus, highlight of ISU's spring activities, will presented on April 22 and 23 at 8 p.m. in Horton Fieldhouse. This is the Circus's 30th annual presentation.

Gamma Phi, gymnastic fraternity, is composed of members of the student body, as well as faculty and staff. Anyone is eligible to attend Monday night practices first semester to learn and develop gymnastic acrobatic skills.

In February, tryouts are held for the Circus squad. Members of the squad then devote two nights each week to practice for the Circus.

Features of the 1966 include two free exercise routines by 14 ISU coeds; an Indian fire dance, where two Indian maidens search for a sun goddess, dancing with hoops and a ring of fire; two Gamma Phi members performing daring hand-to-hand stunts on a high trapeze; and spinning wildly on the big demonstrating their balance coordination.

Performers selected for different gymnastic stunts include: on the balance beam — Carol Herman, Dinah Mobus, Kathy Mulligan, and Betty Komlanc; on the parallel bars — Jeannie Burpee, Cindy Haynie, Diane Harmer, and Paula Poechla; on the webs —Sandy Brenneman, Janet Giugler, Bobbi Goulet, Carol Herman, Paula Polechla, and Nancy Schermerhorn; working the trampoline — Eric Keipper, Mel Wheeler, and Bob Hendron; men on the parallel bars — Jerry Jones, Tod Fassbender, Willy Vrba, and Joe Long; tumbling — Hendron, Mel Wheeler, Bob Court, Cindy Haynie, Jeannie Burpee, Kathy Mulligan, Debbie Smith, and Joyce Zetterlind; riding unicycles — Dave Nesbit, Dan Heagstadt, Dick Schuler, Bob Hendron, Bill Dueringer, Dave Kerns, Tom Best, Tom Honn, Sandy Brenneman, and Sue Weast.

Tod Fassbender and Joe Long will perform on the high Working the muscle-demanding rings will be: Jerry Jones, Fassbender, Joe Long, Bob Lesley Sheets, Nancy Schermerhorn, and Mary Knouse.

Gordon Kinkelman, Chuck Strayer, Willy Vrba, Bill Stark, Eric Keipper, Karl Heien, Herman, Diane Harmer, Karen Pinney, Jeannie Burpee, Judy Brown, and Cheri Moore are members of this year's vaulting squad.

This spring Larry Pennie will be featured with the slack rope. Also featured will be Bobbi Goulet and Tom Honn demonstrating great balance on the ball. Participants in the big wheel act will be chosen from the entire squad.

Like all good circuses, Gamma Phi Circus will be attended by three clowns. The members of the Circus, are Heagstadt, Karl Heien, and Pennie.

Trapeze artists include Hendron, Cheri Moore, Janet Giugler, and Lesley Sheets. Kathy Mulligan and Cindy Haynie will do Indian Fire Dance.

The members of ball gymnastic routines arc as follows: Peterson, Mary Knouse, Becky Stone, Lesley Sheets, Judy Brown, Bobbi Goulet. Dinah Mobus, Sue Weast, Diana Harmer, Karen Pinney, Paula Polechia, Carol Herman, Giugler, and Nancy Schermerhorn.

Thrilling the audience with feats of courage and skill on the high trapeze will be Dale Finfrock and Cheri Moore.

Cost for this year's performance will be $1 for adults and 50 cents for children. Gamma Phi, under the direction of Arley G. Gillett and assistant sponsor Alan W. Weith, organized in 1928 by Dr. C. Horton, head of the department of physical education for men. At first, the organization was limited to men and exhibited only formal gymnastic work. Circus acts were gradually introduced into program. In 1961, women allowed to join and have added graceful talent to the Circus.

The Circus, which has been an annual event on ISU's campus since 1930, is self-supporting and owns most of the gymnastic equipment and all of the costumes used in the circus.

Members of Gamma participate or head responsible for the entire organization of the circus. This year's committees and their chairmen are costumes, Diane Harmer and Karen Pinney; decorations, Jeannie equipment, Willy Vrba; lighting, Karl Heien; Music, Carol program, Larry Pennie; publicity, Paula Polechla; queen, Burpee and Larry Pennie; Social hour, Paula Polechla; and Gordon Winkelman.

Committees are under the direction of the 1965-66 Gamma Phi officers. This year's officers are president, Gordon Winkleman; vice president, Larry Pennie; secretary, Jeannie Burpee; treasurer, Carol Herman; and social chairman, Paula Polechla. Mrs. Arley F. Gillett is costume supervisor.

The week before the circus at ISU, on April 14, the entire circus will travel to Decatur to perform at an all-school assembly at Stephen Decatur High School. afternoon they will again perform at the Eisenhower High School. At 8 p.m. on May 6, they will perform at Joliet East High School.

Mar 31, 1966 (front page)
Gamma Phi Invite Queen Nominations
With Gamma Phi approaching. each organization on the ISU campus has been invited to nominate one girl to run for queen of the annual event, to be held on April 22 and 23 in Horton Fieldhouse. A queen and a court of four will be selected from nominated in an all-school election scheduled for Wednesday. April 13.

After everyone has found his seat in the fieldhouse. the queen will be crowned and will give her royal command for the circus to begin. The queen and her court will reign over both on-campus performances and an off-campus performance, if the circus travels to her highness' hometown for an off campus performance.

Last year's queen was Barb White, then a sophomore in health and physical education Her court consisted of Karen Bock. Donna Doetch. Margie Craig, and Gloria Thomas.

Elections this year will be held April 13 in the I man, and Morton Fieldhouse Each polling place will have a list of the candidates and a picture of each.

Apr 19, 1966 (page 3)
Gamma Phi Circus Opens Friday; Highlights Little Sister Weekend
The annual spring Gamma Phi Circus will highlight this year's Little Sister Weekend. The circus's 30th presentation will begin at 8 p.m. this Friday and evening in Horton Fieldhouse.

Members of the co-educational gymnastic fraternity will perform on the balance beam, women on the uneven parallel bars and men on *the even parallel bars, on the webs, the trampoline, tumbling, unicycles, the high bar, the rings, and a routine of vaulting.*

Larry Pennie will be featured with the slack rope, while Bobbi Goulet and Tom Honn demonstrate balance on the ball. Participants in the big wheel act will be Janet Guigler and Nancy Schermerhorn.

One of the special features of the performance will be a ball gymnastics routine by 14 coeds. Dressed in black and gold, the girls will execute movements while holding balls. Another highlight of the circus will be an Indian fire dance performed with flaming hoops. Kathy Mulligan and Cindy Haynie will do the dance dressed in Indian costumes.

Other features will include hand-to-hand and foot-to-foot stunts on a high trapeze and a display balance and timing on a large wheel while it continuously turns through the air.

Spotlights will be placed several of the acts. The finale will consist of a formation of circus members in one large pyramid with three smaller ones beside it.

Friday night the Gamma Phi Queen will be crowned by Gordy Winkleman, president of Gamma Phi. The five members of the Queen's Court, to be escorted into the arena by male members of Gamma Phi, are Joanne Adams, nominated by the Industrial Arts Club; Sherrill nominated by Women Off Campus; Mary Brady, from the Lowell Mason Club; Arden Leiter, Student Senate; and Alice nominated by APO.

Tickets are being sold every day this week from 8 a.m. to 4 p.m. in the Union and at the door both nights. Seats are not reserved.

According to Paula social chairman and chairman publicity, "It's going to be a great circus, even if we don't have any elephants."

HOLD IT RIGHT THERE—Gamma Phi Circus performers enter into their final week of practice as the annual circus opens this Friday at Horton Fieldhouse.

April 19, 1966 (page 3)

Apr 28, 1966 (front page)

Old Circus Days Relived At ISU

By Edith Kenyon

Days have passed when prospect of seeing the traveling circus created excitement and wonder in kids and grownups as well. The circus is a dying form of American entertainment, known to most only through the movies, in literature, or through the tales old-timers tell of having seen the real thing.

In this town the circus is not dead. Granted, it was not held under the Big Top with three rings and a sawdust floor. Barnum and Bailey or the Cole Brothers were not here. There were no lions or elephants or even one little dog who could walk a tightrope. But there were plenty of viewers on hand munching popcorn, waving balloons and giggling at the ridiculous antics of the clowns. Most important of all, the freely exhibited enthusiasm, and the performers showed pride in their work.

"THERE SHE IS—Miss Gamma Phi Queen." One of these ISU coeds—left to right, Cheryl Anderson, Arden Leiter, Alice McGrath, and Mary Brady—Joanne Adams, who is not pictured, will reign over the annual Gamma Phi Circus in Horton Fieldhouse Friday and Saturday.

April 21, 1966 (front page)

397   A Circus in the Paper

No, the performers were professionals, and they made a lot of mistakes. However, they did revive the true spirit of the circus with their determination and optimism.

"As Queen of the 1966 Gamma Phi Circus, I command performance to begin," Queen Mary Brady ordered the performers. Queen Mary and her court, Joanne Adams, Arden Leiter, Alice McGrath, and Sherrill Anderson, added to the excitement and color of the circus atmosphere.

The audience, despite its receptiveness. received one black mark for behavior during performance of the "Spoke Benders," the troupe of cyclists. The group had difficulty in maintaining balance and precision on their cycles. While the routine was not intended to be of a comic nature, the audience seemed to find it amusing. I felt the behavior of audience was uncalled for. It must be remembered that these performers are amateurs without experience necessary to execute flawless performance. They deserved a better reception than extended.

It is difficult to select any one performer as being because the amount of displayed was excellent. Lesley Sheets, performing in "Ringos," "Bells of the Ball," "Unmatched Perils." and "Swing in the Wind," displayed outstanding ability. Lesley's poise and skill made her perhaps outstanding performer of the circus.

An extraordinary amount of flexibility was indeed evident throughout the "Flexibility Extraordinary," a routine by Bob Hendron, Mel Wheeler, Bob Court. Cindy Haynie, Jeannie Burpee, Kathy Mulligan, Joyce Zetterlind, and Debbie Smith.

The performance of Nancy Schermerhorn and Janet Giugler in the opening number "Wheel Around" was fascinating. I felt my stomach do a double-take with each turn of the double wheels.

The finale, involving the entire circus troupe, was impressive. I feel safe in taking the liberty of saying for all those present at the opening night of the 30th Annual Gamma Phi Circus, the color excitement of the old-time circus was reborn at ISU.

The Circus Continues...

With his promotion, Dr. Gillett relinquished the position of Director/Sponsor of Gamma Phi Circus. That represented a transition between the initial era of Gamma Phi and the ones that follow.

From 1929 until 1966, Pop Horton and Dr. Gillett were responsible for maintaining the stability and success of the organization.

Dr. Truex's tenure in Gamma Phi had begun.

...

Gamma Phi as an organization started as a gymnastics group with lofty standards. It persevered through two world wars and a national Depression to continue supporting many communities through education, training, performances, and charitable work.

Members of Gamma Phi served the country--several giving the ultimate sacrifice.

To this day, members of Gamma Phi continue promoting its original ideals and continue performing around the country, and even throughout the world!

...

An initially small Midwestern Chapter of Gamma Phi has done well for itself, and for countless others.

The story of the Gamma Phi organization will continue...

BIBLIOGRAPHY

1 Ohio State Lantern; Mar 18, 1908

2 University of Wisconsin; The Daily Cardinal; Mar 27, 1905

3 The Ohio Wesleyan Transcript; Mar 18, 1920

4 The Ohio Wesleyan Transcript; 1921

5 Priscilla (Landis) Gilroy-Green, The Development of Gamma Phi Honorary Gymnastic Fraternity from 1929 to 1975, 1975

Entire Page, The Vidette, p. 1, March 12, 1952. [Online]. https://videttearchive.ilstu.edu

"G. D. C. on a Hike," The Vidette, p. 2, March 21, 1917. [Online]. https://videttearchive.ilstu.edu

"VIDETTE CIRCUS BIG SUCCESS," The Vidette, pp. 5, 8, March 3, 1915. [Online]. https://videttearchive.ilstu.edu

"RUSSELL TROUPE—STATIONARY PYRAMID," The Vidette, p. 1, March 3, 1915. [photograph] [Online]. https://videttearchive.ilstu.edu

"THE DANCING GIRLS," The Vidette, p. 5, March 3, 1915. [photograph] [Online]. https://videttearchive.ilstu.edu

"Miss Lydia Clark," The Vidette, p. 5, March 3, 1915. [photograph] [Online]. https://videttearchive.ilstu.edu

"Mr. Harrison H Russell," The Vidette, p. 5, March 3, 1915. [photograph] [Online]. https://videttearchive.ilstu.edu

"Dwight M Ramsay," The Vidette, p. 5, March 3, 1915. [photograph] [Online]. https://videttearchive.ilstu.edu

"Russell Troupe ladder pyramid," The Vidette, p. 8, March 3, 1915. [photograph] [Online]. https://videttearchive.ilstu.edu

"Should the Circus Become an Annual Affair?," The Vidette, p. 1, March 3, 1915. [Online]. https://videttearchive.ilstu.edu

"Clifford E. Horton, Baseball Coach at Clark University, Named as Russell's Successor," The Vidette, p. 1, May 30, 1923. [Online]. https://videttearchive.ilstu.edu

"COACH HORTON TO STUDY UNDER DR. MEANWELL," The Vidette, p. 1, June 18, 1923. [Online]. https://videttearchive.ilstu.edu

"Dr. Meanwell, of the U. of W...," The Vidette, p. 3, June 25, 1923. [Online]. https://videttearchive.ilstu.edu

"COACH HORTON VISITS THE NORMAL, UNIVERSITY," The Vidette, p. 3, June 25, 1923. [Online]. https://videttearchive.ilstu.edu

"OUR NEW COACH," The Vidette, p. 3, Sept 8, 1923. [Online]. https://videttearchive.ilstu.edu

"Introducing Coach Horton to New ISNU Men," The Vidette, p. 1, Sept 16, 1927. [Online]. https://videttearchive.ilstu.edu

M. Scherer, "Clifford Horton: 'Mr. Fieldhouse'," The Vidette, p. 8, July 23, 1977. [Online]. https://videttearchive.ilstu.edu

"Former ISU athletic director Clifford Horton...," The Vidette, p. 8, July 23, 1977 [photograph] [Online] https://videttearchive.ilstu.edu

"Horton's Tumblers Please Crowd at DeKalb Game," The Vidette, p. 3, Jan 31, 1928. [Online]. https://videttearchive.ilstu.edu

"Tumbling, Boxing, and Wrestling to be Featured," The Vidette, p. 1, Mar 7, 1929. [Online]. https://videttearchive.ilstu.edu

"GAMMA PHI, NEW FRATERNITY MEETS," The Vidette, p. 3, Nov 11, 1929. [Online]. https://videttearchive.ilstu.edu

Priscilla (Landis) Gilroy-Green, The Development of Gamma Phi Honorary Gymnastic Fraternity from 1929 to 1975, 1975

"GAMMA PHI PLEDGES HOLD FIRST MEETING," The Vidette, p. 3, Nov 18, 1929. [Online]. https://videttearchive.ilstu.edu

Group Gamma Phi Picture, The Index, p. 149, 1930 [photograph] [Online]. https://library.illinoisstate.edu/collections/yearbooks/index.php

"GAMMA PHI TUMBLERS SHOW THEIR CLASS IN EXHIBITION THURSDAY," The Vidette, p. 3, Dec 9, 1929. [Online]. https://videttearchive.ilstu.edu

"GAMMA PHI, P. E. FRAT, HOLDS INITIATION BANQUET," The Vidette, p. 6, Dec 16, 1929. [Online]. https://videttearchive.ilstu.edu

"P E. MEN ARE BEING TAUGHT TAP DANCING," The Vidette, p. 3, Jan 13, 1930. [Online]. https://videttearchive.ilstu.edu

"GAMMA PHI PREPARES FOR DEMONSTRATION AT COOKSVILLE," The Vidette, p. 3, Jan 13, 1930. [Online]. https://videttearchive.ilstu.edu

"When the Gamma Phi boys marched out...," The Vidette Edition 02, p. 3, Jan 30, 1930. [Online]. https://videttearchive.ilstu.edu

"Editorial - Deems Conduct Unsportsmanlike," The Vidette, p. 4, Feb 10, 1930. [Online]. https://videttearchive.ilstu.edu

"GAMMA PHI TO GIVE ATHLETIC DEMONSTRATION," The Vidette, p. 6, Feb 10, 1930. [Online]. https://videttearchive.ilstu.edu

"GAMMA PHI TO HOLD PLEDGE MEETING," The Vidette, p. 6, Mar 3, 1930. [Online]. https://videttearchive.ilstu.edu

"Gamma Phi Athletic Show Draws Large Number of Sporting Fans Despite Inclemency of Weather," The Vidette, p. 3, Apr 7, 1930. [Online]. https://videttearchive.ilstu.edu

"Eugene Hill, Track Star, Appointed to Normal Coaching Staff...," The Vidette, p. 3, June 23, 1930. [Online]. https://videttearchive.ilstu.edu

Group Gamma Phi Picture, The Index, p. 150, 1931 [photograph] [Online]. https://library.illinoisstate.edu/collections/yearbooks/index.php

"Bill Muhl and Shorty Unsicker would like the attention...," The Vidette, p. 3, Oct 10, 1930. [Online]. https://videttearchive.ilstu.edu

"GAMMA PHI GROUP IS TO STUNT AT NEXT GAME," The Vidette, p. 3, Oct 27, 1930. [Online]. https://videttearchive.ilstu.edu

"Gamma Phi is Host to Physical Education Men," The Vidette, p. 3, Nov 3, 1930. [Online]. https://videttearchive.ilstu.edu

"GAMMA PHI TO ENTERTAIN WOMEN'S P. E. CLUB TONITE," The Vidette, p. 3, Dec 8, 1930. [Online]. https://videttearchive.ilstu.edu

"The basketball squads from Forrest Township...," The Vidette, p. 3, Jan 19, 1931. [Online]. https://videttearchive.ilstu.edu

"Intramural Finals ," The Vidette, p. 4, Mar 16, 1931. [Online]. https://videttearchive.ilstu.edu

"Intramural Track...," The Vidette, p. 4, Mar 23, 1931. [Online]. https://videttearchive.ilstu.edu

"TWENTY-FOUR TO BE INITIATED INTO GAMMA PHI," The Vidette, p. 4, Mar 23, 1931. [Online]. https://videttearchive.ilstu.edu

"Awards Presented to Students In General Exercises Tuesday," The Vidette, p. 1, June 8, 1931. [Online]. https://videttearchive.ilstu.edu

"The McCormick Gymnasium In November," The Index, p. 176, 1932 [photograph] [Online] https://library.illinoisstate.edu/collections/yearbooks/index.php

Group Gamma Phi Picture, The Index, p. 64, 1932 [photograph] [Online]. https://library.illinoisstate.edu/collections/yearbooks/index.php

"The Pictures," The Index, p. 231, 1932 [photograph] [Online]. https://library.illinoisstate.edu/collections/yearbooks/index.php

"The Gamma Phi Tumblers," The Index, p. 233, 1932 [photograph] [Online]. https://library.illinoisstate.edu/collections/yearbooks/index.php

"Gamma Phi, Intramural Winners," The Index, p. 233, 1932 [photograph] [Online]. https://library.illinoisstate.edu/collections/yearbooks/index.php

"C. E. Horton Speaks at Stag Party Held by Varsity Club," The Vidette, p. 5, Oct 5, 1931. [Online]. https://videttearchive.ilstu.edu

"GAMMA PHI SPONSOR GET ACQUAINTED PARTY," The Vidette, p. 3, Oct 12, 1931. [Online]. https://videttearchive.ilstu.edu

"The Gamma Phi, athletic fraternity…," The Vidette, p. 3, Feb 29, 1932. [Online]. https://videttearchive.ilstu.edu

"First Annual Circus to be Given by Gamma Phi Friday," The Vidette, p. 1, Mar 7, 1932. [Online]. https://videttearchive.ilstu.edu

"GAMMA PHI TO PEORIA," The Vidette, p. 3, Apr 4, 1932. [Online]. https://videttearchive.ilstu.edu

"INTRAMURAL TROPHIES AWARDED BY MANAGER," The Vidette, p. 3, Apr 4, 1932. [Online]. https://videttearchive.ilstu.edu

"Gamma Phi Will Meet To Select Pledges In Its Spring Initiation," The Vidette, p. 6, Apr 11, 1932. [Online]. https://videttearchive.ilstu.edu

"GAMMA PHI TO HAVE CLUBROOM IN GYM," The Vidette, p. 6, May 2, 1932. [Online]. https://videttearchive.ilstu.edu

"GAMMA PHI HOLDS SMOKER," The Vidette, p. 3, May 9, 1932. [Online]. https://videttearchive.ilstu.edu

"John Ad Kinneman Reads Paper Before Gamma Phi Members," The Vidette, p. 5, May 16, 1932. [Online]. https://videttearchive.ilstu.edu

"GAMMA PHI TO INITIATE AND HOLD BARBEQUE," The Vidette, p. 5, May 31, 1932. [Online]. https://videttearchive.ilstu.edu

"P. E. SENIORS ENTERTAINED," The Vidette, p. 1, June 6, 19232. [Online]. https://videttearchive.ilstu.edu

"HONOR GRADUATES en," The Vidette, p. 2, June 6, 1932. [Online]. https://videttearchive.ilstu.edu

Group Gamma Phi Picture, The Index, p. 141, 1933 [photograph] [Online]. https://library.illinoisstate.edu/collections/yearbooks/index.php

"Brown to Speak to Men at Stag Party for All Men Tonight," The Vidette, p. 3, Sept 19, 1932. [Online]. https://videttearchive.ilstu.edu

"GAMMA PHI TO HAVE CHANGE OF NORMAL CHEERLEADER," The Vidette, p. 2, Oct 17, 1932. [Online]. https://videttearchive.ilstu.edu

"Homecoming Festivities are to Open This Evening at 8:15," The Vidette, p. 1, Sept 16Nov 4, 1932. [Online]. https://videttearchive.ilstu.edu

"TUMBLING TIME HAD AT CONVOCATION," The Vidette, p. 1, Nov 14, 1932. [Online]. https://videttearchive.ilstu.edu

"Second Annual Gym Circus To Be Presented Feb. 16-17," The Vidette, p. 1, Jan 19 1933. [Online]. https://videttearchive.ilstu.edu

"CIRCUS PLANS ARE GETTING UNDERWAY," The Vidette, p. 6, Jan 16, 1933. [Online]. https://videttearchive.ilstu.edu

"ILL. NORMAL BAND AND CIRCUS TO JOURNEY TO MACOMB THIS WEEK," The Vidette, p. 5, Feb 27, 1933. [Online]. https://videttearchive.ilstu.edu

"GAMMA PHI, HONORARY GYM FRATERNITY, PLEDGES 22," The Vidette, p. 1, Mar 21, 1933. [Online]. https://videttearchive.ilstu.edu

"GAMMA PHI MEETING," The Vidette, p. 7, Mar 27, 1933. [Online]. https://videttearchive.ilstu.edu

"Gamma Phi Gym Fraternity Stages Initiation Services," The Vidette, p. 3, Apr 3, 1933. [Online]. https://videttearchive.ilstu.edu

"Gamma Phi Stages Formal Initiation for Seventeen Men," The Vidette, p. 6, Apr 10, 1933. [Online]. https://videttearchive.ilstu.edu

"GAMMA PHI PUTS ON EXHIBITION AT PEKIN," The Vidette, p. 6, Apr 17, 1933. [Online]. https://videttearchive.ilstu.edu

"Announcement Made of Groups Chosen for V. C. Stunt Show," The Vidette, p. 1, May 1, 1933. [Online]. https://videttearchive.ilstu.edu

"On Friday night the annual Stunt Show will hold the spotlight...," The Vidette, p. 1, May 8, 1933. [Online]. https://videttearchive.ilstu.edu

"GAMMA PHI AWARDS CIRCUS QUEEN SISTER PIN," The Vidette, p. 8, May 8, 1933. [Online]. https://videttearchive.ilstu.edu

"W.A.A. AND ART CLUB WIN TOP HONORS IN ANNUAL STUNT SHOW," The Vidette, p. 1, May 15, 1933. [Online]. https://videttearchive.ilstu.edu

"GAMMA PHI HOLDS PICNIC AT LAKE BLOOMINGTON," The Vidette, p. 1, June 5, 1933. [Online]. https://videttearchive.ilstu.edu

1934 "Set up for opening spec," THIRD ANNUAL I.S.N.U. CIRCUS, [photograph] Group Gamma Phi Picture, The Index, p. 65, 193 [photograph] [Online]. https://library.illinoisstate.edu/collections/yearbooks/index.php

"GAMMA PHI IN PARADE," The Vidette, p. 1, Sept 29, 1933. [Online]. https://videttearchive.ilstu.edu

"GAMMA PHI BANQUET," The Vidette, p. 1, Oct 27, 1933. [Online]. https://videttearchive.ilstu.edu

"GAMMA PHI TAKES PART IN LEGION SHOW," The Vidette, p. 1, Oct 27, 1933. [Online]. https://videttearchive.ilstu.edu

"GAMMA PHI OFFERS RECREATIONAL PROGRAM," The Vidette, p. 3, Nov 10, 1933. [Online]. https://videttearchive.ilstu.edu

"GAMMA PHI TO HOLD REGULAR MEETING NEXT MONDAY AT GYMNASIUM," The Vidette, p. 3, Dec 8, 1933. [Online]. https://videttearchive.ilstu.edu

"GAMMA PHI ENTERTAINS AG. SMALL GRAIN SHOW," The Vidette, p. 3, Dec 15, 1933. [Online]. https://videttearchive.ilstu.edu

"Gamma Phi, physical educational fraternity at Normal...," The Vidette, p. 3, Dec 19, 1933. [Online]. https://videttearchive.ilstu.edu

"NOTICE!," The Vidette, p. 2, Jan 16, 1933. [Online]. https://videttearchive.ilstu.edu

"A group of Gamma Phi boys...," The Vidette, p. 3, Jan 16, 1933. [Online]. https://videttearchive.ilstu.edu

"Gamma Phi Group to Be Busy During the Remainder of Month," The Vidette, p. 3, Jan 19, 1934. [Online]. https://videttearchive.ilstu.edu

"Gamma Phi Troupe to Show Before Macomb Students January 31," The Vidette, p. 3, Jan 19, 1934. [Online]. https://videttearchive.ilstu.edu

"DIGEST HAS NORMAL PICTURE," The Vidette, p. 1, Jan 30, 19234. [Online]. https://videttearchive.ilstu.edu

"Gamma Phi, local physical education fraternity...," The Vidette, p. 3, Feb 2, 1934. [Online]. https://videttearchive.ilstu.edu

"PLANS MADE FOR ELECTING GAMMA PHI CIRCUS QUEEN," The Vidette, p. 1, Feb 9, 1934. [Online]. https://videttearchive.ilstu.edu

"Gamma Phi, local physical education fraternity...," The Vidette, p. 3, Feb 2, 1934. [Online]. https://videttearchive.ilstu.edu

"PLANS MADE FOR ELECTING GAMMA PHI CIRCUS QUEEN," The Vidette, p. 1, Feb 9, 1934. [Online]. https://videttearchive.ilstu.edu

"Edson White, physical education director...," The Vidette, p. 3, Feb 9, 1934. [Online]. https://videttearchive.ilstu.edu

"Gamma Phi Circus Scheduled To Appear Feb. 23-24 At Gym," The Vidette, p. 3, Feb 9, 1934. [Online]. https://videttearchive.ilstu.edu

"TO CHOOSE QUEEN BY ALL - SCHOOL VOTE THURSDAY," The Vidette, p. 1, Feb 13, 1934. [Online]. https://videttearchive.ilstu.edu

"Queen Chosen by Vote for Gamma Phi Gym Circus," The Vidette, p. 1, Feb 16, 1934. [Online]. https://videttearchive.ilstu.edu

"GAMMA PHI MAKES TEN DOLLAR GIFT TO STUDENT LOUNGE," The Vidette, p. 1, Mar 9, 1934. [Online]. https://videttearchive.ilstu.edu

"Edson White, physical education director...," The Vidette,3p. 1, Mar 9, 1934. [Online]. https://videttearchive.ilstu.edu

"GAMMA PHI PLANS TUMBLING EXHIBIT FOR THIS MONTH," The Vidette, p. 3, Mar 30, 1934. [Online]. https://videttearchive.ilstu.edu

"TO ATTEND BANQUET," The Vidette, p. 3, Apr 20, 1934. [Online]. https://videttearchive.ilstu.edu

"VAUDEVILLE ACTS, MUSICAL COMEDY TO BE PART OF MAY FETE," The Vidette, p. 1, May 1, 1934. [Online]. https://videttearchive.ilstu.edu

"GAMMA PHI TO DEMONSTRATE The Vidette, p. 1, May 18, 1934. [Online]. https://videttearchive.ilstu.edu

"GAMMA PHI IS TO ADD ANOTHER CHAPTER," The Vidette, p. 3, May 23, 1934. [Online]. https://videttearchive.ilstu.edu

"CONFINED IN HOSPITAL," The Vidette, p. 2, May 29, 1934. [Online]. https://videttearchive.ilstu.edu

Group Gamma Phi Picture, The Index, p. 128, 1935 [photograph] [Online]. https://library.illinoisstate.edu/collections/yearbooks/index.php

"Gymnastics, another hobby hour feature...," The Vidette, p. 3, Oct 25, 1934. [Online]. https://videttearchive.ilstu.edu

"Gamma Phi Members Prepare for Circus," The Vidette, p. 3, Nov 6, 1934. [Online]. https://videttearchive.ilstu.edu

"Intramural Party Gives Fellows Chance to Show How Unskilled They Are," The Vidette, p. 3, Nov 23, 1934. [Online]. https://videttearchive.ilstu.edu

"LOOKING FOR MATERIAL," The Vidette, p. 3, Dec 14, 1934. [Online]. https://videttearchive.ilstu.edu

"Ten Men Initiated into Gamma Phi at Meeting This Week," The Vidette, p. 1, Feb 8, 1935. [Online]. https://videttearchive.ilstu.edu

"HAVE BUSY WEEK," The Vidette, p. 3, Feb 12, 1935. [Online]. https://videttearchive.ilstu.edu

"WANTED — A QUEEN," The Vidette, p. 2, Feb 15, 1935. [Online]. https://videttearchive.ilstu.edu

"Gamma Phi Fraternity Presents Acts; Prepares for Annual Gym Show," The Vidette, p. 1, Feb 15, 1935. [Online]. https://videttearchive.ilstu.edu

"SIX ARE NOMINATED TO RUN FOR GAMMA PHI CIRCUS HONORS," The Vidette, p. 1, Mar 5, 1935. [Online]. https://videttearchive.ilstu.edu

"Music, always a part of us will be heard...," The Vidette, p. 2, Mar 19, 1935. [Online]. https://videttearchive.ilstu.edu

"MARGARET NAFFZIGER CROWNED QUEEN OF GAMMA PHI CIRCUS," The Vidette, p. 1, Mar 22, 1935. [Online]. https://videttearchive.ilstu.edu

"APPRECIATIVE AUDIENCE GREETS FINAL GAMMA PHI BIG TOP EVENT," The Vidette, p. 1, Mar 2, 1935. [Online]. https://videttearchive.ilstu.edu

"Professor C. E. Horton Principal Speaker at Anchor High Banquet," The Vidette, p. 3, Mar 29, 1935. [Online]. https://videttearchive.ilstu.edu

"Gamma Phi Tumblers Schedule Three Shows," The Vidette, p. 2, Apr 5, 1935. [Online]. https://videttearchive.ilstu.edu

"GAMMA PHI BANQUET," The Vidette, p. 2, May 21, 1935. [Online]. https://videttearchive.ilstu.edu

"Elephants, Gamma Phi Don't Forget; Walking Back Part of Ritual," The Vidette, p. 1, May 24, 1935. [Online]. https://videttearchive.ilstu.edu

"EARLY HABIT FORMATION ASSET FOR ATHLETES BIG LEAGUER BELIEVES," The Vidette, p. 1May 31, 1935. [Online]. https://videttearchive.ilstu.edu

"GAMMA PHI ELECTS OFFICERS," The Vidette, p. 4, June 7, 1935. [Online]. https://videttearchive.ilstu.edu

Gamma Phi Members pictures, The Index, p. 202, 1936 [photograph] [Online]. https://library.illinoisstate.edu/collections/yearbooks/index.php

"Gamma Phi, honorary gymnastic fraternity...," The Vidette, p. 2, Sept 20, 1935. [Online]. https://videttearchive.ilstu.edu

"Coach Harold E. Frye "Pop" Horton Plans Big Year at First Gamma Phi Meeting," The Vidette, p. 3, Sept 27, 1935. [Online]. https://videttearchive.ilstu.edu

"Gamma Phi to Present All-School Dance...," The Vidette, p. 1, Oct 8, 1935. [Online]. https://videttearchive.ilstu.edu

"Hobby Hour Drawing More Recruits, Director Says," The Vidette, p. 6, Oct 25, 1935. [Online]. https://videttearchive.ilstu.edu

"NOTICE," The Vidette, p. 8, Oct 25, 1935. [Online]. https://videttearchive.ilstu.edu

"Snake Dance Friday" The Vidette, p. 1, Nov 12, 1935. [Online]. https://videttearchive.ilstu.edu

"Gamma Phi Sponsors Snake Dance, Cheers BonFire, Tonight" The Vidette, p. 1, Nov 15, 1935. [Online]. https://videttearchive.ilstu.edu

"Gamma Phi Tumblers to Make Third Bow," The Vidette Edition 2, p. 3, Nov 26, 1935. [Online]. https://videttearchive.ilstu.edu

"Ring Queen to be Chosen Soon by Popular Vote; Clowns to be Super," The Vidette, p. 5, Jan 10, 1936. [Online]. https://videttearchive.ilstu.edu

"Circus Queen Poll on Registration Day," The Vidette, p. 1, Jan 24, 1936. [Online]. https://videttearchive.ilstu.edu

"Normal Tumblers Show at Lincoln," The Vidette, p. 1, Feb 14, 1936. [Online]. https://videttearchive.ilstu.edu

Not Sailors, But Acrobats Prove to Be Best Dates for Fell Hallers," The Vidette, p. 14, Feb 14, 1936. [Online]. https://videttearchive.ilstu.edu

M. Blum, "Cliff Cozart," The Vidette, p. 2, Feb 18, 1936. [Online]. https://videttearchive.ilstu.edu

"Gamma Phi Circus Lists Elaine Good," The Vidette, pp. 1, 5, Feb, 1936. [Online]. https://videttearchive.ilstu.edu

"Introducing Coach Horton to New ISNU Men," The Vidette, p. 1, Feb 25, 1936. [Online]. https://videttearchive.ilstu.edu

"Elaine Good...," The Vidette, p. 1, Feb 25, 1936. [photograph] [Online]. https://videttearchive.ilstu.edu

"Introducing Coach Horton to New ISNU Men," The Vidette, p. 1, Sept 16, 1927. [Online]. https://videttearchive.ilstu.edu

"Gamma Phi Goes Through Pace...," The Vidette, p. 3, Feb 25, 1936. [photograph] [Online]. https://videttearchive.ilstu.edu

L. Poklaske, "Gamma Phi to Reveal Ring Queen as Prelude to Aerial Features," The Vidette, pp. 1, 4 Feb 25, 1936. [Online]. https://videttearchive.ilstu.edu

J. Dohm, "John Finds That Gym Is No Place for Killing Time," The Vidette, p. 6, Apr 24, 1936. [Online]. https://videttearchive.ilstu.edu

"Gamma Phi Banquet at Maplewood Today," The Vidette, p. 4, May 5, 1936. [Online]. https://videttearchive.ilstu.edu

Group Gamma Phi Picture, The Index, p. 160, 1937 [photograph] [Online]. https://library.illinoisstate.edu/collections/yearbooks/index.php

"Only a short program will accompany the annual Homecoming dinner...," The Vidette, p. 12, Oct 30, 1936. [Online]. https://videttearchive.ilstu.edu

"Gamma Phis Have Dinner-Then Hear Fingerprint Talk," The Vidette, p. 6, Jan 15, 1936. [Online]. https://videttearchive.ilstu.edu

"Gamma Phi Circus To Be March 10, 11," The Vidette, p. 1, Jan 19, 1937. [Online]. https://videttearchive.ilstu.edu

"On March 10, Fell Hall will sponsor...," The Vidette, p. 1, Jan 22, 1937. [Online]. https://videttearchive.ilstu.edu

"To Elect Gamma Phi Circus Queen," The Vidette, p. 1, Jan 22, 1937. [Online]. https://videttearchive.ilstu.edu

"Gamma Phi Circus Queen To Reign For Two Nights," The Vidette, p. 1, Jan 26, 1937. [Online]. https://videttearchive.ilstu.edu

"Annual Circus To Be Planned," The Vidette, p. 4, Feb 12, 1937. [Online]. https://videttearchive.ilstu.edu

"Men Discuss P. E. Change," The Vidette, p. 7, Mar 5, 1937. [Online]. https://videttearchive.ilstu.edu

"There will be a meeting of all Men...," The Vidette, p. 8, Mar 19, 1937. [Online]. https://videttearchive.ilstu.edu

"GAMMA PHI, the new P. E. fraternity...," The Vidette, p. 1, Apr 2, 1937. [Online]. https://videttearchive.ilstu.edu

J. Ross, "Gamma Phi Circus | Promises Thrills; Queen Kept Secret," The Vidette, p. 3, Apr 6, 1937. [Online]. https://videttearchive.ilstu.edu

"Circus Plans Now Complete," The Vidette, p. 7, Apr 9, 1937. [Online]. https://videttearchive.ilstu.edu

J. Ross, "Gamma Phi Circus," The Vidette, p. 3, Apr 13, 1937. [Online]. https://videttearchive.ilstu.edu

J. Ross, "Ace Stambach To Introduce Circus Acts," The Vidette, p. 7, Apr 16, 1937. [Online]. https://videttearchive.ilstu.edu

"Six Queens of the Air Show Here at Circus," The Vidette, p. 7, Apr 16, 1937. [photograph] [Online]. https://videttearchive.ilstu.edu

"Women's I-M Department Aids Gamma Phi," The Vidette, p. 8, Apr 16, 1937. [Online]. https://videttearchive.ilstu.edu

"Gamma Phi Queen Thrills to Annual Fraternity Circus," The Vidette, p. 3, Apr 23, 1937. [Online]. https://videttearchive.ilstu.edu

"Queen Clara Myers," The Vidette, p. 3, Apr 23, 1937. [photograph] [Online]. https://videttearchive.ilstu.edu

"Gamma Phis Give Chase," The Vidette, p. 7, Apr 23, 1937. [Online]. https://videttearchive.ilstu.edu

"CHAIR BALANCERS," The Vidette, p. 7, May 7, 1937. [Online]. https://videttearchive.ilstu.edu

"Elect Gamma Phi Frat Head," The Vidette, p. 1, May 11, 1937. [Online]. https://videttearchive.ilstu.edu

"Banquet Planned By Gamma Phi's," The Vidette, p. 7, May 14, 1937. [Online]. https://videttearchive.ilstu.edu

"Clara Myers To Be Guest Of P. E. Frat," The Vidette, p. 1, May 18, 1937. [Online]. https://videttearchive.ilstu.edu

"Horton, Hancock to Study At University of Indiana," The Vidette, p. 3, June 12, 1937. [Online]. https://videttearchive.ilstu.edu

cartoon, The Vidette, p. 6, Mar 4, 1938. [Online]. https://videttearchive.ilstu.edu

"Gamma Phi Holds Meeting Thursday," The Vidette, p. 7, Oct 1, 1937. [Online]. https://videttearchive.ilstu.edu

"Gamma Phi Holds Meeting For All University Men," The Vidette, p. 3, Oct 12, 1937. [Online]. https://videttearchive.ilstu.edu

"Fred Young Speaks To Men's Group," The Vidette, p. 6, Oct 15, 1937. [Online]. https://videttearchive.ilstu.edu

"NOTICE," The Vidette Edition 2, p. 11, Oct 29, 1937. [Online]. https://videttearchive.ilstu.edu

"The float representing Gamma Phi ...," The Vidette, p. 3, Nov 4, 1937. [photograph] [Online]. https://videttearchive.ilstu.edu

"Judging Contest Draws Candidates From 25 Schools," The Vidette, p. 3, Nov 19, 1937. [Online]. https://videttearchive.ilstu.edu

"Gamma Phi, honorary physical education fraternity...," The Vidette, p. 7, Dec 1, 1937. [Online]. https://videttearchive.ilstu.edu

"President Wendel Lewis...," The Vidette, p. 6, Dec 10, 1937. [Online]. https://videttearchive.ilstu.edu

"Physical Education Group to Present Tumbling Show...," The Vidette, p. 6, Jan14, 1938. [Online]. https://videttearchive.ilstu.edu

"Gamma Phi Entertains," The Vidette, p. 3, Jan 18, 1938. [Online]. https://videttearchive.ilstu.edu

"Gamma Phi to Entertain At Intermission of Game," The Vidette, pp. 6, 7, Jan 21, 1938. [Online]. https://videttearchive.ilstu.edu

"The half exhibition put on by Gamma Phi...," The Vidette, p. 3, Jan 25, 1938. [Online]. https://videttearchive.ilstu.edu

"Gamma Phi to Present Annual Circus in March," The Vidette, pp. 6, 8, Feb 4, 1938. [Online]. https://videttearchive.ilstu.edu

"Gamma Phi Busy Preparing Circus," The Vidette, p. 7, Feb 18, 1938. [Online]. https://videttearchive.ilstu.edu

"Gamma Phi Acts Rehearse in Gym," The Vidette, p. 1, Feb 22, 1938. [Online]. https://videttearchive.ilstu.edu

"Gamma Phi to Present 20 All- Student Acts in Annual Gymnastic Circus March 4-5," The Vidette, p. 1, Feb 25, 1938. [Online]. https://videttearchive.ilstu.edu

"Circus man," The Vidette, p. 1, Feb 25, 1938. [photograph] [Online]. https://videttearchive.ilstu.edu

"Gamma Phi tumblers at State Normal...," The Vidette, p. 8, Feb 25, 1938. [Online]. https://videttearchive.ilstu.edu

"Giant Swing, Dance Team, Flying Trapeze to Hold Circus Spotlight," The Vidette, p. 1, Mar 1, 1938. [Online]. https://videttearchive.ilstu.edu

"Wendell Lewis," The Vidette, p. 1, Mar 1, 1938. [photograph] [Online]. https://videttearchive.ilstu.edu

"Gamma Phi Plans Dinner Dance for May 20," The Vidette, p. 1, May 10, 1938. [Online]. https://videttearchive.ilstu.edu

"P. E. Group Holds Dinner," The Vidette, p. 6, May 20, 1938. [Online]. https://videttearchive.ilstu.edu

"Make Plans For Circus," The Vidette, p. 6, June 23, 1938. [Online]. https://videttearchive.ilstu.edu

"McCormick Gymnasium Is Scene of School Circus," The Vidette, p. 3, July 7, 1938. [Online]. https://videttearchive.ilstu.edu

"swinging ladder," The Vidette, p. 3, July 7, 1938. [photograph] [Online]. https://videttearchive.ilstu.edu

"Normal Gymnasts Present Exhibition at CCC Camp," The Vidette, p. 5, Aug 4, 1938. [Online]. https://videttearchive.ilstu.edu

Group Gamma Phi Picture, Illinois State University's Special Collections, Milner Library, 1939

"Gamma Phi Week to End With Stag Party," The Vidette, p. 4, Oct 4, 1938. [Online]. https://videttearchive.ilstu.edu

"Physical Education Seniors Meet, Outline Year's Schedule of Events," The Vidette, p. 3, Nov 8, 1938. [Online]. https://videttearchive.ilstu.edu

"Gamma PM Holds Formal Initiation in Gym Monday," The Vidette, p. 1, Dec 2, 1938. [Online]. https://videttearchive.ilstu.edu

B. Smith, "Horton Elaborates on Background Of Coming Gamma Phi Production," The Vidette, p. 3, Feb 14, 1939. [Online]. https://videttearchive.ilstu.edu

"Selection of Gamma Phi Circus Queen Set for Party on March 3," The Vidette, p. 1, Feb 17, 1939. [Online]. https://videttearchive.ilstu.edu

"Gamma Phi Issues Plea for Redhead," The Vidette, p. 1, Feb 21, 1939. [Online]. https://videttearchive.ilstu.edu

"EUGENE HILL," The Vidette, p. 4, Feb 24, 1939. [photograph] [Online]. https://videttearchive.ilstu.edu

B. Smith, "Hill Gives Views On Gamma Phi," The Vidette, p. 4, Feb 24, 1939. [Online]. https://videttearchive.ilstu.edu

"The Gamma Phi has been hesitant...," The Vidette, p. 6, Feb 24, 1939. [Online]. https://videttearchive.ilstu.edu

"Gamma Phi Selects Five Nominees For Annual Circus Queen Contest," The Vidette, p. 1, Feb 24, 1939. [Online]. https://videttearchive.ilstu.edu

"Tumblers Go To Towanda For Program," The Vidette, p. 8, Feb 24, 1939. [Online]. https://videttearchive.ilstu.edu

"Bevy of Beauteous Brunettes Appear at Party, Aspire to Honor of Selection as Circus Queen," The Vidette, p. 1, Mar 3, 1939. [Online]. https://videttearchive.ilstu.edu

B. Smith, "Veterans Perform in Gamma Phi Circus," The Vidette, p. 6, Mar 3, 1939. [Online]. https://videttearchive.ilstu.edu

"Clowns Galore Display Talent To Circus Goers," The Vidette, p. 7, Mar 3, 1939. [Online]. https://videttearchive.ilstu.edu

"Jack LaBounty," The Vidette, p. 7, Mar 3, 1939. [photograph] [Online]. https://videttearchive.ilstu.edu

"Large Crowd Sees Gamma Phi Circus," The Vidette, p. 1, Mar 15, 1939. [Online]. https://videttearchive.ilstu.edu

"Parsons Member Of Gymnast Team," The Vidette, p. 3, Mar 31, 1939. [Online]. https://videttearchive.ilstu.edu

"Gamma Phi, men's physical education fraternity…" The Vidette, p. 8, Apr 14, 1939. [Online]. https://videttearchive.ilstu.edu

"Trio of Acrobats Appear in Circus," The Vidette, p. 7, May 5, 1939. [Online]. https://videttearchive.ilstu.edu

"Gamma Phi Dance Routine Is Popular," The Vidette, p. 3, May 23, 1939. [Online]. https://videttearchive.ilstu.edu

"Gamma Phi to Present Gymnastic Carnival," The Vidette, p. 6, June 22, 1939. [Online]. https://videttearchive.ilstu.edu

"Metropolitan Tenor Carter Appears on Artist Series," The Vidette, p. 7, June 29, 1939. [Online]. https://videttearchive.ilstu.edu

"Gamma Phi Holds Circus," The Vidette, p. 1, July 20, 1939. [Online]. https://videttearchive.ilstu.edu

"It's Amazing," The Vidette, p. 6, July 20, 1939. [photograph] [Online]. https://videttearchive.ilstu.edu

"Hope No One Sneezes," The Vidette, p. 8, July 20, 1939. [photograph] [Online]. https://videttearchive.ilstu.edu

"Gamma Phi Holds Outdoor Gym Circus Friday Night," The Vidette, p. 14, July 27, 1939. [Online]. https://videttearchive.ilstu.edu

"Gamma Phi Circus Held; Audience Numbers 1500," The Vidette, p. 13, Aug 3, 1939. [Online]. https://videttearchive.ilstu.edu

"Notice," The Vidette, p. 3, Oct 13, 1939. [Online]. https://videttearchive.ilstu.edu

"Gamma Phi has taken a progressive step…," The Vidette, p. 5, Oct 13, 1939. [Online]. https://videttearchive.ilstu.edu

"Nine Pledges Get Gamma Phi Honors From Initiation," The Vidette, p. 6, Oct 20, 1939. [Online]. https://videttearchive.ilstu.edu

"Gamma Phi Invites Women to Become Acrobats, Tumblers," The Vidette, p. 6, Nov 10, 1939. [Online]. https://videttearchive.ilstu.edu

"Gamma Phi Men's Invite Accepted," The Vidette, p. 6, Nov 17, 1939. [Online]. https://videttearchive.ilstu.edu

"Second Co-op Party Features Ted Fio Rito," The Vidette, p. 1, Dec 1, 1939. [Online]. https://videttearchive.ilstu.edu

"Gamma Phi Works," The Vidette, p. 3, Dec, 1939. [Online]. https://videttearchive.ilstu.edu

"Jesse Parsons," The Vidette, p. 5, Dec 20, 1939. [photograph] [Online]. https://videttearchive.ilstu.edu

"Intramural Cagers Prepare For Boom on Hardwood," The Vidette, p. 6, Feb 2, 1940. [Online]. https://videttearchive.ilstu.edu

"Gamma Phi Prexy Receives Call to Arms; Accepts Professorship," The Vidette, pp. 6, 7, Feb 9, 1940. [Online]. https://videttearchive.ilstu.edu

"Circus Queen Petitions Are Due Friday," The Vidette, p. 1, Feb 20, 1940. [Online]. https://videttearchive.ilstu.edu

"Gamma Phi Queen Will Be Chosen At Friday Dance," The Vidette, p. 1, Feb 27, 1940. [Online]. https://videttearchive.ilstu.edu

"Cox to Occupy Throne Of Honor at Circus," The Vidette, p. 45, Mar 13, 1940. [Online]. https://videttearchive.ilstu.edu

"Curtain Goes Up on 1940 Gamma Phi Circus Tonite," The Vidette, p. 1, Mar 15, 1940. [Online]. https://videttearchive.ilstu.edu

"Want to Join Gamma Phi? Horton Gives Low-Down," The Vidette, p. 3, Mar 15, 1940. [Online]. https://videttearchive.ilstu.edu

"Gamma Phi Elects," The Vidette, p. 1, May 21, 1940. [Online]. https://videttearchive.ilstu.edu

"Gamma Phi Opens Contest For 1941 Circus Queen," The Vidette, p. 1, Feb 21, 1941. [Online]. https://videttearchive.ilstu.edu

"Notice," The Vidette, p. 4, Feb 28, 1941. [Online]. https://videttearchive.ilstu.edu

"Nine Petitions in For Circus Queen As Deadline Nears," The Vidette, p. 1, Mar 7, 1941. [Online]. https://videttearchive.ilstu.edu

"Meet the Misses," The Vidette, p. 6, Mar 14, 1941. [Online]. https://videttearchive.ilstu.edu

"Busy Man," The Vidette, p. 5, Mar 14, 1941. [photograph] [Online]. https://videttearchive.ilstu.edu

"Andy Kamp Deserts Texts for Tents," The Vidette, p. 7, May 29, 1941. [Online]. https://videttearchive.ilstu.edu

"Gamma PM Meets," The Vidette, p. 3, Sept 30, 1941. [Online]. https://videttearchive.ilstu.edu

"Gamma Phi had a "Bronze Men"...," The Vidette, p. 3, Sept 30, 1941. [Online]. https://videttearchive.ilstu.edu

"Fedanzo Is Gamma Phi Star, Former Marine," The Vidette, p. 7, Oct 17, 1941. [Online]. https://videttearchive.ilstu.edu

"New equipment is installed for use in the 1942 circus...," The Vidette, p. 3, Nov 18, 1941. [Online]. https://videttearchive.ilstu.edu

"Know the Students," The Vidette, pp. 3, 4, Dec 2, 1941. [Online]. https://videttearchive.ilstu.edu

"Horton's quote about the war...," The Vidette, p. 3, Dec 12, 1941. [Online]. https://videttearchive.ilstu.edu

"Now's the Time to Reorganize ISNU's Extracurricular Life," The Vidette, p. 8, Feb 20, 1942. [Online]. https://videttearchive.ilstu.edu

"Gamma Phi Takes Over Sponsorship Of Physical Fitness Program," The Vidette, p. 7, Mar 18, 1942. [Online]. https://videttearchive.ilstu.edu

"Gamma Phi will hold its first meeting...," The Vidette, p. 4, Oct 13, 1943. [Online]. https://videttearchive.ilstu.edu

"Conducted by Mona Eisenhower," The Vidette, p. 2, Dec 8, 1943. [Online]. https://videttearchive.ilstu.edu

"Notice," The Vidette, p. 4, July 29, 1944. [Online]. https://videttearchive.ilstu.edu

"Summer Session Show Coming," The Vidette, p. 2, Aug 2, 1944. [Online] https://videttearchive.ilstu.edu

"Hileman Sisters," The Vidette, p. 4, Aug 2, 1944. [photograph] [Online] https://

videttearchive.ilstu.edu

"Band, Navy Drill Are Featured In Summer Show This Evening," The Vidette, p. 1, Aug 9, 1944. [Online] https://videttearchive.ilstu.edu

"Prize Stunt Will Be Given," The Vidette, p. 1, July 25, 1945. [Online]. https://videttearchive.ilstu.edu

"Crowds of 3,500 Applaud Talent Acts Of Last Week's Summer Show at Field," The Vidette, p. 4, Aug 15, 1945. [Online]. https://videttearchive.ilstu.edu

"Gymnastic Organization Begins Year's Activities," The Vidette, p. 1, Oct 17, 1945. [Online]. https://videttearchive.ilstu.edu

"The Gamma Phi circus is scheduled...," The Vidette, p. 7, Mar 13, 1946. [Online]. https://videttearchive.ilstu.edu

"Gamma Phi To Plan A Circus," The Vidette, p. 3, Mar 20, 1946. [Online]. https://videttearchive.ilstu.edu

"Gamma Phi Plans Circus Saturday," The Vidette, p. 1, Apr 3, 1946. [Online]. https://videttearchive.ilstu.edu

"Gamma Phi Circus Returns," The Vidette, p. 2, Apr 10, 1946. [Online]. https://videttearchive.ilstu.edu

"Gamma Phi Circus Smashing Success," The Vidette, p. 3, Apr 10, 1946. [Online]. https://videttearchive.ilstu.edu

"Ike Labounty and Chuck Greenwood...," The Vidette, p. 3, Apr 10, 1946. [photograph] [Online]. https://videttearchive.ilstu.edu

"WRA Playnight Features Games, Gymnastic Skit," The Vidette, p. 4, Jan 29, 1947. [Online]. https://videttearchive.ilstu.edu

"NOTICE," The Vidette, p. 1, Feb 5, 1947. [Online]. https://videttearchive.ilstu.edu

"Gamma Phi Circus Marks Highpoint on Fun Calendar," The Vidette, p. 7, Mar 12, 1947. [Online]. https://videttearchive.ilstu.edu

Group Gamma Phi Picture, The Index, p. 106, 1948 [photograph] [Online]. https://library.illinoisstate.edu/collections/yearbooks/index.php

"to direct Gamma Phi publicity . . .," The Vidette, p. 8, Oct 31, 1947. [Online]. https://videttearchive.ilstu.edu

"Gamma Phis Norma Bland...," The Vidette, p. 8, Oct 31, 1947. [photograph] [Online]. https://videttearchive.ilstu.edu

"Gamma Phi Holds Circus March 12-13," The Vidette, p. 1, Mar 3, 1948. [Online]. https://videttearchive.ilstu.edu

"Hi Ho Come To The Fair; Circus Friday," The Vidette, p. 1, Mar 10, 1948. [Online]. https://videttearchive.ilstu.edu

"Competition for Gamma Phi queen...," The Vidette, p. 5, Mar 5, 1949. [Online]. https://videttearchive.ilstu.edu

B. Soldewedel, "Gamma Phi Opens Big Top For Annual Circus Frolics," The Vidette, p. 1, Mar 15, 1949. [Online]. https://videttearchive.ilstu.edu

"Queens," The Vidette, p. 1, Mar 15, 1949. [photograph] [Online]. https://videttearchive.ilstu.edu

"Bob Thomas," The Vidette, p. 7, Mar 15, 1949. [photograph] [Online]. https://videttearchive.ilstu.edu

"Gen Witherspoon," The Vidette, p. 7, Mar 15, 1949. [photograph] [Online]. https://videttearchive.ilstu.edu

"ON THE AIR WJBC Tower Studios Cook Hall," The Vidette, p. 2, Mar 15, 1949. [Online]. https://videttearchive.ilstu.edu

B. Findley, "Lowell Kuntz Heads Gamma Phi Band," The Vidette, p. 4, Mar 15, 1949. [Online]. https://videttearchive.ilstu.edu

"Gamma Phi Performers Thrill Capacity Crowd," The Vidette, p. 3, Mar 22, 1949. [Online]. https://videttearchive.ilstu.edu

"Bob Thomas," The Vidette, p. 3, Mar 22, 1949. [photograph] [Online]. https://videttearchive.ilstu.edu

"We liked that Gamma Phi circus…," The Vidette, p. 5, Mar 22, 1949. [Online]. https://videttearchive.ilstu.edu

"Circus Sidelights," The Vidette, p. 6, Mar 22, 1949. [Online]. https://videttearchive.ilstu.edu

1950 Gamma Phi Circus Group Picture, Gamma Phi Circus, ISNU [photograph]

"Gamma Phi Initiates Three," The Vidette, p. 6, Oct 11, 1949. [Online]. https://videttearchive.ilstu.edu

"Gamma Phi Movies Shown At Reception," The Vidette, p. 10, Oct 11, 1949. [Online]. https://videttearchive.ilstu.edu

M. Eggenberger, "P. E. POINTERS," The Vidette, p. 15, Nov 1, 1949. [Online]. https://videttearchive.ilstu.edu

"Gamma Phi Circus Dates Postponed; Practice Held," The Vidette, p. 3, Mar 8, 1950. [Online]. https://videttearchive.ilstu.edu

"TEETH ARE vitally important…," The Vidette, p. 3, Mar 21, 1950. [photograph] [Online]. https://videttearchive.ilstu.edu

"Gamma Phi Sets Up The Big Top," The Vidette, p. 3, Mar 21, 1950. [Online]. https://videttearchive.ilstu.edu

"Gamma Phi Queen Heads Weekend Panorama," The Vidette, p. 1, Mar 28, 1950. [Online]. https://videttearchive.ilstu.edu

"GAMMA PHI ACROBATS…," The Vidette, p. 1, Mar 28, 1950. [photograph] [Online]. https://videttearchive.ilstu.edu

"Joan Model, Queen of Circus, Reigns With Court of Four," The Vidette, p. 4, Apr 4, 1950. [Online]. https://videttearchive.ilstu.edu

"JOAN HODEL, FRESHMAN…," The Vidette, p. 4, Apr 4, 1950. [photograph] [Online]. https://videttearchive.ilstu.edu

"Heard tell of war weary veterans…," The Vidette, p. 2, Apr 11, 1950. [Online]. https://videttearchive.ilstu.edu

"Gamma Phi Circus to Give Weekend Benefits…," The Vidette, p. 1, Apr 18, 1950. [Online]. https://videttearchive.ilstu.edu

J. Bonney, "P.E. Club Wins Stunt Show," The Vidette, p. 1, May 9, 1950. [Online]. https://videttearchive.ilstu.edu

"Russell Taylor Head Gamma Phi Executive," The Vidette, p. 8, May 23, 1950. [Online]. https://videttearchive.ilstu.edu

1951 Gamma Phi Circus Group Picture, Gamma Phi Circus, ISNU [photograph]

"Gamma Phi President Taylor Sends Out Call for Gymnasts," The Vidette, p. 2, Sept 28, 1950. [Online]. https://videttearchive.ilstu.edu

"Gamma Phi to Meet Tonight…," The Vidette, p. 7, Oct 3, 1950. [Online]. https://videttearchive.ilstu.edu

"Homecoming," The Vidette, p. 5, Nov 8, 1950. [Online]. https://videttearchive.ilstu.edu

"Gamma Phi Circus Set for March 9,10; Arley Gillett Heads Gymnastic Troupe," The Vidette, p. 8, Feb 14, 1951. [Online]. https://videttearchive.ilstu.edu

"Queen, Court of Four Will Reign Over Circus; Gamma Phi Members Prepare for March Shows," The Vidette, p. 6, Feb 28, 1951. [Online]. https://videttearchive.ilstu.edu

"JACK DALEY...," The Vidette, p. 6, Feb 28, 1951. [photograph] [Online]. https://videttearchive.ilstu.edu

"GAMMA PHI CIRCUS OPENS FRIDAY NIGHT," The Vidette, p. 1, Mar 7, 1951. [Online]. https://videttearchive.ilstu.edu

"Honorary Gymnastics Initiate 17 Pledges Into Gamma Phi Fold," The Vidette, p. 1, June 6, 1951. [Online]. https://videttearchive.ilstu.edu

1952 Gamma Phi Circus Group Picture, Gamma Phi Circus, ISNU [photograph]

"Gamma Phi Schedules Workout, Open House," The Vidette, p. 8, Sept 26, 1951. [Online]. https://videttearchive.ilstu.edu

"Gamma Phi Opens Doors To Aspiring Gymnasts," The Vidette, p. 4, Oct 3, 1951. [Online]. https://videttearchive.ilstu.edu

"Homecoming," The Vidette, p. 1, Oct 31, 1951. [Online]. https://videttearchive.ilstu.edu

"Gamma Phi Sets Dales For Annual Circus," The Vidette, p. 1, Feb 13, 1952. [Online]. https://videttearchive.ilstu.edu

"Candidates for Queen May Pick Up Petitions," The Vidette, p. 4, Feb 20, 1952. [Online]. https://videttearchive.ilstu.edu

"Gamma Phi to Preview Circus in Assembly," The Vidette, p. 8, Feb 27, 1952. [Online]. https://videttearchive.ilstu.edu

"Students to Elect Gamma Phi Queen Today, Tomorrow," The Vidette, p. 1, Mar 5, 1952. [Online]. https://videttearchive.ilstu.edu

"Gymnasts Present Annual Circus This Week," The Vidette, p. 1, Mar 12, 1952. [Online]. https://videttearchive.ilstu.edu

"DARWIN HANY AND PAT MEYER...," The Vidette, p. 1, Mar 12, 1952. [photograph] [Online]. https://videttearchive.ilstu.edu

D Patterson, "Horton Founder Of Honorary Group On ISNU Campus," The Vidette, p. 1, Mar 12, 1952. [Online]. https://videttearchive.ilstu.edu

"MISS JOAN ALLEN...," The Vidette, p. 1, Mar 19, 1952. [photograph] [Online]. https://videttearchive.ilstu.edu

"Gamma Phi Draws 3,010 to Circus; Plans Additional Show for 1953," The Vidette, p. 4, Mar 26, 1952. [Online]. https://videttearchive.ilstu.edu

"Russell Steele, of the publicity office...," The Vidette, p. 3, Apr 2, 1952. [Online]. https://videttearchive.ilstu.edu

1953 Gamma Phi Circus Group Picture, Gamma Phi Circus, ISNU [photograph]

"Gamma Phi Circus In Off-Campus Benefit," The Vidette, p. 7, Apr 2, 1952. [Online]. https://videttearchive.ilstu.edu

"Gamma Phi Gymnasts To Hold Tryout Monday," The Vidette, p. 6, Sept 24, 1952. [Online]. https://videttearchive.ilstu.edu

"Gamma Phi's Equipment Buy Incites Spring Circus Plans," The Vidette, p. 6, Nov 5, 1952. [Online]. https://videttearchive.ilstu.edu

"Federal Bank Building Scene for Circus Party," The Vidette, p. 3, Dec 17, 1952. [Online]. https://videttearchive.ilstu.edu

"Cardinals Even Conference Slate Against Western," The Vidette, p. 6, Feb 11, 1953. [Online]. https://videttearchive.ilstu.edu

"Campus Clubs to Nominate Gamma Phi Queen and Court," The Vidette, p. 1, Feb 18, 1953. [Online]. https://videttearchive.ilstu.edu

"Gymnasts Plan Assembly," The Vidette, p. 4, Feb 25, 1953. [Online]. https://videttearchive.ilstu.edu

"Gamma Phi Releases Club Nominees For Queen and Lists Acts of Circus," The Vidette, p. 1, Mar 4, 1953. [Online]. https://videttearchive.ilstu.edu

"Letter to the Editor," The Vidette, p. 2, Mar 4, 1953. [Online]. https://videttearchive.ilstu.edu

"'Circus Artists Invade Gym' Announces Gamma Phi," The Vidette, p. 8, Mar 11, 1953. [Online]. https://videttearchive.ilstu.edu

"Delores Lauf Reigns Over Gymnastic Circus," The Vidette, p. 1, Mar 18, 1953. [Online]. https://videttearchive.ilstu.edu

"DELORES LAUF...," The Vidette, p. 1, Mar 18, 1953. [photograph] [Online]. https://videttearchive.ilstu.edu

"PICTURED ABOVE...," The Vidette, p. 2, Mar 18, 1953. [photograph] [Online]. https://videttearchive.ilstu.edu

"Delores Lauf Overcomes Handicap To Become Outstanding Student," The Vidette, p. 8, Mar 25, 1953. [Online]. https://videttearchive.ilstu.edu

"STUDENT TEACHES BRAILLE SYSTEM," The Vidette, p. 8, Mar 25, 1953. [photograph] [Online]. https://videttearchive.ilstu.edu

"Gamma Phi Receives Twenty-One Members," The Vidette, p. 4, May 6, 1953. [Online]. https://videttearchive.ilstu.edu

1954 Gamma Phi Circus Group Picture, Gamma Phi Circus, ISNU [photograph]

"Homecoming," The Vidette, p. 1, Nov 4, 1953. [Online]. https://videttearchive.ilstu.edu

"Gym Club Plans Open House for All Interested in Circus," The Vidette, p. 7, Nov 30, 1953. [Online]. https://videttearchive.ilstu.edu

"Basketball game against Eureka ld," The Vidette, p. 4, Dec 16, 1953. [Online]. https://videttearchive.ilstu.edu

"Gymnasts Make Early Start on Circus," The Vidette, p. 2, Feb 17, 1954. [Online]. https://videttearchive.ilstu.edu

"Gamma Phi Readies for Circus Opening Night," The Vidette, p. 3, Feb 24, 1954. [Online]. https://videttearchive.ilstu.edu

"Circus Shows Sneak Preview," The Vidette, p. 2, Mar 3, 1954. [Online]. https://videttearchive.ilstu.edu

"Four Women to Grace Crown Wearer's Court," The Vidette, p. 1, Mar 10, 1954. [Online]. https://videttearchive.ilstu.edu

"TV Station To Review Circus Acts Via Film," The Vidette, p. 3, Mar 17, 1954. [Online]. https://videttearchive.ilstu.edu

"Activities Rate Merit," The Vidette, p. 2, Mar 31, 1954. [Online]. https://videttearchive.ilstu.edu

J. Martin, "The Press Box," The Vidette, p. 5, Mar 31, 1954. [Online]. https://videttearchive.ilstu.edu

"Gamma Phi Initiates 41 New Members; Elects 1954-55 Officers," The Vidette, p. 2, May 26, 1954. [Online]. https://videttearchive.ilstu.edu

Gamma Phi Executive Board Picture, The Index, p. 88, 1955 [photograph] [Online]. https://library.illinoisstate.edu/collections/yearbooks/index.php

"Student Council, Gamma Phi Supply Funds for New Campus Markers," The Vidette, p. 5, Sept 22, 1954. [Online]. https://videttearchive.ilstu.edu

"'N' Club To Greet Alumni," The Vidette, p. 4, Oct 13, 1954. [Online]. https://videttearchive.ilstu.edu

"ISNU Gymnastics Fraternity Urges Interested Students To Perform in Annual Circus," The Vidette, p. 4, Nov 22, 1954. [Online]. https://videttearchive.ilstu.edu

"Gamma Phi Tells 1955 Plans," The Vidette, p. 1, Feb 16, 1955. [Online]. https://
videttearchive.ilstu.edu

"Riley Pittman Speaks To Assembly Goers On Brotherhood Week," The Vidette, p. 2, Feb 23,
1955. [Online]. https://videttearchive.ilstu.edu

J. Martin, "The Maze," The Vidette, p. 2, Feb 23, 1955. [Online]. https://
videttearchive.ilstu.edu

"The Circus Comes to Town," The Vidette, pp. 1, 5, Mar 2, 1955. [Online]. https://
videttearchive.ilstu.edu

"QUEEN CANDIDATES," The Vidette, p. 1, Mar 2, 1955. [photograph] [Online]. https://
videttearchive.ilstu.edu

"Gamma Phi Presents Preview of Circus In Assembly," The Vidette, p. 4, Mar 2, 1955.
[Online]. https://videttearchive.ilstu.edu

"DICK WUTHRICK SAILS THROUGH THE AIR...," The Vidette, p. 4, Mar 2, 1955.
[photograph] [Online]. https://videttearchive.ilstu.edu

"Gymnasts Ready Acts for Opening Night Performance," The Vidette, p. 1, Mar 9, 1955.
[Online]. https://videttearchive.ilstu.edu

"The Maze," The Vidette, p. 1, Mar 9, 1955. [Online]. https://videttearchive.ilstu.edu

"Vidette Offers Praise d," The Vidette, p. 2, Mar 16, 1955. [Online]. https://
videttearchive.ilstu.edu

"Stunt Show Participants Play for Keeps This Year," The Vidette, p. 1, Apr 17, 1955. [Online].
https://videttearchive.ilstu.edu

Gamma Phi Executive Board Picture, The Index, p. 105, 1956 [photograph] [Online]. https://
library.illinoisstate.edu/collections/yearbooks/index.php

"Gamma Phi . . .," The Vidette, p. 5, Sept 28, 1955. [Online]. https://videttearchive.ilstu.edu

"Gamma Phi...," The Vidette, p. 5, Oct 26, 1955. [Online]. https://videttearchive.ilstu.edu

"Gamma Phi Reveals Program," The Vidette, p. 6, Nov 9, 1955. [Online]. https://
videttearchive.ilstu.edu

"Gamma Phi...," The Vidette, p. 3, Nov 23, 1955. [Online]. https://videttearchive.ilstu.edu

"Gamma Phi...," The Vidette, p. 4, Jan 16, 1956. [Online]. https://videttearchive.ilstu.edu

"Gamma Phi...," The Vidette, p. 3, Feb 8, 1956. [Online]. https://videttearchive.ilstu.edu

"Organizations Nominate Eleven ISNU Women For Gamma Phi Queen," The Vidette, p. 4,
Feb 22, 1956. [Online]. https://videttearchive.ilstu.edu

"Polls Open Tomorrow For Circus Queen Vote," The Vidette, pp. 1, 3, Feb 29, 1956. [Online].
https://videttearchive.ilstu.edu

"Gamma Phi queen candidates...," The Vidette, p. 1, Feb 29, 1956. [photograph] [Online].
https://videttearchive.ilstu.edu

"Circus Comes to Capen Next week's assembly...," The Vidette, p. 2, Feb 29, 1956. [Online].
https://videttearchive.ilstu.edu

"Gamma Phi Brings '56 Circus to Town," The Vidette, pp. 1, 3, Mar 7, 1956. [Online]. https://
videttearchive.ilstu.edu

"Students See Preview of Coming Attractions; Gamma Phi Performs Under Capen Big Top,"
The Vidette, p. 2, Mar 7, 1956. [Online]. https://videttearchive.ilstu.edu

"Queen Martha Gronemeier...," The Vidette, p. 1, Mar 14, 1956. [photograph] [Online].
https://videttearchive.ilstu.edu

"The Gamma Phi performers returned...," The Vidette, p. 6, Mar 21, 1956. [Online]. https://
videttearchive.ilstu.edu

Group Gamma Phi Picture, Illinois State University's Special Collections, Milner Library, 1957

"Lions Club Gives Gift To Scholarship Fund," The Vidette, p. 4, Aug 1, 1956. [Online]. https://videttearchive.ilstu.edu

"Gamma Phi...," The Vidette, p. 5, Oct 3, 1956. [Online]. https://videttearchive.ilstu.edu

"Gamma Phi...," The Vidette, p. 6, Oct 10, 1956. [Online]. https://videttearchive.ilstu.edu

"Two Gamma Phi Acts Head WRA Playday On Saturday," The Vidette, p. 7, Oct 24, 1956. [Online]. https://videttearchive.ilstu.edu

"Men's PE Club Changes By-Laws; Gillett Relates Gamma Phi Functions," The Vidette, p. 6, Dec 5, 1956. [Online]. https://videttearchive.ilstu.edu

"Gamma Phi...," The Vidette, p. 5, Dec 12, 1956. [Online]. https://videttearchive.ilstu.edu

"Gamma Phi Circus Goes Into Action," The Vidette, p. 1, Feb 27, 1957. [Online]. https://videttearchive.ilstu.edu

"Gamma Phi Holds Queen Election Tomorrow," The Vidette, p. 1, Mar 6, 1957. [Online]. https://videttearchive.ilstu.edu

"UP IN THE AIR, JUNIOR BIRDSMAN!," The Vidette, p. 4, Mar 6, 1957. [photograph] [Online]. https://videttearchive.ilstu.edu

"'Greatest Show On Earth' Comes to Campus," The Vidette, p. 4, Mar 6, 1957. [Online]. https://videttearchive.ilstu.edu

"ISNU Gamma Phi Circus Opens Tomorrow," The Vidette, p. 8, Mar 13, 1957. [Online]. https://videttearchive.ilstu.edu

"Ron Tinsley...," The Vidette, p. 8, Mar 13, 1957. [photograph] [Online]. https://videttearchive.ilstu.edu

"Leo Benson...," The Vidette, p. 8, Mar 13, 1957. [photograph] [Online]. https://videttearchive.ilstu.edu

"Gamma Phi Circus Troupe Schedules Tour; To Perform Before Four Area High Schools," The Vidette, p. 3, Mar 27, 1957. [Online]. https://videttearchive.ilstu.edu

"Truex, Harris Join ISNU PE Staff," The Vidette, p. 4, July 10, 1957. [Online]. https://videttearchive.ilstu.edu

"Wayne Truex," The Vidette, p. 4, July 10, 1957. [photograph] [Online]. https://videttearchive.ilstu.edu

"Clarence (Pat) Patterson...," The Vidette, p. 5, July 31, 1957. [photograph] [Online]. https://videttearchive.ilstu.edu

Gamma Phi Executive Board Picture, The Index, p. 96, 1958 [photograph] [Online]. https://library.illinoisstate.edu/collections/yearbooks/index.php

"Gamma Phi Orients Pledges, Concentrates On Homecoming," The Vidette, p. 4, Sept 25, 1957. [Online]. https://videttearchive.ilstu.edu

"Gamma Phi...," The Vidette, p. 4, Oct 17, 1957. [Online]. https://videttearchive.ilstu.edu

"Homecoming...," The Vidette, p. 3, Oct 23, 1957. [Online]. https://videttearchive.ilstu.edu

"Mr. Truex, one of Gamma Phi sponsors...," The Vidette, p. 6, Oct 30, 1957. [Online]. https://videttearchive.ilstu.edu

"Rules For Gamma Phi," The Vidette, p. 7, Oct 30, 1957. [Online]. https://videttearchive.ilstu.edu

"Gymnasts' Party Includes Caroling, Games, Dancing," The Vidette, p. 5, Dec 11, 1957. [Online]. https://videttearchive.ilstu.edu

"Truex, Five Men Attend Open Gymnastic Meet," The Vidette, p. 6, Dec 18, 1957. [Online]. https://videttearchive.ilstu.edu

"Gamma Phi Journeys To Champaign; Views Gymnasts of Germany," The Vidette, p. 5, Jan 15, 1958. [Online]. https://videttearchive.ilstu.edu

"Gymnasts Travel To Minonk," The Vidette, p. 5, Feb 12, 1958. [Online]. https://videttearchive.ilstu.edu

"Gymnastic Coach Wayne Truex would like it announced...," The Vidette, p. 6, Feb 12, 1958. [Online]. https://videttearchive.ilstu.edu

"Circus Searches For Queen," The Vidette, p. 5, Feb 19, 1958. [Online]. https://videttearchive.ilstu.edu

"WL Readies Midway For Carnival," The Vidette, p. 8, Feb 19, 1958. [Online]. https://videttearchive.ilstu.edu

"Roscoe Spechts...," The Vidette, p. 8, Feb 19, 1958. [photograph] [Online]. https://videttearchive.ilstu.edu

"Gamma Phi Pounds Stakes For March 13 Opening Date," The Vidette, p. 8, Feb 26, 1958. [Online]. https://videttearchive.ilstu.edu

"With the greatest of ease . . .," The Vidette, p. 8, Feb 26, 1958. [photograph] [Online]. https://videttearchive.ilstu.edu

"Gamma Phi's 3-Night Stand Brings Set of New Gymnastic Troupe Arts," The Vidette, p. 8, Mar 5, 1958. [Online]. https://videttearchive.ilstu.edu

"THE BIG WHEEL," The Vidette, p. 8, Mar 5, 1958. [photograph] [Online]. https://videttearchive.ilstu.edu

G. Goodhart, "Annual Gamma Phi Show Opens Tomorrow," The Vidette, p. 1, Mar 12, 1958. [Online]. https://videttearchive.ilstu.edu

"RON'S ROUNDUP," The Vidette, p. 6, Mar 19, 1958. [Online]. https://videttearchive.ilstu.edu

many pictures, The Vidette, p. 8, Mar 19, 1958. [photographs] [Online]. https://videttearchive.ilstu.edu

"Gamma Phi Hits Road; Performs Out of Town," The Vidette, p. 7, Apr 16, 1958. [Online]. https://videttearchive.ilstu.edu

"The Gamma Phi performers returned from Warrensburg...," The Vidette, p. 6, Apr 30, 1958. [Online]. https://videttearchive.ilstu.edu

"RON'S ROUNDUP," The Vidette, p. 6, May 14, 1958. [Online]. https://videttearchive.ilstu.edu

"Course Prepares Gymnasts," The Vidette, p. 11, May 28, 1958. [Online]. https://videttearchive.ilstu.edu

Group Gamma Phi Picture, The Index, p. 117, 1959 [photograph] [Online]. https://library.illinoisstate.edu/collections/yearbooks/index.php

"Gamma Phi...," The Vidette, p. 3, Sept 17, 1958. [Online]. https://videttearchive.ilstu.edu

"Just a brief bit from Gamma Phi...," The Vidette, p. 6, Oct 1, 1958. [Online]. https://videttearchive.ilstu.edu

"Gamma Phi Gymnasts Receive Letters," The Vidette, p. 5, Nov 5, 1958. [Online]. https://videttearchive.ilstu.edu

"Danish Gymnasts Slate Performance," The Vidette, p. 8, Nov 12, 1958. [Online]. https://videttearchive.ilstu.edu

"Danish Gymnasts Demonstrate Techniques," The Vidette, p. 2, Nov 19, 1958. [Online]. https://videttearchive.ilstu.edu

"Gamma Phi...," The Vidette, p. 3, Dec 3, 1958. [Online]. https://videttearchive.ilstu.edu

"Gamma Phi Announces 1959 Queen Contest," The Vidette, p. 9, Feb 1, 1959. [Online]. https://videttearchive.ilstu.edu

"'59 Gamma Phi Circus Comes To McCormick Gym March 12," The Vidette, p. 3, Feb 25, 1959. [Online]. https://videttearchive.ilstu.edu

"ONE WILL BE CROWNED," The Vidette, p. 8, Mar 4, 1959. [Online]. https://videttearchive.ilstu.edu

"Pictured above ...," The Vidette, p. 8, Mar 4, 1959. [photograph] [Online]. https://videttearchive.ilstu.edu

"Select Gamma Phi Queen Friday," The Vidette, p. 8, Mar 4, 1959. [Online]. https://videttearchive.ilstu.edu

M. Childers, "Big Top Goes Up For Circus; 50 Performers Head Yearly Show," The Vidette, p. 1, Mar 11, 1959. [Online]. https://videttearchive.ilstu.edu

"Dance Will Climax Annual Gamma Phi Circus Production," The Vidette, p. 4, Mar 11, 1959. [Online]. https://videttearchive.ilstu.edu

"Doris Carmichael...," The Vidette, p. 3, Mar 18, 1959. [photograph] [Online]. https://videttearchive.ilstu.edu

"Students, Faculty Select Four Stunts For Annual University Club Show," The Vidette, p. 8, Apr 22, 1959. [Online]. https://videttearchive.ilstu.edu

"Gamma Phi To Hold Election," The Vidette, p. 4, Apr 29, 1959. [Online]. https://videttearchive.ilstu.edu

Group Gamma Phi Picture, The Index, p. 55, 1960 [photograph] [Online]. https://library.illinoisstate.edu/collections/yearbooks/index.php

"Gamma Phi Needs Pledges; Starts Homecoming Project," The Vidette, p. 4, Sept 20, 1959. [Online]. https://videttearchive.ilstu.edu

"Gamma Phi Plans Open House," The Vidette, p. 5, Oct 21, 1959. [Online]. https://videttearchive.ilstu.edu

B. Borovausky, "STEP RIGHT UP LADIES, GENTS...," The Vidette, p. 7, Oct 21, 1959. [Online]. https://videttearchive.ilstu.edu

"Queen Sharon Palmer Reigns At Weekend's Homecoming Activities," The Vidette, p. 8, Oct 28, 1959. [Online]. https://videttearchive.ilstu.edu

"Gamma Phi Holds Tryouts," The Vidette, p. 4, Nov 11, 1959. [Online]. https://videttearchive.ilstu.edu

"Gamma Phi Has Tryouts; Plans Workout Period, Annual Christmas Party," The Vidette, p. 3, Dec 2, 1959. [Online]. https://videttearchive.ilstu.edu

"Gamma Phi...," The Vidette, p. 4, Jan 20, 1960. [Online]. https://videttearchive.ilstu.edu

"Gamma Phi...," The Vidette, p. 4, Feb 17, 1960. [Online]. https://videttearchive.ilstu.edu

"Gamma Phi Stages Circus March 17, 18, 19," The Vidette, p. 4, Mar 2, 1960. [Online]. https://videttearchive.ilstu.edu

"Carnival Night Arrives on Saturday; Booths Represent 28 Organizations," The Vidette, p. 1, Mar 9, 1960. [Online]. https://videttearchive.ilstu.edu

"Martha Klinefelter and Al Martling...," The Vidette, p. 5, Mar 9, 1960. [photograph] [Online]. https://videttearchive.ilstu.edu

"Diane Alt, DeVee DeRocker, and Sharon Schillinger...," The Vidette, p. 1, Mar 16, 1960. [photograph] [Online]. https://videttearchive.ilstu.edu

"Gamma Phi Presents Circus in McCormick," The Vidette, p. 1, Mar16, 1960. [Online]. https://videttearchive.ilstu.edu

"Campus Elections, Student Senate Actions Attract Interest," The Vidette, p. 2, Mar 16, 1960. [Online]. https://videttearchive.ilstu.edu

"Election. Outstanding Senior Selection Retain Limelight," The Vidette, p. 2, Mar 23, 1960. [Online]. https://videttearchive.ilstu.edu

"Gamma Phi...," The Vidette, p. 4, May 18, 1960. [Online]. https://videttearchive.ilstu.edu

"Gamma Phi... The Vidette, p. 4, May 25, 1960. [Online]. https://videttearchive.ilstu.edu

Group Gamma Phi Picture, The Index, p. 50, 1961 [photograph] [Online]. https://library.illinoisstate.edu/collections/yearbooks/index.php

"Campus Graduates Perform In New "Teachers Of Tomorrow" Color Film," The Vidette, p. 8, Sept 21, 1960. [Online]. https://videttearchive.ilstu.edu

"GAMMA PHI, gymnastics organization...," The Vidette, p. 4, Feb 15, 1961. [Online]. https://videttearchive.ilstu.edu

"Gillett Accepts Names," The Vidette, p. 3, Feb 22, 1961. [Online]. https://videttearchive.ilstu.edu

"Gamma Phi Prepares Show," The Vidette, p. 8, Mar 1, 1961. [Online]. https://videttearchive.ilstu.edu

"Gamma Phi Presents Circus, Elects Queen," The Vidette, p. 5, Mar 8, 1961. [Online]. https://videttearchive.ilstu.edu

"Gamma Phi To Crown Queen," The Vidette, p. 1, Mar 15, 1961. [Online]. https://videttearchive.ilstu.edu

"Members of the Gamma Phi Court...," The Vidette, p. 1, Mar 15, 1961. [photograph] [Online]. https://videttearchive.ilstu.edu

A. Kelly, "Reporter Features Non-Academic Employees," The Vidette, p. 3, Apr 26, 1961. [Online]. https://videttearchive.ilstu.edu

"Skip Rounds...," The Vidette, p. 8, Mar 22, 1961. [photograph] [Online]. https://videttearchive.ilstu.edu

"Devee De Rocker...," The Vidette, p. 8, Mar 22, 1961. [photograph] [Online]. https://videttearchive.ilstu.edu

"Janet Buxton...," The Vidette, p. 8, Mar 22, 1961. [photograph] [Online]. https://videttearchive.ilstu.edu

F. Kaempfer, "'Pop' Horton Retires After 38 Years," The Vidette, p. 6, May 10, 1961. [Online]. https://videttearchive.ilstu.edu

F. Kaempfer, "'Pop' Horton Retires After 38 Years," The Vidette, p. 6, May 10, 1961. [photograph] [Online]. https://videttearchive.ilstu.edu

Group Gamma Phi Picture, Illinois State University's Special Collections, Milner Library, 1962

"Gamma Phi," The Vidette, p. 4, Nov 8, 1961. [Online]. https://videttearchive.ilstu.edu

"Gamma Phi...," The Vidette, p. 4, Nov 15, 1961. [Online]. https://videttearchive.ilstu.edu

"Horton Turns Spade For Field House," The Vidette, p. 1, Dec 15, 1961. [Online]. https://videttearchive.ilstu.edu

"Clifford "Pop" Horton," The Vidette, p. 1, Dec 15, 1961. [photograph] [Online]. https://videttearchive.ilstu.edu

"P E Plant To Bear Horton's Name," The Vidette, p. 1, Dec 15, 1961. [Online]. https://videttearchive.ilstu.edu

"GAMMA PHI QUEEN," The Vidette, p. 2, Feb 8, 1962. [Online]. https://videttearchive.ilstu.edu

"GAMMA PHI PRACTICING," The Vidette, p. 4, Feb 22, 1962. [Online]. https://videttearchive.ilstu.edu

"Gamma Phi Selects New Club Members," The Vidette, p. 3, Mar 1, 1962. [Online]. https://videttearchive.ilstu.edu

"'Open House' Releases Broadcast Schedule," The Vidette, p. 1, Mar 8, 1962. [Online]. https://videttearchive.ilstu.edu

G. Cardarelli, "Ziert Drifts From Tap Dancing To Gymnastics," The Vidette, p. 3, Mar 8, 1962. [Online]. https://videttearchive.ilstu.edu

"Annual Circus To Highlight New Show Acts," The Vidette, p. 1, Mar 13, 1962. [Online]. https://videttearchive.ilstu.edu

"Marti Staab," The Vidette, p. 1, Mar 13, 1962. [photograph] [Online]. https://videttearchive.ilstu.edu

"Carole Butler," The Vidette, p. 1, Mar 13, 1962. [photograph] [Online]. https://videttearchive.ilstu.edu

"Students To Select Gamma Phi Queen," The Vidette, p. 1, Mar 13, 1962. [Online]. https://videttearchive.ilstu.edu

"Circus Lists Chairmen," The Vidette, p. 1, Mar 15, 1962. [Online]. https://videttearchive.ilstu.edu

"School Picks Court," The Vidette, p. 1, Mar 20, 1962. [Online]. https://videttearchive.ilstu.edu

"Gamma Phi To Start Three-Day Run," The Vidette, p. 1, Mar 22, 1962. [Online]. https://videttearchive.ilstu.edu

"Red Cross Mobile To Visit ISU," The Vidette, p. 2, Mar 22, 1962. [Online]. https://videttearchive.ilstu.edu

"Reporter Appraises Gamma Phi Performance," The Vidette, p. 8, Mar 27, 1962. [Online]. https://videttearchive.ilstu.edu

"Attendants Linda Fortna...," The Vidette, p. 8, Mar 27, 1962. [photograph] [Online]. https://videttearchive.ilstu.edu

"Bill Hunt and Dale Manning...," The Vidette, p. 8, Mar 27, 1962. [photograph] [Online]. https://videttearchive.ilstu.edu

"Gamma Phi," The Vidette, p. 4, May 22, 1962. [Online]. https://videttearchive.ilstu.edu

"Dr. Gillett Obtains New PE Position," The Vidette, p. 1, June 27, 1962. [Online]. https://videttearchive.ilstu.edu

Group Gamma Phi Picture, The Index, p. 51, 1963 [photograph] [Online]. https://library.illinoisstate.edu/collections/yearbooks/index.php

"Gamma Phi," The Vidette, p. 4, Sept 20, 1962. [Online]. https://videttearchive.ilstu.edu

"Red Door Sponsors 'Roaring Twenties'," The Vidette, p. 1, Nov 13, 1962. [Online]. https://videttearchive.ilstu.edu

"Gamma Phi Selects 28 Pledges," The Vidette, p. 8, Feb 7, 1963. [Online]. https://videttearchive.ilstu.edu

E. Ceres, "Ziert Wins 'Athlete of Week' Honors," The Vidette, p. 7, Feb 21, 1963. [Online]. https://videttearchive.ilstu.edu

M. Lyons, "Annual Spring Carnival Promises Gala Festival," The Vidette, p. 1, Feb 28, 1963. [Online]. https://videttearchive.ilstu.edu

J. Yeast, "Everyone Loves Gamma Phi Circus!," The Vidette, p. 8, Feb 28, 1963. [Online]. https://videttearchive.ilstu.edu

"Gamma Phi unicyclists...," The Vidette, p. 8, Feb 28, 1963. [photograph] [Online]. https://videttearchive.ilstu.edu

J. Yeast, "Circus Creates Suspense, Sensation," The Vidette, p. 8, Mar 7, 1963. [Online]. https://videttearchive.ilstu.edu

"17 COEDS VIE FOR CROWN . . .," The Vidette, p. 1, Mar 12, 1963. [Online]. https://videttearchive.ilstu.edu

J. Yeast, "Circus Begins Ticket Sale Tomorrow," The Vidette, p. 4, Mar 14, 1963. [Online]. https://videttearchive.ilstu.edu

"Neil Barton," The Vidette, p. 4, Mar 14, 1963. [photograph] [Online]. https://videttearchive.ilstu.edu

"Barb Messman," The Vidette, p. 4, Mar 14, 1963. [photograph] [Online]. https://
videttearchive.ilstu.edu

"WIOK Presents...," The Vidette, p. 8, Mar 14, 1963. [Online]. https://videttearchive.ilstu.edu

J. Yeast,"Gamma Phi Circus Features Aerialists. Cyclists, Jugglers," The Vidette, p. 1, Mar 19,
1963. [Online]. https://videttearchive.ilstu.edu

"Circus Crowns Queen at Annual Fling," The Vidette, p. 1, Mar 21, 1963. [Online]. https://
videttearchive.ilstu.edu

"One of these coeds...," The Vidette, p. 1, Mar 21, 1963. [photograph] [Online]. https://
videttearchive.ilstu.edu

"Union Board Hosts Students at Roman Banquet," The Vidette, p. 7, May 9, 1963. [Online].
https://videttearchive.ilstu.edu

"John Carroll Speaks To Sixty At UU Annual Roman Banquet," The Vidette, p. 4, May 16,
1963. [Online]. https://videttearchive.ilstu.edu

"Stage Band To Present Jazz Concert," The Vidette, p.8, May 23, 1963. [Online]. https://
videttearchive.ilstu.edu

"Board Slashes Vidette '63-'64 Budget," The Vidette, p. 1, May 28, 1963. [Online]. https://
videttearchive.ilstu.edu

L. Cains, "Campus Impresses Finnish Educator," The Vidette, p. 1, May 28, 1963. [Online].
https://videttearchive.ilstu.edu

Group Gamma Phi Picture, The Index, p. 43, 1964 [photograph] [Online]. https://
library.illinoisstate.edu/collections/yearbooks/index.php

"Clubs Brew Hospitality," The Vidette, p. 4, Oct 24, 1963. [Online]. https://
videttearchive.ilstu.edu

"The blueprint of a dream...," The Index, p. 12, 1963 [photograph] [Online] https://
library.illinoisstate.edu/collections/yearbooks/index.php

"Whirlo's Perform On Amateur Hour," The Vidette, p. 4, Dec 10, 1963. [Online]. https://
videttearchive.ilstu.edu

"Clubs Nominate Twenty Coeds For Gamma Phi Circus Queen," The Vidette, p. 1, Mar 17,
1964. [Online]. https://videttearchive.ilstu.edu

"Perfect Balance," The Vidette, p. 4, Mar 17, 1964. [photograph] [Online]. https://
videttearchive.ilstu.edu

"Gamma Phi Performs Circus In Horton Gym," The Vidette, p. 4, Mar 19, 1964. [Online].
https://videttearchive.ilstu.edu

"Spanish Whips," The Vidette, p. 4, Mar 19, 1964. [photograph] [Online]. https://
videttearchive.ilstu.edu

"Kathy Vignocchi," The Vidette, p. 4, Mar 19, 1964. [photograph] [Online]. https://
videttearchive.ilstu.edu

"John Fussner," The Vidette, p. 4, Mar 19, 1964. [photograph] [Online]. https://
videttearchive.ilstu.edu

"Carol Herndon," The Vidette, p. 4, Mar 19, 1964. [photograph] [Online]. https://
videttearchive.ilstu.edu

"Gamma Phi Displays Bright Colors, Pageantry; Clowns, Tumblers Thrill Audience With
Daring," The Vidette, p. 3, Apr 9, 1964. [Online]. https://videttearchive.ilstu.edu

"Annual ISU Sports Banquet Features Northwestern Director Stu Holcomb As Main Speaker
For I Men, Guests," The Vidette, p. 6, Apr 9, 1964. [Online]. https://
videttearchive.ilstu.edu

"Dale Manning crowning Janet Drew," The Vidette, p. 1, Apr 14, 1964. [photograph] [Online].
https://videttearchive.ilstu.edu

"Union Honors Seventy ISU Students At Annual Roman Banquet Wednesday," The Vidette, p. 1, May 12, 1964. [Online]. https://videttearchive.ilstu.edu

Group Gamma Phi Picture, The Index, p. 92, 1965 [photograph] [Online]. https://library.illinoisstate.edu/collections/yearbooks/index.php

"Organizations Join In Parade Saturday," The Vidette, p. 4, Oct 29, 1964. [Online]. https://videttearchive.ilstu.edu

"Sign Warns Residents Of Peddling Unicyclist," The Vidette, p. 3, Feb 25, 1965. [Online]. https://videttearchive.ilstu.edu

"THROUGH TRAFFIC," The Vidette, p. 3, Feb 25, 1965. [photograph] [Online]. https://videttearchive.ilstu.edu

"Gymnasts Perform Acrobatic Feats At 29th Annual Gamma Phi Circus," The Vidette, p. 1, Mar 11, 1965. [Online]. https://videttearchive.ilstu.edu

"Queen Candidates," The Vidette, p. 1, Mar 16, 1965. [photograph] [Online]. https://videttearchive.ilstu.edu

"Ad for Queen Candidate Donna Doetch," The Vidette, p. 2, Mar 16, 1965. [photograph] [Online]. https://videttearchive.ilstu.edu

"Calypso Music…," The Vidette, p. 1, Mar 18, 1965. [Online]. https://videttearchive.ilstu.edu

"Ad for Gaye Burke for Queen," The Vidette, p. 2, Mar 18, 1965. [photograph] [Online]. https://videttearchive.ilstu.edu

"Head Coach Truex, Six Squad Members Depart For NAIA National Gymnastics Meet In Kansas," The Vidette, p. 4, Mar 18, 1965. [Online]. https://videttearchive.ilstu.edu

"Strains of calypso music echo in Horton Fieldhouse…," The Vidette, p. 4, Mar 23, 1965. [Online]. https://videttearchive.ilstu.edu

3 non-labeled pictures, The Vidette, p. 4, Mar 23, 1965. [photograph] [Online]. https://videttearchive.ilstu.edu

"Gamma Phi Show Starts Friday," The Vidette, p. 1, Mar 25, 1965. [Online]. https://videttearchive.ilstu.edu

"MORE BOUNCE TO THE OUNCE…," The Vidette, p. 1, Mar 25, 1965. [photograph] [Online]. https://videttearchive.ilstu.edu

"'ROUND AND ROUND WE GO…," The Vidette, p. 1, Mar 25, 1965. [photograph] [Online]. https://videttearchive.ilstu.edu

"Barb White Queen," The Vidette, p. 3, Mar 30, 1965. [photograph] [Online]. https://videttearchive.ilstu.edu

J. Cipfl, "Ziert Concludes Memorable Career," The Vidette, p. 4, May 13, 1965. [Online]. https://videttearchive.ilstu.edu

Group Gamma Phi Picture, Illinois State University's Special Collections, Milner Library, 1966

"Gamma Phi Works Out," The Vidette, p. 4, Oct 7, 1965. [Online]. https://videttearchive.ilstu.edu

"Dignitaries, Camel, Floats Highlight Saturday Parade," The Vidette, p. 1, Oct 21, 1965. [Online]. https://videttearchive.ilstu.edu

"Homecoming Calendar," The Vidette, p. 11, Oct 21, 1965. [Online]. https://videttearchive.ilstu.edu

"ISU Sets Scoring Record; Defense Lags In NIU Loss," The Vidette, p. 4, Jan 11, 1966. [Online]. https://videttearchive.ilstu.edu

"Gillett Named ISU Athletic Director," The Vidette, p. 4, Feb 24, 1966. [Online]. https://videttearchive.ilstu.edu

"Arley Gillett," The Vidette, p. 4, Feb 24, 1966. [photograph] [Online]. https://videttearchive.ilstu.edu

"Carnival Mood Prevails At AWS 'Midterm Midway'," The Vidette, p. 1, Mar 24, 1966. [Online]. https://videttearchive.ilstu.edu

"Acrobatics, Clowns Enliven Gamma Phi Circus," The Vidette, p. 1, Mar 29, 1966. [Online]. https://videttearchive.ilstu.edu

"Gamma Phi Invite Queen Nominations," The Vidette, p. 1, Mar 31, 1966. [Online]. https://videttearchive.ilstu.edu

"Gamma Phi Circus Opens Friday; Highlights Little Sister Weekend," The Vidette, p. 3, Apr 19, 1966. [Online]. https://videttearchive.ilstu.edu

"Vaulting practice," The Vidette, p. 3, Apr 19, 1966. [photograph] [Online]. https://videttearchive.ilstu.edu

"Queen Candidates," The Vidette, p. 1, Apr 21, 1966. [photograph] [Online]. https://videttearchive.ilstu.edu

E. Kenyon, "Old Circus Days Relived At ISU," The Vidette, p. 1, Apr 28, 1966. [Online]. https://videttearchive.ilstu.edu

INDEX

18-foot pole, 150
25-foot pole, 146
50-foot wire slide, 160

A

acts
  adagio, 104
  aerial, 3, 103, 199, 225, 249, 365
  animal, 181, 224, 276
  balance, 144, 265, 271
  balance beam, 242, 252, 257, 264–65, 267, 304, 313, 323, 339, 344, 352–53, 368, 374, 379, 392, 395
  balancing, 140, 146, 149–51, 205, 232, 254, 264, 377–78
  balls, 96, 199, 214, 218, 233, 255, 257, 292, 323, 344, 352, 356, 358–59, 368, 374, 392, 395
  bars, 1, 38–39, 76, 121, 140, 149, 208, 223, 298, 359, 376
    parallel, 1, 232, 244
    uneven parallel, 275, 312, 354, 376, 380, 395
  baton twirling, 180, 183–86, 200–201, 232, 275–76, 291, 313
  beams, 170, 354, 359
  bronze, 119, 143
  chair balancing, 106, 108, 125, 140, 146, 151, 173, 175, 189, 199, 210
  circus, 138, 232, 264, 273, 290, 321, 323, 338, 379, 393
  cloud swing, 119, 160–61, 187, 199, 209, 224, 233, 242, 275–76, 292, 313
  clowns, 2, 7, 68–69, 77, 79, 81, 88, 101, 119, 135, 141–42, 147, 150–51, 161, 164, 173, 175, 179, 184–85, 188–89, 192, 199, 208–10, 215–18, 224–25, 234–35, 244–45, 255, 259, 264, 267, 270, 276, 311, 314, 323, 339, 341, 345, 352, 356, 359, 368, 374, 378–79, 391–92, 397
  flying rings, 53, 69, 81, 140, 150–51, 154, 161, 172–73, 207, 293
  horizontal bars, 1, 42, 121, 151, 185, 249, 254, 270, 297, 304, 323, 353, 374, 379
  horse, 1–3, 23–24, 210, 297, 378
  jaw, 201
  juggling, 3, 69, 155, 162, 174, 187, 244, 249, 252, 254, 258, 263, 339, 358

ladders, 1, 3, 53, 69, 81, 89, 92, 94–95, 118–19, 125, 135, 150, 160–61, 170–71, 184, 189, 199, 202, 234, 267, 269, 291, 304, 338, 343, 352, 359, 377–78
parallel bars, 2–3, 27, 32, 54–55, 69, 77, 92, 94, 115, 118, 127, 140–41, 143, 155, 173–75, 188, 190, 199, 202, 209, 217, 223–24, 241, 249, 265, 267, 270, 293, 297, 304, 323, 341, 344, 356, 368, 374, 378, 392, 395
perch pole, 3, 104, 140, 142, 146, 149, 154–55, 161, 175, 198–99, 203, 208, 210, 267, 304
pyramid building, 20, 41–42, 53, 64–65, 71, 73, 78, 89–90, 105, 108, 119, 125, 143, 161, 189, 198, 224, 312
revolving ladder, 42, 173, 185, 358
roller skating, 105, 242, 249, 256–58, 298, 344
Spanish Webs, 304, 353, 365
springboard, 92, 103, 105, 109, 118–19, 125, 127, 150–51
strong-man, 164
swinging ladders, 119, 143, 151, 153–54, 160, 181–83, 208, 218, 224, 254, 267, 269, 293, 304, 323, 344, 356
swinging perch pole, 204, 217, 224, 234, 270, 292, 311
sword, 189
tightwire, 76, 119, 125, 143, 147, 149–50, 153–55, 160–61, 164, 171, 174–75, 187, 189, 204, 230, 338, 341, 344, 353, 356
trampolet, 374, 380
trampoline, 3, 188, 198, 201, 208, 218, 222, 224, 233, 249, 263, 265, 267, 270, 275–76, 297, 304, 311, 313, 323, 335–36, 344, 349, 352–53, 359, 368, 377–78, 385–86, 392, 395
trapeze, 1–3, 7, 103, 119, 121, 187, 208, 222, 234, 249, 254, 267, 276, 293, 302, 304, 313, 323, 330, 344, 351–52, 358–59, 363, 365, 368, 374, 379, 392–93, 395
triple trapeze, 209, 224
tumbling, 1, 3, 20, 22, 24–27, 32–33, 35, 41–42, 50–54, 58, 64–66, 69, 71–73, 76, 78, 80, 87, 89, 91, 94, 96, 100, 105, 117–19, 127, 143, 153, 161–62,

425   A Circus in the Paper

184–85, 187, 189, 198–99, 214, 222, 224, 229, 232, 249, 254, 256–59, 265, 270, 276, 297, 311, 335–36, 344, 349, 351–52, 356, 368, 374, 377–78, 380, 385–86, 392, 395

tumbling and pyramid building, 64–65, 71, 78

unicycles, 3, 94, 101, 149, 151, 160, 232–33, 244, 252, 255, 257, 259, 264, 269, 276, 290, 323, 341, 344, 352, 358–59, 368, 372, 374, 378, 392, 395

vaulting, 174, 302, 311, 344, 352, 368, 375, 380, 395

Wampus, 79, 119

Whirl of Death, 253, 259

zouaves & floor pyramids, 172

Adams, Don, 101

Adams, Jane, 363

Adams, Joanne, 395, 398

Adeline Bach School, 103

admission, 10, 42, 80, 86, 89, 104, 106, 119, 145, 161, 180, 195, 225, 231, 233–34, 263, 305, 338, 369

Aeillo, John, 25

Alamo, 45, 47, 57, 59, 82

Albright, Sally, 293

Alderson, Mary, 217

Aldridge, Vic, 173

Alexander, Holly, 363

Allan, Robert, 200

Allen, Joan, 223, 225

Allen, Mabel Clare, 182

all-school election, 67–68, 70, 164, 217, 265, 275, 363, 394

Almquist, Lydia, 220, 232–33, 244

Alt, Diane, 310, 312, 333–34, 338–40, 342, 345

American Red Cross, 176, 327

Anchor High School, 81

Anderson, Carter, 43

Anderson, Judy, 339, 342, 356–57

Anderson, Mary, 304

Anderson, Nancy, 348

Anderson, Russell, 51, 57–58

Anderson, Sheila, 292

Anderson, Sherrill, 395, 398

Anderson, William, 122–23, 127–28, 132

Angleton, Doris, 100

Annual Christmas Party, 274, 300, 310

annual circus, 43, 51, 65, 68, 72, 88, 100, 106, 109, 112, 121, 153, 156, 163, 169, 171, 186–87, 191, 197, 201, 204, 208, 221, 229, 231, 245, 249–50, 258–59, 276, 278, 298, 313, 319–21, 330, 333–34, 338, 365, 368, 372, 377, 379

Annual Gamma Phi, 64, 68, 70–71, 78–80, 89, 97, 102–4, 118, 127, 157, 191, 196, 209, 214, 217, 265, 292, 341, 343, 351, 372, 376, 398

Anson, Ronald, 342

apparatus, 20, 76, 203, 253, 269, 280, 292–93, 297, 300, 347, 353–54

Archibald, Joyce, 208

Arlington Heights, IL, 235, 307

Armitage, John, 77

Armstrong, Marilyn, 303, 310

Arnold, Wayne, 220

Art Club, 59–60, 232, 234

Aschenbrennen, Conrad, 220

assembly, 90, 141, 165–66, 196, 222–23, 231–32, 241–42, 250–51, 256–57, 259, 266, 268, 270, 394

athletics, 2, 14–15, 17–18, 20, 23, 29, 31, 38, 74, 81, 101, 108, 110, 246, 327–28, 332, 335–36, 389–90

attendants, 80, 88, 106–7, 143, 159, 165, 196, 209, 235, 252, 265–66, 275, 320

audience, 22, 33, 53, 58, 65, 94, 130, 138, 142, 144, 146, 150, 161, 185, 189, 201–2, 212, 231, 244, 338, 345, 351, 353–54, 356, 362, 365, 393, 398

awards, 2, 36, 49, 71, 84, 110, 123, 299, 345, 349, 359–60, 369, 377, 385, 387

Axelson, Jan, 363

Ayres, John, 77

B

Backman, Paul, 358

Baier, Marie, 245

Baier, Rosemarie, 243

Bair, Nancy, 310–11, 313

Baird, Betty, 51

balance, 81, 91, 125, 140, 147, 203, 209–10, 214, 222, 224, 233, 259, 267, 269–70, 291–93, 344, 354, 356, 359, 368, 372, 377–78, 392, 395, 398

Ball, Lyle, 192, 198, 202

Ballister, Bill, 310

Ball State, 335

Baltes, John, 310, 334, 338–39, 342

band, 41–42, 68–69, 71, 89, 105, 119, 149, 179–80, 182, 184, 199, 242, 250, 267, 276–77, 296, 379

pep, 199–200

band members, 200, 281, 342

banquet, 25–26, 47, 71–72, 81–83, 85, 87, 97, 109–10, 326, 328, 370

Barclay, Harry, 123
Barclay, Otis, 77, 81
Barclay, Owen, 43, 91
Bardo, Bill, 138
Barnum & Bailey, 104, 180, 192, 309, 323, 397
Barr Brothers, 42
Barto, Margaret, 26, 54, 59, 73, 106
Barton, Neil, 334, 338, 352, 354, 358, 361
baseball, 12, 14–17, 24, 96, 327
basketball, 3, 12, 14–15, 17, 31, 41, 43, 49, 73, 96, 115, 129, 138, 156, 195, 200, 310, 327
basketball games, 13, 15, 17, 20–21, 78, 115, 130, 138, 156, 195, 241
Baskovic, Robert, 342
Batman, Margaret, 208
baton twirlers, 185, 275–76
Bauman, Marilyn, 159–60
Baumgardner, Gabriel, 342
Bavo, Philip, 35
Beales, Ronald, 239
Beardsley, Janet, 323
Beardstown, IL, 319, 321, 375, 380
Beesley, Jerry, 348, 353
Behnke, Dean, 310
Belknap, Helen, 106
Belleville, IL, 232, 235, 237, 299, 301
Bennett, Richard, 57–58, 62–64, 69, 103, 105
Benson, Bernadine, 107
Benson, Leo, 254–55, 257, 269–70, 286
Berning, Penny, 348, 356
Berthold, Carol, 340
Best, Tom, 392
Bjorkman, Phyllis, 201
Blackford, Diana, 321, 339, 342, 353
Blakeley, Scott, 267
Blattner, Don, 254, 269, 293
Bleyl, Karl, 181, 183
Blish, Barbara, 255
Bliss, Jean, 160
Bloomington, IL, 6–7, 34, 39, 46–47, 53, 63, 65, 68, 70, 72, 77–78, 89, 92, 103, 106, 110, 115, 117, 122–23, 140, 143–44, 155, 170, 189, 219, 227, 230, 232, 238, 265, 273, 281, 308–9, 311, 321, 323, 334, 341–43
Blum, Maurine, 90
Boaden, Judy, 304, 311
Bock, Karen, 379, 394
Boehm, Barbara, 243, 247, 254
Bone, Robert G., 332, 389
Bonney, Joan, 211

Bookwalter, Irene, 179, 181–83
Borchers, Evan, 220
Bordner, Eloise, 80
Borovausky, Bev, 308
Bourn, Bessie, 304
Bova, Philip, 38
boxing, 2, 4, 22, 27–30, 43
Bradshaw, Jean, 365
Brady, Mary, 395, 398
Brandt, Bob, 247, 254
Brauer, George, 173
Breen, Stanley, 152
Brenneman, Sandy, 365, 374, 380, 389, 392
Brinderhoff, John, 255
Brown, Gloria, 374, 377, 380
Brown, Joyce, 232
Brown, Judy, 392–93
Brown, Mary Lynn, 254, 262, 267, 269, 286
Browne, Richard, 28, 46, 387
Brubaker, Charles, 254
Brumbach, Diddy, 136, 139, 143, 158
Brumbach, Mary, 136
Brummett, Bob, 54, 57, 62, 72
Bryan, Bill, 26
Buckley, Sally, 303
Buckman, Lois, 303
Buckowich, Al, 218
Burda, Don, 270–71
Burgess, Aline, 79
Burmeister, Kay, 244
Burnett, George, 94
Burpee, Jeannie, 348, 356–57, 374, 380, 392–93, 398
Bury, Pauline, 196
Busch, Elmer, 239
Busch, Harry, 255
Buss, Ken, 192, 198–99, 202, 204–5, 207–9
Butler, Carole, 334, 338–39, 342
Butler, Dawn, 243
Butler, Sarah, 243, 247, 251, 254–55, 269–70
Buxton, Janet, 310, 312

C
Cade, Carrol, 28
campus, 3, 11, 17, 25, 33, 39, 41, 49, 51–53, 57, 82, 87, 92, 100, 102, 114, 124, 128, 147, 149, 152, 156, 167, 171, 177, 179, 186, 188, 194–95, 204, 206, 213, 216, 221–22, 225, 227–29, 232, 236, 238, 245–46, 248–49, 253, 260, 265, 267, 276, 301, 315, 317–20, 332, 334, 341, 345–46, 359, 361, 378, 390, 395

Campus Inn, 85, 87, 100
campus organizations, 117, 132, 231, 275, 288, 318
candidates, 13, 35, 70, 79, 82, 99–100, 114, 131, 136–38, 157–58, 165, 195–96, 206, 216, 222–23, 231–33, 250, 265, 288, 290, 303, 314–20, 333, 354, 394
Canham, Norma, 236
Cannell, Barbara, 266
Cannon, Jacquie, 251, 253, 255, 269, 273
Capponi, Carol, 365
Cardosi, Cel, 223, 225
Carlock, Burton, 28
Carlson, John, 250, 255
Carmichael, Doris, 303–4
Carnahan, James, 61
Carney, Mary, 254, 257, 259, 269, 286, 290, 293
carnival, 180, 221, 289, 312, 391
Carpenter, Bonnie, 305
Carr, Dick, 217, 219–20, 222, 229, 232, 241
Carstensen, Nancy, 292
Carter, Bonnie, 354
Carter, Harry, 29
Carter, Russ, 42, 54
Caruso, Jerry, 244
Casner, Betty, 201
Catenacci, Ray, 220
ceremonies, 36, 159, 161, 182, 184, 192, 202, 204, 208–9, 218, 243, 332
Chandler, Dodie, 269, 284, 286, 293, 299, 304
Chapman, Edna Mae, 208, 212, 214
Chapman, Kay, 310
Chaudoin, George, 220
Chicago, 12, 53, 89, 141, 169, 174, 196, 217, 219, 223, 226, 271, 290, 323, 334–36, 362
Chilton, Sandy, 365
Chmielewski, Marie, 323
Chouinard, Rhea, 374, 380
Christensen, James, 99
Christiensen, Lavernne, 86, 97, 101–2, 107, 109–10, 114, 118, 135
Chung, Cyril, 254, 265, 269
Churchill, Connie, 209
Churchill, Robert, 239
circus, 4, 7–8, 10–11, 20–21, 24, 34, 37, 39, 42–43, 51–54, 60, 65, 67–68, 70–71, 75–76, 78–79, 88–90, 94, 98–103, 117–18, 124–25, 130–32, 134–35, 137–46, 149–50, 157–59, 164–66, 168, 170, 180, 186–88, 191–92, 195–96, 198–201, 203, 205, 208–11, 216,

221, 223–24, 226–27, 230–33, 235, 240–45, 250–57, 263–70, 272, 275, 280–81, 288–89, 291–93, 301–2, 304–5, 309, 313–14, 320–21, 339–40, 343, 345, 347–48, 351–54, 356–59, 365, 368, 372, 374–75, 379–80, 382, 391–99
acts, 138, 232, 264, 273, 290, 321, 323, 338, 379, 393
band, 198–99, 201, 217, 225, 227, 231–32, 251, 253, 256, 267, 296, 304, 311, 320–21
clowns, 202, 251, 374, 380
first, 48, 52, 79, 130, 134, 144, 192, 344
queen, 51–52, 66–67, 70, 79, 88, 100, 106, 110, 132, 138, 164–65, 192, 195, 209, 225, 231, 234, 243, 245, 340
See also Gamma Phi Queen
squad, 287, 301, 310, 320, 348, 365, 379–80, 391
troupe, 217, 224, 276, 280, 292, 312, 320–21, 323, 339, 368, 398
circuses, 2, 6, 23, 42, 91, 102, 134–35, 140, 144, 195, 239
Clark, Wanda, 339, 342
Clarke, Richard, 241, 244, 254–55
Clark University, 12–13, 16, 326
Clendenin, Robert, 108, 119, 121
Clendenin, Tony, 118–19, 135, 161
Cleveland, Carol, 269
Clifton, Jack, 270
Clinton, IL, 89, 214, 219, 221, 231, 241, 245, 251, 303, 309
Cluts, Ray, 251, 253–55, 259
coaches, 12–18, 30, 38, 49, 63, 84, 89, 91, 98, 194, 222, 225, 246, 253, 267, 281, 290, 327, 337, 349, 390
Coach Russell, 13, 15
Coal City, IL, 89
Coal Valley, 299, 334, 340, 345
Coatney, Dorothy, 208
Cockerill, Forest, 43
Cogdal, Joseph, 53
Cole, Marcia, 266
Colebar, Leona, 243
Cole Brothers, 119, 397
Colfax, IL, 108, 114
college circuses, 1, 5
Collegiate Digest, 66
Collins, 64
Colteaux, Theodore, 49
Conder, Barbara, 257, 259
constitution, 23, 101
Cook, Marjorie, 51, 69

Cook Hall, 18, 20, 114
Copeland, Ray, 26, 35
Cordova, 284, 286
Cornell, 114, 340
coronation, 70, 94, 104–5, 139, 192, 201,
    224, 234, 253, 276, 338
costumes, 1–2, 179, 198, 215–16, 230, 241,
    243, 267, 276, 288, 290, 306, 309,
    321, 339, 342, 345, 359, 365, 393
Cotterell, Lavaughn, 254, 269
Cottingham, Joanne, 303
court, 158–59, 165, 195, 198, 209, 216–17,
    223, 225, 231, 241, 245, 265–66,
    268, 275, 278, 303–4, 313, 321, 333,
    340, 343, 354, 368, 379, 394, 398
Court, Bob, 392, 398
Courtney, Dorothy, 209
Covey, Edward, 25–26, 173
Cox, Betty Lou, 159, 161–62
Cozart, Clifford, 56–58, 62, 64, 69, 76, 78–
    81, 84, 86–92, 94, 127
Cozart team, 95
Craig, Margie, 394
Craig, Steve, 379
Creve Coeur, IL, 334, 369
Crochett, Ken, 241–42
Crotchet, Nola, 257, 286, 293
Crotchett, Jim, 218, 289, 293
Crotchett, Ken, 209, 217, 220, 241, 244
Crotchett, Nola, 269
Croutcher, Clarence, 30
Crush, Alice, 79
Cruze, Gene, 232–33, 239, 241–42, 244, 247
Cunningham, Roger, 241, 244, 250–52,
    254–55, 257, 270, 272–73
Curley, Sharon, 363
Curtis, Francis, 220
Cutter, Roberta, 257

D
Daggett, Bill, 149
Daggitt, Betty, 348, 357, 374, 376, 379–80
Dale Manning, 338–40, 342, 345, 353, 356,
    358
Daley, Jack, 198–99, 201–2, 207–9, 211–12,
    215–17, 222
Dalton, Eleanor, 158–59, 162, 165
Dalton, Ray, 334, 339, 342
Damotte, Judy, 290, 293, 305, 308
dance, 33, 42, 50, 62, 81, 87, 118, 158, 160–
    61, 285, 305, 347, 392–93, 395
dancers, 33, 131, 139, 147, 160, 166
Danforth, IL, 334
Daniel, Charlotte, 338–39, 342

Danish Gymnastic Team, 205, 299
Danvers, 189
Darby, Judy, 269, 293
Darr, Ken, 198
Davis, Lee, 348, 357, 374–75, 380
Davis, Lois, 107, 136, 139, 158
Davis, Richard, 342
Day, Esther, 180, 217, 219–20, 243
Dean, Harris, 72
Dearth, Jack, 310
DeBosker, Nancy, 357
Decker, Charles E., 124
Decker, Renate, 293, 308
Deer Creek, IL, 46–47
Deerfield, IL, 262, 270
Deetz, Ralph, 77–78, 84, 86–88, 99–104,
    113, 123
DeGraff, Melvin, 199, 204, 207–8
DeKalb, 21, 27, 116, 200, 221, 227, 229,
    346
departments, 10, 15, 25, 38, 52, 58, 80, 101,
    115, 123, 326–28, 332, 339, 359,
    378, 389–91
    Agricultural, 181
    Athletic, 15
    Biology, 358
    Commerce, 171
    Health and Physical Education, 187, 195,
        225, 241–44, 247, 251–52, 254–55,
        257, 262, 265–67, 272–73, 276, 299,
        303–4, 307, 318–21, 324, 345–47,
        372, 394
    Intramural, 156, 192–93
    Science, 183
DeRocker, Carol, 269, 276, 290, 299
DeRocker, DeVee, 292, 302, 312, 321
DeRocker, Nancy, 338, 342
Desch, Leo, 285, 293, 299–300, 307–8, 314
Dickey, Bob, 192
Dietz, Ralph, 88, 101
Dillon, Lawanda, 223
Doenitz, Mary, 311, 321
Doetch, Donna, 379, 394
Dohm, John, 95
Doman, Marjorie, 244
Dombrosky, Pauline, 278
Donar, Ramona, 253, 255
Donovan, Marie, 69
Doran, Ramona, 251
Dorrence Darling, 35
Doss, Bert, 309
Douglass, Tom, 26, 46, 208–10
Drake, Edgar A., 180
Drew, Janet, 363

Dreyer, Cheryl, 348, 356
Drum, Gerald, 26
DuBois, Margaret, 239
Dueringer, Bill, 392
Dueringer, Carol, 318, 321
Dueringer, Sharon, 334, 338, 342
Dunbar, Carl, 332
Dunham, Sandy, 355
Duvick, Caroline, 239
Dwyer, Carolyn, 363
Dziadula, Dorothy, 275

E
East Bay Camp, 145, 149, 170, 327
Easterbrook, Roger, 115, 125, 150–51, 161
Eastern Illinois University, 377
East Peoria High School, 336
Eckstein, Roger, 293
Edgerton, Carmelita, 363
Edwards, Richard, 6
Edwards Hall, 260
Eggenberger, Margaret, 205
Eickmeyer, Elaine, 232
Eisenhower, Mona, 179
Elliot, Lois, 79, 100
Elliott, Edward, 243
England, Lois, 208
Enos, Gene, 208–10
Evans, Orville, 108
Ewing, Arthur, 200
exhibitions, 1, 20, 27, 30, 32–33, 39, 54, 58,
    62, 64, 66–67, 70–72, 77–78, 81–82,
    89, 94, 115–17, 125, 130, 160, 181,
    195, 267, 292–93, 299, 304, 321
Eyer, Lois, 160, 169–71

F
Fager, Ginger, 215, 217, 219
Fager, Jan, 204, 207–8, 214–15, 217–18
Fassbender, Kathy, 374, 380, 392
Fassbender, Tod, 374, 379, 392
Faulkner, Sue, 250, 254–55, 257
Fedanzo, Tony, 169–70, 173, 178
Feirn, Janet, 284
Felmley, 12–14, 18, 20–22, 28–29
Fender, John, 247, 255, 257, 270
Ferguson, Don, 199
Findley, Barbara, 199
Finfrock, Dale, 356, 393
Finland, 361
Fissell, Fred, 49
Fitzgerald, Edward, 56–57
Fitzgerald, Russell, 254, 257, 259, 269, 288,
    290, 293, 301, 305, 339, 358, 362

Fitzgerald, Shirley, 339, 358
Fitzpatrick, Bonita, 232, 234–35
Fitzsimmons, Don, 141, 143, 150–52, 158,
    161, 173
Flaminio, Emma, 232–33, 239, 241, 244
Flatt, Terry, 289, 293
Florent, Pat, 275, 305
Flying High Circus, 98
Flying Lamars, 175
Flying Wards, 7, 309
Foeller, George, 320, 338, 341, 345, 359,
    374, 379
Fogler, Ralph W., 124, 136
football, 12, 15, 17, 24, 31, 46, 109, 238,
    327
Forneris, Jim, 290
Fortna, Linda, 340–41, 343
Fortney, Carol, 374, 380
Fosdick, Cecil, 35, 51
Foster, Chuck, 174
Foy, John, 160
Fraley, John F., 35
Frances, Anna, 94
FranCoeur, Bill, 310
free exercise, 292, 335–36, 349, 368, 374,
    377–78, 380, 385–86
Freesmeyer, Dean, 243
Frey, Harold E., 188
Fricke, Lloyd, 35
Friedrich, Patricia, 257
Frink, Warren, 161, 163, 169, 172
Frink, Willis, 219
Frye, Dave, 312
Frye, Harold, 53, 76, 85–86, 128, 189
Furrow, Jim, 334, 339, 342, 353, 357, 374,
    377, 380
Fussner, John, 334, 339, 356–57, 375, 377–
    78, 380

G
Gaffney, Virgil, 188–89
Gallagher, Kathy, 257
Gallion, Gene, 276
games, 22, 26–27, 34, 38–39, 46, 63–64,
    76–77, 83, 96, 115–16, 230, 274,
    285–86, 347
Gamma Phi, 1–4, 6, 11, 17, 20, 23, 25–29,
    31–36, 38–39, 41, 43–52, 54–69, 71–
    91, 94–119, 121–25, 127–32, 134–
    46, 149–50, 152–54, 156–75, 178–
    80, 184, 186–88, 191–92, 194–99,
    201–9, 211–14, 216, 219–27, 229–
    33, 235–36, 238–47, 249–50, 252–
    56, 258–68, 270–76, 280–81, 283–

92, 296–300, 306–11, 313–14, 316–
21, 323–24, 327–28, 330, 333–34,
338–41, 343, 345–48, 350–54, 356–
61, 365, 368–70, 372, 376–79, 385–
86, 388–95, 399
activities, 75, 85–86, 184, 324
exhibitions, 58, 118
meetings, 56, 128, 249, 308
organization, 17, 76, 100, 248, 298, 371
Charter Member, 134, 186
Group Pictures, 204, 213, 220, 229, 240,
272, 330
Membership, 153–54, 162
Pledges, 24–26, 28, 44–46, 55–57, 75, 77,
82, 128–29, 152, 194, 219, 230, 260,
263–64, 272, 280, 284–86, 307, 310,
318, 334, 340, 348
Queen, 48, 51, 94, 98, 152, 165, 206, 265,
304, 315, 319, 333, 354, 363, 371,
395
See also circus queen
Sponsors, 58, 86, 109, 123, 160, 214, 242,
244–45, 252, 265, 285, 288, 316, 333
Gamma Phi Circus, 6, 8, 20, 51, 78, 80, 86,
92–93, 99, 101–2, 104, 108, 110,
121–22, 130, 140, 142, 150, 159,
170, 188, 208, 211, 213, 217, 222,
227, 234, 274–75, 278, 280, 301–3,
314, 322, 325, 333–34, 340, 343,
346, 351, 353, 357, 360–63, 375,
379, 391–92, 394, 398–99
first, 4, 8, 37, 188–89
Gantz, Genevieve, 165
Gasper, Diane, 338–39, 342, 345, 353–54
Gecan, Kay, 254–55
George, Dick, 339, 342
Gerard, Linda, 342
Gerold, Nancy, 254
Gibson, Audrey, 254, 269–70, 273
Gibson, Harold, 248
Gifford, Dick, 220, 243
Gillett, Arlene, 217, 220, 242, 259, 281
Gillett, Arley, 75, 77, 91, 94, 97, 99, 101–2,
109, 118, 135, 144, 174, 191–92,
194, 196, 198–99, 203–4, 213–14,
216–17, 220–22, 224–27, 229–30,
232, 239, 242, 244–45, 250, 252–54,
259, 262–65, 267, 271–72, 274, 281,
284, 287–88, 290–91, 296, 298, 307,
311, 319–22, 324, 331, 333–34, 339,
345–48, 357, 359, 372, 378–79, 389–
91, 393, 399
Gillett, Bari, 334, 338–39, 342, 353, 356
Gillett, Jay, 217, 220, 242, 287

The Gilletts, 254
Girard, Linda, 339–40
Giugler, Janet, 392–93, 398
Glasgow, Arthur, 22
Glass, Louise, 310, 338, 342
Glassman, Becky, 244
Glover, Nancy, 334, 342, 353
Gobush, Joyce, 254
Good, Elaine, 92, 94
Goodhart, Gladys, 284, 286, 288, 292–93,
313
Gooding, Ralph, 136, 181, 184
Gorens, Deacon, 76
Gould, Patricia, 165
Goulet, Bobbi, 348, 353, 392–93, 395
Gove, Nancy, 266
Graack, George, 26
Grebner, Florence, 254, 269
Green, Jane, 275
Greenwald, Jan, 290, 292
Greenwood, Charles, 161, 174, 186–90
Gridley, IL, 114, 222, 235
Griffith, Francis, 128–29
Grimes, Burleigh, 83–84
Gronemeier, Martha, 266
Gruever, Roylene, 290, 292
Guigler, Janet, 395
Guthrie, John, 50, 56–57
Guttstein, Fred, 109
Gwaltney, Louise, 251, 253, 255, 273
gym circus, 72, 99, 116–18, 124–25, 127,
144, 188, 192–93, 195, 225, 249,
252, 267, 285, 288, 292, 311
gymnastic fraternity, 34–35, 41, 52, 64, 71,
73, 88–89, 99, 204, 213–14, 216,
232, 264, 272–73, 348, 391
gymnastics, 2, 6, 14–15, 20, 24, 33, 38, 53,
75, 78, 118, 140, 145, 154, 187, 190,
195–96, 205, 221, 245, 281, 291,
297, 335–37, 347, 350, 353, 385–86
gymnastic team, 1–2, 14, 143, 326, 331, 335
gymnasts, 2, 13–14, 20, 118–19, 121, 125,
132, 143, 155, 213, 231, 241, 287–
88, 292, 299, 304, 335, 338, 341,
349, 352, 369, 377, 384, 390

H
Haas, Gert, 292
Haemeker, Joyce, 255
Hafner, Jim, 274
Hahn, Pam, 374, 380
Halane, Elizabeth, 166
Hall, Barton, 306, 309
Hall, Charles, 146

Hall, Harold, 77, 86
halves, 17, 21–22, 25, 27, 32, 35, 64, 66–67, 77–78, 115, 130
Hamilton, Don, 269
Hamilton, Marvin, 128
Hammond, Robert, 249
Hancock, Howard, 46, 49, 86, 110, 332
Hancock, Nancy, 254, 269–70
Handy, Barbara, 217
Hannah, Wade, 178
Hanson, Carolyn, 293, 308
Hanson, Milford, 58
Hanus, Dick, 347
Hany, Darwin, 217–18, 220–22, 229, 232–35
Hargis, Virgil, 161
Harmer, Dianne, 374, 380, 392–93
Harmon, Dorothy, 51
Harms, Phil, 374, 380
Harraden, Charles, 209, 215–16, 218
Harris, Allan, 342
Harris, Cynthia, 239, 241–43, 247, 250, 255, 262, 267, 270
Hart, Betty, 89
Hartshorn, Irene, 208–9
Hartung, Jan, 365
Harvey, Darrell, 310, 314
Hase, Paulette, 292
Haskins, Jack, 98, 141
Hasler, Elsie, 269
Haughey, Max, 152, 161
Haynie, Cindy, 392–93, 395, 398
Headley, Charles, 219
Heaton, Lucille, 160
Heckel, Ray, 143
Heien, Karl, 374–75, 380, 392–93
Hendron, Bob, 392–93, 398
Herman, Carol, 348, 353, 356, 374, 379, 392–93
Herman, Margie, 379
Hermer, Diane, 374, 380
Herndon, Bob, 374, 379–80
Herndon, Carol, 348, 353, 374, 379
Herrick, Buell, 141, 150–51, 161
Hickman, Gloria, 220, 244
Higginbothan, Glen, 58
Hileman, Esther, 179
Hileman, Jane, 180
Hileman Sisters, 183–84
Hill, Arthur, 28
Hill, Gene, 26, 31, 43, 96, 124, 128, 134–35, 176, 186, 188, 194
Hinds, John, 270, 284–86, 291, 293, 296, 299, 301, 304, 307–8

Hinman, Kathryn, 158–59, 162, 165
Hinshaw, Jane, 217
Hoblit, Helen, 342
Hodel, Joan, 208–9
Hodgson, Donna, 257, 259
Hoff, Bob, 220
Hoffa, Carol, 255
Hoffman, Gene, 246
Hoffman, Jan, 215, 219
Holloway, Charles, 53
Holmes, Hal, 350
Holmes Paul, 350
Holt, Camilla, 244–45
Holt, Marion, 107
Homecoming, 50–51, 186, 191, 195, 211, 214, 221, 240, 249, 284–85, 361
Honn, Tom, 392, 395
honorary gymnastic fraternity, 50, 73, 77, 85, 145, 191–92, 201, 219–21, 249, 252, 262, 264, 276, 284–85, 298–300, 321, 372, 379
honorary member of Gamma Phi, 132, 137, 158–59, 165
Hopp, Jim, 305, 308
Horn, Fred, 335
Horton, Clifford E., 3–4, 8, 12–18, 20–26, 31, 33, 36, 38–39, 41, 46, 49, 53–54, 56–58, 61, 63, 65, 71–73, 76–77, 81–82, 84–87, 89, 91, 101, 109–10, 114–17, 123–25, 127–30, 135, 140, 143–45, 149, 153–54, 160, 162, 166, 172, 176, 178, 180–81, 183, 185–88, 192, 194, 204, 207, 222, 225, 253, 267, 280, 321, 326–29, 331–33, 362, 365, 380, 388, 393, 399
Horton Fieldhouse, 18, 21, 362–63, 365, 368, 372, 376, 378–79, 388, 391, 394
Houser, Lou, 29–30
Houston, Victor, 109
Howard, Arthur, 239
Howard, Bettye, 275
Howard, Judy, 275
Howarter, Janice, 304, 311
Hoyl, 150
Hrebik, Bill, 209, 218
Hrebik, Louise, 218–19
Hrvatin, Joanne, 348
Hubbard, Nate, 334, 353, 357
Huber, John, 342
Huggins, Clarabelle, 136, 139, 158
Hughes, Sonny, 290, 293, 305, 325, 339, 358
Hunsinger, Carol, 223, 225, 232, 234–35
Hunt, Bill, 310, 312, 334, 338–39, 341–43, 345, 348, 352, 356–58

Hunt, Phyllis, 310, 312, 342, 358
Hunt, Starkey, 100
Hunter, Valerie, 199, 209, 215, 217–18, 346
Hutmacher, Paul, 43
Huxtable, Mary, 100

I

Illinois State, 335, 337, 339, 341, 346, 351–52, 362, 377, 379, 385–86
Illinois State Normal University. *See* ISNU
Industrial Arts Club, 232, 234, 244, 248–49, 314–17, 341, 343, 354, 363, 371, 379, 395
Irwin, Bette Jane, 342
ISNU (Illinois State Normal University), 6, 12, 17, 23, 31, 44, 62, 81, 106, 166, 171–72, 176–77, 181–82, 186–88, 192, 197–98, 205, 211–12, 225, 237–38, 245–46, 248, 252–53, 267, 281, 284, 292, 308–9, 319–20, 323, 326–28, 332–34, 357
ISNU Circus band, 208, 235, 253, 269
ISNU President, 6, 332
ISU president, 6, 18, 183, 240, 260, 270, 301, 303

J

Jablonovich, Milan, 217, 219–20, 222
Jablonski, Christine, 208
Jackson, Charlotte, 51, 69
Jackson, Judy, 303
Jacobs, Joyce, 165
Jacobs, Lanida, 290, 293, 308
Jacobs, Shirley, 275, 278
Jacquath, Virginia, 89
Janecke, Judy, 389
Jarke, Ernest, 160, 174
Jessman, Sally, 339, 342, 353, 356
Johnson, Donna, 340
Johnson, Kaye, 363
Johnson, Lou, 192, 198–99, 205, 208
Johnson, Lowell, 122–23, 128–29
Johnson, Mary, 340
Jones, Jerry, 392
Jones, Norma, 293
Jones, Ruth, 348
Jordan, Preston, 335
Jordon, Charles, 50
jugglers, 103, 105, 269, 348, 357
juggling duet, 254, 259
juggling quartet, 242

K

Kafer, Lois, 215, 223, 225

Kaiser, Bruce T., 360
Kallenbach, Merrill, 220, 232–33, 239, 267, 269
Kamp, Andy, 168
Kamp, Carole, 269
Kaszynski, Gloria, 270, 293
Kearney, Fred, 84, 86
Keipper, Eric, 392
Kelly, Emmett, 263
Keltner, Gene, 174
Kennedy, Ann, 215, 217, 219
Kennedy, Judy, 340
Kenyon, Edith, 396
Kerns, Dave, 392
Kerrick, Tom, 56–58, 63
Kerrihard, Tom, 220
Kerwood, Lewis, 123
Ketchmark, Gloria, 244
Kewanee, IL, 307, 318–19, 321, 341
Kidder, Glenn, 94, 108, 118, 121
Kilburn, Shirley, 251, 253, 255
Killian, Pat, 208–9
Kimmel, Joy, 275, 278
King, Harland, 77, 81, 91
King, Lyle, 175
King, Roger, 239, 243, 255
Kinkelman, Gordon, 392
Kinneman, John A., 45
Kirkpatrick, Dave, 220
Kirkton, Roger, 220
Kistner, Kenneth, 342
Klinefelter, Martha, 310
Kmetz, Michael, 200
Knepp, Margo, 348
Knouse, Mary, 392–93
Komlanc, Betty, 392
Kordewick, Tom, 334, 338–39, 342, 353, 356–57, 374, 377
Kracmer, Lorraine, 363
Krase, Dick, 348, 357, 374, 380
Kunkel, Doris, 94
Kuntz, Lowell, 199, 201, 208
Kuosmanen, Paavo, 361
Kuybida, Pat, 363

L

LaBedz, Barbara, 340
LaBounty, Ike, 175, 186, 188
LaBounty, Jack, 118–19, 141, 143, 147, 150, 152, 159, 161, 189
Lafferty, John, 46, 172
Laird, Martha, 323
Lake Bloomington, IL, 46, 60–61, 123, 127, 247, 327

Lake Forest, 303
Lake of the Woods, 318
Lake Zurich, IL, 250, 252
LaMance, William, 25
LaMasters, Doris, 67–68, 79–80, 99
Lambdin, Barbara, 243–44
Landgraf, Sue, 354
Lanham, Lucy, 198–99, 207–9
Larsen, Al, 332
Larsen, Arthur H., 332
Larson, Carl, 310, 314
LaSalle-Peru, IL, 144, 217, 375, 380
Lauderback, Martin, 43
Lauf, Delores, 232, 234–36
Leasman, Rudolph, 38
Leemon, Jean, 266
Lehmann, Anne, 348, 353
Leigh, Barney, 138
Leismeister, Marilyn, 254, 257
Leiter, Arden, 395, 398
Lemanski, Adel, 266
Leonard, Carl, 29
LeRoy, IL, 31, 114, 127, 136, 139, 219
Lesmeister, Marilyn, 273
Lessen, Sheryl, 303
Lester, Howard, 128–29
Lewis, Barney, 56–57
Lewis, Wendel, 97, 101, 108–9, 112, 114–
    19, 121–25, 127, 145–47, 150–51
Lexington, IL, 50, 56, 72, 114, 143
Libby, Robert, 269
Liberti, Anne Marie, 365, 374, 380
Libertyville, IL, 284, 299
Lientz, Gene, 128
Lighted Indian Clubs, 69, 149
Lindberg, Imogene, 217, 220, 229, 231, 239
Linder, Rich, 348
Lindsey, Elmarie, 304
Little, Norma, 232
Litton, Jeanne, 314, 317
Litwiller, Arthur, 50–51, 58
Litwiller, Herbert, 56
Litwiller, Howard, 57, 63
Long, Joe, 374, 379, 392
Lovelock, Patti, 160
Loveridge, Robert, 254, 267, 270–71, 273
Lowey, John, 270, 276, 284, 286, 289, 293,
    305
Lutie's party house, 62, 71
Lyons, Kathleen, 232, 234–35

M
Macek, John, 217
Mackinaw, 114

Macomb, 33, 54, 64–67, 71
Maddrey, George, 201
Madigan, Paul, 46
Maile, Delores, 196
Malloy, 334, 339, 342, 374–75, 377–78, 380
Marecsak, Janis, 338, 342, 354
Marlin, Kenneth, 51
Marquardt, Carl, 56, 63
Marquardt, Neil, 69
Marquiss, Sandy, 363
Martin, Jack, 246, 252
Martin, Kendrick, 61–63, 72, 76
Martin, Kenneth, 50, 84
Martling, Allan, 310
Massachusetts, 14–16, 20, 326
Matthews, George, 128–29
McBain, Phil, 198, 202, 208–9
McCain, Gerry, 165
McCarthy, Marilyn, 196
McCormick Gymnasium, 33, 35, 39, 41, 44,
    51, 53, 57, 62–65, 68, 71, 76, 78–80,
    85, 87–88, 94, 106, 110, 112, 114–
    16, 118, 121, 125, 129–30, 134, 142,
    149, 156, 159, 164, 169, 186–89,
    191–92, 195, 197, 201, 206, 208–9,
    213–14, 217, 220–21, 225, 231–32,
    234, 249, 252, 256–57, 263, 266,
    268–69, 273, 275–76, 278, 284–85,
    288, 290–93, 296, 299–301, 303–4,
    306, 310–11, 313, 319–23, 330, 333–
    35, 338–39, 341, 343, 347, 351, 357,
    362
McDaniels, Clement, 77–78
McDermand, Charles, 270
McEhliney, Maurice, 22
McGrath, Alice, 398
McKay, Jacquelyn, 266
McKay, John, 270
McKinley, Malinda, 251, 254–55
McKinley, Robert, 220, 239, 241–42, 251,
    254–55
McQueen, Bill, 42
meetings, 28, 38–39, 44, 48, 50, 63–64, 71,
    75, 77, 85, 102, 109, 112, 114, 122,
    128–29, 153–54, 169, 177–78, 187,
    204, 213–14, 216, 230, 233, 238–40,
    263, 274, 285, 288, 298, 306, 315,
    347
Meidel, Jerry, 274
Melcher, Nancy, 254, 257
members, 3–4, 20, 22–25, 27–28, 31–35,
    37–38, 45–47, 52, 55–56, 58, 60–61,
    65–69, 72, 74, 77–79, 82, 84, 86, 91–
    92, 99–100, 103–4, 107–8, 112–15,

117, 119, 122–23, 129–30, 134, 137–39, 141, 143–44, 153–54, 178, 182, 195, 205, 213, 224–27, 229, 231–32, 239, 242–43, 245, 247, 251, 267, 274, 280, 286, 288, 291, 299–300, 307–11, 317, 320, 327, 331–32, 334–36, 339, 343, 345–46, 348, 360, 365, 377–78, 385–86, 389, 391–94
former, 13–14, 194–95, 328
new, 47, 55, 57, 76, 110, 112, 114, 247, 249, 263, 306, 365
membership, 24, 28, 44, 84, 101, 110, 129, 152, 162, 169, 195, 225, 253, 267, 280, 321, 386, 390
Mendota, IL, 67, 196, 205, 211, 227, 229, 231, 241, 245, 264, 270, 272, 280, 342, 352, 366
Menne, Margaret, 254, 257, 270, 273, 281
Merdian, Robert, 220
Messman, Barbara, 334, 339, 342, 352–53, 356
Metcalf, Thomas, 70, 142, 196, 198, 208, 217
Meyer, Clara, 117
Meyer, Pat, 205, 208, 217–18, 220, 222, 227
Meyer Sisters, 202, 209, 212, 218, 222, 224
Mickey, 69
Mien, Geneva, 89
Mikel, Grace, 89, 97, 99
Milford, 196
Miller, 150
Miller, Campbell, 52, 54, 56
Miller, Evelyn, 244–45
Miller, Janet, 301, 304, 321, 339, 342, 358
Miller, Jean, 354
Millikan-Macomb, James, 64
Milner Library, 308
Mindrup, Dorothy, 71
Miss Barto's Class, 69
Miss Bauman, 159
Miss Brenneman, 375
Miss Brown, 374, 380
Miss Burpee, 374–75, 380
Miss Chilton, 375
Miss Daggitt, 374–75
Miss Davis, 139
Mitchell, Carolyn, 314
Mitchell, Eleanor, 275
Moberg, Jan, 304
Mobus, Dinah, 365, 374, 379, 392–93
Mondrzyk, Ruth, 269
Monette, Art, 309
Montgomery, Dale, 270, 276, 284, 286–88, 291, 293, 296, 299, 304

Montross, Raymond, 200
Mooney, Jack, 26
Mooney, Joe, 38, 51, 54, 58
Moore, Carol, 303–4
Moore, Cheri, 392–93
Moore, Glenn, 22
Moore, Roy, 21–22, 25–26, 30, 35
Moore, William, 101
Morgan, Lucy R., 348
Morhun, Konstantin, 220, 223, 232, 241
Morris, Lindsey, 128–29, 132
Morris, Norma, 165
Morrissey, Bill, 132, 138, 140–41, 144–45, 149, 151–52
Morser, Jill, 334, 338–39, 342, 353, 358
Muhl, Bill, 25–26, 32–33, 35–36, 43, 51, 54, 58, 62–64, 69, 72, 81, 94, 125, 145, 149, 151
Muhl, Frank, 42, 47, 51, 54, 58, 61–64, 72
Mulkern, Mary, 212
Mulligan, Kathy, 392–93, 395, 398
Murdock, John, 56–57
Murphy, Dave, 293, 305, 308, 314
Murphy, Kay, 303
Murphy, Malinda, 243
Murray, Leslie, 64, 69, 76, 78–79, 81, 84, 89, 91, 94–95, 97, 108, 127, 132, 135, 220, 222
Myers, Clara, 106–7, 110

N
Naffziger, Margaret, 79–80, 99
Nafsiger, Tish, 84
Nally, Karen, 310
Nardin, Janet, 310–11, 321, 338–39, 342
Nardin, Sandra, 288, 290–91, 305, 308, 313
Neil Barton coaching Ginny Reiger, 352
Nelle, Dick, 51, 58
Nemitz, Darlene, 220
Nenne, Margaret, 274
Neponset, IL, 321
Neuman, Milt, 348, 358, 374
new acts, 131, 159, 204, 242, 253, 259, 270, 290–91, 302, 311, 338, 368
Newman, Milt, 352, 356
Newman Club, 232, 234, 257, 275, 314, 354, 363, 379
New York, 73, 328, 336
Nicewander, Mary, 201
Nickoley, Barbara, 284, 290, 299
Nobk, Clyde, 308
Noe, Rachel, 51
Nordberg, Judy, 314
Norden, Barbara, 257

Novak, Frances, 275, 278
Novak, Toni, 257, 259
Nowers, Henry, 284, 288, 293

O

O'Brien, Sandy, 303
O'Byrne, Arthur, 175
O'Dell, Bob, 292, 299
Odell, Charles, 254, 265, 269, 274, 284,
    286, 290, 292
Ohio Wesleyan University (OWU), 3, 12–
    14, 16, 20, 25, 194
Olson, Beverly, 201
O'Mohundro, Carol Ann, 354
Opperman, Nancy, 339, 342
organization, 2, 4, 17, 20, 27, 31, 33, 35, 38–
    39, 44–46, 48, 55, 57–59, 71–72, 77–
    78, 84, 86, 88, 100, 109–10, 112–13,
    115–17, 122–23, 127–28, 130, 152–
    53, 156, 162–63, 169, 177–78, 186–
    88, 194–96, 198, 204, 207, 214, 216,
    219–21, 225–27, 230, 233–34, 239,
    241, 246–48, 250, 260, 262–68, 284,
    301, 312, 319–21, 327, 333–34, 339,
    345, 352, 354, 359–60, 365, 385,
    391, 393–94, 399
Orr, Marie, 86
Ortgiesen, Julie, 254, 257
Ortman, Rosemary, 192, 201, 207, 209–10
Otto, Bruce, 342

P

Packard, Russell, 28
Pagel, Irene, 284, 293
Pager, Jan, 208
Palmer, Sharon, 309
Park, Karen, 339, 354, 357
Park Forest, IL, 334
Parkinson, Ruth, 121, 136, 139, 145, 147,
    149–50, 152–53, 155, 160–61, 163,
    166
Parsons, Gilford, 109, 123–24
Parsons, Jesse, 109, 115–19, 121, 132, 138,
    140, 142, 144–46, 149–51, 153, 159–
    61, 163–64, 166, 170, 175
Parsons, Robert, 173
Patterson, Cartherine, 188–89
Patterson, Charlaine, 215–19
Patterson, Clarence, 255
Patterson, Don, 225
Patterson, Pat, 262, 266–68, 270, 273, 275,
    281
Patton, Margaret, 244–45
Patton, Phyllis, 340

Pedigo, Lynn, 363
Pennie, Larry, 356, 358, 374, 380, 392–93,
    395
Peoria, IL, 43, 72, 88, 124, 318, 321, 331,
    342, 345, 362
Peoria YMCA, 32, 336
perch pole, 3, 104, 140, 154–55, 161, 175,
    198–99, 203, 208, 267
performances, off-campus, 321, 341, 366,
    394
Perhach, Andy, 203
Perrill, Irwin, 30
Peru, IL, 270, 391
Peter, Joyce, 301
Peter, Nancy, 293, 299–300, 304
Peters, Sharon, 310, 338, 340, 342, 357
petitions, 52, 54, 66–67, 70, 78, 88, 100,
    131, 157–58, 164–65, 206, 216, 222,
    250, 265, 288, 320, 333
Petitions for queen candidates, 158, 320
Petrie, Herbert, 146
Pfeiffer, Jackie, 354
Phillips, Gene, 215, 218–19
physical education, 15–16, 22–23, 26, 29,
    31, 33–34, 53, 69–71, 73, 77, 91,
    101–2, 108–10, 112, 117, 122–23,
    128, 145–46, 149, 162, 178, 187,
    195–96, 207, 223, 225, 227, 241–44,
    247, 251–55, 257, 262, 265–67, 272–
    74, 276, 289, 299–300, 303–4, 307,
    318–21, 323–24, 326–27, 330–31,
    341, 345–47, 352, 361, 372, 390,
    393–94
physical education club, 130, 205, 211, 244,
    274, 310
physical education department, 4, 23, 34, 43,
    63, 73, 76, 106, 108–9, 114–15, 117,
    124, 128, 130, 143–44, 167, 178,
    183, 188, 192, 222, 225, 297, 321,
    331–32, 365, 393
physical education fraternity, 27, 33, 45, 57,
    62–64, 68, 72–73, 77, 81, 86–88, 97,
    102, 108, 110, 112–17, 122–23, 127,
    129, 144, 152, 157, 162, 164, 171
physical education majors, 39, 52, 100, 128–
    29, 160, 192, 195, 220, 274, 328
Pilarski, Marian, 340–41, 343
Ping, James, 254, 257, 270–71
Pinney, Karen, 374, 380, 392–93
Pitchford, Sheila, 284–86, 288
Pittman, Riley, 251
Pitts, Hank, 30
Pittsburg, 168, 385
pledges, 24–26, 28, 44–46, 55–57, 75, 77,

82, 128–29, 152, 194, 219, 230, 260,
   263–64, 272, 280, 284–86, 307, 310,
   318, 334, 340, 348
Ploss, Doug, 251, 253, 255, 270
Pluxtable, Mary, 79
Poechla, Paula, 392
Pohle, Ernest, 116
Poklaske, Lee, 94
Polechia, Paula, 372, 392–93
Polivka, Rosemary, 340
Pontiac, 78, 101, 103, 114, 140–41, 219,
   271, 273, 281, 286, 341, 343
Pontiac circus, 103, 141, 143
Popejoy, Bert, 335
Porter, Kathryn, 107
Powell, Porter, 115, 118, 124–25, 127, 150–
   51
Preno, Judy, 348, 353, 374, 379
Preno, Patricia, 348, 353
president, 7, 12, 17, 33, 35–36, 38, 46, 49,
   57, 84, 101, 112, 117–18, 123, 127,
   143–44, 153, 174–75, 187, 206–7,
   212, 220–21, 229, 234–35, 247, 262,
   267–68, 273–74, 281, 296, 307, 318,
   327, 334, 350, 393
President Bone, 332, 389
President Lewis, 112
president of Gamma Phi, 86, 115, 119, 121,
   124–25, 128, 164, 205, 214, 270,
   275, 334, 352, 386, 395
Pritchett, Ruth, 71, 79–80, 99
Probasco, Lewis, 140
Proehl, Kathy, 355
Ptasnik, Janet, 340–41, 343
Purnell, Paul, 290, 292
Putnam, Jean, 207–8, 215–17

Q
queen, 48, 52–54, 60, 67–71, 78–80, 88, 92,
   94, 97–101, 103–5, 110, 117, 131–
   33, 135–37, 143, 157–59, 161, 164–
   65, 186, 194–96, 198–99, 207–8,
   215–17, 223–24, 231–35, 241, 244,
   252–53, 257, 265–68, 275, 278, 288,
   292, 301, 303, 313–14, 320–21, 333–
   34, 338–41, 343, 354, 359, 368, 379,
   393–94, 398
   candidates for, 131, 138, 157, 206, 222,
     250
Queen, Gamma Phi, 48, 52–54, 60, 66–71,
   78–80, 88, 92, 94, 97–101, 103–5,
   110, 117, 131–33, 135–37, 143, 157–
   59, 161, 164–65, 186, 194–96, 198–
   99, 207–8, 215–17, 223–24, 231–35,

241, 244, 252–53, 257, 265–68, 275–
   76, 278, 288, 292, 301, 303, 313–14,
   320–21, 333–34, 338–41, 343, 354,
   359, 363, 368, 379, 393–94, 398
queen, *See also* Gamma Phi Queen
queen candidates, 158, 165–66, 222, 241,
   251–52, 257, 266, 288, 317, 320
queen committee, 243, 250, 255, 265, 276,
   301, 303, 315, 333, 375
queen contest, 164, 301, 340, 342
queen election, 251–52, 257, 316
queen's court, 164, 209, 234, 238, 316, 343,
   395
Quigley, Maryann, 244
Quimby, Nancy, 214, 216–18, 220, 230,
   232–33

R
Radmacher, Dorothea, 107
Rae Ann Austin, 251, 254–55, 265, 269–70
Ragans, Marie, 340
Rake, Ron, 310
Rakers, Rita, 354
Ramage, Harold, 308
Ramano, Shirley, 243
Rapp, Sharon, 340–41
Rapps, Sandra, 310
Raymond, Glen, 35
Read, John, 334, 339, 342, 357
Reed, Marilyn, 208
Reedy, Sharon, 314
Reeser, Norma, 196
refreshments, 33–34, 39, 102, 112–14, 129,
   205, 213–14, 230, 239, 262, 264,
   274, 391
Rehn, Ann, 291, 305, 308, 313
Reid, Dempsey, 86
Reid, Forrest, 128
Reinhart, Beverly, 251, 253, 255
Renfro, Judy, 254, 257
Renner, Lenore, 275
requirements, 6, 23–24, 34, 55, 195, 263,
   266, 272, 284, 391
Reynolds, Dick, 57
Reynolds, Robert, 56–57
Rice, Kenneth Homer, 56–57
Rich Schuler, 372, 374, 380
Richter, Don, 348, 357
Richter, Doris, 239
Ridenour, Arthur, 72
Ridgley, Douglas C., 13–14
Ridings, Bill, 335
Rieger, Ginny, 334, 353, 358
Riegger, Arnold, 308

Riek, Ron, 274
Rine, Neil, 290, 299
Rinkenburger, Lyle, 149, 151–52
Rivers, Linda, 363
Rivord, Merle, 115
Roan, Carol Ann, 270
Roberts, Glenn, 56–58
Robinson, Sheldon, 128
Roby, Sally, 303
Rockford, 251, 284, 299, 301, 318, 334
Roderick, Byron, 339
Rogers Hotel, 26
Romano, Shirley, 239, 241, 247, 250, 254–
    55, 257, 265, 267, 269
Romary, Judy, 292
rope, 24, 39, 119, 161–62, 201, 352–53,
    358–59, 368
Ropp, Clarence, 332
Rose, Shirley, 275
Ross, John, 102, 104, 107
Rothenberg, Diane, 308
Rounds, Dick, 334, 339, 342
routines, 10, 92, 115–17, 191, 293, 323, 349,
    368, 377–78, 395, 398
Rowe, Bob, 26
Rowe, Susan, 334, 339, 342, 353, 356–57
Royce, Helen, 51
Roznowski, Hillard, 239
Ruebush, Walton, 47
Russell, Dick, 335
Rydeen, Dave, 138

S
Sabador, Arlene, 311
Salima, Marilyn, 243, 251, 253, 255
Salzman, Roy, 200
Sand, Joyce, 275, 278, 293, 296, 299, 301,
    304
Sandee Chilton, 374, 380
Sanders, Dean, 321
Sanders, Herbert, 245
Sanders, Joe, 149
Sandi Kinney, 310, 334, 339, 342, 358
Sarff, Clarabel, 269, 293
Satterfield, Verna, 71
Sawyer, Sally, 363
Scents, Bonnie, 363
Scharlau, Sue, 354
Scherer, Max, 18
Schermerhorn, Nancy, 374, 380, 392–93,
    395, 398
Schillinger, Sharon, 312, 334, 339–40, 342,
    345
Schmitgall, Mike, 357

Schmitt, Patricia, 232, 234–35
Schovin, Pam, 348
Schram, Edward, 175
Schroederus, Connie, 339, 342
Schuermann, Glenn, 234
Schuler, Dick, 392
Schuller, Kathy, 348, 354, 374, 380
Schulte, Joyce, 269, 276
Schumaker, Eileen, 229, 235
Schwenn, Floyd, 124
Scott, Clifford, 50, 56
Scott, John, 132
Scott, Wayne, 35
Seeley, Norman, 274
Seitz, Kenneth, 57
Selberg, Walt, 141, 143, 150–51
Sellers, Beverly, 160
Sellers, Jane, 374, 380
service awards, 48, 82, 123, 345, 359–60
Severns, Janice, 310
Seville, Frank, 255, 270
Shaner, Sandy, 363
Shawn, Ted, 106
Sheahan, Jim, 270
Shearer, James, 128
Sheets, Lesley, 374–76, 380, 392–93, 398
Shelton, Art, 29–30
Sherer, Gail, 365
Sherrard, Don, 200
Sherrard, Wayne, 179–80, 182, 184, 188,
    217, 232, 242
Shields, Robert, 122–23
Shields, Rocky, 128
Shillinger, Sharon, 338
Shiner, John, 25–27, 36, 38, 47
Shippey, Helen, 136, 139, 158
Short, Kay, 243
Shorthair, Sally, 315–17
Shryock, John, 202, 204, 208–9, 217
Shumacker, Bernie, 307
Shumaker, Eileen, 209, 215–18, 220, 222,
    233
Shyrock, John, 215
Sicks, Vangine, 88
Sidell High School, 296
Sieh, Adrian, 160–61, 175
Sigler, Dave, 305, 314
Silvers, Dawn, 254, 269
Simmons, Edmund, 270
Simpson, Judy, 355
Sitwiller, Arthur, 35
Slack, Ron, 274
Sleeter, Eldred, 59
Sloan, Marsha, 363

Slusser, Gerald, 56–57, 61, 64, 66–67, 72, 74
Smith, Betty Ann, 158–59, 162, 165
Smith, Beulah, 223, 225, 239, 241, 243, 247, 254
Smith, Bob, 130, 134, 140
Smith, Curtis, 101
Smith, Debbie, 392, 398
Smith, Don, 160
Smith, Doug, 214, 218–20
Smith, Herbert, 115, 124, 147, 149
Smith, Nelson, 245, 315–18
Smith, Ryan, 338, 342, 353
Smith, Sheila, 355
Smith-Hughes work, 114
Smith-Parkinson team, 150
Smolak, Louis, 43
Snodgrass, Carol, 365
Snodgrass, Harland, 342
Snook, Herb, 219
Solberg, Evelyn, 310
Soldewedel, Bette, 197
Solomon, George, 310
Somers, Phil, 220
Specht, Roscoe, 289, 293
Spellerbreg, Sue, 205, 207–9
Sperry, Warren, 144
Spitery, Sharon, 340
Spokane, WA, 14–15, 326
Springfield, 12–15, 141, 232, 274, 323, 340, 342, 345–46, 390
Springfield College, 13, 15, 191
Springfield YMCA, 326
Staab, Martha, 312, 318, 338–39, 345
Stables, James, 26
Stag Party, 38, 49, 127
Stambach, Ace, 104, 124, 379
Stark, Bill, 392
Starr, Clark, 28, 35, 43, 47
Stearns, Peggy, 365, 374
Steele, Russell, 227, 245
Steelsmith, Forrest, 26, 33, 36
Stephenson, Fred, 109
Stephey, Dick, 220
Stephey, Warren, 220
Sterling, Jo, 196, 199, 303
Sternberg, Louise, 178
Stevens, Gary, 374, 380
Stewart, Kay, 270
Stine, Clair, 128–29, 137, 143
Stine, Marcy, 363
Stock, Susan, 323
Stombaugh, Ray, 249
Stone, Becky, 393

Stoneburner, Kathy, 354
Stoner, Bob, 304, 308, 339
Story, Melvin, 24, 26, 33, 42–43, 47, 58, 62
Strange, Jean, 158–59, 162
Striegal, Louis, 26, 29, 47
student body, 10, 33–34, 44, 50–53, 70, 79, 88, 137, 146, 157, 162, 187, 225, 231–32, 325, 354, 359, 391
stunts, 5, 11, 23, 27, 33, 54, 58–59, 81, 92, 94, 108, 116–17, 149–51, 162, 189, 211, 243–44, 259, 261, 271, 306, 352, 354
Stunt Show, 11, 39, 59–60, 238
Sumner, Bonnie Lee, 340
Sutter, Dale, 269
Swartzbaugh, Harold, 56–57
Sweet, Charles, 35, 43, 54, 57, 64, 69, 76
Swenson, Clara, 266
Swichtenberg, Glenn, 239, 243, 247, 250, 253–55, 262, 267, 269
Switzer, Bob, 118
Switzer, Walter, 108, 123, 146, 150–51, 157, 160–61, 163, 175
Sykes, Kenneth, 57
Symons, Jerry, 255

T
Tatman, James, 35
Taylor, Diana, 340–41, 343
Taylor, Russ, 207–9, 212–14, 217–18, 222
Teofan, Zorine, 314
Terry, James, 332
Thieme, Joanne, 254
Thomas, Charles, 152, 160–61
Thomas, Dave, 241
Thomas, Gloria, 379, 394
Thompson, Barney M., 182
Thompson, Lynn, 257, 259, 266
Thompson, Ron, 334, 339, 342, 357
Thorson, James, 108–9, 114–15, 118–19, 123, 125, 132, 138, 140, 142, 144–46, 149–51, 153, 157, 176
tickets, 54, 80, 103–4, 106, 110, 113, 122–23, 161, 192, 207, 215–16, 231, 233–34, 241, 244–45, 261, 267, 269, 275–76, 278, 288, 299–301, 305, 311, 313, 321–22, 338, 343, 357–59, 369, 375, 378, 382, 395
Tinsley, Ron, 250, 254–55, 270–71, 273, 276, 281, 283–87, 290, 292–93, 297
Tipler, William, 199
Tobias, Betty, 165
Tooke, Florence, 254, 257, 265
Topliff, Jim, 305, 308, 314

Towanda, IL, 137–38, 143, 334
Truex, Wayne, 281, 283, 285–88, 290–91, 296–97, 307, 311, 321, 324, 331, 335–37, 339, 345–49, 359, 369, 372, 377, 379
Truitt, Shirley, 247, 251, 255
tumblers, 68, 70–72, 79, 89–91, 94, 96, 115, 137–38, 143, 153, 223, 252, 264, 290, 350
Turley, Jan, 208–9
Turnbull, Mary, 158–59, 162
Turner, Phyllis, 217, 219
Tursan, Chuck, 124

U

Underwood, Lucy, 304, 307–8, 312
Union, 303, 360, 363, 395
Universities of Wisconsin (UW), 2
University High School, 82, 159, 319
Unsicker, Carl, 25–26, 35–36, 38, 43, 46–47, 51, 58, 63, 339
Urquiza, Bea, 318, 339
US Navy, 173–75

V

V-12 Unit, 176, 182, 327
Van Brannan, Leroy, 57–58
Vance, Arden, 250, 253, 256, 267, 269, 276, 304, 311
Van Gundy, Harry, 56
Van Huss, Wayne, 118–19
Varsity Club, 38, 42, 49, 58–59
Verhunce, Judy, 334, 338–39, 342
Veselack, Richard, 200
Vidette, 8–10, 28, 93, 95, 104, 118, 127–29, 133, 146–49, 155, 167, 172, 190, 200–202, 206–7, 210, 215, 223, 226, 235–36, 252, 256, 258, 260, 268, 271, 277–78, 282, 302, 306, 312–14, 316–18, 322, 324–26, 331, 337, 344, 349–50, 354–55, 364
Vidette Circus, 8–11
Vignocchi, Kathy, 365, 374
Voigts, Herbert, 205, 207
Volk, Margaret, 334, 338, 342
Von Allman, Betty, 160–61
Vrba, Willy, 374, 380, 392–93

W

Wakefield, Janet, 243–44, 251, 254–55
Walker, Dick, 285–88, 293
Walters, Nancy, 354
Walthouse, Tom, 293, 304
Ward, Jake, 42, 52

Ward Barn, 308
Wardell, Donald, 35, 42–43, 47, 51–52, 54, 56, 58
Warren, Jessie Mae, 251, 254–55, 269
Waters, Howard, 176
Watseka, IL, 168, 250, 252, 323
Watson, Margaret, 71
Waukegan, IL, 273, 281, 284, 305
Waynesville, IL, 58, 362
WBBM-TV studios, 362
WBLN, 245
Weast, Sue, 392–93
Webb, Charlie, 30
Weber, Phil, 198–99, 201, 204–9
Weith, Alan, 342, 353, 356, 393
Weith, Marilyn, 291, 301, 305, 307–8
Welch, Lorraine, 165
Weller, Donna, 293
Welsh, Jan, 290
Wendell, Henry, 192
Wendland, Gene, 217–18
Wene, Donald, 86
Werner, Patricia, 304
West Bridge, 216, 231–32, 234, 244, 259–60, 266
Westman, Darlene, 310–11, 313
Whalen, Ginger, 255
Wheat, Bud, 30
Wheeler, Mel, 392, 398
White, Ardene, 254, 257, 267, 269, 273, 276, 281, 284, 288
White, Bard, 394
White, Edson "Scotty", 51, 58, 68, 70, 72
White, Kenneth, 239, 242, 244
Whittington, Neil, 348, 374, 377, 380
Widmer, Gary, 270
Wilcox, Myron, 239
Wilder, Jean, 51, 69
Wilkins, George T., 346
Williams, Nancy, 239, 241, 243
Williamson, Patricia, 239
Wills, Joan, 257
Wilson, Bill, 289, 293
Wilson, Dave, 209
Wilson, Jeanne, 208
Winans, James, 220, 223
Windle, Ralph, 220, 223
Winkleman, Gordon, 348, 357, 375, 380, 393, 395
Winkler, John, 342
Winkler, Phyllis, 251, 253, 255, 270, 273, 276
Wiseman, Gladys, 80, 100
Witherspoon, Gen, 198–99, 201
WJBC, 154, 168, 334

WMBD, 362
Wolf, Barbara, 208, 215–17
Wolff, Carolyn, 51, 69
Wolfinbarger, Sue, 290, 292
Women's Athletic Association, 51, 59, 103
Women's Physical Education, 59, 70, 80, 101
Women's Physical Education Club, 232, 266, 275, 298–300, 341
Woodyah, Kay, 303
WRA, 191, 259, 266, 273, 341, 355, 363, 379
wrestling, 2, 4, 22, 27–30, 43, 104
Wright, Jerry, 310, 318, 321
Wroan, John, 332
Wuthrich, Richard, 220, 232–33, 244, 247, 250, 254–55

Y
Young, Eleanor, 160
Young, Fred, 112–13, 136
Young, Phyllis, 196
Youngren, George, 198, 206–7, 209, 215, 217–18, 220, 227

Z
Zaccagni, Sandy, 363
Zehr, Romaine, 215, 217–18, 220, 241, 243
Zelip, Louis, 108
Zetterlind, Joyce, 374, 380, 392, 398
Ziert, Paul, 334–39, 342, 349–50, 353, 356–57, 361, 369, 374, 377, 379, 384–87
Zimmerman, Wally, 205
Zion, IL, 227, 286

Made in the USA
Monee, IL
02 May 2020